ECONOMIC ADVICE
AND
PRESIDENTIAL LEADERSHIP

ECONOMIC ADVICE
AND
PRESIDENTIAL
LEADERSHIP

The Council of Economic Advisers

EDWARD S. FLASH, JR.

COLUMBIA UNIVERSITY PRESS

New York and London 1965

Edward S. Flash, Jr., is Associate Professor of Public Administration
in the Graduate School of Business and Public Administration,
Cornell University.

TO DORA, DOROTHY, AND STEPHEN

1340325

PREFACE

To me as a public administrator, the fascination of the Council of Economic Advisers has been in the part it has played in the drama of operating politics. The establishment of the Council in 1946 epitomized the evolution of "big government" and its contribution to the nation's economic well-being. The organization and operations of the Council reflect the attempt to achieve rational direction of diverse and complex federal activities through the application of a body of knowledge. Its association with economic policy has given it a role as a developer of economic policies and as a transformer of economic knowledge into political acceptance. Under the aegis of representative government its experiences of success and failure have reflected the give-and-take of political conflict, of relations between staff and line, and of the challenges and pitfalls facing the economist practicing in a political milieu.

But above all, the life and times of the Council symbolize the phenomenon of presidential leadership. In an environment of executive policy initiative, power politics, and bureaucratic procedures, the economist of the Council applies his knowledge, theories, and analytical approaches to economic policy issues in order to help the President fulfill his newest role as "manager of the prosperity." [1] In so doing, the economist works for and with the President as a person; he becomes part of an institutionalized Presidency that overflows from the wings of the White House into the monstrous Executive Office Building, still known to many as "Old State." On behalf of the President and his program, the economist of the Council collaborates with the indispensable idea men, protectors, communicators, and legmen who comprise the White House staff and with the analysts of one of the more significant progeny of twentieth-century bureaucracy, the Bureau of the Budget. As a representative of the Presidency, the Council economist most frequently plies his trade with officials and other professionals in those fiscal-monetary citadels of authority and integrity, the Department of the Treasury and the Federal Reserve Board. Given the perennial concern for profits and employment, he has equally regular association with counterparts in those servant-controllers of management and labor, the Departments of Commerce and Labor. He also works, though more periodically than regularly, with officials and professional counterparts in a variety of other operating agencies. As a manifestation of executive-legislative relations, the Council economist presents himself throughout the year to the members of the congressional Joint Economic Committee, appropriations committees, and relevant subject-matter committees. As a presidential public servant, the Council economist represents his profession and "the Administration" to his professional brethren, to the interest groups, and to the taxpaying voter.

The essence of these far-from-dismal activities is the relationship of economic knowledge to political power. My attempt in writing this book has been to explore the nature of this relationship by focusing less upon economics as such than upon economists and their operating relations with politicians and administrators. The book is about persons and their activities because, as one of the early staff members of the Council observed, "Back of its performance are real people and the situation cannot be made clear without examining the acts, qualities and attitudes of these persons." [2]

My exploration and examination commenced some eight years ago. Much of the literature on the Presidency, on the Council, and on relevant aspects of economics, politics, and organizational behavior has amplified my knowledge and understanding; much of it has been drawn upon in the preparation of this book. The research was based upon (1) analysis of published data, (2) review of available official documents and private papers, and (3)—most important—interviews and correspondence with some seventy individuals who have been involved in or are familiar with the Council's operations.

No account of the research and preparation of this book could do justice as a tribute to the many individuals who have assisted me with advice and information, helpful criticism, and essential editorial work. They have contributed much to such value and significance as the book may possess; they have contributed nothing to the faults, errors, or omissions that no doubt remain and for which I assume full responsibility.

My colleagues at Cornell have provided continuing interest and encouragement. My thanks and appreciation go to Melvin G. de Chazeau, who first directed my attention to the Council and who commented most helpfully on subsequent drafts. Similarly, A. Miller Hillhouse, John G. B. Hutchins, Alfred E. Kahn, Clinton Rossiter, and Paul P. Van Riper have all provided invaluable counsel in their time-consuming review of early drafts and later portions of the manuscript. I am also indebted to Douglas E. Ashford, Robert W. Kilpatrick, and Alan K. McAdams for their comments on particular sections of the book. I am grateful to Robert J. McIntrye for his review of data, references, and quotations and also to his fellow students, Lawrence C. Pierce and Steven E. Rhoads, for their review of Chapters VI through X.

Because of the numbers involved and also because of the request of many to remain anonymous, it is neither possible nor appropriate to identify all the government officials, past and present, to whom I am so greatly indebted for information that was not otherwise available. To them all I express my gratitude. By the same token, it is impossible not to single out the three chairmen whose Councils constitute the focus of this study. In the course of many interviews and considerable correspondence, Leon H. Keyserling, Arthur F. Burns, and Walter W. Heller were extremely generous with their time and helpful beyond measure. I am also grateful to the Council's first Chairman, Edwin G. Nourse, whose book, *Economics in the Public Service*, contributed so much to my knowledge and understanding of the Council's early years.

As is evident in two of the chapters, much of my information on the Keyserling Council comes from the Harry S. Truman Library in Independence, Missouri. I accordingly wish to thank its Director, Philip C. Brooks, and his staff for their considerate and expert assistance. I am also indebted to E. Charles Woods and his

staff in the Bureau of the Budget for office space and countless
helpful courtesies during my many research trips to Washington.

As virtually every academic researcher can appreciate, this study
would not have been possible without financial help. I am therefore especially grateful to Clinton Rossiter for making possible a
grant from the John L. Senior Fund and to the Social Science Research Center at Cornell University for a generous faculty study
grant.

My thanks include recognition of the secretarial staff of the Cornell Graduate School of Business and Public Administration, which
throughout the lengthy process of drafting and redrafting labored
patiently and cheerfully with impossible penmanship and imper-
fect typing. I am also most appreciative of the editorial and review assistance provided during the final rush before the deadline
by Mary and Barron Freeman and Dorothy Van Riper and for
the final manuscript typing by Kathleen Lee, Elaina Carr, Laurie
Myer, and Theresa Slattery. I am also most thankful to the editors and
staff of the Columbia University Press, who have tactfully and ex-
pertly transformed a manuscript into a published volume.

The mere listing of my wife and two children on the dedication
page represents the book's master understatement. My wife's assistance as researcher, critic, editor, and source of encouragement
defies adequate tribute. For eighteen months, being a wife, mother,
and homemaker comprised the sideline activity. My children, whose
patience and good cheer exceeded their comprehension, will be my
creditors for time and company for years to come. I accept the debt
with pleasure.

EDWARD S. FLASH, JR.

Ithaca, New York
February 1, 1965

CONTENTS

ABBREVIATIONS OF
GOVERNMENT AGENCIES

ABEGS	Advisory Board on Economic Growth and Stability
CED	Committee for Economic Development
ECA	Economic Cooperation Administration
FHA	Federal Housing Administration
FNMA	Federal National Mortgage Association
HHFA	Housing and Home Finance Administration
NPA	National Production Authority
NRPB	National Resources Planning Board
NSRB	National Security Resources Board
ODM	Office of Defense Mobilization
OPA	Office of Price Administration
OPS	Office of Price Stabilization
OSS	Office of Strategic Services
OWMR	Office of War Mobilization and Reconversion
VA	Veterans Administration
WPB	War Production Board
WSB	Wage Stabilization Board

ECONOMIC ADVICE
AND
PRESIDENTIAL LEADERSHIP

I. CHALLENGE AND EXPECTATIONS

The right relation of knowledge and power is . . . one of the key problems of our age. The function of advice is one of the crucial points in
that relation.[1]

This book is concerned with the relationship between expert knowledge and political power as revealed in the advisory function. More
specifically, it discusses the relationship between the group of expert
economists who compose the Council of Economic Advisers and the
chief political power in the American government as represented by
the President of the United States. An attempt is made to examine
the relationship between, on one hand, advice on matters of national
economic policy on the basis of command of a particular body of
knowledge and, on the other hand, leadership in the development
and execution of that policy on the basis of command of the resources of government and to inquire into that relationship in the
context of the decision-making process as applied to particular issues
of economic policy significance.

Expert knowledge in this case refers to acquaintance with and
understanding of economic phenomena. Comprehensive and rational
judgment regarding such phenomena of an order not held by the
layman or political leader is implied. The language of the Council's
enabling legislation defines an economist as

a person who, as a result of his training, experience, and attainments, is
exceptionally qualified to analyze and interpret economic developments,

to appraise programs and activities of the Government in the light of the policy declared in section 2, and to formulate and recommend national economic policy to promote employment, production, and purchasing power under free competitive enterprise.[2]

This description implies unusual skill in dealing with the myriad ramifications of fiscal and monetary policy and with such problems as recession and inflation, stability and growth, and domestic and international commerce. Political power in this case refers to the formal, persuasive, and sanctioning powers of the President and includes the formal authority granted to the President by the Constitution, by statutes, and by judicial decisions and by the acceptance of these grants by public officials and private citizens. It comprises also both the President's ability to influence (that is, to persuade) individuals to adopt his judgment as their own and the sanctions (that is, the rewards and punishments) that the Chief Executive, as President and yet at the same time as an individual, seeks or is obliged to apply in the execution of his duties. In accord with Neustadt's description of "a government of separate institutions sharing powers," [3] it recognizes that elements of conflict and cooperation influence the political process. In these terms, the application of power, in whatever combination of authority, persuasion, and sanction, represents the investment or preservation of a leadership resource.

Expert knowledge is concerned with the ability to be right; political power is concerned with responsibility for accomplishment and progress, for welfare and survival. The former is in essence analytical, the latter operational. The correctness of the analysis of the former has no significance apart from the operations of the latter. This is not to say that as in the Platonic concept of philospher-kings knowledge and power become one. Rather it is to accept the hypothesis that there is a functional relationship between the two and that the content and process of the Council's advisory function is essentially and properly part of the President's leadership function.

The objective of this book is thus to explain the nature of the relationship between knowledge and power in terms of the relationship between the Council of Economic Advisers and the President. It seeks to analyze the relationship in action as well as in results and

through such analysis to describe the factors that alone and in combination determine its nature and operating characteristics. It is
hoped that, by contributing a new awareness of the role and significance of the Council and adding depth to the understanding of
the advisory function in the American Presidency, this book will increase the appreciation of the knowledge-power relationship as it
exists in modern bureaucracy and at the same time enhance the
ability of both experts and those in authority to achieve by design
and operation "the right relation between knowledge and power" [4]
of which Bryson wrote.

The approach adopted in this book is that the relationship between the Council and the President can be viewed only from the
perspective of the decision-making process that underlies particular
economic policy issues, for it is in the presidential decisions on these
issues that the knowledge-power relationship between the Council
and the President has its *raison d'être*. Participation in decision-
making for a particular person or organization is normally a combination of direct involvement bearing on the development of
specific decision content and indirect involvement focusing on such
supporting activities as gathering information, preparing arguments,
and drafting ultimate decision statements. The decision-making
process itself encompasses the complex operation—partly rational,
partly irrational, sometimes discretionary, often obligatory—of
choosing among available alternative courses of action. Although
seldom as obvious as the terms imply, it involves first the creative
aspect of developing alternatives and making a choice (even if the
choice is to make no choice) and then the ratifying aspect of
making a commitment to a course of action or inaction.[5]

In substantive terms, the decision-making process as applied to
fiscal and monetary matters is as varied as public housing financing
and international balance of payments. It invokes the participation
of the President, his personal White House staff, the Budget Bureau,
the Council, one or more executive departments, and agencies such
as the Departments of Treasury and Commerce, elements of Congress, and nongovernmental groups. Mechanically, the process is
carried out through instruments as unofficial as the longhand "memorandum for files" or as official as the oft-drafted presidential mes-

sage, as spontaneous as a luncheon conversation or as structured as a formal meeting agenda. In flavor, the process can be as sterile as the press release it often produces or as truly dramatic as the headline that often results.

To examine particular decision-making situations by no means denies the value of the general historical summary nor of an analysis of the Council's economics. Rather it permits a focus on the Council in action, its participation in and contribution to policy-making in different and concrete situations of economic significance that occurred during different presidential administrations under different chairmanships. Such an approach provides an opportunity for both re-creating the operations of different Councils in the respective political and economic milieus in which they operated and for revealing the nature of those operations. It allows for recognition of the complexities and nuances of the knowledge-power relationship and for the distinction between recommendations made publicly and advice given privately. Although concentrating on particular decisions, this approach endeavors to recognize that other issues and other decisions absorb leadership and advisory resources at the same time. The cases chosen are believed to be representative of the Council's operation and hence valid as bases for evaluating both its performance and its relationship with the President.

The Council of Leon H. Keyserling under the Truman Administration during the Korean mobilization of 1950–51 (Chapters II and III) differed from the Council of Arthur F. Burns under the Eisenhower Administration during the recession period of 1953–54 (Chapters IV and V), which in turn differed from the Council of Walter W. Heller under the Kennedy Administration during the development of the 1963 tax proposals in 1961 and 1962 (Chapters VI and VII). Yet all these Councils served Presidents on fundamentally similar economic problems under the mandate of one law, the Employment Act of 1946. All established relationships with the President and components of his administration, all developed patterns of operations and production, and all strove for acceptance and accomplishment. In so doing, each drew upon the experiences of its predecessor, and each had an impact on the profession it represented and institutions it served. Yet marked differences within these similarities come to light in the inquiries into the respective Councils' performance in particular situations.

When Keyserling became Chairman in May, 1950, peace was frail; the adjustment to it at home had been complicated both by price inflation and by mild recession. Truman had committed the nation to world leadership in the strengthening of peace and by his victory in 1948 had won the right to carry out his Fair Deal. Well-known for his outspoken views on economic expansion and anti-inflation policy, Keyserling assumed the chairmanship after six months as Acting Chairman and three years as an active Vice-Chairman under Edwin G. Nourse, the Council's first Chairman. The reputation of the new Council had been tarnished by both internal and external debate over the issue of Council members' testifying before Congress. A new test for the Keyserling Council, which was made up largely of veteran government economists, was to come abruptly and unexpectedly in the form of the Communist invasion of South Korea and the crushing prospect of World War III. Keyserling had to lead his Council in a situation of partial mobilization in association with such Administration leaders as John R. Steelman, Charles Murphy, Stuart Symington, Alan Valentine, Michael DiSalle, and Charles E. Wilson of General Electric. Over the period of June, 1950, to December, 1951, what part did the Keyserling Council play in such specific mobilization issues as passage of the Defense Production Act of 1950, establishment of indirect and then direct price and wage controls, achievement of the Treasury–Federal Reserve accord, and agreement on the stretch-out decision of 1951?

A similar question may be asked concerning the Burns Council: What part did Burns play in the development of the Eisenhower program, and how did he help the first Republican administration in twenty years pull the nation out of the recession of 1953–54? General Eisenhower came to the presidency to make a change and to return to minimum government; similarly, Burns came to Washington to revitalize the Council and to return it from politics to economics. He provided the President and fellow conservatives such as George Humphrey, Sinclair Weeks, and Charles E. Wilson of General Motors, with a renowned expert on business cycles who was not a Keynesian economist. He and his colleagues, predominantly from

the universities, were barely established before they had to deal with
the ghost of 1929, the second such ghost since the war. The Burns
Council's challenge was to prescribe in 1953 and 1954 countercyclical policies that would bring back economic prosperity and preserve the free enterprise system. This Council had to support,
modify, or accept the views of conservative businessmen in contributing to the President's 1954 program—tax revision, housing,
unemployment insurance, public works, and fiscal and monetary
stimulants for an ailing economy.

Again, under the Kennedy Administration, a like situation prevailed. As had been Burns', Heller's immediate task was to wrestle
with recession, the fourth since the war. But, in contrast, Heller assumed the Council's chairmanship as one of the new generation
pushing out the New Frontiers both at home and overseas. Not
merely recovery but growth was to become the issue for a Council
staffed largely by young newcomers to presidential advising. If
President Kennedy advocated a balanced budget at the end of his
first year in office and endorsed tax legislation involving substantial
budget deficits at the end of his second, if, in June, 1964, Secretary
Dillon described the three and a half years since January, 1961, as
constituting "a significant watershed in the development of American economic policy," [6] then what part did the Heller Council play
in the emergence of a new tradition that gave political acceptability
to what economists had long since acknowledged? In an era marked
by persistent unemployment and lagging growth at home, burgeon-
ing economies abroad, and deteriorating balance of payments in between, a major share of the Council's analysis and advice would be
devoted to developing tax reduction measures proposed in 1963 and
ultimately passed in part in 1964. In an environment of pragmatism
and activity, it would have to marshal analysis and advice to counter
prevailing views and particular interests.

The three specific situations in which these three Councils operated represent only some five years of the almost two decades that
the Council of Economic Advisers has survived as a creature of the
Employment Act of 1946 and as the executive embodiment of the
federal government's responsibility for the nation's economic welfare. During its lifetime, the Council has comprised a group of
acknowledged experts representing a profession of scholars and

practitioners who have served visibly as advisers to the nation's acknowledged political leader. To paraphrase Nourse, economics has been in the public service. In fulfillment of this service, the Council has had six chairmen, seventeen appointees to the two remaining membership posts, and much turnover of professional staff.[7] Its annual reports, the statements of its members, and its reported influence on various matters have earned for the Council extremes of both praise and criticism. In applying their expertise, the Council members and staff economists have experienced accomplishment and frustration, assistance and competition, acceptance and rejection. In success they have known the satisfaction of seeing their work accepted and relied upon by the President and his administration, by Congress, and by the public. In failure they have experienced the heat of opposition as well as the freeze of being ignored, of not being summoned, and of seeing carefully worked-out proposals consigned to the wastepaper basket.

The Council's expert advisory function and the President's awesome responsibilities have thus been joined into an association that has stood the test of time. Moreover, the association has been of such duration and of such significance as to warrant attempted analysis of its operation. More specifically, I believe that an analysis of the Council's performance in the three specific cases can yield answers to three summary questions:

1. What has been the nature and extent of the Council's impact on economic policy, to what extent has it fulfilled or deviated from original expectations regarding its performance, and how can its performance be explained? (Chapter VIII)

2. Based upon its performance, what is the nature of the relationship between the Council and the President, what is the process of relating economic knowledge and political power, how can the differences between individual Councils be explained, and what is the Council's emerging tradition? (Chapter IX)

3. What is the relevance of the Council's experience to other staff advisory bodies in both private and public bureaucracies, and what does the analysis of the Council's experience suggest as a possible analytical approach to the understanding, creation, and operation of such bodies? (Chapter X)

Although concerned primarily with the relationship of knowledge to power, the answers to these questions are relevant to the broader considerations of politics, administration, and, to a lesser degree, economics. They bear upon the nature of the Presidency, that is, upon the nature of presidential leadership, power, and need for assistance. As such, they supplement the analyses of Neustadt, Rossiter, Sorensen, and others. They are pertinent to such organizational considerations as staff-line relations, decision-making, professional and institutional orientation, and organizational change. They have meaning, too, for what may be called the "presidential bureaucracy," that is, the professional personnel, temporary or permanent, who make up the Executive Office of the President and who for the most part have orientations internally shared but quite different from their counterparts in operating departments and agencies. Although the answers to the questions (and the case descriptions that precede them) do not attempt to provide new insights into economics as such, they do bear on the development of economic knowledge and of its relationship to political science.

As the Council of Economic Advisers did not just appear in the body politic, an analysis of its performance must take as its points of departure the Council's origins and, more important, the original expectations regarding its purpose and means of operation. Without such a foundation, any appraisal of its influence, politics, and significance lacks a basic dimension.

In 1946, when the Council of Economic Advisers was established, probably the most pervasive and popular expectation of it was that, in cooperation with its legislative counterpart, the Joint Committee on the Economic Report (subsequently renamed the Joint Economic Committee), it would help defend the ramparts against depression. One cannot think back to the immediate postwar period without recalling both the prayerful thankfulness for the end of bloodshed and the determined optimism for a new era of peace abroad and security at home. The harnessing of the atom, the opportunities and commitments of new worldwide responsibilities, vast technological developments, sprawling urbanization, and the hardly forgotten suffering of the Great Depression all brought new challenges to private citizens and public officials alike. But above all, there was the desire to prevent a repetition of the depressions that followed World War I.

It is impossible to read Bailey's *Congress Makes a Law,* an absorbing account of the passage of the Employment Act of 1946, without realizing that these new challenges were being taken up on all sides and, in fact, had been initially tackled in and outside of government well before the climactic landings in Normandy. For all its pummeling by what Bailey characterizes as "a kaleidoscopic and largely irresponsible interplay of ideas, interests, institutions, and individuals," [8] the Employment Act articulated the aspirations and fears of the generation. It set forth new objectives and concepts of public policy, economics, and administration that had their roots in the experiences and events, the theories and convictions of the 1930s and that, nourished by the war, blossomed in such opposing seedbeds as the 1944 Democratic and Republican platforms. In making explicit the federal government's responsibility for using its resources to help avoid recession and hence unemployment, the Employment Act acknowledged Keynesian compensatory fiscal and monetary principles and transformed the issue of conscious governmental intervention in the nation's economic welfare from "whether" to "how."

If the fear of another 1929 had not been so prevalent in 1945 and early 1946, however, it is questionable whether there would have been an Employment Act and thus a Council of Economic Advisers. Moreover, if the Act as a whole gave statutory recognition to objectives that had proved socially imperative, economically sound, and politically necessary, its wording made it abundantly clear that a basic conflict in philosophy reflected opposing sets of expectations as to how these objectives were to be achieved, what constituted fulfillment, and how the Council was to operate. The words and phrases, the qualifications and ambiguities, the said and unsaid, constitute hallmarks of fundamental differences. In no part of the Act is the interplay of conflicting ideas more sharply evident than in the opening policy statement:

The Congress hereby declares that it is the continuing policy and responsibility of the Federal Government to use all practicable means consistent with its needs and obligations and other essential considerations of national policy with the assistance and cooperation of industry, agriculture, labor, and State and local governments, to coordinate and utilize all its plans, functions, and resources for the purpose of creating and maintaining, in a manner calculated to foster and promote free competitive enterprise and the general welfare, conditions under which there will be afforded useful employment for those able, willing, and seeking to work, and to promote maximum employment, production, and purchasing power.[9]

Such conflicting means and ends were echoed in the definition of the Council's duties and functions as being

(1) to assist and advise the President in the preparation of the Economic Report; (2) to gather timely and authoritative information. . . ; (3) to appraise the various programs and activities of the Federal Government in the light of the policy declared in section 2. . . ; (4) to develop and recommend to the President national economic policies to foster and promote free competitive enterprise, to avoid economic fluctuations or to diminish the effects thereof, and to maintain employment, production and purchasing power; (5) to make and furnish studies, reports thereon, and recommendations . . . as the President may request.[10]

Among legislators, administrators, economists, and voters, those who regarded attaining maximum employment, production, and purchasing power as major means of achieving national economic well-being opposed those who saw supporting the free enterprise system as the key to lasting prosperity. Those who did not fear active government opposed those who did. Those who looked to the executive for initiative opposed those who sought reaffirmation of legislative leadership. Stripped of variations and qualifications, this basic schism pitted liberals against conservatives, representatives from urban areas against those from rural areas, labor against management, and Keynesian economists against traditionalists.

Consequently, the Council faced from the beginning a divergence of expectations regarding its brand of economic analysis, its policy recommendations, and its mode of operations. Its mandate under the Employment Act precluded one universal interpretation; it could be judged by the standard of either the original Murray Full Employment Bill as passed by the Senate [11] or the more conservative House version,[12] for the Act in its final form could be considered to be consistent with both.

Judged by the Senate version, the Council would be expected to operate under the banner of "maximum employment, production, and purchasing power." Its advice and recommendations would be consistent with the concept of economic growth and full utilization of productive resources as necessary means of achieving economic stability. It would be expected to favor expanded expenditures to cover a variety of governmental programs and to be quick in urging compensatory fiscal and monetary policies at the first sign of recession. It would presumably be less fearful of deficits, more likely to advocate "easy money" policies, more concerned with the consumer than the investor. It would be expected to apply Keynesian aggregative concepts of economic analysis, including the use of an annually submitted quantitative national budget. As originally set forth in the Murray Full Employment Bill, this would have required the transmitting of

a general program for such Federal investment and expenditures as will be sufficient to bring the aggregate volume of investment and expenditure by private business, consumers, State and local governments and Federal Government, up to the level required to assure a full employment volume of production.[13]

Although this concept was watered down in the Employment Act to requiring an annual report "setting forth the levels of employment, production and purchasing power obtained in the United States and such levels needed to carry out the policy declared in Section 2," [14] the basic idea was left sufficiently intact as to permit some form of discretionary application.

On the contrary, if judged by the House version, the Council would be expected to base its operations on the phrase, "in a manner calculated to foster and promote free competitive enterprise." Its advice and recommendations would reflect the belief that economic growth and stability stemmed primarily from minimum government interference in economic activity, from providing favorable conditions for business' own initiative and expansive powers, from reducing spending and balancing budgets. The Council would be expected to discourage the increase of federal expenditures and, for compensatory policies, to urge withholding of governmental action until economic forces were clearly cumulative. In times of recession it would be expected to advocate placing primary emphasis on

monetary remedies and to favor tax and credit relief over public
works spending. It would presumably stress the need for maintaining business confidence by minimum "tampering" and maximum aid
to investment. Economic analysis would focus primarily on the progress of the business cycle and of the various categories in industry.

Although not mutually exclusive in theory and application, these
sets of expectations were so different and opposite in emphasis and
ideas as to constitute different standards of conduct and different as
well as reciprocal measures of success or failure. Furthermore, they
ramified into varying expectations regarding the nature and extent
of the Council's function and of its relations with the President.

One of the most important ramifications centered in the Employment Act's implicit authorization for economic planning and therefore for the Council's fulfilling a planning function as part of its
larger analysis function. The expectation regarding planning had
two major aspects, the first of which was that planning had substantive or policy significance and therefore involved both predictions
and objectives. Although not viewed in the extreme sense of a
planned, or nonmarket, economy, the nature of the Council's expected planning function did vary with the different interpretations
of the Employment Act.

If, under one interpretation the government was to seek maximum
employment, production, and purchasing power, then mobilization of
resources and predetermined plans would have to set forth desired
and feasible overall objectives and at the same time describe the
component fiscal, monetary, and related economic policies necessary
for their achievement. As a derivative of aggregative economic
analysis and long-range forecasting, such planning would involve the
development of comprehensive budgets and programs outlining
courses of action and standards by which components could be
judged. If, under the other interpretation, relatively free rein was to
be given to the economy, the Council's planning would be a far
more limited operation. Limited forecasting would preclude long-
range policy programs except in the most general terms. In inven-
torying the plans and programs of operating agencies, the Council
would emphasize analysis of the impact of these programs on the
economy as a whole. The planning model of the maximum employ-

ment interpretation was essentially deductive; that is, governmental programs would more or less fit some overall and predetermined objectives. The model of the free enterprise interpretation, on the other hand, was essentially inductive; that is, overall economic policy would be an approximate sum of separate governmental programs evaluated for their impact on the economy as a whole.

Such planning of policy was related to but distinct from the second aspect, in which planning had a procedural or managerial significance. The concern was with coordination in the sense of control, with aiding the President by providing a measure of top-level order and perspective out of the massive and competing demands of separate federal programs. Writing in 1947, Millett defined the job of central planning as "to make sure that plans are prepared by operating agencies; that these plans are reviewed; and that the plans of any one agency do not come into conflict with the plans of another agency." [15] "Planning," he wrote, "is the very essence of administrative management." [16] Millett concludes,

Both the War Mobilization and Reconversion Act of 1944 and the Employment Act of 1946 indicated a Congressional realization that the central planning responsibility in the federal government had to be vested in the President. Presumably, then, there is no basic issue in our government today about providing planning machinery which will seek a reconciliation of interest group points of view, or which will "control" the chief executive and administrative agencies. Planning management has been accepted as Presidential management. [17]

So it was that the Council was made part of the Executive Office of the President rather than an independent "supreme court"; it was staffed by full-time trained professionals rather than operating officials serving on a part-time basis. Such an arrangement did not represent an administrative innovation of the Employment Act so much as an accumulation of fifteen years of coordinating experience and experiment within the Executive Branch dating back at least to Robert M. LaFollette, Jr.'s proposal in 1931 to establish a National Economic Council. Such accumulation included the rise and fall of the National Resources Planning Board (NRPB) and the transfer of the Budget Bureau from the Treasury to the newly established Executive Office of the President under the Reorganization Act of 1939.

It concluded with the example of the Office of War Mobilization and Reconversion (OWMR), which was folding its tent just as the Council was preparing Truman's first *Economic Report* in the fall of 1946.

Establishing the Council within the Executive Office was an additional answer to the call of the President's Committee on Administrative Management in 1937 that "the President needs help." Under the maximum employment interpretation, the Council would help as an active right hand of advice and planning. It would combine the NRPB characteristics of independence and involvement in policy planning with the coordinating and executive nature of OWMR. Under the free enterprise interpretation, the Council's assistance would be more passive. In its emphasis upon analysis, informing, and communicating, it would imitate neither the creativity of NRPB nor the activity of OWMR.

Implicit in the expectations regarding policy interpretation and planning was the related expectation that the Council's relationship to the President would be that of a full-time professional consultant helping the President to meet his economic welfare responsibilities by providing expert advice in an objective manner. As Miss Silverman has noted, "As the CEA began its work, there were many who hoped it would strengthen the quality and rationality of economic decision making in government by injecting at the White House level the advice of three professional economists." [18] Assisting the Council members would be "specialists and other experts," [19] presumably professional economists recruited from government agencies, educational institutions, research organizations, and private firms. To enhance the value of its advisory function, the Council would, as it considered appropriate, consult with outside experts as well as with representatives of labor, management, and agriculture.

By anticipating, analyzing, informing, and advising, the Council would provide a link in the name of the President with operating agencies and with Congress; it would play a general advisory but not an executive role in presidential policy-making. By improving the quality and extent of economic knowledge available and by developing techniques of analysis leading to a national economic policy, the Council would become the nation's center of economics; its chairman would hold "the highest public position to which an economist in this country can aspire." [20] From its Olympian perch the Council could dispense expert advice with objectivity, perspective, and independence. The implication of the qualification for holding office was essentially that of nonpolitical expertise. The Council would not become enmeshed in the passion of advocacy and operation. Moreover, expertise would reveal *the* answers, lead to the setting of correct goals, and provide economic standards for judging specific policies. Truth would harness, perhaps even overcome, but never succumb to partisanship. True to the public administration views of the day, economics, like administration, would be separated from politics. In his letter to President Truman in which he accepted the offer of the Council's chairmanship, Nourse gave perhaps the best statement of the Council's expected objectivity:

The first function of the Council will be to piece together a complete and consistent picture of the economic state of the nation from these official sources and from any nonofficial sources which appear to be useful. The Council must detect errors of method, bias, or inconsistency and, by revealing these shortcomings of the nation's fact-finding machinery, lead to their correction. . . .

The second function of the Council is to interpret all available literal facts into the soundest possible diagnosis as to the state of the nation's economic health and the causes which explain any evidence of current ill health which threaten to produce unhealthy conditions in the future. . . .

The Council of Economic Advisers is conceived as a scientific agency of the Federal Government. Its prime function is to bring the best available methods of social science to the service of the Chief Executive and of the Congress in formulating national policy from year to year and from month to month. There is no occasion for the Council to become involved in any way in the advocacy of particular measures or in the rival beliefs and struggles of the different economic and political interest groups. It should give a clearer and more comprehensive picture than we have ever had as to the economic state of the nation, as to factors which are tending to retard prosperity, and as to the probable effect of various remedial measures which may be under consideration by the Executive or the Congress.[21]

The expectation of professional objectivity was linked to a final expectation that the Council would be an institutional rather than

personal source of advice. Seligman concludes that "as a formal recognition that, in matters of economic policy, leadership was to be
expected from the President, the Full Employment Act reflects a
confirmation of the leadership of President Roosevelt. The President's leadership in economic policy was thus made an institutional
feature of his office." [22] Gross and Lewis have noted that the Employment Act marked the first instance where a particular species of
knowledge and ability had been given separate agency status within
the President's staff.[23] Such status would allow it to follow in the
tradition of the Budget Bureau rather than that of the White House
staff. In this tradition, the Council would soon be joined by the
establishment of the National Security Council in 1947.

In part, the legislative specification of an institutional form for the
Council grew out of a sensitivity to fourteen years of Roosevelt domination and to the Chief Executive's growing control of the executive
branch. Although accepting the need for economic advisory assistance, Congress sought to avoid an enlargement of the coterie of
presidential advisers whom it neither knew nor could control. As
Seligman has observed,

If the President's economic advisers could be made a detached group
delivering learned reports to the President and Congress alike, then the
influence of the President could be reduced. Congress knew well that a
council of economic "bright boys" or a council of economic advisers who
"looked at the President and reported to the country" could only enhance the political effectiveness of the President.[24]

Specifying a Council of three rather than a single adviser, requiring
Senate confirmation of its members, and setting forth certain necessary qualifications would go far toward insuring against such ano-
nymity and, by preventing subjectivity, would enforce objectivity.
Denying the Council any operating authority and limiting annual
appropriations for salaries of members and employees would prevent the development of any elaborate addition to presidential
power and would severely restrict any advocacy role. By establishing the Joint Committee on the Economic Report, the Congress not
only reinforced these restrictions but also made the Council at least
partially beholden to Congress, thereby counterbalancing the President's preeminence in the economic field with an eminence of its

own. Among other duties, the Joint Committee would review the President's *Economic Report* prepared by the Council, conduct hearings, and submit its own reports "containing its findings and recommendations with respect to each of the main recommendations made by the President in the *Economic Report*." [25]

Thus, the Council was expected to prevent depression, interpret the Employment Act, serve as a planning body in the light of that interpretation, provide expert and objective advice, and operate as an institutional form of presidential assistance. As marching orders, these expectations were as broad as they were inconsistent, as discretionary as they were inhibiting. Only in its experiences could the Council fulfill, modify, or change expectations. As the members of the original Nourse Council well recognized, the Council would have to make its way in a bureaucratic environment already populated with agencies and personalities armed with their own aspirations and expectations and their own resources and desires for helping the President and influencing economic policy. As hopes and fears, or speculations and intentions, the expectations regarding the Council would soon be tested by the economic developments and policy decisions of the late 1940s and early 1950s.

II. THE PERIOD OF INFLUENCE

Almost six months elapsed between the time the Employment Act was signed (February 20, 1946) and the time Council membership was completed. On August 9 the Council was sent on its way with the blessings of President Truman, the good wishes of the public and the press, and the wait-and-see cooperation of the bureaucracy. Operating reflections of the legislative struggle lay beneath the harmony of the all-too-brief honeymoon. Another six weeks were to pass before the Council managed to set up shop in the basement of "Old State," giving it, in the words of Nourse, "only sixty days before we would have to deliver a product to the President." [1]

The delay in getting started was itself a reflection of the eager and somewhat frenetic postwar readjustment, the method of presidential operations, and the Administration's initial view of the Council. Truman opens Volume II of his *Memoirs* with the statement, "Within the first few months I discovered that being a President is like riding a tiger. A man has to keep on riding or be swallowed." [2] By grabbing the scruff of the tiger's neck rather than the tail, Truman had ridden through the final stages of winning the war, tackled the major domestic and foreign issues of reconversion, launched the Fair Deal, and, by guiding the nation into the UN, helped turn its back on isolationism. During the Council's formative years, he was to face up to the issues of civil rights, economic stability, and public welfare and win an election in the process. In the early rounds of the Cold War, he was to initiate aid to Greece and

Turkey, the Berlin air lift, European recovery, Point Four, and the North Atlantic Treaty Organization. In a nuclear age he was to focus on such issues as defense unification, rearmament, military and peaceful application of atomic energy, competition with the USSR, and cooperation with our allies. Such were the monumental legacies of the Roosevelt years.

If in issues and objectives Truman was heir to Roosevelt and the New Deal, his operations of the presidency were essentially his own. Neustadt describes a President wanting to set the country's sights in a straightforward way, to accept "the buck that stops here," to make decisions, and to carry on his daily work in openness and attempted order.[3] Truman's accessibility to virtually anyone who wanted to see him and his sense of loyalty to those whom he trusted, along with his feeling for personalities and his willingness to improvise, gave his administration a stamp of directness and informality. The formality of his relationships with James Forrestal, General Marshall, and later Dean Acheson was balanced by the comfortable intimacy with John Snyder, Carl Vinson, and John R. Steelman. The division between the "Murphy side" of the White House staff, supposedly concerned with forward programming and legislation, and the "Steelman side," supposedly focusing on day-to-day operation, existed more in form than in fact. There was much crossing over, cooperation, and inter-dependence and no little confusion between the West Wing team of Charles Murphy, David Lloyd, David Bell, and Richard Neustadt and that of the East Wing comprised of Steelman, Harold Enarson, David Stowe, Robert Turner, and others.

Viewing the federal budget as the measure of the President's program, Truman applied his own fondness for figures to developing a keen interest in budgeting as an end in itself and as a technique of leadership. "The federal budget was one of my more serious hobbies," Truman writes, "but it was also much more than that. In fact, I regarded it as one of the most serious of the responsibilities of the President—a responsibility that never failed to prove thoroughly fascinating."[4] His interest extended well beyond the generalities of policy and probed deep into technicalities of budget preparation and execution. Budget experts attending his annual budget seminars with the press were repeatedly impressed by his grasp of details.

Such command meant reliance upon and prominence for the Budget Bureau and its succession of immediate postwar directors, Harold D. Smith, James E. Webb, Frank Pace, and Frederick J. Lawton.

Given the scope and press of postwar issues, the active nature of presidential operations, and the almost party-machine flavor of the Administration, the Council was welcomed more as a distant cousin than as an established member of the family. Truman had favored but not necessarily championed the passage of the Employment Act. There was no rush in the appointment of the Council members, he did not push its prompt establishment, and, according to Nourse's account of his appointment and swearing-in, Truman had not given extensive thought to the use he would make of it: "Now you gentlemen just keep this national income up to 200 billion dollars and we'll be all right." [5]

Precedent and Prologue

With Nourse as Chairman, the other two Council members were Leon H. Keyserling, then thirty-eight, and Vice-Chairman, and John D. Clark, then sixty-two. The original professional staff was made up of nine economists and one statistician, a majority of whom had seen extensive government service, either as careerists or as recent veterans of wartime agencies. More important, three had participated in the development of the Employment Act; they were Gerhard Colm, Walter Salant, and Bertram Cross.

Immediately prior to his appointment, Nourse had been Vice-President of The Brookings Institution, barely five minutes' walk from his Council office. He had been associated with Brookings since 1923 and at the time of his appointment was deeply involved in work he had not expected to leave. His previous professional activities had included extensive writing and teaching experience, a term as President of the American Farm Economic Association in 1924 and of the American Economic Association in 1942, as well as a three-year term as Chairman of the Social Science Research Council during the war years. At the time he assumed the Council chairmanship he was sixty-three years old.

Although it was generally realized that Nourse was not President

Truman's first choice for the position, he enjoyed the utmost respect of the government officials and professional economists. While not associated with any particular school of economics, Nourse was generally considered to be moderately conservative. He had not been involved in the passage of the Employment Act and at the time of his appointment was only generally familiar with it.[6] As already noted, he none the less was able to give the President a fairly specific idea of his interpretation of the Council's role as a source of expert and objective advice. His interpretation of its underlying economic philosophies would emerge in the course of his chairmanship.

Clark was first a lawyer by training. Forsaking a successful and remunerative career in business, he had resigned from the vice-presidency of Standard Oil of Indiana in his early forties to undertake a second career in the academic world. He completed his Ph.D. in economics in 1931, taught economics for ten years at the University of Denver and at the University of Nebraska, where he served as Dean of the School of Business, and took a crack at Wyoming politics, serving briefly as a Democratic representative in the Wyoming legislature. A maverick among his industry colleagues, he was an ardent Democrat and kept himself available for a variety of presidential appointments during the Roosevelt era. Moreover, he was a close associate of Senator Joseph O'Mahoney, who was one of the sponsors of the Employment Act. In fact, some attribute Clark's appointment to the Council to this association.[7] As Miss Silverman has noted, "Clark did not consider himself a 'conservative' economist, and his position on questions pondered by the Council of Economic Advisers seems to confirm this estimate of himself." [8] Nevertheless, he joined the Council as the practicing economist with a business background.

Because of the focus of this and the following chapter on the involvement of the Council of Keyserling in Korean mobilization policies, it is appropriate to summarize his background in more detail. A South Carolinian by birth and a New Dealer by vocation, Keyserling received his A.B. from Columbia University in 1928 with a major in economics and his LL.B. from Harvard University in 1931. This was followed by some part-time graduate study in economics again at Columbia University. In March, 1933, he was brought to Washington by Rexford Tugwell on the legal staff of Jerome Frank of the Agricultural Adjustment Administration. Then followed four years as legislative assistant to Senator Robert Wagner and two years as a staff member of the Senate Committee on Banking and Currency. From 1937 to 1946 he served in various capacities with public housing agencies, including that of General Counsel for the National Housing Agency.

Keyserling's association with such men as Tugwell, Frank, and Wagner and his participation in numerous Democratic election campaigns, together with his almost ten years of association with housing agencies—the first ten years of public housing—could not help but shape the expansion emphasis of his economics. As a student and practitioner he could not have been oblivious to the new Keynesian economics. During the war, he witnessed the struggle of Robert Nathan, Stacy May, Simon Kuznets, and others in fighting the isolationists before Pearl Harbor and, in their roles as staff members of Donald Nelson's War Production Board (WPB), in developing feasible production goals. Keyserling witnessed, too, the galvanizing effect of Roosevelt's declaration in January, 1942, on production goals for planes, tanks, antiaircraft guns, and shipping that far exceeded the most optimistic calculations.[9]

In 1944, Keyserling won the $10,000 second prize of the Pabst Postwar Planning Awards for his essay, "The American Economic Goal." [10] In this, the first articulation of his emerging economic philosophy, he called for the determination of goals stating that "maximum standards of living depend upon full employment of manpower, skills, plant and resources." He advocated an economic policy based both upon cooperation by industry, labor, and agriculture and upon government incentives manifested in tax policy, research, timely reconversion, government insuring and guaranteeing of private housing, credit aids, and aids to private urban redevelopment. "As bedrock civilized responsibility," we should adopt "a creative offensive against unemployment" that integrates spending, taxing, and regulation as full employment incentives. Keyserling proposed that economic goals be regularly redefined by an American Economic Committee composed of three representatives each from the House of Representatives and the Senate, three members of the

President's Cabinet, and two representatives each from industry, agriculture, and labor. The Chairman would be designated by the President, and the Committee would be supplemented by a small staff of experts. The resulting redefinitions would not be blueprints but goals, voluntarily accepted by an informed public. The ideas set forth in his essay were suggestive to the drafters of the original Full Employment Bill, and throughout "the full employment fight" he participated unofficially as a sounding board and adviser to Senator Wagner and the Banking and Currency Committee staff.[11]

There is little doubt that, once the Employment Act was passed, Keyserling desired appointment to the new Council. Toward this objective Senator Wagner served as his chief sponsor. To Steelman, the Senator wrote:

We do not want a relationship such as developed, unfortunately, between Congress and the National Resources Planning Board. Mr. Keyserling is universally well regarded by many members of both the Senate and the House, particularly members of those committees which deal with economic and employment matters. . . . He is well liked and highly regarded not only by those up here who share his liberal views, but likewise by those with different political viewpoints. . . . I gradually formed the opinion that Mr. Keyserling was not only a first-rate legal technician, but also a first-rate student of economics and of governmental problems. . . . I am enclosing a folder containing some of his quite recent speeches and articles all in support of the objectives of the present Administration.[12]

Keyserling's extensive New Deal–Fair Deal involvements bespeak a man of ability, dedication, and ambition. By the time he joined the Council, there was little doubt regarding his convictions on economic policy. A difficult personality and prodigious worker, to his associates Keyserling often seemed at one and the same time cooperative and garrulous, helpful and irritating. In the words of a former colleague, "he is a man with the heart of a missionary and the ego of a politician, desiring ardently to be actively engaged in the good works at the center of the Lord's battle for right and justice."

Taken together, the differences in background and conviction of the three Council members foreordained a basic incompatibility among these presidential advisers. In addition to the President's apparently superficial interest in the Council along with the pace of the many issues—domestic and foreign, defense and nondefense, fiscal and monetary—that absorbed his time and energies, a basic incompatibility between the Council and its environment was inevitable. As Nourse himself reveals and as has been indicated by Keyserling, by the Clark papers at the Truman Library, by such commentators as Miss Silverman, and by individuals who were associated with the original Council, there were frustrations and disagreement within the Council on many substantive and procedural issues.

Nourse shared Truman's concern for a "hard currency" policy of living within the government's budget and consequently of not increasing defense expenditures, but he had little sympathy with underlying Fair Deal policies [13] and even less with the expansion economics of his own Vice-Chairman or the monetary ease advocated by Clark. Although all three were concerned with inflation and agreed on proposals of levying an excess profits tax and on tightening consumer credit, Nourse was more willing than his colleagues to increase Federal Reserve discretion in controlling the bond market and less willing to endorse selective price and wage controls. The former was anathema to Clark; the latter was a necessity to Keyserling. Their differences on inflation policy carried over to differing countercyclical policies during the recession of the following year. In 1949 Keyserling, Bertram Gross, and other staff members were active proponents of the Spence and Murray bills [14] as resurrections of the original Full Employment Act. Like Truman, Nourse would have nothing to do with either of the measures, neither of which were considered by Congress. He sought an emphasis upon stability rather than upon expansion and thus, for example, supported both the President and prevailing public opinion by arguing against expanding defense budgets beyond $15 billion.[15] By late 1948, the Council could no longer report to the President in a single voice, as memoranda and reports began to incorporate differing individual viewpoints.

No procedural issue was more disruptive to their relationship than the disagreement over testifying before congressional committees. Nourse thought that Council members should not testify before other than appropriation committees, while Clark and Keyserling believed it appropriate to testify before the Joint Committee on the Economic Report as well as before the other committees. The issue was finally resolved on August 3, 1948, by the President in favor of Keyserling and Clark, and Keyserling, with charts and extensive arguments, went before the Senate Banking and Currency Committee the following day to support the President's anti-inflation program.

It was equally irritating to Nourse that he was unable to develop satisfactory relations or channels of communication with the President and the White House. His contacts with the President appear to have been infrequent, off-hand, indirect, and generally unsatisfactory.[16] Keyserling argued that

Dr. Nourse was simply unable to adjust himself to the nature and the problems of the Presidency. He could never understand that the President of the United States has too many things to do to engage in long bull sessions on economics of the kind that take place at The Brookings Institution. He could never understand that the President must delegate, must have confidence in his principal officers, and that these officers have not just cause for complaint when the President not only remains accessible to them but also accepts practically everything that they recommend to him.[17]

Nourse's concept of the service his Council could render to the President remained entirely alien to that of the President. As the *U.S. News and World Report* was to write six months after Nourse's resignation, Truman "doesn't like to deal with scientists and economists . . . does not have an inquiring mind . . . does not ask many questions . . . and is an economic illiterate." [18] Being more operationally and promotionally inclined than Nourse, Keyserling and, to a lesser degree, Clark had little difficulty with the environment but considerable difficulty in getting Nourse to accept it and adjust to it. The root of the difficulty appears to have been Nourse's inability to maintain the scientific objectivity to which he aspired; his economic policy views kept intruding. His advocacy may have been more passive than that of his colleagues, but it existed all the same. His numerous public speeches were no less policy-oriented than the testimony and speeches of Keyserling and Clark. In retrospect, not the issue of testifying before committees of Congress but the issue of conservative versus liberal concepts of economic policy appears as the fundamental conflict.

That the original trio held together for three formative but obviously difficult years is a credit to the good will and sense of purpose of each. However, the basic incompatibility within the Nourse Council and between it and the White House and the Congress could not help but overshadow the Council's substantive work at both Council and staff levels and at the same time affect its prestige. By the time, in early August, 1949, that Nourse had noted in his diary that "it is useless to try to go on in my post under present conditions," [19] the Council had settled to a level well below its original hopes and expectations. Statutory equality merely exacerbated a relationship strained over differences of opinion both in operation and policy.

In these early years, the Council tended to be known less for its contributions to the many substantive issues with which it dealt than for its estrangement from the President and its internal discord. Congress had reduced the Council's budget twice in successive years. The press concentrated on the rumors of resignations and reports of disagreements and paid progressively less attention to the *Economic Reports*. At its annual meeting in December, 1949, the American Economic Association panel on "Stabilizing the Economy: The Employment Act of 1946 in Operation" appeared to be less concerned about the *Economic Reports'* analyses and national budget ideas than about the Council's economics being too politically oriented.[20] The first Hoover Commission had recommended that the Council be replaced by an Office of the Economic Adviser and that it have a single head.[21] In short, by the time of Nourse's resignation in October, 1949, the Council had not yet been able to meet Nourse's ideal of "a truly professional and nonpolitical," [22] scientific agency. Whether or not it was a realistic ideal or whether or not some other standard could make the Council more representative of the operation of economic advice at the presidential level remained for future Councils to demonstrate.

Amid the conflicts of views and personalities, Keyserling assumed much of the day-to-day direction of the Council's operations. Some of the early staff members have commented that, as Vice-Chairman,

Keyserling had a major part in the preparation of the annual *Economic Report* and in the encouragement of the development of quantitative analysis and long-range forecasts, neither of which appealed greatly to Nourse and Clark.

On the same day that Truman accepted Nourse's resignation, Keyserling, not unnaturally, responded to a request of Clark Clifford in the White House by forwarding to him information in support of his candidacy as the Council's next chairman. This was followed in subsequent days by endorsements from a number of predominantly Democratic sources. Prominent in Keyserling's presentation was a six-page summary of his earlier Council experience, his writings in economics, and his testimony and speeches before public and private groups. The document and covering memorandum reveal a keen sensitivity to the criticism that he should not be considered a professional economist because he lacked the formal qualifications of a Ph.D. degree in economics:

There is utterly no basis in the facts for this kind of objection. While 16 years of preoccupation with national economic programs have prevented Mr. Keyserling from following the traditional course of the academic economist, his actual work (including writing) in the field of overall economic policy, stabilization and full employment has been voluminous and constant. Probably there are few economists in the country who have worked as constantly in this particular field of economics. To grade this type of work less highly than the more customary pattern of economics work at a university would be to undervalue the very type of experience and effort which is most closely related to the responsibilities of the Council of Economic Advisers under the Employment Act of 1946.[23]

Although Truman assured Keyserling very early after Nourse's resignation that he would be named Chairman, the fact that six months passed before the appointment was made suggests that Keyserling's sensitivity was not unfounded. Lack of unanimous support for him among the White House staff because of his lack of academic qualifications, in addition to his outspoken support for price and wage controls, no doubt led to active recruitment of alternative candidates. Many may have been approached, but Keyserling denies[24] Nourse's statement that the post was, in fact, offered to a number of professional economists on a White House list.[25] Part of the delay in

announcing Keyserling's appointment seems attributable to the difficulty of selecting a third member. Keyserling's appointment was, in
fact, announced at the same time as that of Roy Blough, who was to
join the Council in June.[26] Aside from any commitment to Keyserling,
the President's known antipathy to economists may have been decisive. In any event, Keyserling assumed active direction of the
Council's activities in November as Acting Chairman, and Clark
continued as the other member.

Keyserling had been Acting Chairman of the Council for barely a
week when he struck his expansion theme in his first "Monthly
Report" to the President:

> We need more than a slight upward trend of business and employ-
> ment. . . . Economic stability requires economic growth, and the maxi-
> mum employment and production objectives of the Employment Act
> require an expanding economy from year to year. . . .
> Only pronounced economic expansion can rescue us from the trap in
> which, as that review shows, we are caught when the economy declines
> or does not expand. . . .
> We believe that your announced goal of a 300 billion dollar economy
> is not just a slogan; it is the central solution to the core problems of our
> economy.[27]

In the January, 1950, *Economic Report to the President,* Keyserling was able to describe the emerging recovery from the mild recession of the preceding year (which had at least dampened much of
the inflationary forces) and to be cautiously optimistic about the
coming year. His analysis of the economy's potential supported the
declarations in the President's *Economic Report* that "Maximum production and maximum employment are not static goals; they mean
more jobs and more business opportunities in each succeeding year.
If we are to attain these objectives, we must make full use of all the
resources of the American economy." [28] In short, there was to be a
renewed emphasis upon economic growth or at least a renewed emphasis upon something on which both remaining Council members
were in essential agreement.

With Keyserling and Clark in early 1950 was a supporting staff
made up of professional economists who had joined the Council during the Nourse period. The most prominent of these was Gerhard

Colm, who had come to the Council after seven years of government experience, first in the Department of Commerce with Richard Gilbert and then in the Fiscal Division of the Bureau of the Budget. It was while Colm was with this division that he developed the concept of the national economic budget that was included in Roosevelt's budget message of 1941 and participated in the genesis of the original Full Employment Bill.[29] He operated in the overall areas of economic analysis, income flows, and national economic budget projections and served in fact if not in formal title as chief of staff. As a staff member recalls,

Gerhard Colm probably was the strongest and most influential man on the staff because Keyserling took him more seriously than anyone else, partly because he probably had a greater average standing within the rest of Government. Gerhard was a balanced fellow. He had Keyserling's sort of compulsive, moralistic compulsion to produce, but he had a much finer technical and statistical sense about what is feasible and professionally respectable in the argument of the case. . . . His own point of view was probably a pretty good center of gravity around which the . . . net position of the agency as a whole came out. However, the public appearance was of course colored by Keyserling's own biases which one would expect because the Chairman has a little better chance to set the public image than anyone else.

With Colm were a group of seven other senior professional economists who, with one exception, could be termed government careerists. Benjamin Caplan had won his governmental spurs during World War II with WPB and the Office of Price Administration (OPA). After seven years of teaching, he returned to the government and handled the Council's price work. John C. Davis, the group's labor economist, had also forsaken a teaching career and come to the Council after four years with the War Manpower Commission, the Bureau of the Budget, the War Labor Board, OWMR, and the National Housing Administration. Walter Salant was another OPA veteran. He had started his government career as an economic analyst with the Treasury in 1934 and had served with the Securities and Exchange Commission, Commerce, Office of Economic Stabilization, and the Price Decontrol Board in addition to OPA. Bailey credits him with being one of the early idea men behind the Employment

Act.[30] In Salant's work with the Council, he concentrated on international economic affairs. Robinson Newcomb, who was to leave the Council soon after the start of the Korean War and return as a consultant in 1953, was the Council's expert in the housing, construction, and public works areas. His thirteen years of prior government work included assignments with the National Recovery Administration, Interior, Commerce, WPB, and the Federal Works Agency. Frederick V. Waugh, the Council's agricultural economist, was perhaps the senior staff member in terms of government service, having been with the Department of Agriculture since 1928.

The exception to the government career pattern was Edgar M. Hoover, whose one year of government service (exclusive of three years with the Office of Strategic Services) had been a quick succession of assignments with NRPB, OPA, and WPB in 1942. Before joining the Council in September, 1947, he had resumed his teaching at the University of Michigan. His specialties with the Council embraced investments, prices, employment, and regional analysis.

Supporting these economists were professional assistants, four of whom came to the Council with previous government experience: Hamilton Q. Dearborn joined the Council from the Foreign Economic Administration having been with the Federal Reserve and WPB, Joseph L. Fisher served with NRPB during the war, Burton H. Klein served briefly with the Commerce Department before the war and later with the U.S. Strategic Bombing Survey before finishing graduate work at Harvard University, Susannah E. Calkins had been with the Budget Bureau and OPA, and Mary Smelker, who was Colm's assistant, had worked in the Department of Labor, OPA, and the Federal Reserve.

Although not professional economists, two other staff members were important in the Council's operation, each in his own way. Bertram M. Gross' government career started in 1938 in the Housing Authority research division. He moved to OPA in 1941 and to the Senate's Small Business Committee staff in the winter of 1942. He joined the Council in October, 1946, fresh from the battles of the Employment Act. According to Bailey, "For fourteen months, Room 15-A, as Gross' office, was the nerve center of full employment activity on Capitol Hill." [31] As assistant to the Chairman and later as

Executive Secretary, he served as the Council's administrative officer. In applying much of the aggressiveness and initiative that had marked his five years of staff experience on the Hill, he played far more of a creative role in the Council's activities than his titles might indicate. The other staff member was Frances James, the Council's chief statistician, to whom fell the responsibility of the Council's statistical data in its annual *Economic Reports*, memoranda, and other materials. She had been in the government for fourteen years and had transferred to the Council from the Bureau of the Budget.

As a group, there were two particularly noteworthy features regarding the Keyserling Council staff that had been for the most part inherited from the Nourse Council. First of all, it is obvious from their backgrounds that the great majority of them had their roots in Washington. They were career civil servants for whom the Council could be either a temporary or permanent base of operations, and they knew their way around not primarily as Council economists but as individual professionals with established reputations and contacts. Two of the eight had served with the Budget Bureau (Colm and Davis), all but Colm had seen service with the wartime emergency agencies, and Newcomb, Salant, and Waugh were—like Keyserling —veterans of the New Deal. The experience of the staff as a whole was predominantly analytical or advisory rather than operational.

It is also clear that, by and large, the convictions of the staff as of early 1950 were essentially congenial with those of Keyserling. (Charles L. Schultze, a latecomer to the staff, recalls that "by and large we agreed with Keyserling and he with us." [32]) They generally accepted the spirit if not all the letters of his expansion economics; they accepted the maximum-employment interpretation of the Employment Act. Such acceptance did not rule out certain reservations or disagreements, nor did it rule out eruptions in working relations between the chairman and the other economists, but it did mean a basic compatibility of viewpoints between the members and staff levels of the Council. Moreover, this compatibility included agreement on the Council's operations.

Keyserling's economic philosophy meant an equally aggressive concept of the Council's role.[33] It was "to help the President formulate, articulate, and obtain acceptance of policies contained in his

Economic Reports . . . to help determine needs and evolve policies
and programs." [34] To be effective, the Council should use its influence where different opinions exist. It should not hesitate to influence decision-makers, to inform the President, or to attempt to
persuade others. The extent and manner of advising depends upon
the individual adviser—his conduct, the vigor of his arguments, his
writings, and his speeches. Even in fulfilling an advisory role, the
Council is part of the President's official family and its members
should testify just like any other Cabinet member: "In the public
eye, I'm a government policy officer confirmed by the Senate. Somebody must exercise the trust; somebody must speak up. Disagreeing
with the President is as old as the government. I did not support the
President when I disagreed with him. Of course, I did not publicly
disagree with him." [35] Keyserling has also commented, "If the gap
is too great to be bridged, a resignation is in order." [36] Significantly,
economic analysis embellished by active advocacy were antithetical
neither to Clark nor to the staff, who were attuned to an active
advisory role on the Washington scene.

Internally, the Council was organized along lines that represented
an approximate melding of specialties of the staff incumbents with
major segments of economic activity—general economic developments, employment, prices, investment, production, monetary and
fiscal affairs, regional development, agriculture, international, construction, and welfare. The work load divided itself roughly into
continuing economic analysis and advice, preparation of the then
semiannual *Economic Report*, and the more routine tasks ranging
from preparing economic data for the UN to answering public
inquiries. These tasks were accomplished by a combination of
individual assignments and staff committees, such as the Reports
Committee.

There is no doubt that Keyserling was the energizing force behind
the Council's operations. Staff members of the period who have been
interviewed agree that Keyserling ruled with a strong hand, that he
drove his staff and could be demanding and impatient, but that
through delegation could also give them a sense of participation. In
his leadership, Keyserling did not adhere to any formal patterns of
giving assignments or holding staff meetings but passed out work as

it came along, sometimes in a continuing manner and sometimes on a crash emergency basis. Sometimes assignments would be direct; at other times they would be made through Colm. Consequently, most of the infrequent staff meetings centered on particular projects and involved only those who were working on them.

Under such circumstances, there was an interpenetration between objective economic analysis and policy questions. In applying technical competence, both Keyserling and his staff expected that the staff as well as the Council would think, research, write, and otherwise operate in terms of policy considerations. True, staff members would not take ultimate responsibility for policy recommendations, but they were expected to think in these terms. Describing the working relationships of the Council, Lewis has commented, "There was no reticence about telling the Council members everything we thought, . . . [we] talked with them freely, . . . we were often arguing with them." [37]

The Council's external operations followed a similar pattern of activity and informality. Keyserling would not hesitate to try to involve the Council in any issues that he thought could have a bearing on economic expansion.[38] Such involvement meant constant contacts by the Council and staff, primarily with the Executive Office but also with other economic agencies. The Council sponsored a number of interdepartmental committees, the most important of which was the Committee on Economic Stabilization Policy. Keyserling left no stone unturned in providing economic information for the President on a weekly, monthly, quarterly, or *ad hoc* basis or in bringing the Council's work to the attention of the White House, the Budget Bureau, and other of its clientele whose support the Council needed or whose opposition it wished to minimize.[39] Keyserling and Clark were able to see the President without difficulty, although the Truman papers indicate that the initiative for most meetings was with the Council and was most frequently exercised at "*Report* time."

As previously noted, Keyserling was more than willing to testify before appropriate committees of Congress. As one former colleague put it, "Keyserling would talk with anyone." And for the most part so would his staff, for it was such individuals as Colm, Gross, and

Caplan who were instrumental in maintaining continuing contact with such White House aides as Bell, Turner, and Neustadt. They maintained a constant link through professional association of long standing with the Budget Bureau, the newly formed National Security Resources Board (NSRB), NSC, and the staff of the Joint Committee on the Economic Report, as well as with such operating agencies as the Treasury, Commerce, Agriculture, and Interior Departments, and the Federal Reserve. Although Keyserling served as ex officio Chairman of the Committee on Economic Stabilization Policy, Colm was its active leader among the agency representatives of top departmental economists and program chiefs.[40]

Since the annual *Economic Report* was the Council's principal production, the preparation of it was a reflection of both internal and external operations. During the Keyserling period, it was essentially a communal process, not only within the Council itself but between the Council and the White House. For an *Economic Report* to be submitted by the President to Congress in January, the Keyserling staff in October prepared a tentative outline of analysis, recommendations, and projections, which was then reviewed and thrashed out in a joint session of Council members and staff. The Reports Committee, usually made up of three senior men, drafted the *Economic Report* based upon these deliberations, which, after countless revisions, would be forwarded to the Council. Despite the work that had gone on before and the general acceptance of substantive parts, Keyserling would not infrequently redraft whole sections, often by dictation.

According to Gross and Lewis, writing the report paralleled the process of preparing the budget. Although there was no counterpart to the call for estimates, *Economic Report* drafts involving policy recommendations were circulated to appropriate agencies for comment and clearance. Resolution of disagreements resembled an appeal procedure, where, if a settlement could not be reached by agency and Council staff, it was referred to Council members or agency heads, or if necessary to the Cabinet, or in the last resort to the President. Only in cases of exceptional conflict did the Council, even in its own reviews, include policy recommendations that did not in large measure grow out of interagency discussions.[41] Because

Keyserling regarded the budget as an operational aspect of the government's economic policy, he arranged to have the *Economic Report* submitted to Congress before the submission of the Budget Message.

1340325

For the *Economic Report* as a whole, the major clearance process was between the Council and the White House, for it had to be consistent with the President's Budget Message and State of the Union Message. Often, Colm or others of the staff would feed early drafts to Turner for his comments, so that, when the completed draft was presented for review as the Council's position, acceptance was more or less assured. Nevertheless, final drafts were reviewed with care by White House economists like Turner and Bell, with the latter serving as a clearing house for the two messages and the *Economic Report*. Normally, changes in the drafts of the President's *Economic Report* would be both substantive, to conform to the President's program, and editorial, to conform to the President's style of writing, whereas changes in the Council's own portion would be only editorial. Reportedly, Keyserling was often reluctant to have any changes made in his work and in late-hour sessions in the White House would frequently insist upon acceptance of "his" version. The final *Economic Report* was, in balance, a Keyserling product: "If the Chairman cannot very importantly influence the *Economic Report*, he's not effective. He should, of course, work with his colleagues, respect their views as well as his own, and strive for maximum reconciliation." [42] Although much of the analysis and sifting of views and ideas that went into the *Economic Reports* were carried on by the staff, the *Economic Report* itself symbolized Keyserling's Council and reflected his concept of its policy advisory operation.

By the time Keyserling received his appointment as Chairman on May 10, 1950, he, Clark, and their staff could take comfort in the status of the economy resurging from the mild contraction of 1948–49. After six months as Acting Chairman, Keyserling himself could look back and with satisfaction note that internal and external operations were working reasonably well. Although he was not a part of the White House inner circle, he maintained satisfactory relations not only with the President and the White House staff, but also with fellow occupants of "Old State"—the Budget Bureau and NSRB. On the personnel side Karl Arndt was soon to come from Nebraska to work with Clark on monetary policy and John P. Lewis would join the staff from Union College for his first government assignment. He attributed his appointment to the Council to his Ph.D. dissertation entitled "Toward an Administratable Price Policy for Full Employment," which had come to the attention of Colm.[43] More important, Blough would join Keyserling and Clark as the third Council member.

Consideration of Blough for appointment to the Council apparently dates back at least to the previous January, when Grover W. Ensley, then Associate Director of the Joint Committee on the Economic Report, sent to Donald Dawson in the White House a copy of Blough's paper on the Council presented at the recent American Economic Association meetings in New York. "I think," Ensley said, "he is sound in every respect. He's available."[44] Blough took his Ph.D. in economics at the University of Wisconsin in 1929 after three years of teaching economics. He worked for the Wisconsin State Tax Commission for five years and then resumed teaching at the University of Cincinnati between 1934 and 1938. For the next eight years, he served as Director of Tax Research for the Treasury Department with a concurrent two-year assignment as Assistant to the Secretary of the Treasury. During the four years immediately prior to his joining the Council, he was a Professor of Economics at the University of Chicago. Blough was apparently a far more reticent man than his colleagues. His views were more moderate; he appeared to abstain from taking definite positions and eschewed controversy. "A professional middle-of-the-roader" was the description of one former associate. Another felt that Blough "was, above all, ill at ease in this position of responsibility and didn't really want to exert very much leadership."

Of perhaps greatest substantive significance to the Council during the spring of 1950 was the Administration's major reappraisal of national security policy. Partially as a result of Russia's detonation of an atomic bomb in August, 1949, three years in advance of intelligence estimates, President Truman on January 31 ordered[45] that work proceed on the development of the hydrogen bomb and that the State and Defense Departments collaborate on a review of the national security situation and on the development of a planning document as a basis for future action. Although a joint effort, the bulk of the task fell to the State Department Planning Staff headed by Paul H. Nitze. After two months of concentrated work, a draft document was sent to the President on April 7.[46]

According to Hammond, Nitze and his staff thought that the military budget should be increased from $13 billion to approximately $35 billion or possibly even $50 billion, while Defense representatives were thinking in terms of a $5-billion increase to $17 or $18 billion.[47] Although the draft apparently argued for a greatly expanded commitment of resources,[48] it gave no indication of what the expansion would cost, apparently because of the irreconcilable differences between State and Defense viewpoints. The draft was so vague that Truman turned it over to the National Security Council with instructions to develop precise information and recommendations as to specific programs and costs. It was at this point that the document was christened "NSC 68" and that a sizable *ad hoc* committee was established under the National Security Council to carry out the President's instructions in a so-called "costing exercise." In addition to the National Security Council staff and representatives of State and Defense, the group consisted of representatives from the Joint Chiefs of Staff, NSRB, Treasury, the Central Intelligence Agency, the Budget Bureau, the Economic Cooperation Administration (ECA), and the Council of Economic Advisers. Although little of a concrete nature was accomplished by the Committee from mid-April to the start of the Korean War, Defense Comptroller MacNeil came up with "flash estimates" of $50 billion for fiscal year 1952 by July 1, which, tentative and unreliable though they might have been,[49] show that, even independent of Korea, the planning document's expansionary note "stuck."

The significance of the "sticking" was that it constituted a split with the prevailing view—legitimized by Nourse,[50] embraced by Secretary of Defense Louis Johnson, and accepted by Budget Director Pace [51]—that the national economy could not endure defense expenditures of more than approximately $15 billion without incurring ruinous inflation, intolerable economic dislocation, or both. The significance to the Council of this split was that Keyserling and individual staff members played a direct and indirect part in the development of the Policy Planning Staff position.

The devotion of one chapter of the planning document to a discussion of the potential of U.S. resources and, as reported by Alsop, Acheson's reference to "mobilizing our total resources" [52] indicates more than a coincidental similarity with the economic expansion views associated with the Keyserling Council. Available evidence does not indicate that the Policy Planning Staff formally consulted with the Council during the pre-April 7 drafting stage. However, Nitze, staff economist Robert Tufts, and others of the group had apparently worked with Council staff members Colm, Dearborn, and Salant at various times in the past, and they could hardly be oblivious to the thinking that had gone into the Full Employment Bill, the Spence and Murray expansion proposals of the preceding year, and Point Four. It seems only natural that such expansionist concepts would in turn form part of the thinking of planners wanting to justify the economic feasibility of the national security increase they considered necessary. It seems equally likely that they would make use of the Council's *Annual Economic Review* of January, 1950, which, in a chapter entitled "Pathways to Economic Growth," repeated Keyserling's argument for increasing gross national product from $258.7 billion in 1949 to $300 billion in 1954 through full utilization of the nation's resources.[53]

The Council's contribution took on a more direct and tangible character through the faithful participation of Keyserling and Dearborn in the costing exercise and through Colm's assistance in the drafting of the chapter on economics of the NSC 68 document approved by Truman shortly after the Korean War started. In their support on economic grounds of the argument for national security expansion, the Council joined NSRB and ECA as allies of the State Department ranged against the Defense Department, the Joint Chiefs of Staff, and the Budget Bureau. As one observer recalled, "Leon Keyserling consistently advocated the view that the economy could afford defense programs of the size contemplated and that it was a politico-military not an economic question as to whether or not we needed such programs for national security."

The views expressed in NSC 68 did not in and of themselves resolve the dispute between the limited and expansionist viewpoints.
The Korean outbreak accomplished this by rendering completely
academic the question of whether or not there should or could be
expansion. There had to be. The arguments for NSC 68 suddenly
switched from peacetime analysis to mobilization necessity. In blunt-
ing the force of the previously dominant view that the nation's economy could stand only so much defense expenditures, the Council
helped to shape the compatibility of national security objectives
with national resources allocations. The overriding significance of
NSC 68 and of the Council's involvement in it was that there
emerged before Korea a common foundation of information and
shared understanding of issues, commitments, and capabilities that
would otherwise have been arrived at in a piecemeal and partial
manner after it was most needed.

As of the third week in June, the existence and certainly the importance of this foundation was scarcely appreciated. The Council
for its part carried on with the costing exercise at the same time that
it completed the final drafts of its *Midyear Report*. With optimism
and reassurance it could describe "stability and growth on a sound
basis," [54] a decrease in unemployment, and an increase in both GNP
and productivity—all of which were favorable for the country at
large and for congressional elections barely four months away. A
sense of well-being for the economy and for the Council itself, soon
to be reinforced by the presence of Blough, Arndt, and Lewis, provided comfortable conditions for the summer pace of work.

The Affirmative Voice of Indirect Controls

The serenity and order of Friday, June 23, changed to the turmoil
and apprehension of Monday, June 26. Painfully reminiscent of
Pearl Harbor, although not as catastrophic, individuals and agencies
could easily envisage the shattering prospect of World War III. Cutting short his visit to Independence, Truman flew back to Washington for Sunday night meetings at Blair House with Acheson,
Johnson, the military service secretaries, the Joint Chiefs of Staff,
and others. While the UN Security Council condemned North

Korean aggression, those at the Truman emergency meeting agreed
with General Omar Bradley that the Russians "were obviously testing us, and the line ought to be drawn now." [55] The commitment of
U.S. forces followed promptly.

For the Council, no less than for the rest of the Washington bureaucracy, the world was different. The arrival of Lewis at the
Council on Monday and Blough three days later was lost in the
shuffle of new problems, new demands, and new opportunities.
Lewis has described the atmosphere he entered:

The staff reaction without exception was there was a hell of a job to be
done. There was nothing but, in a very matter-of-fact unemotional way,
a complete dedication to the job at hand. . . . Everybody worked hard.
The *Report* writing seasons . . . are always heavy overtime, long-
houred affairs, but this kind of pace continued right through the summer. The morale of the Council . . . was first class.[56]

Most immediately and specifically, the *Midyear Report* was suddenly obsolete and would have to be redone. As a newcomer, Lewis
could observe but not participate:

It was a most difficult thing watching them struggle for the next three
weeks and finally come around to the view that the thing had almost to
be thrown away and started all over again. This has always been to me a
great example of the inertia that is inherent in drafting, particularly in
drafting that is a group thinking process where there has been a whole
lot of negotiation and a lot of sweat and blood to get some sort of position established. And once you get that in hand, there is a terrific inertia
against changing it in response to new events. Unfortunately, the Council had been particularly forehanded in this instance and the *Report* was
by June 24 much more fully in hand than was usual at that point in time.
Then, of course, everything blew up. First a little tinkering with the
draft—a new introduction and a little rhetoric was thought to be
enough. Then gradually implications would seep through.[57]

Despite the anguish and pressure of the rush revision, which included two rounds of galleys on two successive days, the *Midyear
Report* was given a quick clearance and sent to the Congress on
July 26, one hectic month after the Korean invasion. Accepting both
the belief that Stalin's ultimate objective was to wreck the major
salient of the free world economy and the assumption that the immediate situation demanded partial mobilization, the Council ar-

gued for the long-term development and maintenance of maximum national economic power: "Economic policy must now be adjusted to the prospect of this long pull." [58] Public policies should be designed to achieve "a quick increase in production," "priority for defense and essential civilian needs," and "protection against the threat of inflation." [59] Of these, increasing production was of greatest importance, not only as an end in itself but as a means to achieving the other two. The recommended methods for this achievement were to increase taxes, to reduce nondefense federal expenditures, to tighten credit, priorities, and allocations for some materials and facilities, and to establish programs of guarantees and loans for capital expansion.[60] The *Midyear Report* nevertheless stated, "We do not recommend the employment of general controls over prices and wages at this time." [61] Instead, with productive potential well above the level of two years before,[62] major reliance would be placed upon (1) the indirect controls of taxation, credit restraints, and allocations and (2) voluntary adjustments by business, labor, and the consumer.[63] At the same time it was stated that

the appropriate agencies of Government should continue and intensify their development of plans for the utilization of more sweeping controls over the price-wage structure and over the utilization of manpower. These efforts should be brought at once to so high a stage of development that, if the need becomes clear, a request to and action by the Congress would enable their immediate application.[64]

The views set forth in the *Midyear Report* became the hallmark of Council views for the months ahead. Moreover, they constituted an articulation of economic expansion directly and indirectly in the name of the President. With his back turned on the pre-NSC 68 assumption of economic limits, Truman in his *Economic Report* said in Keyserling language, "Our economy has the human and material resources to do the job ahead—if we achieve the unity that will enable us to do our best." [65] The same mobilization of resources underlying Keyserling's approaches to reconversion, inflation control, and expansion were now applied to partial mobilization. Operationally, the statement of views demonstrates the Keyserling Council's move into a nonmilitary policy vacuum. The Council assumed this leadership role by taking the initiative to determine a mobilization policy framework that, while not necessarily original or innovative, both encompassed and shaped the quickly emerging though disparate mobilization views and efforts of agencies throughout the government. The Truman files suggest that Keyserling used the clearing of the *Midyear Report* to encourage the exchange of views at the Cabinet level.[66]

On July 19, the President addressed the nation and Congress on the Korean crisis. In speaking of the partial mobilization, he stressed the need for tax increases, credit restrictions, necessary allocation of scarce materials, and responsible action by citizens and government alike. At the same time he forwarded to Congress a request for a $10-billion defense supplemental budget appropriation and also a draft of the Defense Production Act of 1950, the Administration's proposal for mobilization.[67]

The bill, as simultaneously introduced into both houses, was silent on price and wage controls but concentrated on priorities and allocations, authority to requisition, expansion of productive capacity and supply, and control of credit and commodity speculation. The reasons for omitting controls involved recognition of political realities and convictions as to the needs of the moment. Despite any grudging admission of its wartime effectiveness, the OPA of World War II had lost none of its immediate postwar unpopularity; the hangover of antipathy to anything resembling its resurrection was strong. The Administration was badly beaten in its attempt to push price controls as an anti-inflation weapon in 1947 and 1948; Congress had little enthusiasm for the Spence and Murray proposals of 1949. No wonder the Administration wanted if at all possible to avoid the appearance of trying to achieve in an emergency what it could not do under normal circumstances, particularly in an election year. Congressional reaction against controls was judged to be so strong that, in Neustadt's words, Speaker Rayburn advised the President "that without the old divisive price issue his other control measures would pass Congress in a week." [68]

A number of nonpolitical reasons for avoiding controls were of at least equal importance. First, with the partial mobilization expected to absorb only an estimated 10 percent of the nation's resources, economic regimentation of the kind enforced during World War II was considered not only unnecessary but also inhibiting to the expansion that was expected. Hence, the drafters rejected NSRB's proposed twenty-title Emergency Powers Act, which, based on World War II experience, assumed full mobilization. Second, although it was generally recognized that the recovery of 1950 was beginning to generate some price increases even before Korea,[69] the Administration believed and hoped that its proposals would, in fact, be sufficient to check the expected price increases after Korea. Besides, other measures, such as tax increases, were possible. Third, the President wished to assure the Western world that he neither saw nor was planning for World War III.[70] Fourth, although the news from the front told a grim story of continuing defeat and retreat, the Commander-in-Chief knew that MacArthur was pushing his preparations for landings at Inchon and the breakout from the Pusan perimeter.

The sidestepping of wage and price controls was nevertheless short-lived. Neither the public nor Congress was aware of MacArthur's silver lining within the dark war clouds. The dominant feeling was one of alarm over the headlines of war and over rising prices at home. The wholesale price index (1926 = 100), having moved from 154.5 to 157.3 from June, 1949, to June, 1950, shot up to 163.7 in the first month of Korea. In the same thirteen-month period, prices of farm products rose 8 points and food prices 11 points.[71] Although not yet registered in terms of the consumer price level, the increase reinforced fear of national shortages and produced a consequent spate of hoarding.

Bernard Baruch's outspoken testimony before the Senate Committee on Banking and Currency on July 26 for controls far tighter than the loose indirect curbs contemplated at the time ignited a smoldering fire of public and congressional protest.[72] Baruch, the venerable, wise, and experienced adviser, became a champion. His views were backed by congressional leaders like Senator Scott Lucas and Representative Carl Vinson. Congressmen were beseeched by their constituents; pressure on the Administration mounted. Even such highly regarded Administration supporters as Secretary of Commerce Charles Sawyer were unable to stem the tide. Truman was thus forced to modify his position against all controls and, in similar letters to Representative Spence and Senator Maybank, chairmen of the respective House and Senate Banking and Currency committees, indicated a willingness to accept some form of price and wage controls. At the insistence of Maybank, the White House staff developed and furnished Maybank's committee with a draft of standby price and wage control provisions which were introduced on August 2.

Although the draft emerged virtually intact a month later as Title IV, "Price and Wage Stabilization," it had to survive attack both from those who sought to prevent use of direct controls as well as from those of the Baruch persuasion who considered it not strong enough. Representative McKinnon, for example, introduced an unsuccessful amendment that would have made price and wage controls mandatory if prices rose 5 percent above June 15 levels, and, reportedly, Senators Fulbright and Douglas pushed the same "trigger" idea within the Senate Banking and Currency Committee. As a measure of anti-Truman-pro-Sawyer sentiment, the Senate passed an amendment that, if it had not been killed in the conference committee, would have conferred authority for the allocation and priorities program upon the Secretary of Commerce.

In its final form, the bill had also to survive the possibility of a veto; two ex-OPA lawyers, Richard H. Field and Henry M. Hart, Jr., reviewed the bill at length to see whether it provided adequate flexibility for the President.[73] But the President did sign it on September 8, and within an hour the Federal Reserve issued regulations on installment purchasing and borrowing for the purchase of automobiles and other durables as authorized by the Act.

The Administration's handling of the Defense Production Act from the early drafting to the eventual enactment was the work of an *ad hoc* group of Executive Office specialists under the aegis of the White House staff, which provided day-to-day field leadership. The group included Charles H. Kendall, NSRB general counsel and veteran of WPB, Edward Hollander from the Department of Labor, Milton Kayle from the Budget Bureau's legal staff, Matthew Hale, who, as Secretary Sawyer's acting solicitor and also a veteran of WPB, enjoyed considerable acceptance by those who counted on the

Hill, and, for the Council, Caplan and Gross. Although Neustadt's office became the base of operations, the early drafting sessions took place in the office of another White House aide, Stephen J. Spingarn. Hollander, Kayle, and, to a lesser degree, Caplan were the ones who did most of the negotiating with the congressional staff, particularly Joseph P. McMurray and James Barrier of the Senate and House Banking and Currency committees. According to Neustadt, "Hale served as chief troubleshooter, while I manned the switchboard at the White House. Hale took his economic advice chiefly from me, and I, in turn, took it from Caplan, Hollander, and others." [74]

The Council's contribution through the participation of Gross and Caplan was twofold—general and particular. Regarding the former, Gross' contribution represented the Council's basic thinking. "Actually," Gross later recalled, "the Act can be regarded as a third step in a series started by the Spence Bill and the Murray Economic Expansion Bill, particularly the third title, "Expansion of Productive Capacity and Supply." [75] Gross provided the back-up material and, as an inveterate operator in the legislative process, encouraged the exchange of ideas and intelligence between the Hill and the White House and within the Executive Office. Sensitive to the importance of both production expansion and congressional acceptance, he urged brief and appealing labels for what might be an unappealing, even if necessary, set of provisions. In giving the Act its title, "The Defense Production Act," he put the emphasis on expansion, thereby directing attention away from the control and stabilization aspects. As late as July 13 it was called the "Allocation Act of 1950," a label with a far more negative impact.

Caplan was not only regarded as a competent career economist, but, as an OPA veteran, he was one of the most knowledgeable available experts on the problems at hand in mobilizing the nation's economy. Moreover, according to Lewis, he "was a ball of fire in any sort of a crash situation where you had to come up with some specific solution." [76] Consequently, it fell to Caplan to draft the discretionary standby price and wage control provisions as ordered by Maybank. Caplan did the drafting over the weekend of July 30, drawing largely upon applicable portions of World War II control laws, his own experience, and the control portions of the formerly proposed Spence Bill. His Title IV, "Price and Wage Stabilization," was the most crucial, the most debated, and, three months later, the most important portion of the Defense Production Act. Caplan's performance on the Defense Production Act typified the operating nature of the specialist's advisory role.

The day-to-day participation of Gross and Caplan as members of an *ad hoc* group that in three weeks turned out a draft bill and in another five guided it through the intricacies of congressional action to ultimate passage was significant on two counts. First, it illustrated the Council's central involvement in the most pressing economic policy issue of the day—the extent and nature of controls—and, second, it typified the individual and almost free-lance nature of that involvement. Gross and Caplan applied their expertise largely at their own discretion and initiative; they volunteered almost at the same time that they were called upon, primarily because of their knowledge and experience and secondarily because of their association with the Council. This order of importance does not depreciate the significance of the Council but rather indicates the nature of much of its early operations.

The day after signing the Defense Production Act President Truman addressed the nation and issued Executive Order 10161 delegating responsibilities pursuant to the Act. In his speech, Truman emphasized the necessity of increasing defense production, of operating on a pay-as-you-go basis, and of preventing inflation. He also spoke of increasing defense spending from the $15 billion intended before Korea to $30 billion by June, 1951. Both Keyserling and Caplan were among those who participated in the preparation of the speech. As Caplan has recalled, "Although we discussed the rate at which defense spending could be stepped up, that figure of $30 billion was in a sense pulled out of the air." [77] In neither the speech nor the Executive Order was there any mention of exercising the authority to control prices and wages. Nor was such exercise contemplated. Quite clearly, reliance on indirect controls was to continue.

By Ackley's definition, indirect controls are controls "which attempt to remove the excess of demand over supply by policies which inhibit demand—which curtail the aggregate of spending decisions." [78] This was in contrast, in Ackley's terms, to direct controls, "which attack the problem by making all except specifically permitted price and wage increases illegal." [79] As Ackley continues, the advantages of indirect controls include decentralized decision-making, better allocation of resources, simpler administration, maintenance of individual freedom, and no accumulation of unsatisfied demand. On the other hand, they might be ineffective or, if effective, injurious in terms of equity, incentives, and price relationships. Direct controls have the contrasting virtues and liabilities. They are usable when indirect controls are ineffective, they can enforce stability in relative income and prices, and they preserve the *status quo*. By precisely this preservation, they paralyze variations in price and income and impose that which is socially and politically undesirable, a managed economy.[80]

The reliance on indirect controls before and after the passage of the Defense Production Act represented a consensus among presidential advisers and executive officials concerned with mobilization policy. Typical of this consensus, the Keyserling Council in its new "Weekly Reports on the Economic Situation" addressed to the President advocated both intensified action on tax increases, credit measures, and expanded production and holding controls available on a standby basis.[81] Thomas McCabe, Chairman of the Federal Reserve Board, wrote to the President of his attempts to encourage Secretary Snyder, Senator George, and Congressman Cooper "to consider a more realistic tax bill," his discussing ways and means of slowing down the housing boom with Raymond Foley, the Housing Administrator, and the Federal Reserve's intention to institute realistic credit regulations.[82] In early September John Brownlee, Henry Hart, and Donald Wallace, consultants to Symington, urged prompt enactment of tax increases and firm credit controls, as well as strong allocation measures. They concluded, "We do not recommend a general price freeze or other overall controls at this time because it takes time to organize and implement, public opinion is not yet ready, inflationary spiral is not that imminent, and they might do more harm than good and impair availability when needed." [83] After conferring with Secretary of the Treasury Snyder, Blough wrote in his diary, "He [Snyder] thinks that the largest fraction of military expenditures should be financed through taxation in view of economic situation and the size of the public debt." [84] More than reinforcing consensus, these views pointed to the actions that were being initiated.

On June 29, four days after the start of hostilities in Korea, the House of Representatives capped four months of consideration by approving the 1950 tax bill,[85] directed primarily at reducing excise taxes and at the same time closing corporation tax loopholes. Within two weeks the gears had ground into reverse, and what had started out as a measure primarily to reduce taxes became one to increase them. The Senate began action on the original bill on July 5, but under pressure from both the President and Secretary Snyder, the Senate Finance Committee dropped the matter. In the meantime, the Treasury tax staff had developed a substitute stopgap measure providing for a tax increase of over $5 billion. On July 24, Representative Robert C. Doughton, Chairman of the House Ways and Means Committee, and Senator Walter F. George, Chairman of the Senate Finance Committee, agreed to consider the measure as an amendment to the first bill in order to obviate returning it to the House as an original money bill. To expedite matters further, it was decided to limit hearings to questioning Treasury and congressional tax experts in executive session. The bill was debated in late August, passed on September 1, approved by the conference committee by September 22, and signed into law the following day as the Revenue Act of 1950.

The major threat to the bill had lain in the possibility of including an excess profits provision. To the Administration this addition would have jeopardized the immediate passage of the bill, and to the legislators it was too risky before election. Consequently, a separate excess profits tax bill was introduced after Congress reconvened in late November and was signed on January 3, 1951. This was followed by the Revenue Act of 1951. On a full-year basis revenues were expected to be increased by $5.8 billion from the Revenue Act of 1950, by $4.2 billion from the excess profits tax, and by $5.4 billion from the Revenue Act of 1951, the total increase being $15.4 billion.[86] These tax measures were a major part of the government's effort to control inflation and at the same time channel the nation's economic resources into the defense effort.

The Council's contributions to this major effort were both catalytic and substantive. As Blough recalls, "Particularly during the fall of 1950 we were interested in seeing that a tax bill was developed and kept moving." [87] Moreover, Dearborn told Blough that the Council should not give up its position as coordinator of financial policies. Largely by virtue of his familiarity with tax issues and lengthy previous association with Treasury, the major share of this coordinating role fell to Blough. He was invited to join a Treasury study group charged with preparing a tax program. The group included representatives from Labor, Agriculture, and Commerce (but not from the Budget Bureau, Federal Reserve, or the White House staff).[88] At an initial Treasury tax policy meeting, the Council was invited to attend as the only "outside" participant.

In addition to the Treasury group, Blough established an informal tax policy discussion group composed of himself, Colm, David Bell from the White House staff, Samuel Cohn of the Budget Bureau, Laslo Ecker-Racz, head of the Treasury Tax Advisory Staff, occasionally Grover Ensley from the staff of the Joint Committee on the Economic Report, and Charles W. Davis, clerk of the House Ways and Means Committee.[89] Ecker-Racz' concern no doubt focused upon specific Treasury policy and particular provisions; Bell had to consider the consistency of tax possibilities with the President's overall program. Cohn thought in terms of matching revenues and expenditures. Blough and Colm were also concerned with the President's program but with greater emphasis upon the impact of the tax bite or lack of it upon different phases and processes of the economy.

The frequent communications among members of this group did more than provide a basis of understanding and consensus; it served to coordinate efforts to keep pressure on the President, Secretary Snyder, and the Congress, and they enabled the Council to assert a degree of leadership initiative not otherwise possible. For example, within three days of the President's signing the stopgap Revenue Act of 1950 the Council recommended to the President that he submit to Congress "at the earliest feasible moment" a second-stage tax bill designed to yield more than $10 billion in additional revenue to be derived from an excess profits tax and increases in payroll, corporate ("to around 50 per cent"), personal, and excise taxes. "A third stage of tax increases may be somewhat longer delayed, pending further clarification of the trend of expenditures and their impact upon the economy." Three weeks later the Council reiterated its recommendation and even suggested that a $15-billion increase might be necessary.[90] Undoubtedly such a proposal was thoroughly considered by Blough's group beforehand, even to the extent of circulating drafts. From the following excerpts of a memorandum from Bell to Murphy, it is clear that the recommendation as sponsored by the Council contributed to White House deliberations and ultimately to the President's request for an excess profits tax in November and a third-stage $10-billion increase the following February:

On page 7, the Council recommends a "second stage" tax program which would include an excess profits tax, plus increases in payroll taxes, corporate income taxes, personal income taxes, and excise taxes—the total to yield more than $10 billion of additional revenue. I do not know enough about the problem at this time to have any judgment on the various pieces of such a tax program, aside from the excess profits tax to which the President is already committed. It strikes me, however, that this is an exceedingly ambitious tax program to be presented to the Congress at its short session beginning in November. Charlie Davis told me the other day his offhand opinion is that it might be wise to limit the November tax bill to excess profits tax alone, in order to have a chance of enacting a bill at all, and in order to reduce the possibility of the Senate tacking on various special interest provisions. Laslo Ecker-Racz told me at lunch on Friday that he was tentatively thinking of an excess profits tax bill for the November session and a larger package in January. All in all, there is obviously a difficult problem of legislative strategy presented here, to which we will need to give consideration. Personally, I am convinced enough of the danger of inflation to urge that the President should recommend as big a package in November as could feasibly be enacted, but as yet I have no idea of how big such a package would be.[91]

Because of the central importance of tax policy to the mobilization program and because of the liaison the Council, largely through Blough, was able and permitted to maintain, the Council's contribution was not so much to make decisions as to clarify and to create the substance about which decisions had to be made.

Credit controls were scarcely less important, but the Council's contribution was, in contrast, almost peripheral. As already noted, the Federal Reserve issued regulations on consumer installment credit (Regulation W) within minutes of the signing of the Defense Production Act on September 8. Regulation W established a general minimum down payment of one-third on automobiles and 15 percent on home appliances and specified a maximum installment maturity of twenty-one months on automobiles and eighteen months on other items. At the same time, the Regulation tightened terms on VA-insured and FHA-guaranteed loans to take effect September 18 as a temporary step until Regulation X, then being developed, could be issued. The terms of Regulation X, issued on October 11, covering conventional loans on new one- and two-family dwellings and also government-insured or -guaranteed loans, constituted a comprehensive tightening on down payments and lengths of mortgages.

Throughout the period from August through October, the Council in its communiqués to the White House harped on the need for tighter credit restraints, reminding the President and his immediate advisers of the growth of consumer credit outstanding (27.5 percent above the level of August, 1949), urging prompt tightening of mortgage and installment credit, and criticizing the Federal Reserve regulations as "too limited and too mild." After the revision of Regulation W and the issuance of X, the Council, while finding encouragement in the tightening of consumer credit, urged the development of regulations governing multifamily structures and the strengthening of rent controls.[92]

Available evidence suggests that these urgings were those of an outside commentator rather than of an inside participant in the development of consumer credit regulations. Recommending a one-third down payment in late August appears less as the Council's original idea than as an articulation and support of the thinking that emerged as formal regulation less than two weeks later. The chief participants and formulators apparently were Guy Noyes, Winfield Riefler, and Raymond J. Saulnier (consultant) of the Federal Reserve, Neil J. Hardy of the Housing and Home Finance Administration, P. N. Brownstein of the Veterans Administration, Joseph E. Reeve of the Budget Bureau, and Robert Turner from the White House. In the development of Regulation X, Noyes and

Hardy were the day-to-day legmen and Turner wrote the enabling Executive Order.[93] Keyserling actually appears to have been reluctant to be drawn into the deliberations. On September 13 he wrote Steelman that "I have received your letter of September 7, enclosing a 'Statement of Policy for Control of Real Estate Credit.' We shall be guided by it to the extent that we are drawn further into this matter." [94] As late as September 25, in an internal memorandum on the pending Regulation X, one of the participants reported that, "Our most recent efforts have been devoted to bringing the Economic Council and NSRB into the picture to the maximum feasible extent."

The reasons for this lesser role appear to be twofold. One, consumer credit was sufficiently specialized in its nature and sufficiently independent in its Federal Reserve institutional roots that extensive participation by other than those operationally involved was difficult. Two, although Keyserling was convinced of the need for tighter control and sufficiently knowledgeable to play a part, his mind and efforts were too riveted to mobilization efforts as such to devote detailed attention to specific consumer credit controls. Similarly, Blough was concerned with fiscal matters, Clark with debt management and interest rates, and at the staff level there was no one available to play the positive role necessary for contribution in day-to-day deliberations.

By October the freshening current of good news that accompanied MacArthur's northward crossing of the Thirty-eighth Parallel not only bore out Truman's description of the Korean War as "a police action" but also served to validate the appropriateness of both indirect controls and partial mobilization. This validation was buttressed by the increases in production and leveling of prices in September and October. There crept into current thinking a sense of relief that all-out war, Russian-inspired inflation, and a controlled economy had all been avoided. Perhaps pressures would melt in the glow of Indian summer.

The Council, of course, could share in the general reaction to these developments, but at the same time it, particularly Keyserling, still had its collective eye on the long haul of Cold War pressure and on the necessity to expand production. In its late September and October reports to the President, the Council voiced concern over the emerging influence of enlarged defense expenditures, which were beginning to register in increased personal incomes, higher employment, extended weekly hours of work, higher wages, and higher profits.[95] These elements would inevitably accumulate into a wage-price spiral irrespective of short-term developments north or south of the Thirty-eighth Parallel. Only enlarged productive capacity for both military and civilian goods could ameliorate the long-term inflationary pressures. But such enlargement required affirmative action, not defensive reliance on controls. Although there was within the Council an underlying support for Keyserling's position, Blough and a number of the staff were reputedly more concerned with the immediate problem of price stability, and they attempted with some success to exert pressure in this direction.[96] A White House observer notes that Keyserling and Blough had differences over details but not over basic points: "Leon kept his eye on the big issue and was therefore amenable to some changes of detail." [97] Military progress and momentary price stability in September made indirect controls more effective, and the threat of direct controls was thereby reduced. But, to Keyserling's concern, the pressure was correspondingly lessened for the organization of agencies that were to direct and coordinate the mobilization of production resources and thus provide the key to expanding production. This was the problem that absorbed a major share of Keyserling's attention.

The mobilization ferment of the summer and fall of 1950 spilled over into organizational developments as rapidly as it did into defense, fiscal, monetary, and control policies. The early drafts of the Defense Production Act recognized the necessity for new authorizations, delegations, and generally expanded activities, as well as the inevitability of manpower shortages. Congressmen, Senators, and Administration spokesmen were no less aware of the impending organizational implications. Within the bureaucracy the prospect of renewed activity reminiscent of World War II meant all kinds of organizational realignment and innovation. "Organization and methods" shops, no less than their personnel and budget counterparts, began piling up overtime. Temporary buildings, eyesores that scarred much of the area between the White House and the Potomac, were conceded a new lease on life.

In the Department of Commerce, Secretary Sawyer convened a special meeting of the Business Advisory Council on July 26 for an off-the-record discussion of mobilization, economic controls, and organizational alternatives. In attendance were such notables as Lucius Clay, Sidney Weinberg, and William Yandell Elliot. Its *ad hoc* Committee on Organization recommended the establishment of a production agency comparable to the World War II WPB but under the jurisdiction of the Secretary of Commerce.[98] At the same time, Bernard Gladieux, Executive Assistant to the Secretary, and Ralph Heltzel, Director of the Office of Program Planning, initiated a related organizational planning effort. They were informally aided by Lyle Belsely, who had been with NSRB, was at the time serving with the Federal Security Agency, and would reenter the mobilization field on the staff of the National Production Authority (NPA) before the year was out. Seeking to benefit from the organizational lessons of World War II, their thinking ran toward the creation of a standby organization within Commerce similar to the Civilian Production Administration that had been established as the successor to WPB. The prospect of Commerce directing the mobilization effort was encouraged by a move in the Senate to have the Defense Production Act assign allocation and priority authority to the Secretary of Commerce.

This prospect ran directly counter to the views of both the Budget Bureau and the Council, which were disposed toward greater centralization. As described by Rosenberg, Charles B. Stauffacher, the Budget Bureau's Assistant Director in charge of administrative management, wished to preserve presidential authority for both constitutional and managerial reasons. Stauffacher reasoned that only at the presidential level could the diverse activities of various departments and agencies be coordinated in the event of full mobilization. The President could not delegate his constitutional authority to make decisions; hence, mobilization responsibility should not be centered in one department nor in NSRB, which should focus on long-range planning and advising, not on active coordination.[99]

The Council agreed with the Budget Bureau on the need for centralizing decision-making authority with the President but disagreed on the role of NSRB, which the Council thought should have "adequate authority to coordinate and expedite the various segments of the program assigned to a number of agencies . . . more than the right to receive information and make suggestions." [100] Behind the Council's arguments on behalf of centralization within NSRB was its own desire to be fully involved in mobilization activities. Delegation of the activities out of the Executive Office of the President would deny the Council a market for general economic analysis and expansionist emphasis: "The channels should be clear for the President to receive advice not only from the coordinating agency but in the same manner also from such primary staff agencies as the Council of Economic Advisers and the Bureau of the Budget." [101]

The prospect of direction by the Department of Commerce struck a competitive chord in operating agencies like Agriculture and Interior, which, not unnaturally, wished control over their own operations. It registered similarly with NSRB, which, under Symington, viewed overall coordination of defense mobilization as falling within its province. Fully aware of the activities within Commerce and the favorable legislative prospects for its leadership, Symington intensified his new agency's own organizational preparations and had his staff prepare plans for an enlarged administrative structure. On the day Truman signed the Defense Production Act, NSRB completed a detailed 103-page plan that called for the establishment of an Office of National Mobilization which would function as the central coordinating and directing agency, by implication under the general aegis of NSRB.

Neither Commerce nor NSRB could be satisfied with either the Act or the implementing Executive Order 10161, which upheld the Budget Bureau's position of lodging essential decision-making authority with the President. The Order authorized the establishment of the Economic Stabilization Agency (ESA) and two major components, the Office of Price Stabilization (OPS) and the Wage Stabilization Board (WSB). The order delegated the programs to establish allocations and priorities to the Department of Commerce and the Department of the Interior. Although it gave NSRB policy-planning functions, it limited coordinating powers to mediating interagency disputes, transmitting policies, obtaining progress reports, advising the President, and such other activities as the President might determine. In no sense was NSRB to be a link in the delegation of authority for specific parts of the mobilization effort to the new agencies or to Interior, Commerce, Agriculture, Army, Navy, Air Force, the Interstate Commerce Commission, or the General Service Administration, each of which shared in the delegations.

Despite the rebuff to NSRB and to Symington, the Council's continued involvement in mobilization policy was assured; policy-making was not moved beyond its advisory reach. Moreover, it managed to have a wedge inserted in the Executive Order:

> The Council of Economic Advisers shall adapt its continuing studies of employment, production and purchasing power needs and objectives so as to furnish guides to the agencies under this Executive Order in promoting balance between defense and civilian needs and in avoiding inflation in a stable and growing economy. In the performance of this function, the Council shall obtain necessary information from the agencies concerned and engage in regular consultation with them.[102]

Keyserling was thus free to direct his fire on what was to him the fundamental necessity of programming the mobilization. He sought full exploitation of authority under Title III of the Defense Production Act for guaranteeing loans, buying raw materials, encouraging exploration of critical materials, and reselling agricultural commodities. Even before the Act was passed, he was concerned about the uncoordinated nature of early mobilization efforts. His concern continued after the Act's passage, and he criticized such developments as the alleged independence of Federal Reserves operations [103] and the lack of specificity and firmness in Defense Department estimates.[104] He protested delays in basic priorities regulations, which hung fire in the Department of Commerce's new NPA awaiting decisions as to priorities and allocations for specific commodities. In the meantime, inventory control regulations remained ineffectual.[105] NSRB's apparent inability to settle a feud between Commerce and Interior over the control of nonferrous metals [106] epitomized the general bungling and confusion, and reinforced Keyserling's concern.

Keyserling's difficulty was that, weak as NSRB was, it was the best means available—in addition to the Council—for obtaining any sort of mobilization coordination. For this reason, Keyserling led his Council into close association with NSRB and did what he could to strengthen it. As an illustration, he prodded NSRB into developing a resources and needs budget, which he then forwarded to the White House in an attempt to promote the agency's operations.[107] In mid-October he appealed to the President without success to enlarge the coordinating powers of NSRB. Keyserling regularly attended the meetings of NSRB's Interagency Controls Coordinating Committee and always shared as much as possible in NSRB responsibilities. Although not administratively involved, the Council took substantial interest in NSRB's interdepartmental tax amortization committee and tried to implement its views. The mutuality of their programs and their propinquity within "Old State" enhanced the frequent association between the principals and staffs of the two agencies.

In retrospect, the explanation for the association between the Council and NSRB lies in the reactions of two men to complementary and interdependent factors. Both Symington and Keyserling thought in terms of increased defense build-up, Symington because it would provide the necessary strength against Russia, Keyserling because it meant, in addition, greater productivity for the nation. Symington's apparent readiness to impose controls for full mobilization did not at this point clash with Keyserling's opposition to them for partial mobilization. For the Council, association with NSRB meant a stronger hand in at least accelerating the mobilization effort. For NSRB, association with the Council meant a stronger, even if indirect, contact with the White House and an ally when it had virtually none. Symington's advocacy of full mobilization kept him out of step with Administration thinking and hence at arms' length from the President. Association with the Council meant staff resources when NSRB had few; Rosenberg saw the Council as NSRB's *de facto* economics staff.[108] As relatively new advisory agencies without established operating responsibilities they could help one another in an Executive Office dominated by the Budget Bureau.

The association had its rough edges; the Council's impatience with NSRB's seeming delays and incompetence was matched by NSRB's annoyance at the Council's aggressiveness and persistence. Keyserling had the competitive advantage of being on the right

track with a going organization. Nevertheless, the association functioned with some positive results. In a retrospective evaluation,
Ackley concludes,

With the success of the U.N. counterattack beginning in mid-September,
the urgency of control measures seemed to lessen. Such activity as there
may have been was centered in the National Security Resources Board
and the Council of Economic Advisers, since the Economic Stabilization
Agency existed only on paper.[109]

The Council's contribution to the organizational aspects of mobilization lay in the prominence it gave to the programming of mobilization operations. This prominence presented a centralizing force
against the divisiveness of departmental independence and NSRB's
inability to exact any real measure of coordination. Although the
strength of the Council contribution was limited to advice rather
than extending to command, the Council did encourage production
and hence a degree of interim price stability, it did help forestall the
imposition of direct controls, which turned out to be a mixed blessing, and it did press for the establishment of mobilization agencies,
even if only by exhortation.

Although others determined specific mobilization policies—the
President and his aides, Congress, the Budget Bureau, NSRB, Defense, Treasury, and the Federal Reserve, among others—the major
dimensions of the policies as they emerged during the summer and
fall of 1950 were fundamentally consistent with what had been the
Council's viewpoint since the beginning of the Korean War. By no
means was this a matter of the Council's originating and then gaining acceptance for the Administration's mobilization program. The
experiences of World War II provided too common a body of knowledge for that, and operating agencies already had too firm ideas of
what should be done. Through the activities of Keyserling, the other
appointed Council members, and the individual staff professionals,
however, the Council articulated a consensus and an approach to
policy alternatives. It gave these an attitude of, in one of Keyserling's
favorite phrases, "affirmative action." Its constant urging of increased
production, planning, and indirect controls from the vantage point

of the Presidency produced a sense of impetus and direction that were more forceful than were echoes of decisions made elsewhere. In providing an overall viewpoint acceptable to the Truman Administration, the Council served as the focal point of mobilization leadership. In the full range of its advisory operations, the Keyserling Council was largely responsible during the first five months of the Korean mobilization for directing the mobilization policy away from rather than toward direct price and wage controls and for directing attention toward rather than away from objectives of expanding both civilian and military production.

The reasons for the Council's influence appear to be fourfold:

1. Korea provided a compelling rationale for expansion economics. The maximizing of the nation's productive capacity that Keyserling had been arguing for to fight recession and inflation now became the major "nonsecret weapon" for national security. The potential to handle the defense expansion envisaged in NSC 68 turned overnight into a necessity.

2. The emergency created the need and expectation of greater government participation in the nation's economic affairs and correspondingly the expectation within the government of an almost wartime measure of central direction and coordination.

3. The partial mobilization put effective mobilization leadership in limbo. That is, it was enough of a mobilization so that the President was almost solely concerned, along with the NSC, with the military and foreign policy aspects of the emergency and thus could not lead on the domestic front as well. But it was not extensive enough to warrant the naming of a mobilization czar for consolidated coordination of effort; at least, Truman was not willing so to designate Symington or to turn NSRB into a latter-day OWMR. In the situation of mobilization authority decentralized under the Defense Production Act, NSRB ineffective in terms of leadership, the Budget Bureau immersed in budgetary and organizational phases, and the White House staff too close to the President to take coordinating initiative itself, the Council stepped in. No other agency was effectively functioning as an overall coordinating body. Although created in October, the Economic Stabilization Agency was not to become operative until the following January.

4. Until December, 1950, the major decisions regarding mobilization policy had not been locked up. Instead of commitment to programs that could be delegated to operating agencies, consideration of policy alternatives continued, thereby permitting the Council to participate and press its views. True, stopgap tax legislation had been enacted, a supplemental budget request had been rushed through, the Defense Production Act had been passed, and credit controls established. But, as illustrated by the standby nature of the wage and price control authority of that Act, thinking was more in terms of handling contingencies than of making long-term commitments. Keyserling, no less than anyone else, wished to avoid controls. The immediate characterization of the war as a limited engagement—a view at first threatened by ominous retreats but later justified by MacArthur's advances up the Korean peninsula—only served to lessen pressures for decisions and to keep the decisions themselves fluid.

To this combination of circumstances, the Keyserling Council was both willing and able to respond. It shared the galvanizing sense of urgency. A burden was to be shouldered, a job to be done, and, most important of all, there was a demand for its services. This was not a demand limited to the appropriateness and void-filling acceptance of Keyserling's expansion economics but extended to the more detailed and technical contributions of its staff. Lewis' recollections are revealing:

As a small outfit, an outfit that could improvise, it had good enough professionals with enough experience so that they could be popped in to hurry up first draft jobs, get some sort of order together, begin to sketch out the requirements—administrative and organization and so on for a control agency. My own impression is that the Council and its staff were very effective—possibly more as a reservoir of individual consultants than as a single integrated or coherent agency.[110]

Under Keyserling's chairmanship, the work of Gross and Caplan on the Defense Production Act provides perhaps the most specific example of this, but it would also apply to Davis on labor matters, Hoover on production problems, such as tax amortization, and Salant on international affairs. In other words, both in their external and internal relationships the Council staff members were able to link their expertise with decisions. The staff was able to back up and complement its Council.

The rhetorical question of the time might have been, will the Council's influence last? The gathering momentum of increased defense expenditures was forcing a resumption of price increases and hence an acceleration of the wage-price spiral. Even more ominous, in early November the Chinese Communists crossed the Yalu to oppose the UN forces in North Korea.

III. THE PERIOD OF FRUSTRATION

Overnight, the Chinese intervention in the Korean fighting meant virtually a new war both at the front and at home. The new crisis cast over the oncoming Christmas season a gloom that was as intense over Washington as over the rest of the nation and the free world. The changed situation meant new strategy for MacArthur and revised policy on both sides of the Potomac. Indirect price and wage controls were threatened as retreat from the Yalu forced the mobilization effort into urgent expansion. Military requirements skyrocketed. The budget for the fiscal year 1952 was obsolete before it was presented, while a second supplemental to the budget for fiscal year 1951 raised the year's total defense budget to $48.2 billion from the original $13 billion. For the nation's economy, another wave of scare buying, joined with the groundswell impact of already expanded defense procurement on top of the growing shortage of material and manpower resources, produced another turn of the wage-price spiral. The question was not so much whether or not there should be price and wage controls but what controls, how imposed, when, and by whom.

Although these were questions much in need of answers, it was six weeks before any decisive action was taken and another five weeks before mandatory controls went into effect. For the most part, Administration officials vacillated, at least in their public statements, in an on-again-off-again cycle of favoring and opposing the imposition of controls. While in mid-November Truman saw no price and wage controls "right now," [1] Symington said they would be applied gradually,[2] and the new Secretary of the Army, Frank Pace, warned of a long period of sacrifices and high taxes.[3] Later in the month, Keyserling spoke of expansion without regimentation by government controls.[4] In early December Symington expected all-out controls as the situation went from light to dark gray,[5] while Senator O'Mahoney urged their prompt imposition,[6] and Secretary Snyder viewed them as coming eventually.[7] At the same time, Alan Valentine of ESA, along with his new Price Administrator, Michael DiSalle, and Wage Administrator, Cyrus Ching, were pictured as reluctant to embrace controls.[8] The Attorney General, Paul McGrath, opposed them unless there was a full emergency.[9] Senators Maybank, O'Mahoney, Ives, and Capehart urged mandatory controls on prices and wages after Ford and General Motors refused to rescind their recently announced price increases.[10] Simultaneously, Keyserling reluctantly predicted some wage and price controls soon,[11] and Steelman saw rationing on scarce materials unless output increased.

Not until mid-December, when the Communists had almost encircled the First Marine Division, the Gallup poll reported that 55 percent of the nation thought World War III was at hand, and another wage-price spiral was clearly in sight, were any sort of concrete steps taken. On December 7, the Council sent a memorandum to the President entitled "Further Action on Price and Wage Controls," which stated in part,

Mr. Clark emphatically urges an immediate freeze of all prices and of wages of industrial and utility workers. . . . Mr. Keyserling and Mr. Blough, while recognizing the forces of this argument, feel strongly that, due to a combination of economic, administrative and public reaction reasons, price and wage controls should be imposed through a rapid sequence of steps and not in one fell swoop. They recommend a strong program along these lines.

(1) Immediate centralization of purchases from abroad of essential and scarce materials which are being bought in large quantities. . . .

(2) Very prompt imposition of controls on basic industrial raw material prices, starting at once with some nonferrous metals such as copper and zinc . . . accompanied by effective wage stabilization where ceilings are placed on prices. . . .

(3) Conferences with selected groups of management and labor, starting with the most important commodity fields. . . .

(4) In addition, . . . staffing and preparation should be rushed forward as rapidly as possible.[12]

Truman reacted by asking Steelman to arrange a meeting for December 9, but it was apparently not held until December 11.[13] Symington and Clark reportedly urged controls and proclamation of a national emergency, while Valentine, Keyserling, and Blough opposed these moves on the grounds that a proclamation would accomplish little and that the agencies were not staffed to handle more than gradual controls.[14] According to Ackley, the conferees did agree to urge the adoption of voluntary standards, to send telegrams to leading firms urging voluntary restraint, to consult with appropriate representatives of business regarding action on commodity prices, to seek a roll-back of the recent automobile price increase, and to develop a stabilization field organization.[15] The group did not, however, take action on the Council's most clear-cut recommendation of imposing controls on basic raw materials.

As an outgrowth of the meeting, the President on December 15 declared a national emergency, spoke to the nation about an increase in military expansion and accelerated production, established an Office of Defense Mobilization (ODM) with Charles E. Wilson of General Electric as Director, and said that controls on wages and prices would follow. The following day, prices on automobiles were rolled back to December 1 levels and on December 23 automobile industry wages were frozen. By the beginning of the new year, however, some eight weeks after the Chinese intervention, there was still no broad and concrete action on wage and price controls beyond assurance to the general public and ample advance warning to producers that they were somehow, sometime coming.[16] This combination of indecision, confusion, promise, and inevitability of outcome led Ackley to conclude, "In short, the Administration record of the stabilization agency and the whole presidential high command in this period is one of miserable failure." [17]

The explanation for this failure lay in the complex of uncertainties surrounding the entire Korean War situation, the general reluctance to respond to the more immediate developments, and the woefully unprepared conditions of mobilization organization. Perhaps Neustadt was correct in suggesting that Truman, unlike Roosevelt, could not or would not shift from "Dr. Fair Deal" to "Dr. Win-the-War," for normally firm leadership did not come from the White House on the matter of controls. Truman's antipathy for the control provisions of the Defense Production Act appears to have been coupled with uncertainty about Communist intentions even as he tried to prevent the spread of fighting. While his own attention and that of the State and Defense Departments were thus focused on Korea, his mobilization officials and advisers proved unable to take up the delegation of leadership on the home front.

Valentine himself had little stomach for direct controls. Ackley quotes a memorandum from Valentine to himself, apparently some thoughts written as he assumed his duties as Director of ESA:

Important to recognize the precedents of a three to four year hot war do not necessarily apply to a five to ten year "cold war," economically, sociologically, psychologically.

1. In situation we face, productive capacity must be constantly increasing, not only military goods but nearly all goods.

2. Increased production is perhaps the best single factor to curb inflation.[18]

On December 11, the day of Truman's meeting, Valentine circulated a memorandum to his staff containing twelve reasons for not considering a general price freeze. One of the most important of these was ESA's inability so far to staff and develop an adequate organization to police a comprehensive controls program. Moreover, his economic advisers were not in agreement regarding the imposition of price controls. On one hand, James Brownlee clung to reliance upon voluntary action with possibly some selective controls, and Richard Heflebower shied away from a general freeze because of the difficulty of controlling prices of consumer items such as food, the purchase of which could not be postponed. On the other hand, Griffith Johnson favored the imposition of an immediate freeze of nonagricultural raw material prices, and Caplan, advising from the Council, saw comprehensive controls as inevitable by the early part of 1951. He recommended the imposition of selective controls immediately, starting with nonferrous metals and moving to finished products, and ultimately to the wholesale level.[19]

Valentine's concern over organizational and staffing problems appeared to be an extremely valid one, as controls without an administrative and enforcement organization would be worse than no controls at all. Manpower shortages existed at all levels of ESA, OPS, WSB, and NPA. Regular agencies, willing to lend personnel to the new emergency organizations, could not be too generous without handicapping their own operations. The uncertainties attending the partial mobilization cooled the willingness of business executives, lawyers, and other specialists to take positions, particularly of those who had served with the World War II emergency organizations. It was on the basis of this argument of inadequate organization and management that the Budget Bureau reputedly supported Valentine on postponing direct price and wage controls. Moreover, a situation stringent under the best of circumstances was made worse by the press of other year-end activities. The White House, the Budget Bureau, and the Council were racing to prepare the three presidential messages. Striving to get some specific budget data from the Defense Department on the costs of the arms buildup, the Budget Bureau was not in position to invest resources in the price and wage controls problem.

As for the Council, it is true that it had recognized the accumulating inflationary pressures during October and November, had frequently reported these developments to the President, and had urged tighter indirect controls, more extensive programming of resources and needs, and accelerated organization of mobilization agencies. As early as November 8, Colm favored prompt action to freeze selected prices that were already reacting to the Chinese intervention.[20] Clark's preference for a freeze and Caplan's favoring of selective controls has already been noted. Fred Waugh, the Council's agriculture man, and John Lewis also favored prompt stabilization action.[21] The Council's December 7 memorandum to the President, particularly its recommendation to impose controls on raw materials, stands as a consensus acceptable to the Council as a whole but apparently not one to which Keyserling could subscribe heartily or publicly. To accept the consensus was one thing; to promote its substance, especially the controls, was something else. As Lewis recalls,

His attitude toward the advisability of introducing price controls shifted like some other people's after the Chinese intervened and thinking about mobilization shifted from something like a 10 percent to a 25 percent one. Of course, whether his own views shifted or not, the Administration's did and he had to go along to a degree. But he still didn't want price controls to get in the way of the production effort.[22]

Six days after sending the December 7 memorandum to Truman and just two days before the President was to proclaim a national emergency, Keyserling and his colleagues met with the Business Advisory Committee of the Department of Commerce. After introductory comments by its chairman, the Council received a consensus that was predictable but still quite different from its own. Executives such as Marion Folsom, Fred Lazarus, Jr., Blackwell Smith, and John D. Biggers were against controls; they were not needed now, would hamper production, wouldn't work: "For the long pull, we kid ourselves if we expect to control prices generally." [23] They were also opposed to the excess profits tax, then nearing congressional enactment, which, to the government advocates of indirect controls, was vital to the stabilization program. In answer to these objections, Keyserling asked whether a line could be drawn between areas that must be controlled and those that need not; he also countered that now was the time to commence action on selective types of controls.[24]

In its published statements, the Council was more neutral than it had been on December 7. In its annual report to the President, entitled *The Economics of National Defense,* the Council emphasized the need to expand production, program requirements and supplies, maintain pay-as-you-go taxation, and encourage voluntary efforts. On a note of unwelcome inevitability, it acknowledged that "the die has now been cast for price and wage controls." [25] Not until its own *Economic Review* of January 9, 1951, published with the President's *Economic Report,* a full two months after the Chinese intervention, did the Council openly support direct controls and even then its discussion of controls, in terms of relationships and general policy guides, was noncommittal and unenthusiastic.

It is clear from his statements and from his whole approach to mobilization policies that Keyserling resisted supporting direct price and wage controls as long as he did primarily because of what he considered to be their restrictive impact on expanded production. Direct allocation and priority controls had at least the advantage of being positive inducements to the production that was necessary. The build-up of inflationary pressures in November and December, of which Keyserling was perfectly aware and which were of such concern to his Council colleagues, failed to shake his single-minded attachment to comprehensive production programs and indirect controls. Moreover, the impressions gained from Council colleagues of the time is that Keyserling hung back from urging the imposition of controls at least in part because he simply did not wish to be identified with the leadership of any move to impose them; he did not wish to attract the antagonism of those who would be made uncomfortable by such controls. Such hesitancy was not a matter of courage or principle or lack of these qualities, but rather of prudence and discretion. He could not publicly veer too far from the views of Truman, as had Symington; in addition, he could well remember the criticism he had absorbed for his active encouragement of controls in 1947, 1948, and 1949.

At the risk of oversimplification, the evaluation of the Council's performance during this period carries an inference of what might have been. Having done much in the Truman manner, to set the sights in the economic part of the mobilization effort during the four months of July through October, the Council entered the November–January period in a position of influence. It enjoyed a central role in the policy-making process at a time when partial mobilization made indirect controls feasible and bearable, when a cross between dread of another war and optimism over a "police action" inhibited a firm commitment to mobilization, and when neither ESA nor NSRB was fully effective and ODM was not yet established. The confusion and indecision following the Chinese offensive was grounded largely in precisely these failures to organize, program, and expedite during the preceding months that Keyserling had warned against. Yet the conclusion remains that by the Council's own indecisiveness and failure to change course quickly and firmly, the Council itself contributed to rather than ameliorated the confusion when the situation did, in fact, become critical. Because of the Council's role and composition, it was the agency theoretically most capable of changing course quickly. Because of the promptness of its response to the initial crises in July and the affirmative nature of its voice during the intervening months, it was perhaps the agency most expected to change course, or to set a course.

It seems all too possible that the Council could have exerted a clarifying force if it had itself been more responsive to the changed situation. In retrospect, it appears that there should have been a price freeze established by December 15 and that such a move could have provided the necessary pressure for overcoming the organizational bottleneck. It would have provided in addition a legal basis for enforcing a freeze and possibly a subsequent roll-back of prices once enforcement was organizationally possible.[26] Frustrated and paralyzed by the conflict between its basic expansion philosophy and the necessity for controls, the Council lost its capacity for exerting influence. Quite out of character, it failed to fill a decision-making void that desperately needed filling. In its failure, it became a swing factor in sustaining the hiatus that existed before anti-inflationary controls were finally established in late January.

A Battle Won and a Battle Lost

It was not until after the start of the new year that paralysis in the presidential high command began to give way to action and progress. While the establishment of wage and price controls in the near future was being widely advertised by administrative spokesmen, including Truman,[27] steps toward what would be called the "January price freeze" were being taken on the organizational front and at the professional level.

Under the terms of Executive Order 10193, by which ODM was established, Wilson had been given extremely broad powers as defense mobilizer. Despite efforts of the Budget Bureau to limit the implied delegation of presidential authority, Wilson was virtually an assistant President responsible for the entire mobilization effort, or, as the *Reporter* expressed it, a "Byrnes and Nelson rolled into one." [28] By the early weeks of January, ODM and two subsequently established adjuncts, the Defense Mobilization Board and the Defense Production Administration, were gradually gathering staffs and getting under way. Replaced by ODM, Symington and his NSRB were out of a job and many of its personnel transferred to the successor agencies. Moreover, DiSalle, who had become head of OPS in early December, was more favorably disposed toward the immediate imposition of controls than his boss, Valentine. At increasing odds with Valentine, DiSalle soon learned that he had to, and could, circumvent him to establish a direct and more effective alliance with Wilson and his aide, Eric Johnston. Although Valentine was able to persuade Wilson to reject DiSalle's early January proposal of a thirty-day temporary freeze, the combination of pressure, conflict, and frustration led to Valentine's resignation and to its quick acceptance on January 18. Even his last-minute summoning to a secret meeting on January 17 of former OPA chiefs Leon Henderson, Paul Porter, and Chester Bowles for advice on formulating a general freeze to be imposed the next day did not alter the desire for his resignation. The closer ESA-OPS alliance thus strengthened their respective organizations, an improvement that was matched by Cyrus Ching's development of WSB.

In the meantime, the professionals at the working level were desperately trying to hammer out some sort of price-control regulations. On January 15, Harold Leventhal, a Washington lawyer and young veteran of OPA days, joined DiSalle's OPS staff. He immediately pulled together the staff-level draft efforts that had been accumulating since early December and started preparing a general freeze order. Caplan, who had worked with Johnson in drafting the regulations for certain commodities,[29] turned to drafting the general "Statement of Consideration." [30]

What proved most difficult was the problem of establishing a suitable roll-back of prices in order to reverse the price-increase trend, penalize speculators and those attempting to "beat the freeze," and fulfill an obligation to reward those who had responded to government requests by voluntarily withholding price increases against both increasing costs and decreasing profit margins. However, price-cost relationships had become too distorted during the December–

January inflation scramble to push prices back to December 1 levels, much less to those of mid-November or the previous June. Despite the advantage given speculators over those who had heeded government requests, the solution proposed by the Leventhal group on January 24 was a freeze order involving both a roll-back of prices and a base period of at least a week. Besides being administratively feasible, such an arrangement would penalize the worst price-raising offenders and at the same time give at least token recognition to those who had not raised prices. This solution was apparently sufficiently acceptable to DiSalle that he was able to forecast the prompt issuance of general controls before the Joint Committee on the Economic Report.[31]

Immediate opposition to this solution came from the top administrative level. In its meeting on January 24 the Cabinet, with Keyserling in attendance, discussed price- and wage-control policy. While in no sense attempting to pass judgment on the technical aspects, it did, with Truman's assent,[32] accept Keyserling's argument that prompt establishment of controls should not be complicated by either a roll-back or a base period. According to Ackley, Keyserling led the argument against the roll-back to December 1, having been persuaded of its impracticability by his aide, Caplan, who had been instrumental in shaping the opinion of OPS.[33]

Promptly informed of the Cabinet's view, Leventhal and his colleagues were much upset and obtained permission to attempt to change Keyserling's mind. At a meeting on either the same or the following day, Leventhal succeeded in convincing Keyserling of the necessity of a base period on the practical grounds that hundreds of products did not turn over on the market every day. But Keyserling would not budge on the roll-back. What upset Leventhal was that Keyserling disputed the judgment of the Leventhal group, not on policy grounds but on technical grounds—"*our* area of competence" —and insisted that a roll-back could not be administered.[34] Even Caplan was believed to consider Keyserling wrong in objecting to a one-week roll-back.[35]

Leventhal made a last-ditch presentation to Johnston on January 26 at a final meeting prior to the issuance of the freeze order that evening. Although Johnston appeared to believe that Leventhal's arguments were sound, he telephoned Keyserling for his side of the story, for he said, "I'm not the expert, Keyserling's the expert." [36] Keyserling immediately joined the meeting and made what has been described as an emphatic argument for no roll-back, insisting that the decision had been made at the Cabinet level and should not be reversed by technicians. Moreover, as Keyserling has stated it,

emphasis on roll-backs, base periods, etc., and all the administrative paraphernalia that would go with them would direct attention away from the major problem of relying upon planned expansion of production as the main long-range method of stopping inflation and focus it instead on procedures. . . . It was administratively cumbersome and involved taking up too many people's attention. We had to consider the larger issues, not just roll-backs.[37]

The Keyserling viewpoint prevailed partly out of agreement and partly out of necessity. If there had been a roll-back, the order could not have become immediately effective because, being ex post facto, it would have automatically created thousands of violations. In consideration of this problem, the OPS proposal contemplated an effective date two weeks after issuance. As Clay, acting for Wilson, and Johnston were opposed to any further delay, the professionals conceded defeat. Into the early hours of January 27, OPS mimeographers ran off and gave to the press a page at a time a general price freeze effective immediately that provided for a base period extending from December 19 to January 25 but no price roll-back.

To Keyserling the outcome was "a justifiable battle won." [38] The reasons behind his successful participation in this particular matter appear to be threefold:

1. It is difficult to overestimate the force of the constant and overwhelming concern for expanding production, particularly during a time of crisis. To Keyserling the more simple the control mechanism, the less it would hamper the increase of productive capacity. His arguments proclaiming the inhibiting effects of too much administration registered with mobilization officials from business and labor who wanted to start moving.

2. The necessity for immediate establishment of price and wage controls of some sort was obvious to all; Keyserling's advocacy was part of a swelling chorus rather than a solo performance.

3. He could move into the January price-freeze situation and win because of the still amorphous and unconsolidated positions of ESA and its constituent OPS. Their policies, their organizations and communications, and their leadership were as yet undeveloped. ODM was itself far from being fully operational. All three were woefully undermanned. Johnston had been in office only a few weeks, his boss Wilson and subordinate DiSalle not much longer. Working relationships, both formal and informal, had not yet been established among professionals such as Leventhal, Stephen Ailes, Johnson, and Edward Phelps. These fluid and highly formative circumstances were favorable to Keyserling, who must have wanted his Council to rebound from eight weeks of uncharacteristic indecisiveness and regain the initiative necessary for constructive policy involvement. Nevertheless, it would be the continuing evolution of these circumstances that would make this victory climactic rather than part of a developing trend for the Council.

While OPS ground out its long-awaited freeze order, ODM began to accumulate operating momentum as it pushed defense production to the center of the mobilization stage. On the military front, the fighting was beginning to stabilize around the Thirty-eighth Parallel. At the same time, the Council was posting a new series of inflation storm warnings that would soon appear in its February *Economic Indicators*. Consumer, commodity, farm, and stock prices continued their upward climb, led by foods at the farm, wholesale, and retail levels. Disposable income for the 1950 fourth quarter continued to gain despite an increase in savings; consumer credit was up slightly. Commercial bank loans continued to expand, privately held money supply had reached a new high by January, and preliminary estimates indicated a $367-million federal government cash deficit for the 1950 fourth quarter.

For OPS itself, January's policy problems of roll-back and base periods became February's operational problems of enforcement and adjustment.[39] The problem that absorbed the major energies of OPS officials for the ensuing two months centered on price regulation for the great manufacturing segment of the economy. To DiSalle and his professionals the demands of the problem were fourfold:

1. Adjustments had to be worked out within the limits of the General Ceiling Price Regulations (GCPR) in order to close loopholes and handle inequities.

2. The commitment to rescue those who had voluntarily refrained from raising prices had to be fulfilled.

3. Price stability had to be achieved without further distortion of cost-price relationships inherited from the preceding seven months of inflation and indirect controls.

4. OPS had to secure compliance with the regulations it promulgated. Of these, the first was perhaps the most immediately apparent, but the second became the most compelling force in shaping the Manufacture Price Regulation, better known as CPR-22. Inasmuch as the GCPR imposed no price roll-back, OPS felt that it had an obligation to help or, in its terms, "bail out" the American business firms who had voluntarily held the price line. Moreover, as Leventhal recalls, "My concern was on equitable as well as moral grounds. . . . The reference to equity indicates that there is a legal consideration as well. And it is also practical since any government program involves the voluntary cooperation of the regulated in ways too numerous to mention." [40]

The outcome of almost two months of deliberations, trial proposals, and modifications was a proposal that attempted a tolerable compromise among these demands. OPS proposed not to restore pre-Korean War prices but rather pre-Korean War cost-price relationships at whatever levels possible. Its approach to this objective and to price relief for cooperative manufacturers was not to impose broad-scale roll-backs on those who had hiked prices. Instead, OPS would attempt a combination of roll-backs and roll-forwards, that is, certain price increases and decreases beyond the January 26 freeze that would extricate the conscientious, restrain the opportunists, and in the process restore cost-price relationships. Achieving such two-way price adjustments would be by each industry's own calculation of cost-price data required by OPS rather than by OPS determination and enforcement. As soon as possible, such individual calculations would be replaced by OPS regulations tailored to each industry. The emphasis was to be on roll-backs, with roll-forwards limited only to firms with unsatisfactory profit positions.

The Council's link with CPR-22 was primarily via Caplan, who kept in frequent and extensive contact with OPS personnel directly involved in its development, including members of its economic staff.[41] Moreover, Keyserling had reportedly discussed the matter with Johnston, and the Council's mid-February "Monthly Report" to the President underlined a "need for quick and further clarification of price policy." It implicitly criticized OPS, however, for its excessively flexible approach to price controls and indicated that the Council was "working actively with other interested parties in the furtherance of such a [general price stabilization] policy." [42] Keyserling's opposition to CPR-22 appears to have become more pronounced during the latter rather than earlier stages of the regulation's preparation. At an April 3 meeting, intended to be a review of the final draft of the regulation and attended by representatives of OPS, ESA, the Council, and the White House, Keyserling attacked the proposals. He objected to the principle of restoring price-cost balance, believing that only price increases would result. He objected to the roll-forwards as a bad application of the principle, one that would provide too liberal a "bail out" for manufacturers and thus make a shambles of price-control efforts. He did not object to roll-backs but believed price increases should be allowed only in cases of clear hardship.

Keyserling was not alone in his views, for both the White House and Johnston were worried by the possibility of further price increases. They were particularly sensitive to the recently published retail margins, which were widely interpreted as price increase margins. By the same token, NPA objected to further roll-backs because of the complicating effect they would have on procurement already far behind schedule. The period following the meeting was marked by three weeks of discussions, debates, and exchange of memoranda between OPS officials, Keyserling, and the staff of both ESA and the White House. In the Council's "Quarterly Report" to the President, Keyserling urged that the "price control program should now move toward relatively less emphasis upon the correction of 'inequities' and relatively more emphasis upon *holding the line. . . .* A hold-the-line policy requires a much sterner absorption of cost increases instead of translating them into price increases." [43] Despite the Administration's reluctance to see further price increases, Bell told Blough that he and Neustadt thought the principle of the order was sound and that Neustadt felt "the pressure for the provision of the price order was too strong to stand against." [44]

In the end, however, OPS insistence upon making good to those manufacturers who had not raised their prices won out, and CPR-22 as issued on April 25 provided for roll-forwards in cases of "unsatisfactory profit position." [45] Unfortunately, CPR-22 did not turn out to be very successful. Enforcement on the basis of the industry's own calculation proved to be impractical. The Capehart amendments to the 1951 renewal of the Defense Production Act extending the permissible period of recalculation and limiting the extent of roll-backs softened much of the bite that the original regulations had possessed. In the end, the leveling and, in some cases, dropping of prices that started as early as March and April denied CPR-22 a real test.

Nevertheless, in this, its first major project after the January freeze order, OPS successfully overruled Keyserling. As Keyserling himself conceded, "It was a fair battle lost." [46] Having themselves lost out to Keyserling on the January price freeze, OPS professionals tended to have little sympathy for his views. Moreover, it appears that they resented what they regarded as his "pseudo-toughness" on price policy after the freeze when he had previously failed to advocate an early freeze. There was also the feeling that he was anxious to have the Council participate in an area from which it had been largely eliminated. In any event, the Council entered deliberations late and played a minor role. Not only was the substance of the matter limited to one particular phase of price controls handled by one operating agency, but the regulation was also developed in the general area of mobilization policy being quickly staked out by ESA and ODM. The very experience of producing the regulation helped crystallize the sphere of activities for these agencies. These were circumstances of policy, organization, and operations that in many ways closed CPR-22 to the Council.

The Treasury–Federal Reserve Accord: An Inside Entente

Direct controls painted only part of the Korean mobilization picture, which by early spring of 1951 was still colored with urgency and uncertainty. The concern for financing a defense budget that had grown in six months from $13 billion to $48 billion for the fiscal year of 1952 brought to the surface the fundamental issue of monetary policy that had been smoldering since the close of World War II. Was the primary objective of that policy an effective combating of inflation, that is, economic stabilization, or was it the promotion of the rate of private expansion at the risk of inflation? Corollary to this basic issue were means-and-ends questions of debt management operations, possible effectiveness of restrictive interest rates as an anti-inflationary device, and the relationship of monetary policy to other forms of economic controls. One viewpoint held that government-supported easy credit would help reconversion and spur investment and long-range economic progress. Any significant hike in interest rates would add to the already huge debt burden, would complicate and increase the cost of Treasury financing, and would disrupt the money market and produce capital depreciation for bond holders. Disruption in the money market would discourage private investors from entering the market. Interest rates sufficiently high to stifle inflation would yield not stability but deflation. The contrary view was that reliance upon broad independent monetary controls could not only provide the desired stability but achieve it through the free interplay of financial market forces upon which economic progress depends.

The Truman Administration, specifically the Treasury Department, subscribed to the former viewpoint; the Federal Reserve Board to the latter. Between the Treasury and the Federal Reserve Board, the basic issue was whether the Federal Reserve Board would be obliged to continue supporting the Treasury in its debt management operations or whether it could regain its independence. The Federal Reserve Board had waged war for freedom on grounds of sound monetary policy—a free money market and operational independence as the necessary monetary requisites for stability. In July, 1947, it had let ninety-day obligations rise from ⅜ to ⅞ of 1 percent and over a year later obliged the Treasury to accept an interest boost in others of its short-term issues. The Federal Reserve Board did continue, however, to protect the 2½ percent yield of long-term bonds. Then in August, 1950, it again withdrew support from the Treasury's thirteen-month notes and ninety-one-day bills and, in so doing, set the stage for an open conflict between the two points of view.

The main support for the Treasury's position came from the President and the Council. Truman has stated that he "felt strongly that in the moment of impending crisis we should not take deliberate steps that could possibly disturb public confidence in the nation's financing." [47] In discussions of the problem, he frequently referred to the World War I Liberty Bonds, in which many individuals suffered losses in the subsequent collapse of the bonds' market value.[48] This situation, he argued, must not reoccur.

In Keyserling and Clark, the President and Secretary Snyder had staunch advocates. Neither hesitated to argue for low interest rates. The Truman files are studded with colorful letters from Clark to the President and White House aides criticizing the Federal Reserve policies. In the January, 1948, *Economic Report,* the Council said that "such actions as may be taken [to control inflation] will not involve withdrawing support from the Government bond market." [49] In response to Truman's request for comments on the report on monetary credit and fiscal policies by the Joint Committee on the Economic Report,[50] Keyserling wrote in early 1950, "Our view is that low interest rates are always desirable." Both the 1950 *Midyear Report* and the 1951 *Economic Report,* however, were silent on this theme. Instead, the Council commented to the President on the confusion and uncertainty following the Federal Reserve's action in August, "at the very time when quiet and confidence in the financial markets are of the utmost importance." [51]

By the end of 1950, the rate on Treasury bills had increased from 1.09 percent in January to 1.38 percent. The yield on nine-to-twelve-month issues averaged 1.44 percent in the fourth quarter of 1950 compared with 1.09 percent for the 1949 fourth quarter. Open market rates for short-term loans moved correspondingly.[52] With the Federal Reserve Board announcement in late December that reserve requirements would be increased in January and February, the conflict between the two financial agencies shifted from a minor to a major key.

In an unprecedented move, the President on January 31 summoned the Federal Reserve Open Markets Committee to meet with him in an effort to resolve the dispute:

I was given assurance at this meeting that the Federal Reserve Board would support the Treasury's plans for the financing of the action in Korea. This assurance was given entirely voluntarily. At no time during the conference did I attempt to dictate to the Board or tell them what specific steps they ought to take. I explained to them the problems that faced me as Chief Executive, and when they left I firmly believed that I had their agreement to cooperate in our financing program. I was taken by surprise when subsequently they failed to support the program.[53]

A release to the press of Truman's letter thanking the Federal Reserve Board for its pledge to back the Treasury program [54] brought a prompt denial from the Federal Reserve Board plus a boomerang release by Board member Marriner Eccles giving his version of the meeting. According to him, no such commitment had been made.[55] Four days later, Board Chairman McCabe wrote the President a conciliatory but straightforward letter in which he promised to work out with the Secretary of the Treasury as promptly as possible a program that would be practicable, feasible, and adequate in the light of the defense emergency, that would safeguard and maintain public confidence in the values of outstanding government bonds, and that at the same time would protect the purchasing power of the dollar.[56] At best this was only a short truce.

Some sort of enduring settlement was imperative. Truman's economic advisers told him on February 15,

In any event, however debatable may be the substance of this issue, there can be no doubt that there must be an end to the continuing uncertainty and undermining of confidence which must result to the business community and to the public at large when there is on display an unresolved conflict between two major organs of public policy with no apparent means of resolving it. The consequences of leaving the issues in suspense will be most dangerous.[57]

On the same day Truman asked Wilson to mediate the Federal Reserve–Treasury split on the grounds that it had a direct bearing on his responsibility for defense mobilization.[58] This request was formalized at a much-publicized meeting on February 26, at which the

President asked Wilson, Secretary of the Treasury Snyder, Chairman McCabe of the Federal Reserve, and Keyserling as Chairman of the Council to study—as a committee—ways and means of reconciling the two objectives of restraining private credit expansion and at the same time maintaining stability of the government securities market. The President requested that there be no change in the interest rate pattern while the study was in process, and Wilson expressed the hope that his committee could report to the President in ten days to two weeks.[59] Attending the meeting besides Wilson, McCabe, and Keyserling were Edward Foley, Under Secretary of the Treasury (Secretary Snyder was ill at the time); William McChesney Martin, Assistant Secretary of the Treasury; Charles Murphy, Special Counsel to the President; Allan Sproul, Vice-Chairman of the Federal Reserve Open Market Committee; and Harry A. McDonald, Chairman of the Securities and Exchange Commission. To an observer at the meeting, its purpose was to knock heads together, hopefully with results favorable to the Treasury's low interest rates position.

Instead, on March 3, only five days after the President's meeting and well before Wilson's committee could get under way, much less submit a report, the Treasury and the Federal Reserve Board announced that an accord had been reached. The net effect of the accord was to give the Federal Reserve Board discretion in permitting fluctuations in the yields and prices of marketable federal issues. Although the terms of the accord were not revealed, the Treasury acknowledged one provision of it when, in announcing plans to refund the 2½ percent marketable long-term bonds, it offered nonmarketable twenty-four-to-twenty-nine-year bonds at 2¾ percent. As subsequently revealed, other provisions of the accord included agreement that the short-term rate was not to be supported, that the rediscount rate was to stay at 1¾ percent and to be changed only in case of virtual catastrophe—then only upon consultation with the Treasury—that both parties were to join equally in supporting some securities to be exchanged, but not others, and that their support was to be at par plus $2\frac{2}{32}$ until approximately April 15 with no commitment thereafter, and that total Federal Reserve funds to be devoted to this support would be limited to an undisclosed total figure.[60]

The suddenness of the accord on the heels of an apparent impasse raises questions of how and why the accord was reached and what part, if any, the Council played in the negotiations.

Despite their estrangement on this particular issue the Treasury and the Federal Reserve Board have historically stood not worlds apart, but, because of their interdependence and constant association, side by side. The conflict was not a battle between traditional enemies; rather, it was a strain *en famille*, as painful to one member as to the other. Not conquest but reconciliation was the desired solution. The move to rapprochement was started some six weeks earlier, quietly, informally, and behind the scenes. Martin, who doubled as personal adviser to Secretary Snyder on monetary policy and Assistant Secretary for International Affairs, sought and received Snyder's approval to arrange a luncheon with Winfield Riefler, the Federal Reserve Board's top career economist and Assistant to the Chairman. For over two hours at the Metropolitan Club, these men reviewed the entire problem, established grounds for agreement, and probed for areas and means of reconciliation.[61]

By no means the single act that produced the accord, the meeting did none the less ignite a series of constant, informal, and confidential working-level discussions from which the accord ultimately emerged. Additional participants on the Treasury side included George C. Haas and Robert P. Mayo of the Office of the Technical Staff; Thomas Lynch, General Counsel; Edward F. Bartelt, the fiscal Assistant Secretary; and his assistant, William T. Heffelfinger. Besides Riefler, Federal Reserve Board participants included Woodlief Thomas, Economic Adviser to the Board; Ralph A. Young, Director of the Research and Statistics Division; and Guy A. Noyes of Young's staff. Blough gives an interesting and revealing account of the final deliberations:

Talked with Martin, Foley, Young and Thomas about agreement announced March 3. I think they did not tell me everything. . . . Apparently staffs resumed meeting Wednesday, February 21 and reached an agreement. Martin headed Treasury staff and had authority from the Secretary. Open Market Committee, both retiring and incoming members, were brought to Washington, and Martin and Bartelt met with them Thursday morning for three hours. Martin did the talking. He went over every point (mostly this is from Martin) and every member present was asked by McCabe for his questions and comment. Bartelt stayed over the noon hour to be available and Martin returned in the afternoon to be available until they broke up. I believe he said about 7 p.m. The next day the Committee met again and agreed to the staff proposals. The announcement was delayed until approval of the Secretary was approved and the President gave clearance. . . . Federal Reserve people enthusiastic that great progress made and very enthusiastic about Martin negotiations. Foley somewhat skeptical about achievement but recognizes that the Treasury, in view of public opinion, was forced to make an agreement.[62]

Quite clearly the Council had no direct part in the development of the accord itself. Those familiar with the negotiations agree that it was unlikely that Keyserling or Clark would have provided additional information of help in designing a solution. Moreover, their views in favor of Federal Reserve market support operations were so outspoken as to preclude effective participation in delicate and difficult negotiations. On the other hand, Blough's moderate position, his tactful circumspection, and his former association with Treasury earned him an acceptance not accorded his colleagues. As a newcomer to the Council, he was not associated with the Keyserling and Clark position. He had refrained from adding his name to some of the earlier Council memoranda addressed to the President that were critical of the Federal Reserve Board's position. The restrained nature of the Council's plea for "the maintenance of an orderly public market in United States securities" in its *Economic Review* for January, 1951, seems at least partially attributable to Blough's modifying influence, such was the price of Council unanimity on that issue. As a result of his general attitude, Blough was kept privy to much of the detailed negotiations as they developed toward the ultimate accord. Undoubtedly he responded with reactions, ideas, information—a sounding board that helped to keep things going. As Blough recalls, "My keeping tabs was a constant reminder to the negotiators that the White House was interested in a solution and in this way exerted an indirect and implied pressure to reach a decision." [63]

Blough's kibitzing was backed up by Colm, hardly a novice at bureaucratic byplay and negotiation. Working with Charles Abbot, who was an adviser to Wilson, Haas of Treasury, and Young of the Federal Reserve Board, Colm prepared a memorandum concerning debt management policy and Federal Reserve support of Treasury debt management. Although it did not bear on the accord itself, it was related to the same basic problem, and its imminent submission to the President was believed to have helped prompt Treasury and Federal Reserve officials to reach an accord before the President could act on the memorandum. No doubt strategically distributed, it appears to have comprised one of the many working papers from a respected professional source that contributed a freshet to the constant stream of communications and added an increment to the substance of negotiation.

Aside from joining with Clark in objecting to the terms of the accord itself, Keyserling was more than irked by his and the Council's exclusion from the accord negotiations. More had been confided to Blough privately than to the Council officially.[64] It was to Keyserling "a confusing situation. I really don't know how it worked out. The [Wilson] committee did not function in the negotiations. Actually, it was a matter of basic economic policy, and my views should have been more adequately considered." [65]

In all probability, the *threat* of his involvement did its bit to force an accord. It was not only his potential involvement but that of the Wilson committee as a whole that exerted a strong pressure to reach an accord without delay. Negotiations were coming along, progress was being made, specifics of agreement were taking shape; the last thing Treasury and Federal Reserve officials wanted was for the boat to be rocked by outside interference. Opening up the whole problem to a four-agency committee would drown out all that had been accomplished and hopelessly swamp the knowledge and rapport so essential to solution. To suggest that President Truman was fully mindful of this potential impact does not stretch credulity. Although the White House lieutenants were not participants in the negotiations, they undoubtedly knew of their progress and could gauge the likely result of outside pressure. Presumably the President wanted a decision without delay, if favorable to the Treasury, so much the better, but in any case a decision. Besides indicating presidential concern to the public, the February 26 meeting and establishment of the Wilson committee could be seen as a strongly implied injunction to reach an accord.

Another outside pressure for solution came from the Hill. Both Senator Robertson of Virginia and Senator Douglas of Illinois had voiced concern over the dispute. Douglas was particularly critical of the President's infringement on the Federal Reserve Board's independence. But more specifically, both men were aware of the dispute's crippling effect on national economic policy and believed that an investigation would be necessary if a solution was not soon forthcoming. If anything, this prospect must have been even more upsetting to the negotiators than the threat of the Wilson committee's interference.

The accord as it finally emerged was clearly the product of direct negotiations between the two branches of the financial family. It was an inside entente. To the traditional independence of the Treasury, the Federal Reserve Board could bring not only its *de jure* independence in terms of the Federal Reserve Act of 1913 but also a *de facto* independence in terms of daily operations. The mutual recognition of this institutional equality was as important as the policy decision to free the Federal Reserve Board from the market support commitment. The decision favorable to the Board was not without its cost, however. Shortly thereafter, McCabe resigned from his post as Chairman. He was replaced by Martin, who had played a prominent part in the negotiations. In terms of personalities, Martin symbolized the accord.

The specifics of debt management and interest rates were peculiarly the province of these two agencies, and other agencies could not intrude. The crisis of mobilization increased their vulnerability to outside interference, but at the same time was essentially a fire that heated their determination to reach their own accord. The Keyserling share of the Council's contribution was part of this fire. Blough's and Colm's roles also had their influential aspects but of a catalytic nature; they acted as interested relatives who could not interfere directly, but whose abilities, interests, and responsibilities prohibited their standing idly by. Precluded from entering the arena of decision, they formed part of the environment in which it was made. As important as their performance was in reaching *a* decision, the Council was on the whole not substantially influential, for the accord paralleled neither the thinking of the President and his Secretary of the Treasury nor the formal position of the Council.

Partial Mobilization: The Stretch-out Decision

If during the Korean period, the defensive campaign against inflation was waged in battles such as the January price freeze, CPR-22, and the Treasury–Federal Reserve Board accord, then the offensive was directed toward adequate mobilization of our national resources. NSC 68, the Defense Production Act of 1950, and attempts at material allocation and programming had been early beachheads toward this latter objective. Under the pressure of the crises in 1950, first of attack and then of military reversals, questions of military requirements had largely answered themselves—everything possible must be done. "Expedite" became the procurement officers' battle cry; economy considerations were dumped into the back seat as budget supplementals were rushed to the Hill. Controls came out of their retirement in anticipation of more guns and less butter. But, in the first half of 1951, as retreat switched into advance and as, after the initial Chinese offensive, extensive combat gave way to discretionary stalemate, divisiveness replaced cohesion and the confusion of urgency became the confusion of competing values, different interpretations, and varying institutional interests.

Even in the gloomy period of December, the Korean War had been waged with only partial mobilization, under the pale sun of which military urgency as an energizing force for the defense build-up was diluted by cautious estimates of feasibility. Secretary of Defense Lovett's reduction of initial service budget estimates for the fiscal year of 1952 from $104 to $61 billion in the midst of the Chinese intervention crises [66] suggests the maintenance of a minimum necessary approach. Feasibility and necessity were matters not so much of the all-out productive effort typical of World War II as of discretionary judgment. A balancing of military needs and non-military political and economic values emerged from judgments regarding such factors as productive capacity, division of this capacity between military and civilian sectors of the economy, extent and nature of military requirements, and restrictions of budget ceilings (or "plateaus"), each with its own qualifications. Each impinged upon the other; singly and in combination, these judgments were altered by a complex of military and home-front developments. All were poured into the mix of partial mobilization policy and operations that Wilson inherited when he went to Washington to organize and lead ODM.

The mobilization effort of early 1951 was far less a rational set of carefully priced and scheduled requirements than a bewilderment of goals, estimates, schedules, and specifications. Despite the urgings of men like Keyserling and the accomplishments of the services and of the separate departments involved in mobilization, little had been effected in programming the mobilization. Only after Wilson had the nucleus of an organization and had worked his way through the initial emergencies of price freezes and early price- and wage-control regulations as well as the accord was he able to attempt to bring some order out of the confusion. After extensive deliberation and negotiation, ODM issued on March 14 Defense Mobilization Order No. 4, which, within its eight paragraphs and approximately 1,000 words,[67] ratified the basic principle of limited mobilization. In establishing priorities for material allocation, it put primary emphasis upon the production of immediately needed weapons and military end items, raw materials, and facilities at the expense of expanding industrial capacity and stockpiling. The order severely limited expansion of productive capacity, such as additional oil refineries, pipelines, and tankers, that is, not geared to the support of existing military programs.[68]

As an ideal ordering of priorities, the order was a helpful guide but was not necessarily representative of the two major problems faced by ODM during 1951—vagueness of defense requirements and lagging production. Requirements for military hardware and complementary production schedules were based not so much on actual military demands and production estimates as on budget ceilings and production incentive targets. In some cases, budget estimates for military hardware called for rates of expenditures exceeding reasonable rates of delivery. The plateau theory of stable budgets notwithstanding, the individual military services frequently complemented their failure to base orders on productive capacity with an irresistible urge to create a backlog of authorized expenditures against the inevitable rainy day of budget cuts. With ODM reluctant to get into the budgetary aspects of mobilization, the main task of pumping some realism into budget estimates and hence into military requirements as a whole fell to the Bureau of the Budget. Rosenberg credits one of its senior analysts, William Schaub, and Defense Department Comptroller Wilfred McNeil with pressuring the services into establishing realistic dollar figures for material they wanted and could obtain.[69]

Adding to the difficulty of determining requirements was the fact that each of the military services with different budgets and different Korean combat experiences was developing different requirements under different procurement programs. Moreover, with the leeway of partial mobilization, the services were insisting on exacting specifications, repeated design changes, and extensive testing.[70]

By summer, many of the procurement programs were falling so far behind schedule that Wilson's principal task became one of urging more rapid production rather than presiding over some form of orderly and restrained expansion. Furthermore, the lags were not limited to delivery of jet engines, aircraft, and ammunition [71] but existed also in development of machine tools and the availability of steel, copper, and aluminum. It seemed that the more the fighting in Korea stabilized, the greater was the opportunity for discretion in procurement programs, the more continuing the delays in deliveries, and the greater the discrepancy between the predicted and actual increases in defense expenditures and—more important—the less the pressure for realizing the rate of defense build-up contemplated at the beginning of the year.

From the Council of Economic Advisers, Chairman Keyserling viewed these developments with alarm. His belief in the necessity to expand the nation's productive capacity to meet the mobilization needs did not diminish, nor did his urging upon the President of overall programming and acceleration of the defense effort.[72]

In order to have some impact on the mobilization effort, Keyserling endeavored to break into the policy-making deliberations. To do this he concentrated his attention on ODM, in part because of its

specific responsibilities and in part because of Wilson's close relationship to the President. Although the difference in basic mobilization views between Keyserling and Wilson precluded any really
close rapport, both men were concerned with production and were
capable of understanding one another. Both left it to the military to
decide *what* was needed; they, in their respective jobs, were concerned with *how* it would be obtained. The relations between the
two men were, to one observer, "interesting and somewhat volatile
—hot and cold." [73] Keyserling attempted to attach the Council to
ODM as its economic adviser in much the same relationship it had
had to NSRB in the pre-Chinese days.[74] He represented the Council
at meetings of the Defense Mobilization Board [75] and sat in on meetings of the Defense Mobilization executive staff, which was comprised of representatives of the immediate defense mobilization
agencies, such as ODM, ESA, OPS, and WSB. Keyserling also encouraged his staff to develop and maintain contacts with the working levels of these organizations. A number of the staff, for instance,
collaborated with James Sundquist in putting together the ODM
Quarterly Reports, which, incidentally, Keyserling regarded as du-
plicating the Council's own semiannual reports.[76]

In spite of problems and delays, the prospect of increased military
procurement expenditures in an economy already going full steam
ahead made the nation and the Administration sensitive to the threat
of inflation. A major section of the President's *Economic Report* for
January, 1951, had been devoted to "The Inflationary Danger" growing out of an increase from 7 to 18 percent of national output going
into defense during the year.

Since our economy has recently been running full blast, the defense
program will have to pull men and materials, as well as plants, away
from existing peacetime uses. . . . We must put heavy restraints upon
nonessential business activity. . . . The excess of consumer demand
over available goods will rise by many billions of dollars, . . . [causing]
intense and mounting inflationary pressures which must be counter-
acted.[77]

The Council's "Review" in the same *Report* spoke of defense expenditures increasing from $18 billion for fiscal year 1950 to an an-

nual rate of $45 to $55 billion by the end of calendar year 1951.[78] The Council's *Quarterly Report* of April reiterated the same warning of increasing inflationary pressures.[79] Keyserling's testimony before the Joint Committee on the Economic Report in January and before the Senate Banking and Currency Committee in May carried a similar message. In response to Truman's request in June for a brief up-to-the-minute appraisal of the economic situation and outlook, the Council wrote to the President:

> Before the middle of next year, the annual rate of expenditures for national security will be more than twice as high as the current annual rate. This means an increase of more than 30 billion dollars at an annual rate. This stark fact alone, made necessary by the world situation, is in itself compelling evidence that inflationary pressures will mount. . . .
> The greater dangers ahead do not mean that we *must* have more inflation. They do mean that we *will* have more inflation if we relax our efforts, or fail to strengthen the weak links in the chain of effective controls.[80]

Far from being a voice in the wilderness, the Council was part of a chorus. Truman, Wilson, Johnston, and DiSalle all joined the Council in speaking of inflationary pressures inherent in the defense build-up. From the other end of Pennsylvania Avenue, the Joint Committee on the Economic Report published a report in which it labeled inflation the enemy's Sixth Column and predicted that, under alternative federal expenditure possibilities, consumer demand would exceed consumer supply by amounts varying from $3 billion to $16 billion.[81]

Yet beneath these repeated inflation warnings there were indications as early as March and April that prices were softening, that there was a lull in inflationary pressures. Franz B. Wolf, as Director of Research and Statistics for OPS, wrote a review in which he foresaw "slight" pressure until after the middle of the year. He cited the sharp reduction in consumer demand, actual federal expenditures less than anticipated in January, delays in mobilization programming, and the prospect of only a mild decline in civilian output.[82]

It was at this time that Wolf and a number of his colleagues began privately to discount official projections of national security expenditures.[83] Although such doubts could not be made public, they were shared with the staff members of related agencies with whom they were in constant touch, including, of course, the Council. By working with OPS, the Defense Production Administration, and the Budget Bureau, as well as by their own analysis, men such as Caplan, Colm, Klein, and Lewis became familiar with the innumerable problems of design, material shortages, dollar estimates, contracting confusion, and consequently with the increasing discrepancy between production goals and deficiencies. As these complications persisted into the summer and fall of 1951, Council staff members saw the inflationary lull grow from possibility to probability to certainty and from a temporary to a long-term phenomenon.[84]

These were developments of which the Council members themselves were equally aware. Internal memoranda and their October *Quarterly Report* to the President present the same analysis of defense expenditures smaller than had been expected, of decreased personal consumption matched by increased personal saving, and of both military and civilian production expansion. They also attributed growing stability in part to the bite of increased taxes and credit controls and to price and wage controls that exerted both practical and psychological restraints.[85] Yet in spite of these developments the Council continued to fly its inflation warnings: "The balance of forces is moving toward inflation. Rising government expenditures will lift spendable personal income. . . . The output of consumer goods cannot be expected to keep pace with income." [86]

The reasons for this continuation are not hard to discern. In the first place, the nature of the military stalemate made caution necessary. In no sense were two giant forces faltering under exhaustion; rather, backed by tremendous military power and armed reserves, each was applying just enough pressure to keep the other in check. Wishing to contain the fighting and not provoke Russia, we were on the military and diplomatic defensive. The Administration's belief that the fighting could explode again if Stalin wanted it to kept us on guard. Expansion of military capability remained the objective regardless of the relative combat serenity of the moment. Second, short of a change in policy or the world situation and despite production difficulties, the Council had to assume continued mobilization expansion and consequent economic impact sooner or later. Third, price and wage controls which had been a long time in coming could not be dropped at the first sign of their either working or being unnecessary. The almost certain adverse effect of dropping them was acutely felt because of pressure to dilute the Defense Production Act through the Capehart amendments and the impossibility of maintaining wage ceilings if price controls were dropped or weakened. The scheduled renewal of the steelworkers' contract by December 31, 1951, made the latter a particularly sensitive consideration. Besides, the personnel of control agencies had fought hard to establish their overdue programs, and they did not wish to be denied a *raison d'être* so quickly. Fourth, there was the very real possibility of consumer demand rebounding from its satiety of six months previously. To Keyserling there was a more compelling reason tying all of these together: To relax the anti-inflation pressure would be to relax the pressures for expansion, to accept the delays in mobilization, and, by implication, to accept the argument that inflation was the threat to expansion and therefore the rationale for not expanding. In short, the lag produced the lull; and to erase the lag would be to threaten the lull.

The relationship between mobilization lag and inflation lull took on decisive significance in October and November, when military programs for the fiscal year of 1953 were reviewed in accordance with the Truman promise in his Budget Message of the preceding January. Reappraisal was undertaken before a background of continuing production problems at home, patrols and prisoner exchanges in Korea, and the possibility of major political change twelve months later. The basic question centered in whether or not the target dates for achieving the force levels determined in December, 1950, should be reaffirmed or revised to allow for extension into the future. By the delays encountered so far, some stretch-out was inevitable; the question was really how much? By the very dimensions of military, international, economic, and political significance, the range of top-level policy agencies were involved. The determination of force levels was developed by the Joint Chiefs of Staff and recommended to the President by NSC. The costing aspects would be covered in the President's budget document being prepared by the Budget Bureau and its counterparts in the Defense Department. The defense production aspects were the concern of ODM. The decision would be the President's.

The report that came to the President recommended that the following force levels be reached by July 1, 1954: Army—21 divisions; Navy—408 combat vessels and 16 carrier air groups; Marine Corps —3 divisions and 3 air wings; Air Force—143 wings to be combat-effective by December, 1954. To match this, Lovett submitted to the President a proposed budget for the fiscal year of 1953 of $57 billion.[87] The target date of July 1, 1954, meant a stretch-out of two years. Called "the period of greatest danger," [88] it was none the less a new target date determined primarily by multidimensional feasibility.

The preponderance of information converging on the President was favorable to a stretch-out. Wilson had before him reports on scheduling and design difficulties and on continued production delays, as, for example, in the medium-tank program, where only 70 percent of the original schedule could be expected by December, 1952.[89] On December 1 he reported to the President that production increases would be slight because of the existing shortages and bottlenecks and that in any event the services would have trouble obligating the funds already available to them.[90] Three weeks later Wilson informed Truman that to meet even the material requirements of the proposed program would require curtailing production of civilian durables. Thus, new inflationary pressures would be created and the plateau theory for the military budget would be jeopardized.[91] In other words, stretch-out was necessary, inevitable, and without alternative. Wilson's viewpoint was supported by NPA, the Defense Comptroller, and the Budget Bureau.

To all this Keyserling entered a strong dissent:

I knew perfectly well that the defense effort was being stretched-out, I was not impervious to the fact that this would lessen inflationary pressures. But I was *against* the stretch-out, I was *against* our losing or tying a demonstrative war, I was against those who were using exaggeration of the damage done by inflation to justify the stretch-out, e.g., "Inflation is a greater danger than Stalin." [92]

Keyserling believed that, besides ignoring the nation's expansion capabilities, the stretch-out argument was in part based upon data of material shortages the validity of which he and Burton Klein of his staff questioned.[93] Based upon his investigations, Klein regarded the shortages as hoarding in anticipation of military production orders larger than actually occurred. Keyserling and Klein had support from Colm and others within the Council and also from Acheson and Bohlen of the State Department.[94]

In early November Keyserling urged Truman to undertake acceleration, not stretch-out, supporting his recommendation with long-range GNP projections of expansion possibilities. To Truman's White House advisers on such matters, this argument was irrelevant; the problem was neither long-range nor essentially economic. It was an immediate production problem of breaking bottlenecks. The stretch-out proposal simply recognized the facts as they were; its impact as an actual stretching-out of the mobilization program would not be felt until 1953. Consequently, no decision had to be made in December, 1951, on long-term mobilization goals.

The President's acceptance of stretch-out was hardly a surprise. As announced on December 28 before a formal meeting of top Administration officials, the decision approved the force levels recommended by the Joint Chiefs but pushed attainment from 1954 to 1955 and, for some phases, to 1956. It also cut the 1953 defense budget to $52.4 billion.[95]

As analyzed by Rosenberg, Truman's decision was based primarily on the premise that a general war was unlikely within the fiscal year of 1953.[96] Rosenberg believes that the controlling factor in extending force-level target dates and in shaving almost $3 billion from budget estimates was not only an aspect of production feasibility as argued by Wilson but also consideration of the statutory debt limit.[97] Based on tax rates existing at the time, Truman's budget advisers estimated that military expenditures within 10 to 20 percent of those proposed would extend the Treasury beyond the statutory debt limit of $275 billion. The President would be forced to choose between seeking an increase either in the debt limit or in taxes and cutting back on the budget. As Rosenberg has emphasized, the President weighed factors of maximizing a pay-as-you-go anti-inflation tax policy, his own pride in not exceeding the debt limit, the political dynamite of a Democratic Administration seeking a debt-limit increase in an election year, the known aversion of Congress to such a proposal, and the possibility that 143 wings was "an Air Force grab for funds [against] less predictable times." [98]

Granting that the decision was weighed primarily in budget terms, the debt limit factor seems controlling only in the sense that the basic requirements of the national security situation were believed to have been met. If the debt limit had not been a factor, the defense budget might have been larger, but if maintaining the debt limit was believed to be endangering national security, the limit would have been sacrificed. As Bell has stated it, "Truman would not have jeopardized national security for such a reason." [99] The President could afford to think of the debt limit. Truman himself has commented, "The *situation* made this a good decision." [100] In more abstract terms, the stretch-out decision gave mobilization feasibility and politics a common bond—the art of the practicable.

In this decision, the Keyserling Council's views were rejected, perhaps not even seriously considered. As Blough summarizes it, "Once Korea passed into the military production stage, the Council's influence waned." [101]

Regarding policy values, Truman ignored Keyserling's acceleration argument because the situation and outlook in December, 1951, led him to think in other terms. More basically, partial mobilization became tantamount to minimum mobilization. With the luxury of a truce in Korea, albeit an uneasy one, anti-NSC 68 values were reasserted. In view of assorted production difficulties, expansion was considered impractical; in view of inflationary dangers, to which the Council repeatedly alluded, expansion was considered dangerous. That many shortages in fact evaporated in the revelation of miscalculations, overstated requirements,[102] and hoarding, that defense expenditures continued to fall short of expectation, and that price stability did remain were all beside the point.

It is true that basic economic issues were at stake, but the decision being considered was within the triangle of national security requirements, productive capacity, and budget policy, all of which were beyond (or really beneath) the Council's range. Although the

Council indeed had a valid concern in the matter, the very scope of its advisory area gave it no specific entree, no readily available issue for inserting itself into the deliberations stream, no integral linkage between its own expertise and what was really an applied problem.

The substantive exclusion was matched by an organizational and procedural one. The dominance by spring of ODM, ESA, and OPS, each with its own economics staff, largely removed the Council from the chain of mobilization organizations, not entirely in the informal, or operating, sense but in the formal and structural sense. Once under way, ODM became "The Voice of Mobilization," [103] a voice that went directly to the President, precisely as Truman had intended. In mobilization matters it had, relative to the Council, pre-empted the economic advisory function. Although this exclusion was by no means complete, the repeated reminders in various reports to the President of the value of the Council's work and the importance of its being more closely involved in mobilization activities suggests that it was constantly having to promote its own services.[104] Of course, the Council maintained its contacts, provided information and viewpoints, served testing and catalytic functions, spoke for the Administration regarding inflationary dangers, and participated in various standing and *ad hoc* committees, but it did not carry the same force as during the 1950 phase of the Korean mobilization. Both as an organization and as an assemblage of individuals, it participated in the mobilization program of 1951 but as an auxiliary, valuable as such a role may be, rather than as a leading performer.

Conclusion: The Price of Prematurity

Throughout Keyserling's association with the Council, expansion economics was his guiding principle. What he originally espoused in the Pabst contest in 1944 was evident in his participation in the passage of the Employment Act of 1946. It was the basis of his support of the Administration's anti-inflation efforts in 1947 through 1949 and of the Spence and Murray bills in 1949; it was the basis, too, of his participation in the NSC 68 costing exercise and was the theme running through speeches, testimony, and reports. During the Korean War it was the rationale, in 1950, behind the emphasis on

production in the Defense Production Act, reliance upon indirect
controls, urging of mobilization, and, in 1951, behind the objection
to OPS price-control activities, the Treasury–Federal Reserve accord, and ODM stretch-out policy. Keyserling continued his emphasis on expansion during the reconversion efforts of 1952 and
made it the primary objective of his development of the Conference
on Economic Progress, which he established after leaving the Council in 1953.

In its constant focus on expansion economics, the Keyserling
Council provided economic rationale for the Truman Fair Deal. The
aggregative approach to economic analysis, stressing long-term estimates of potential economic activity, was congenial with the Administration's programs of growth, welfare, and active government. As
Bell recalls from his own days as a White House aide,

The President let Nourse go and promoted Keyserling because Keyserling fitted better the economic tone the President wanted for his Administration. A 5 percent annual increase in GNP would not have been
a natural way for Mr. Truman to have described his objective, but what
Keyserling was driving at appealed to his understanding, convictions, and
hopes for the nation.[105]

Such acceptance was matched by a basic agreement among Keyserling, his colleagues, and his staff. Clark's dogged insistence on low
interest rates, his concern for human welfare, and his willingness to
have the Council attempt active participation in economic policy
deliberations coincided with Keyserling's convictions and methods of
operations. Short of constituting disagreement, Blough's concern for
a balance between growth and stability and his concept of the
Council's assuming a more passive advisory role provided a counterbalance to Keyserling and Clark. His successful liaison with the
Treasury gave the Council an important link with a major source of
fiscal and monetary policy. In their acceptance of expansion economics, such staff members as Colm, Caplan, and Salant did much
to expand the scope of the Council's operations. As well-known and
respected career economists, they developed and maintained contacts that Keyserling, as one man, was unable to handle; they
smoothed over what he may have ruffled and acted largely on their

own initiative. As complements to Keyserling's leadership, they carried the Council rather than the other way around.

The rise and fall of the Keyserling Council during the Korean period of from mid-1950 to late 1951 indicates, however, that the Administration's acceptance of the Council's rationale and the general comity of values within the Council were not translated into adaptation of economic expansion as an objective of economic policy. The initial period of emergency and possible World War III mobilization gave to the concept of expansion economics short-run viability and acceptance and to the Council a climax of policy influence and leadership. But the return to normal as evidenced by the stretch-out decision and concern for inflation indicated that expansion economics failed to take in any lasting way. This failure suggests that the decline of the influence in 1951 constituted the price of prematurity. Governmental and popular consensus regarding values of economics and advice did not coincide with the Council's anticipation of needs and opportunities concerning the nation's economic welfare. Expansion economics was more a philosophical adjunct to the Fair Deal than a continuing guide to specific economic policy. It had less acceptance within the Administration than in some quarters of Congress. A conservative in regard to fiscal policy, Truman was primarily interested in stability; his coolness to expansion policies was reinforced by antipathy towards economic expertise.

White House views were apparently both shared and influenced by those of the Defense Department, the Budget Bureau, and ODM. The short shrift given Keyserling's opposition to stretch-out were reminiscent of the opposition to the expansionist tone of NSC 68. In addition, undoubtedly genuine fears of inflation were engendered in part by the mobilization itself and in part by the conviction that the inflation brought on by increased investment expenditure for the greater productivity Keyserling sought would be too high a price to pay for the ultimate stability supposedly growing out of such productivity. That increased production contributed to price stability during the early months of the Korean mobilization appeared to be largely ignored.[106] A nation could not be expected to spend itself out of inflation. Moreover, there were objections to the long-range planning that expansion economics involved, with regard to both the Keynesian aggregative analysis on which expansion was based and the centralized coordination of governmental activities that would be involved.

The Keyserling Council's sequence of success and failure in influencing economic policy during the Korean period had something of a controversial counterpoint in the reaction to its operations. Because he seldom hesitated to articulate his views and ran his Council, still a fledgling agency trying to establish itself, in an unfavorable climate, Keyserling was himself controversial. Those who accepted his views recognized his considerable abilities as an economist and administrator, his contribution to New Deal and Fair Deal policies, and his leadership of the Council. They accepted his concept of an activist role for the Council along with his application of theoretical analysis on behalf of expansion objectives. Congressmen among his supporters recognized his abilities as a witness. Staff associates could appreciate his supervisory practice of involving them in the full range of Council activities. To his supporters, such qualities were more important than his not having a Ph.D. degree and his often difficult personality.

Those who rejected Keyserling's views, who thought him too wedded to expansion and insufficiently concerned with inflation, tended to discount his abilities; competence in the field was not equated with standing in the economics profession. They objected that his aggressive role for the Council was making it into a political agency. Advocacy was not equated with expert and passive objectivity. Conflicts in personal and working relationships only served to reinforce these negative evaluations.

By the end of his chairmanship, Keyserling had blazed a trail far different from that attempted by Nourse; he had set new precedents of policy exposition for the Council and had expanded the range of its functions.[107] During the first six months, when it was able to assume a role of leadership, it enjoyed a measure of acceptance and support as well as internal unity and momentum that it did not have in 1951. As one staff member recalls, "once the period of frustration set in, things got tense." Blough did not remain until the end of the Truman Administration but resigned from the Council in 1952 to become the principal director of the UN Department of Economic Affairs.

Unhappily and perhaps inevitably the Keyserling Council shared in the nadir of the Truman Administration. As Keyserling himself concedes in commenting upon the stretch-out decision, the Administration was becoming tired and weak.[108] Although the last-minute proposal made on the floor of the House by Edward H. Rees (Republican from Kansas) to reduce the Council's budget for the fiscal year of 1953 by 25 percent grew largely out of a potentially lame-duck environment [109] and an economy move against a number of agencies, it also reflected a resurgence of long-standing conservative opposition to the Council's expansion philosophy. As it turned out, a group of Senators who supported the Council (including Ellender, Maybank, O'Mahoney, Saltonstall, and Taft) were able to take advantage of the forthcoming change of presidential leadership to have the amount of funds approved by the House applied to the three quarters of the year extending from July through March rather than stretched at a 25-percent reduced level over all four quarters. This action restored the amount of funds available for three quarters to the level originally requested by the Council and obviated its having to curtail its activities or reduce its staff. By the exact same token, it denied the Council any funds for the fourth quarter of the year extending from March through June, and thereby passed the buck of the Council's future to Truman's successor.

IV. INDUCTIVE ECONOMICS FOR A REPUBLICAN PROGRAM

As President Eisenhower soon learned, first in the helpful but restrained post-election briefing sessions conducted for him by Truman and Acheson and then in the early months of his own administration, he had inherited many of the problems and issues that had plagued and challenged his predecessor. Domestically, he too would have to deal with price and wage controls, welfare programs, constantly increasing budgets, fiscal and monetary problems, the McCarthy menace, and such specifics as the St. Lawrence Seaway. On the international front, he too would have to face the Soviet threat, not only in the Korean truce negotiations, but also in the crises in Indo-China and Iran, in the divisive pressures within the European Defense Community, and in the development of nuclear energy. He too would be concerned with the paramount issues that straddled both domestic and foreign problems—the programs, organization, and costs of national defense. Inherited problems or not, the popular and certainly the overwhelming political mandate was for a "clean sweep down fore 'n' aft," and the first Republican Administration in twenty years was determined to oblige by manning brooms that were both new and, if possible, different.

The "new" economic policies, as Arthur F. Burns and his Council of Economic Advisers would soon see them, would be directed toward balanced budgets, debt and tax reductions, fiscal and monetary

checks on inflation—all as "incentives that inspire creative initiative." [1] As a vital concomitant, government interference with the nation's economy would be reduced, planning would be avoided, and
the operation of welfare programs would proceed with minimum
interference and financing from the federal government. The 1953
conservatives regarded economic slumps as normally self-curing
events in which the government should not attempt extensive interference.[2] Without repudiating the New Deal–Fair Deal, the Eisenhower Administration intended to put into practice its belief in the
eternal American verities and its loyalty to the principles of the Taft
wing of the GOP. As Marquis Childs has written, the practitioners
summoned to lead the economic way "shared an orthodoxy based on
simple precepts which had filtered down out of the eighteenth and
nineteenth centuries." [3] George Humphrey, Charles E. Wilson of
General Motors, and Sinclair Weeks were all of the same generation
and basic economic persuasion. In addition, as accomplished business administrators, these men would establish business efficiency
and business competence over the sprawling, overlapping, and waste-
ful bureaucracy.[4] By implication, there was a direct correlation between public servants and budget deficits, and both were bad.

Eisenhower paralleled this conservatism of business and economics in his own concepts of office and administration, concepts
that were not born so much of thought and study as of values and
background. In Rossiter's words, "His cast of mind was that of the
genuine conservative, . . . his character . . . that of the peacemaker,
. . . his methods those of a man with a distaste for aggressive politics
and a horror of administrative detail." [5] The Council, no less than
the rest of government, would witness his adherence, during his first
year, to the Whig concept of partnership with Congress and to his
quest for order, unity, and procedures. More particularly, the Council would share with the other components of the Executive Office
the impact of the elaboration of the presidential staff structure—the
formalization of the Cabinet, of National Security Council operations, of the executive officer's function of Sherman Adams, along
with the creation of a coterie of special assistants. Of these, the
most important to the Council in terms of both immediate and enduring significance would be Gabriel Hauge. Himself an economist,

Hauge had joined the Eisenhower team during the 1952 campaign and had become the President's Administrative Assistant responsible for economic affairs. In his opinion, "Bringing Arthur [Burns] down was one of my most significant accomplishments." [6]

The Revitalized Council

Burns was brought down from Columbia and the National Bureau of Economic Research as a prominent economist well known for his work with Wesley Mitchell on business cycles and for his disenchantment with Keynesian economics.[7] He completed his Ph.D. in economics at Columbia in 1934 and taught at Rutgers from 1927 to 1941, at which time he joined the faculty of the Department of Economics at Columbia. He became a member of the research staff of the National Bureau of Economic Research in 1930 and was the Director of Research at the time of his appointment to the Council. He was in effect Mitchell's successor at both Columbia and the Bureau. Outside of some brief consulting stints during the Roosevelt Administration, the Council chairmanship represented his first Washington assignment.

As a disciple of Mitchell, Burns was labeled a champion of empirical, or inductive, economics, preferring to draw conclusions and base policy upon observable facts rather than deductively from theoretical relationships and models. Three years before becoming Chairman of the Council he wrote, "Subtle understanding of economic change comes from a knowledge of history and large affairs, not from statistics or their processing alone—to which our age has turned so eagerly in its quest for certainty." [8]

Burns' knowledge of the past served as the foundation for his anti-Keynesian beliefs. To Burns, the "great and obvious virtue of the remedies proposed by the Keynesians is that they seek to relieve mass unemployment; their weakness is that they lean heavily on a speculative analysis of uncertain value." [9] Denying what he held to be Keynesian acceptance of a relatively stable "consumption function" and of investment as the dynamic variable, he contended that

imposing schemes for governmental action that are being bottomed on Keynes' equilibrium theory must be viewed with skepticism and the

Keynesians lack a clear analytic foundation for judging how a given fiscal policy will affect the size of national income or the volume of employment.[10]

Burns acknowledged the usefulness of Keynesian theory as a passive "apparatus" that is "merely an analytical filing case for handling problems of aggregate income and employment. . . . Keynes' files are labeled 'propensity to consume,' 'marginal efficiency of capital,' 'liquidity preference,' and 'supply of money.' " [11] However, he argued that

the Keynesian theoretical apparatus is one thing, the Keynesian general theory of income and employment is another, and the Keynesian theory of income and employment in the current institutional setting is still another. My essay was concerned with the second and third, not the first. I questioned the determinacy of Keynes' general theory on the ground that it proceeds on a tacit assumption that is open to grave doubt—namely, the independence of the consumption function and intended investment from the adjustment processes of a free enterprise system.[12]

Such questioning by no means ruled out research of a Keynesian nature, much of which was sponsored by the National Bureau, nor was it an across-the-board rejection of Keynes' own theories. As much as anything, it was an objection to the attempt of Keynes' disciples to base a theory of the business cycle upon his theories of depression and unemployment.[13]

Considering Burns' views, it is small wonder that Hauge sought him out for the Council. Reciprocally, as Burns himself recalls, he was attracted by Eisenhower's campaign promise of applying an anticyclical policy of mobilizing the nation's economic resources to combat recession.[14] However, according to Burns,

I did not jump for the job, but took my time to accept. I was, after all, deeply involved in work at the National Bureau. On the other hand, I was drawn to the post by the idea that there was an opportunity to serve and that the President thought he needed me. There was also a chance to rebuild the Council, which had fallen into pretty bad disrepute—witness the unprecedented action of Congress in giving it only a nine months' appropriation for fiscal 1953.[15]

By the time Burns went to Washington in March, 1953, the Council he sought to rebuild was very much in limbo. The three-quarter-year appropriation for the fiscal year 1953 as provided by the previous Congress had expired, and the new Administration inherited the problem of arranging for fourth-quarter funds in accordance with its own wishes. The nature of these wishes, however, were no more apparent then than they had been in the weeks immediately following the inauguration. For a number of reasons, the Council's future was considered uncertain at best. It had not been involved in the post-election conferences between the new and the old Administrations, there had been no indication regarding its reestablishment, the dismissal of the entire staff was believed imminent, and the Administration's big-business orientation was not considered sympathetic.[16] In considering a supplemental appropriation, the new House Appropriations Committee under the chairmanship of John Taber rejected the request for $75,000 for the balance of the year for the Council and, instead, allowed $25,000 to be used by the President for one adviser and a small staff. Taber's assertion that Eisenhower concurred in the Committee's action increased speculation regarding the President's wishes and also suggested that the cut was a stratagem in the underlying desire to clean the Council's slate and rebuild anew.[17]

Following the House action, both the President and Sherman Adams confused matters by appealing to Styles Bridges, Chairman of the Senate Appropriations Committee, for sufficient supplemental funds to see the Council through the fourth quarter. "I have found since assuming office," the President wrote Bridges, "that the Council of Economic Advisers did not have the status that it should have. . . . My intention is to reinvigorate that body."[18] The President indicated that recommendations toward this end would be submitted for the coming year. Although the Senate Committee responded by voting $60,000, this figure was whittled down in the conference committee to $50,000 and appropriated not to the Council but, in line with the House's action, to the President for the single adviser and staff.

It was during the course of the conference committee deliberations that the President announced Burns' nomination as a member of the Council, with the understanding that he would become Chairman when the pattern of the Council was finally set. Thus, "with the

Fair Deal slate wiped clean . . . the President will begin to form an agency reflecting the economic thinking of his Administration." [19] Within a week of Burns' nomination the appointments of the remaining Keyserling staff members were terminated, and the Truman Council passed out of the picture. When Burns started to work on March 19, he was in the anomalous position of being a presidential adviser and also of having been confirmed for membership in a body that did not exist. Nevertheless, he immediately undertook the Council's reestablishment.

Burns' tasks centered on acquiring a small staff of personal assistants and developing plans for reconstituting the Council. He was able to rehire three former Council staff members, David Lusher, Joseph Fisher, and Frances James. With the assistance of Fisher and the management staff of the Budget Bureau, Burns concentrated on the development of a suitable Council reorganization. What emerged was Reorganization Plan No. 9, which was submitted to Congress on June 1 and permitted by that body to go into effect just two months later. In full, it reads as follows:

The functions vested in the Council of Economic Advisers by section 4(b) of the Employment Act of 1946 (60 Stat. 24), and so much of the functions vested in the Council by section 4(c) of that Act as consists of reporting to the President with respect to any function of the Council under said section 4(c), are hereby transferred to the Chairman of the Council of Economic Advisers. The position of Vice Chairman of the Council of Economic Advisers, provided for in the last sentence of section 4(a) of the said Act, is hereby abolished.[20]

The most important feature of this modification was the designation of the Chairman as the operating head of the Council. The function of reporting to the President was transferred from the Council to the Chairman, as was the responsibility for staff appointments. No longer merely first among equals, the Chairman now had at least the official means of avoiding the disputes which had racked the Council during Nourse's chairmanship. While maintaining the collaboration of three advisers, such a reorganization tacitly recognized the Hoover Commission proposal to substitute a single adviser for the Council.

In his transmittal message to Congress, rather than in the Reorganization Plan itself, the President, in accepting another Burns innovation, announced that he was "also asking the heads of several departments and agencies, or the representatives they may designate, to serve as an Advisory Board on Economic Growth and Stability [ABEGS] under the chairmanship of the Council of Economic Advisers." [21] Besides the Council, the following departments and agencies would be represented: Treasury, Agriculture, Commerce, Labor, Federal Reserve, Budget Bureau, and the White House. As an advisory body, ABEGS was to keep the President "closely informed about the state of the national economy and the various measures necessary to aid in maintaining a stable prosperity." [22]

Burns' convictions on the Council's role in the development of economic policy reflected his empirical concern with cyclical economic phenomena, his evaluation of the earlier Council as manifested by the centralizing features of Reorganization Plan No. 9, and his objective of increasing the standing of economic science. To him the Employment Act "expresses the plain intent of the Congress that members of the Council should function as professional economists, giving their views on economic problems and policies in an objective, nonpartisan manner." [23] He would stress business competition as the great economic energizer and a basic determinant of our higher productivity, and, in his role as Chairman, would avoid speeches and political activity.[24]

He told Senator Sparkman that "my own personal inclination would be to stay out of the limelight, make my recommendation to the President, indicate to him what the basis for the recommendation is . . . and then having done that, to remain eternally quiet." [25] He "would not justify policy, but help frame it." [26] This disposition was not self-restraint of the Nourse variety, which, on principle, eschewed involvement in policy-making, for helping to frame policy would certainly necessitate involvement. More accurately, Burns' early attitude revealed an approach that was restrained by his concern for economics as a discipline and by "a feeling of uncertainty whether a professional economist could function well in a political environment." [27]

With the inclusion of funds for its operation in the fiscal 1954 budget, the Council was back in business. Burns was renominated and reconfirmed as a member of the Council in late July and designated its Chairman on August 8. As his professional staff at that time was limited to Lusher, Fisher, and Miss James, his major effort was concentrated on creating a new Council around this nucleus of holdovers and himself. For a number of reasons, this was not a simple task. In order to be able to select the professionals he wanted on the basis of their ability, Burns had to resist pressure, both from within the Administration and from Congress, to ignore economists —despite their qualifications—who had been associated with the previous administration. After all, 1953 was the first Republican patronage season in twenty years.

By the same token, many possible Council members and staff experts, regardless of past affiliations, were not anxious to become stamped as Republican economists. In an atmosphere marked by McCarthyism and a pervasive disdain for the public service, particularly for those intellectuals on its payroll, government work could hardly be termed "attractive employment." One observer of the time believed that some potential candidates for Council membership did not care to be subordinates on a three-man Council with only one acknowledged head. From a practical standpoint, available economists who met Burns' standards of professional excellence were not in plentiful supply. It was especially difficult to recruit from college and university faculties when many of those who otherwise might have been available felt committed to their teaching or research posts for the ensuing academic year. The best that Burns could do was to attempt to meet his immediate needs by appointing qualified economists who could obtain a one-year leave of absence to serve on a full- or part-time basis and then obtain replacements for them the following year. Although this rotation system was presented as providing a highly desirable exchange between government and the campus, it was motivated primarily by necessity.

The first addition to the new staff was Asher Achinstein, who joined by taking a leave of absence from the Library of Congress. He, too, had been a student of Mitchell's, and his views were similar to those of Burns and the National Bureau. His particular responsibilities were to cover general economic analysis and business cycles.

He was soon joined by Raymond J. Saulnier, like Burns from Columbia University and the National Bureau, who was to serve on a part-time consulting basis and operate in the mortgage and finance areas as he had done for the previous three years with the Federal Reserve Board and the Farm Credit Administration. Neil Jacoby from the University of California at Los Angeles, Melvin G. de Chazeau from Cornell University, and Louis Shere from Indiana University enlarged the ranks in September, Jacoby as the second Council member, De Chazeau on a part-time basis to handle problems of general economic instability and private enterprise policy, and Shere to concentrate on the tax policy areas. Shere's appointment in the face of his fourteen New Deal years as an economist with the Treasury Department must be interpreted as a successful attempt by Burns to resist partisan standards of acceptability.

In October, Clarence Long, on a year's leave of absence from Johns Hopkins University, joined the staff to handle labor economics, as did William H. Nicholls on a similar basis from Vanderbilt University to work in agriculture. At the same time, Burns prevailed upon the Federal Reserve Board to detail Albert Koch to the Council for a four-month period to assist in the monetary area and in the preparation of the first *Economic Report*. Collis Stocking transferred from ODM and, although he initially worked on manpower problems, eventually assumed the position of the Council's Administrative Officer. Robinson Newcomb, who had been with the Nourse and Keyserling Councils, rejoined on a part-time consulting basis and concentrated on construction, and Walter W. Stewart headed the November and December additions as the third Council member. He was followed by Robert Triffin from Yale University, who was to handle international economic affairs on a part-time basis, Albert Riefman on a short-term loan from the State Department to assist in the international economics area, and Irving H. Siegel from the Twentieth Century Fund to work on general problems of productivity. By December this group of three Council members and fifteen staff economists was hard at work on the 1954 *Economic Report*. In the following March, the staff was joined by Charles Schultze, who had spent a year with the previous Council and who was to assist Lusher in GNP analysis.

At the time of his appointment as the second Council member, Neil Jacoby was serving as Dean of the Graduate School of Business at the University of California at Los Angeles. A Canadian by birth, he completed his Ph.D. at the University of Chicago and taught there for ten years. He had been associated with the Saskatchewan Department of Finance and Tax Commission in the 1930s and was a member of the research advisory board of the Committee for Economic Development from 1942 to 1948 and of the research staff of the National Bureau of Economic Research from 1940 to 1945. At the time of his appointment to the Council he was forty-four years old, five years younger than Burns.

Walter W. Stewart was the elder statesman of the Council, being sixty-eight at the time of his appointment and the only one of the three who had seen full-time service on the Washington scene. Although not a Ph.D., he was described by the New York *Times* as a "gifted economic theorist" [28] and by Ogden Mills as "the greatest living authority on gold and foreign exchange." [29] In addition to having been a successful investment banker, he had taught at his Alma Mater, the University of Missouri, as well as at the University of Michigan and at Amherst College. During World War I he had been a member of the price section of the War Industries Board and six years later had become the first Director of the Federal Reserve Board's Division of Research and Statistics. Montague Norman appointed him as the first American member of a special advisory committee considering German reparations under the Young Plan. Serving as an economic adviser to the President was not a new experience for Stewart, since he had performed in similar capacities for Coolidge, Hoover, and Franklin Roosevelt. Prior to joining the Council, he had been associated with the Institute of Advanced Studies at Princeton and had been Chairman of the Board of Trustees of the Rockefeller Foundation.

The 1953 Council as a whole was less a grouping of government careerists than of academicians for whom the Council experience was deliberately a temporary assignment. Although they accepted stretches of duty in Washington, their primary career roots were in colleges and universities rather than in bureaucracies, and their primary functions were as teachers, consultants, and researchers rather than as operating economists. Washington was new to Burns and Jacoby, and Stewart's experience had been in a previous generation. Of the staff, seven of the sixteen accurately could be termed career public servants. But of these, two were on temporary loan to the Council for a few months (Koch and Riefman), one planned to remain for only a year (Achinstein), and another left by October, 1954 (Fisher). Only three of these careerists had had previous Council experience (Lusher, Fisher, and Miss James). Of the eight academicians, all, in fact, had government experience but they had come to the Council from academic or (in Siegel's case) research posts. Three were to serve on a part-time basis with the Council, commuting to Washington two to four days a week (De Chazeau, Saulnier, and Triffin), and four were to return to their teaching posts within a year (De Chazeau, Long, Nicholls, and Triffin). In addition to Lusher, Miss James, and Stocking of the careerists, Saulnier and Siegel were to maintain their association with the Council throughout the Eisenhower Administration, with Saulnier succeeding Burns as Chairman in 1956.

With regard to the government careerists–academician dichotomy, four could be described as hybrids. Newcomb could be termed a careerist on the grounds of eighteen years of federal service, including three years of earlier association with the Council, but his base of operation during his second tour with the Council was his own Washington consulting firm. Shere from Indiana University and Triffin from Yale University had previously had fourteen and nine years, respectively, with the federal government in economic posts and were thoroughly familiar with Washington operations. Siegel joined the Council after two years with the Twentieth Century Fund, which had been preceded by two years of teaching and research at Johns Hopkins University. He had had also nine years of statistical and economic experience with federal depression and military emergency agencies. It is interesting to note that, in addition to Burns, Jacoby and four staff members had been associated with the National Bureau of Economic Research—Koch, Long, Saulnier, and Siegel.

The Council was thus revitalized along Burns-Eisenhower Republican lines just in time to meet a compelling demand for its services.

Programs Take Precedence

Before leaving New York for Washington in March, 1953, Burns pointed out to the Board of Directors of the National Bureau that "The shrinkage of private spending during 1951, when public spending was rapidly expanding, is another warning that the present boom will not last forever." [30] As he settled into his new position as economic adviser to the President, he found sufficient confirmation in professional agreement and economic developments to transform a safe prediction of inevitable change into an uneasy concern for the immediate months ahead.

On the occasion of his appointment in September, 1952, as Blough's replacement on the Keyserling Council, Robert Turner had outspokenly predicted that the leveling and subsequent decline of defense expenditures would mean a recession. Three months later in their last review to President Truman, Keyserling, Turner, and Clark raised the question whether or not the combination of increased productivity and moderating defense outlays would produce deflation and unemployment. [31] In March, Jules Bachman, for example, warned of a decline later in 1953, pointing to possible weaknesses in investment, defense spending, housing debt financing, and farm income. [32] By late April, Burns could notice a weakening in four of the National Bureau's set of eight leading economic indicator series—a drop in stock market prices that had started in February, a parallel decline in the average weekly hours of work, a decline of new construction, and in March a lessening of the usual seasonal upswing in housing starts.

At the same time that the Administration was following a restrictive budget policy in their planning for fiscal 1955, Budget Bureau staff working on economic projections were expecting a leveling of GNP in the second half of 1953 or the first half of 1954, followed by a decline in GNP extending into 1955. Coming to similar conclusions, the Bureau of Employment Security in the Department of Labor notified state employment security agencies of a downturn expected by the middle of 1954. [33]

Yet, even taking into account their disquieting significance for the future, these economic developments hardly justified sounding an alarm or initiating a counterattack. Latest reports showed that GNP for the first quarter of 1953 (at seasonally adjusted annual rates) rose to an estimated $363 billion, which was $3 billion above the rate for the fourth quarter of 1952 and $20 billion above that for the 1952 third quarter, that consumer prices decreased slightly, that unemployment was down to 2.7 percent of the civilian labor force, and that industrial production was maintaining the new post-World War II high reached in March.[34] Besides, the new administration had already started to encourage free-enterprise expansion. Wage controls and price controls on a variety of consumer goods were terminated in March, amendments to the Defense Production Act [35] removed all control authority except over allocations and priorities regarding defense items, and the Rent Control Act ended federal rent control on all but critical defense housing.[36]

On the government spending front, Eisenhower cut Truman's fiscal 1954 proposed budget appropriation from $72.9 billion to $64.4 billion, most of it deleted from defense, foreign aid, and related areas. Additional reductions were urged upon government departments and agencies as part of a generally restrictive budget policy for both 1954 and 1955.[37] In April, the Treasury offered $1 billion in 3¼ percent long-term fully marketable securities as the first step in an attempt to lengthen the debt structure. On its own initiative, the Federal Reserve Open Markets Committee in May "began operating to ease pressure on bank reserves, not primarily because it foresaw at that time a recession in the making, but because of the sudden appearance of more tension in the financial markets than it considered appropriate." [38] This was followed by a reduction in reserve requirements in July. The Federal Reserve's explanation was that "The effect of these two actions combined was to increase reserve funds available to member banks by over $2 billion and to change the tone of the money markets from one of restraint to one of ease."[39]

At the same time in May that Burns was working on Reorganization Plan No. 9 and preparing to relaunch the Council, the Administration was concerned not with economic decline but with operating deficits. Even with the $8.5-billion slash in the fiscal 1954 budget, appropriations expenditures were expected to exceed receipts by an estimated $6.6 billion.[40] Consequently, commitments to tax reduction were temporarily shelved while the President secured from a reluctantly obliging Congress a six-month extension of the excess profits tax, which had been imposed as an anti-inflation measure and was scheduled to expire on June 30, in order not to lose $800 million of needed revenue. He was not so successful, however, in a seemingly ill-conceived and half-hearted fight with Senators Byrd and Millikin to lift the debt ceiling from $275 billion to $290 billion. A request made on July 30 for an increase of the ceiling to insure the government's ability to pay its bills was passed by the House on July 31 and rejected by the Senate Finance Committee on August 1. The adjournment of Congress on August 3 left the measure permanently shelved.

Although Burns was kept informed and was consulted regarding these matters, his role in these early actions does not appear to have been a major one. In part this was because he was occupied with setting up his own shop, in part because he probably was in accord with the Administration policies, thereby making his involvement unnecessary, and in part because the steps taken in excess profits tax extension, Treasury financing, and Federal Reserve easing did not call for "outside" advice. The New York *Times* reported, for example, that there was "no prodding from the Administration" [41] on the Federal Reserve's relaxation of reserve requirements.

By August, the persistent shadows of recession had impressed an increasingly deep concern upon the newly reconstituted Council. One of Burns' first moves was to ask Achinstein, Lusher, and Saulnier to prepare recommendations on possible anticyclical steps that could or should be taken if warranted by the evolving situation. True, the latest data covering June and July as summarized in the *Economic Indicators* showed a late July upturn in stock prices after a five-month decline. Similarly, the decrease in average weekly hours of work had leveled off, commercial construction was steady, the downward trend in new housing starts was not serious compared with an even sharper decline in the summer of 1952, and farm income was up slightly.

The continuing sharp rate of business inventory accumulation and the decrease in total business sales, however, signaled an ominous imbalance between the two and pointed to the possibility of impending liquidation. These signs were not lost on Burns and his colleagues. As one of his first assignments, Achinstein undertook a study of the inventory developments. He later commented, "I concluded that inventories were way out of line and that a recession was on the way." [42] The decrease of federal expenditures, even if matched by a drop in receipts, and the prospects of budget cuts for the next fiscal year served only to heighten the concern of the new crew of economic experts.

As individual economists joined the staff during September and October, they promptly became embroiled in the Council's concentration on recession possibilities, which permeated general discussions and debates and became the rationale behind particular assignments. Interagency task forces were established as part of ABEGS to conduct "an intensive study of measures to promote the stability and growth of our economy and specific economic programs and policies to be pursued *in the event of a general slowing down of economic activity*." [43]

In September Burns reminded his staff that "attention should be focused upon measures to be taken within, say, the next six months —when, by whom, for what purpose, and with what probable effect." [44] Such attention meant consideration of a great variety of measures, some of which emerged as definite proposals, others of which survived initial discussion and exploration but never saw the light of formal approval, and still others for which suggestion and rejection were virtually simultaneous. The Council's thinking included possibilities involving modernizing and repairing homes, revising the unemployment compensation system, liberalizing federal credit aids to construction, revising the tax system, planning public works, expanding employment through community and business programs, and strengthening the financial system as a means of contributing to economic stability.

At the same time, industrial observers reminded the Council economists that they were not alone in feeling, as the New York *Times* reported, that "the Eisenhower Administration might be heading into the first test of the adequacy of a hands-off approach to the national economy." [45] At an early ABEGS meeting, Burns brought the sub-Cabinet level of policy-makers up to date on the economic situation as viewed by the Council, for Burns saw ABEGS as a way of "preparing the mind for future acceptance of things that would have to be done to counter the recession." [46] On September 25, he told the Cabinet that a "readjustment" might be on the way. As the situation was not yet critical, however, he was not contemplating drastic action [47] but rather was concentrating on preparations for actions that might become necessary.

Secretary Humphrey was much concerned and told Burns, "We must not let this happen; you must tell us what to do." [48] At Burns' instigation, Humphrey encouraged the business world by telling the American Bankers Association in Washington that the way was clear for the tax cuts on personal income and for the expiration of the excess profits tax to become effective on January 1, 1954, as already scheduled, and that there would be no request for a further extension.[49] Given the difficulty recently experienced in gaining congressional approval for the extension of the excess profits tax beyond June 30, 1953, the normal aversion to tax increases during an election year, and the fact that Congress was not then in session, to do otherwise would have been in Donovan's terms, "well-nigh politically impossible." [50] Under these circumstances, Humphrey's pronouncement seems largely gratuitous. However, according to Burns,

There was considerable uncertainty in the business community whether the scheduled tax cuts would actually take place. Humphrey was reluctant to make a categorical statement and wanted to leave the way open for continuing the taxes if it later proved necessary or desirable, but I persuaded him to come out with solid reassurance to the business community that the cuts would go through as scheduled. It was a necessary psychological move to gain confidence against recessionary developments.[51]

As great as may have been the concern that accompanied the appearance after only nine months in office of the Republican ghost of 1929, attention and interest were largely directed toward a more attractive prospect—the President's program for 1954. Regardless of the economic storm warnings, conceiving, preparing, and presenting the first Republican program in twenty-five years constituted the Administration's major day-to-day activity from early fall on into January. Dealing with a recession, still more prospective than present, would have to wait, and, except for some small-scale assistance in October and November to depressed areas,[52] it did wait. This situation denoted neither a conflict of attitudes between concern for the economy and concern for Republican opportunities in the coming year nor irresponsibility with regard to the nation's economic well-being. Rather, the objectives of economic proposals were to stimulate the economy in the short run and lay the basis for growth in the long run. The course to be followed represented commitments to effect a reconversion from the Korean mobilization, reduce expenditures, balk inflation, balance the budget, and improve governmental efficiency. These ends and means were founded upon Republican values; they evolved from the early experiences and reactions of the new Administration, and, by the autumn of 1953, assumed immediacy under the press of the annual messages, the first Eisenhower budget, and the 1954 congressional elections.

As Neustadt made abundantly clear in his article on the presidency and legislation,[53] plans and preparations for 1954 were both elaborate and comprehensive. Even before Inauguration Day in January, 1953, Budget Director Joseph M. Dodge had begun to brief future agency heads by having Budget Bureau staff members inform each "about 'his' legislative program (compiled the preceding fall), its existence in form and fact, its usefulness for orientation, its potential for planning and control, its liability to renewal on Budget's call." [54] Resurrecting a practice of the Truman Administration, the request for estimates for the fiscal 1955 budget sent to agencies in June, 1953, was accompanied by a request for proposals for the President's 1954 legislative program.

A month later, the President wrote Cabinet members asking for their ideas regarding the forthcoming State of the Union Message, "these ideas to be based on a 'thorough rethinking of the mission of your department and the . . . means to achieve it.' " [55] The legislative proposals and ideas that accumulated in the Budget Bureau and White House during September and October necessitated a detailed reviewing that extended into November and involved members of the White House staff from Sherman Adams on down, the Budget Bureau (principally careerist Roger W. Jones, then the Assistant Director for Legislative Reference), and Burns of the Council. The period was marked by a continuing process of consideration, elimi-

nation, negotiation, modification, and final drafting. Once the particular components of the President's program were developed, there
had to be the final determination of the best vehicle for their presentation, that is, the State of the Union Message, the Budget Message,
the *Economic Report*, or a Special Message.

Throughout the constant give-and-take of the program's final development, Burns was a "prime participant." [56] He was in on many
of the two-to-three hour "skull sessions" and was frequently in direct touch with White House and with Budget Bureau officials as
well as with those of various departments. Available evidence points
to an essentially refining and catalytic contribution—commenting on
the economic significance of particular proposals already in advanced form, discussing substance and strategy with Cabinet secretaries, launching trial balloons in ABEGS, drawing ideas from the
task forces to inject into the main stream of decisions, and, most
important, orienting the President on proposals that would sooner
or later come to him for approval. At the same time, Burns was both
gathering information and getting his bearings for the preparation
of the 1954 *Economic Report*. Not only did he have to report on the
nation's economy, he had also to help set the economic tone of the
Administration. What better way was there to do this than to be in
on the program's development? What better way was there to sell
the *Economic Report* as a vehicle for presenting at least part of the
program? In this respect, Burns' participation was as much a matter
of take as of give.

Once developed, the program was subjected to a series of White
House dry runs followed by three weeks of formal full-scale Cabinet
presentations extending into mid-December. Polished by these final
treatments, the program was then elaborately unveiled to Republican congressional leaders on December 17, 18, and 19, and finally
—with suitable preliminary publicity—presented to Congress and
the nation by a special presidential radio address on January 4. The
State of the Union Message followed on January 7 and the Budget
Message on January 21; the *Economic Report* was released on January 28, and seven special messages were delivered in the weeks
immediately following.

What finally emerged were, by Neustadt's count, some sixty-five
legislative proposals covering everything from atomic energy to revi-

sion of the Taft-Hartley Act—"a comprehensive and coordinated inventory of the nation's current legislative needs, reflecting the President's own judgments, choices and priorities in every major area of Federal action; in short, his 'legislative program.'" [57]

The scope and diffuseness of the program to which Eisenhower gave his name and upon which the Council gave its advice reflected the conflict between the new Administration's preconceived ideas of leadership and policy, on the one hand, and the realities of existing commitments and responsibilities on the other. The very operation of executive initiative in developing a legislative program negated the thought that "Congress proposes, the President disposes." Disdain for the bureaucrat shrank before the new (even if grudging) awareness that it was the expertise and hard work of the career public servant that nurtured ideas and demands through to acceptable and finished form.[58] Most important of all, hopes for budget balancing, tax reduction, and reduced government interference in the private economy could not withstand the massive demands of national security and the constant pressures to renew and extend New Deal–Fair Deal programs such as social security, public housing, and unemployment compensation. Burns' involvement, in reconciling the largely antithetical goals of liberalism in social affairs and conservatism in economic affairs,[59] reveals a measure of his—and the Council's—advisory contribution. This involvement is illustrated in the development of tax revision, housing proposals, and unemployment compensation proposals as components of the President's program for 1954.

Tax Revision for the Goose That Lays the Golden Egg

As if in keeping with the Republican campaign advocacy of balancing the budget and at the same time reducing expenditures and taxes, the House Ways and Means Committee, chaired by Daniel A. Reed of New York, undertook a thorough study of the tax system during the summer of 1953. In addition to hearing some 500 witnesses comment on forty major topics,[60] the Committee reviewed approximately 14,000 separate suggestions submitted in response to a questionnaire distributed by the Joint Committee on Internal

Revenue Taxation. After the hearings, recommendations were drafted as the basis for the 1954 tax revenue bill, which was subsequently labeled "the first general tax revision in seventy-five years." [61]

In introducing his basic tax recommendations, the President noted in his Budget Message that the "proposed revisions are the result of a year's intensive work. The collaboration between congressional and Treasury staffs in the development of the tax revision bill has been very close." [62] Those participating in the collaborative effort were primarily the staffs of the Ways and Means Committee, of the Joint Committee on Internal Revenue Taxation, and eight or ten *ad hoc* study groups within the Treasury. Principal participants included Colin F. Stam, Chief of the Joint Committee staff, Dan Throop Smith, a Harvard University professor of finance who had joined Humphrey as Assistant to the Secretary for Tax and Debt Analysis, and Kenneth W. Gemmill, a Philadelphia lawyer who served as Assistant to the Secretary for Tax Legislation. According to Smith,

The basic features of the measure—for instance, whether or not to push depreciation reform—were worked out in the Treasury and at the White House level and included discussions with the Director of the Budget, the Council of Economic Advisers, and various interested departments. This was not done formally but informally by 'phone or meetings at lunch or in someone's office. It became tacitly assumed that we would do thus and so. There were also almost continuous meetings with Colin Stam and his staff and on major matters with key members of the Congress. The detailed provisions were worked out by the Treasury and congressional committee staffs. When the bill was being considered before the Ways and Means Committee and the Senate Finance Committee, Stam, Gemmill, and I made joint presentations. Facing them in a semicircle, we reviewed the proposed changes. Gemmill and I from the Treasury Department were able to state the Administration's position on congressional reaction to points which were questioned by the congressional committees and to proposals which were made by committee members. It was really a unique example of executive-legislative participation. We worked together in a constant and informal manner.[63]

The reform measures as listed in the Budget Message consisted of twenty-five proposals designed to reduce inequities, loosen restraints

on production, promote investment, and simplify tax law and prevent abuses. The measures themselves in many cases paralleled the
topic headings used in the Ways and Means Committee hearings
and were grouped in three main areas—aid to individuals, aid to
business, and improved administration. Reducing inequities covered
a host of specific measures including relief to widows and widowers
employing assistance for child care, to individuals with heavy medical expenses, and to annuitants whose savings were subject to
income tax—all "at comparatively small loss of revenue." [64]

More significant, expensive, and politically "loaded" were the
major measures for reducing the double taxation of corporate dividends, liberalizing depreciation allowances, extending the loss carry-
back from one to two years, permitting write-off or capitalization of
current research and development expenses, easing the penalty for
accumulation of earnings, and reducing the taxes on business income from foreign sources. Other provisions involved a variety of
specific changes ranging from improving accounting definitions to
allowances for soil conservation expenses. As Smith has pointed out,

There was nothing magic about twenty-five proposals, nor did the estimated price tag for all this of $1.4 billion in tax deductions represent
the total cost of a complete list of desired reforms. Twenty-five was a
good number—comprehensive but not overwhelming. We grouped our
priority items within this limit. When some of the key Republican members of the Ways and Means Committee objected to one of our proposals
just before submission of the Budget Message, we brought out another
that had been held in reserve—the figure had already gone to the President. The price tag was worked at from both ends; the cost of reforms
we wanted versus what we thought would be acceptable to the Congress
in terms of both amount and incidence. Not an easy job, but on the
whole we were satisfied.[65]

Not to have sought greater reductions represents not merely a
calculation of congressional reaction but, in addition, a process of
compromise and balance among basic Administration goals of tax
cuts, expenditure cuts, debt reduction, balanced budget, and reduced government interference in the nation's economy. The emphasis placed upon aid to corporations, largely in the form of
accelerated depreciation, and upon the dividend exclusion and credit

provision, which together comprised approximately two-thirds of the reduction, reveals the Administration's thinking on tax policy. As confirmed in its public justification, revisions favoring the investment sector of the economy would lead to greater and more efficient production which would boost employment. Secretary Humphrey told the Joint Economic Committee:

> We have developed what I believe . . . is a very sound program for depreciation that will promote modernization of plant and equipment which does so many things. In the first place, it increases the market for the making of the new machinery that is to be bought. It gives a man a new machine which lets him produce more goods, which lets him earn more by operating that machine. It lets the business prosper more by having that better machine.
>
> That puts more payrolls out. That puts more money into circulation. The goods that are made on the new machine are cheaper than the goods that are made on the old machine. That induces people to buy.
>
> Mr. Fulbright, the goose that lays the golden egg is production, and it doesn't make much difference. If you haven't got a payroll, you haven't got consumers. Payrolls are what make consumers. Payrolls are the things that get the money out to the people, and you stop the payrolls, and you stop the consumption automatically.[66]

Thus, the Eisenhower Administration proposed to Congress the enactment of tax legislation that, by encouraging the investment sector of the economy, would stimulate long-term economic growth. Throughout the process of its formulation, Burns and his Council provided reinforcement, modification, and refinement to proposals that were in the main developed elsewhere. Burns himself has stated,

> The Council had to keep in mind both the immediate needs and the government's responsibilities for the future. We had to consider economic principles and—regarding taxes—how much to cut, for whom, and when. In view of the tax cuts already made in January, 1954, my main interest and area of participation was the liberalization of depreciation and more favorable treatment of dividends. I did not bother much about minor individual items such as medical expenses.[67]

For both immediate and long-range significance, reforms in these areas held the highest potential for releasing the regenerative forces of a free economy, by "providing more powerful incentives for work, investment, employment, and efficient management, and making the tax structure more stabilizing in its operation." [68] Sensitive both to congressional reaction and continuing deficits, Secretary Humphrey was reluctant to push reform terms that would extend the overall reduction beyond $1.4 billion. Yet, as Burns has recalled, "We wanted to go further than the Treasury. We prodded and stiffened its stand." [69] The urging of further cuts upon a reluctant Humphrey suggests a picture of the President's chief financial officer not only frustrated by the clash of his distaste for deficits with his yearning for tax cuts but also unwilling to modify his stand—even by late 1953—in view of a possible recession. It suggests, too, a companion picture of the President's chief economic adviser willing to make the concessions, less concerned about budget imbalances in the short run, sensitive to the general economic well-being, and looking for opportunities—no matter how small—to serve both long-run growth and immediate contracyclical ends.

By providing ammunition and support, Burns did more to fortify than to change the Treasury's proposals. In part the ammunition and support took the form of offering reassurance on negotiating tactics with the Hill, in part it consisted of suggesting substantive ideas for extending what was already an investment incentive, an approach that had, to Burns, welcome consequences which were aimed at counteracting the recession. Smith has recalled that Burns contributed at least two ideas: extension of loss-carryback provisions from one to two years and a pass-through of savings on tax-exempt securities from the investment company owning the securities to its own shareholders.[70] The former was incorporated as a proposal in the final tax program, but the latter was returned to the shelf until it could be included in the President's 1955 *Economic Report* among the Council's recommendations for "Expanding State and Local Works." [71]

Perhaps Burns' greatest contribution was in briefing the President on the significance and possibilities of the forthcoming program. The weekly sessions with Eisenhower on progress and problems and on what the Chief Executive could expect gave the Council Chairman the opportunity to widen the President's own dichotomous view of liberal welfare and conservative economics to include the divergent but not necessarily conflicting concerns of the Treasury and the Council. These briefings, conducted with tact and restraint, paid off. Smith, who accompanied Humphrey and Folsom to their meetings with Eisenhower in which he approved the proposed revisions, recalled that the President had a good understanding and definite views on the specific contents of the tax program and a full grasp of its significance.[72]

Once the tax proposals became an accepted part of the President's program, Burns helped gain government and public support for them in the *Economic Report*. As a supplement to formal and itemized presentation of them in the Budget Message, he provided a clear and persuasive summary description and defense of what the Administration regarded as essential revisions.[73]

Throughout the development and consideration of the tax reform measure, the process of Burns' participation was primarily one of frequent and informal contact with Marion Folsom, Humphrey, and Smith. In Smith's words, "Burns and I were in frequent touch with each other and he passed on to me whatever he thought was useful from his staff, and of course raised many major points with Secretary Humphrey or Folsom." [74] Burns has described the process in the following terms: "Our discussions were marked by informality. We did not wish to be in the position of reviewing and commenting on drafts. It meant too much of a firm commitment on both sides, of arguing from assumed positions. It was better to keep things fluid and formative." [75] This maintenance of oral and noncommitting flexibility was a Burns technique which had originated during the previous spring in the preparation of the President's message on extending the excess profits tax: "With some disturbing signs in the economy, we wanted to retain some flexibility and freedom for maneuver through the actual wording of the message." [76] Throughout the deliberations on the proposed provisions, Burns was the only Council participant except, occasionally, Jacoby. According to Burns, Louis Shere, as the Council's tax man, "served as a technical backstop for me and did not deal with the Treasury directly." [77]

Factors determining the Council's essentially supporting rather than primarily substantive contribution to the shaping of the tax reform measure were threefold. First, the Treasury and the two congressional committees were the joint instigators and developers of the reform from its beginning in early 1953 through its incorporation into the President's program and on into its congressional enactment. The investment-incentive approach to the revision of business taxes as revealed in Under Secretary Folsom's testimony before the Select Committee on Small Business in May, 1953,[78] was developed before the Council had been reconstituted. Folsom's proposals for the "Reduction of Tax Barriers to Growth" included liberalization of depreciation rates, alleviation of double taxation of dividends, and revision of the surtax on surplus accumulation.[79] With the exception of the loss-carryback proposal, the President's recommendation to "reduce the more serious restraints on production and economic growth [and to] promote investment" [80] conformed to the topical headings previously developed by the Ways and Means Committee. Moreover, as Neustadt has pointed out, during the actual legislation preparation, "Treasury presented draft language piecemeal to the House Ways and Means Committee as a 'technical drafting service' in elaboration of the President's proposals preparatory to the framing of a *committee* bill." [81] The Council was a latecomer; as a peripheral participant it had little to do with shaping the great mass of ideas and suggestions into the reform's major dimensions and content.

Second, within the executive branch, tax matters were by tradition, practice, and expertise the province of the Treasury—an institution historically jealous of its independence and influence and therefore not likely to seek the advice and counsel of outside agencies, especially presidential advisory agencies. Most particularly was this so when the Secretary of the Treasury was an individual like Humphrey, who was reputed to have laid down to Eisenhower one condition for his acceptance of his post: "I want you, if anyone asks you about money, to tell them to go and see George." [82] This did not mean that there was a lack of communications between the Council and the Treasury, for, as has been indicated, there was a good deal, but rather that the taking of action based upon the communications was largely at the discretion of the Treasury. The exchanges, at least at the staff level, were not really on equal terms. For example, the Treasury did not participate in the Council's staff Task Force on Tax

Policy, thus limiting its creative usefulness. As Smith has recalled, "We had more urgent things to do than to spend much time with them." [83]

Lastly, Burns agreed with the program of revisions and therefore needed only to support it. Smith has recalled that "We were all eager, enthusiastic, and in basic agreement—Burns included. He was in on White House discussions." [84] Burns' agreement was not so much rooted in tax reform as an end in itself or in production as the principal energizer in the economy but rather in private investment as a spur to both immediate needs and long-term growth. Consequently, his best service to the reform measure was in adding the Council's expertise to its development and in articulating the major premises underlying its importance. If, as Burns said, his primary interest in the tax area was in providing liberal treatments for both depreciation rates and for dividends, then he contributed to the prominence of these treatments in the final presentation. If, as he contended, he was concerned about overall economic conditions, he helped to identify the tax reform part of the President's program with growth and stability. If he had not been on the scene, virtually the same tax program would have emerged but possibly somewhat less extensive in cuts and probably somewhat less polished as a product of dynamic conservatism.

Housing Proposals for Welfare and Stabilization

Although there was no reference to federal housing policies in the 1952 Republican platform, they could not be ignored in the President's program for 1954. Not only did housing represent too great an issue to be sidestepped, but, in addition, the new Administration inherited the Housing Act of 1949, which, in its "Declaration of National Housing Policy," spoke of

the realization as soon as feasible of the goal of a decent home and a suitable living environment for every American family, . . . thus contributing to the development and redevelopment of communities and to the advancement of the growth, wealth, and security of the nation. The Congress further declares that such production is necessary to enable the housing industry to make its full contribution toward an economy of maximum employment, production, and purchasing power.[85]

In conjunction with these aims, federal housing programs were to be administered "in such manner as will encourage and assist . . . the stabilization of the housing industry at a high annual volume of residential construction."[86] Encouragement and assistance meant government involvement in an industry of tremendous size, of considerable political force, and of both short- and long-term significance for economic policy. During the postwar period from 1946 to 1953, expenditures for new residential construction, including alterations, constituted over 20 percent of gross private investment and some 43 percent of all privately financed new dwelling units involving government-insured or -guaranteed loans. In 1952, the residential mortgage debt made up 45 percent of the total net private long-term debt. Between 1937 and 1953 some 400,000 dwelling units were completed or under construction under the government low-rent public housing programs.[87] Employment in the industry approximated a million construction workers and thousands more in related industries.

Behind such magnitudes lay associations representing the building trades, home builders, financial intermediaries, and realtors, to say nothing of civic groups interested in such objectives as better housing and slum clearance. The implications in the "Declaration of National Housing Policy" notwithstanding, policies favorable to these interests under the 1949 Housing Act meant potential conflict with the responsibility for the growth and stability of the nation's economy as a whole. Federal support for housing might be desirable for housing precisely when goals of overall price stability called for cutting back in housing credit and expenditures as part of an overall policy of monetary and fiscal restraint.[88]

The new administration's welfare and economic responsibilities for housing may have been reluctantly embraced, but the significance of these responsibilities was no less compelling for having first been recognized by the previous New Deal–Fair Deal. The Eisenhower approach to housing would represent another attempt to balance liberalism in welfare with conservatism in economics. To help develop an appropriate liberal-conservative housing program, Eisenhower, in September, 1953, established the President's Advisory Committee on Government Housing Policies and Programs. Chaired by Albert M. Cole, Administrator of HHFA, the twenty-two-man committee was composed of nine bankers and insurance company executives, three business executives, two representatives from the National Association of Home Builders, a representative each from the CIO and AFL, two architects, two housing experts, a lawyer, and an economist. The work of the Committee was divided among five subcommittees with individual members serving on one or more. Each subcommittee was assisted by staff advisers, an executive secretary, or both, normally appointed from the upper career echelons of HHFA.

As was the case in the development of tax policies, the housing recommendations that emerged from this Committee's work to become the backbone of the President's program on housing were not geared to meet any immediate situation but to establish bases of government participation in housing for the years ahead. Such bases were directed less toward realizing "decent homes and suitable living environment for every American family" and encouraging "a high annual volume of residential construction," as specified in the Housing Act of 1949, than toward, in the words of the Committee's report,

facilitating the operation of [a strong, free, competitive economy in order] to provide adequate housing for all the people, *to meet demands for new building*, to assure the maintenance, restoration, and utilization of the *existing stock of housing*, and the elimination of conditions that create hazards to public safety and welfare and to the economic health of our communities, and *that only those measures that prove to be successful in meeting these objectives should be continued.*[89]

As drawn up with minor modifications from the Committee's recommendation, the President's housing program that was presented to the Congress in a Special Message on January 25[90] stressed assistance to localities for urban renewal, support to low-income housing on an experimental basis, rehabilitation of existing homes on terms comparable to those granted for new home construction, equal opportunities for minority groups in urban redevelopment projects, and the easing of terms on VA-guaranteed and FHA-insured mortgages. It proposed a public housing program of 140,000 units to be built over a four-year period at 35,000 units per year, a reorganization of the Federal National Mortgage Association (FNMA, or "Fanny Mae"), the establishment of a secondary mortgage market, and an administrative reorganization of HHFA. In addition to echoing the Advisory Committee's recommendations, the President asked for discretionary authority to adjust the terms of FHA and VA mortgages as a countercyclical tool.

The inclusion of the 140,000-unit four-year public housing program was actually achieved over the objections of the President's Advisory Committee. Although the members incorporated a public housing recommendation in their report, they did so without enthusiasm. In the words of one participant, "it was an issue that split, rocked, and nearly ruined the Committee." The Committee debated heatedly the proposal of its public housing subcommittee for a continued and possibly expanded program over that of the 1949 Housing Act but could not agree on an adequate substitute. That the idea of public housing in some form survived the argument was due to this lack of an adequate substitute, the persistence of the sponsoring subcommittee, and the availability of a conviction-saving compromise. It was rationalized that a modified public housing program might be justifiable, but it might also be made superfluous by the hoped-for success of the Committee's companion proposal for especially easy-term government-guaranteed *private* financing for low-income families. The Committee indicated its objections to public housing by passing the more specific questions of size and methods of financing on to the Administration and the Congress and stating that "The Committee is unanimous in its belief in the objective of a more effective operation of the private housing market so as to lessen steadily the need for direct subsidies." [91]

Consequently, the specifics of the proposal regarding the number of publicly financed units to be built (140,000) and the period of time over which construction would be stretched (four years) were provided by HHFA, not by the President's Committee, and the proposal was submitted to the Cabinet on December 9 by Cole as part of the presentation of his 1954 program. This particular number of units did not represent any specific objective or estimated need but rather a four-year multiple of the approximately 35,000 that had been built on an average annual basis under authorization of the

1949 Housing Act. The survival of the recommendation through White House and Cabinet considerations has been attributed to Ernest Bohm, a Cleveland housing official who was also a member of the public housing subcommittee of the President's Committee. He is reputed to have convinced Secretary Humphrey that Cole's proposal should not be rejected. Quite as unwanted by the Administration as by the Advisory Committee, its inclusion in the housing program was jocularly referred to as "Cole's Christmas present."

The President's housing program as summarized in his *Economic Report* (which was in turn prepared by the Council) included the request for discretionary authority to adjust mortgages but, despite Administration approval, omitted the public housing recommendations. This omission stemmed from Burns' belief that the short-term antirecessionary significance of the public housing—particularly of only 35,000 units—was not great and that the immediate recession (which was by December becoming his main concern) was not going to be sufficiently deep to warrant an all-out public expense effort.[92] As Hauge has recalled, "Burns and the rest of us were not so much opposed to public housing per se; rather, we wished to see its emphasis put on slum clearance and urban renewal." [93] Consistent with the nature of the overall housing program, Burns emphasized neighborhood rehabilitation as an end in itself as well as an investment outlet for long-term growth and stability.

It was the potentiality of immediate contracyclical impact, however, that led Burns during the final deliberations to propose the granting of specific authority to the President to alter the terms of government-guaranteed loans within statutory limits. Until 1949 such authority had been implicit under the terms of the 1934 National Housing Act but had applied only to FHA-insured loans and not to VA-guaranteed loans. Moreover, the practice of operating at the statutory limits of the terms had set a pattern of inactive Executive discretion. The discretionary authority given to the President in the 1949 Housing Act was limited to acceleration, not deceleration, and was applicable only to the relatively small public housing and urban renewal programs involving lead times that were too long to be of much contracyclical help. The Defense Production Act of 1950 authorized the President to prescribe regulations "in order to prevent or reduce excessive or untimely use of a fluctuation in such credit." [94] In spirit and letter, however, the measure was essentially an anti-inflationary control and not concerned with economic stability as such. At Burns' instigation,[95] a limited step toward granting discretionary authority on economic grounds was taken in the Housing Amendment of 1953,[96] whereby the President was allowed to ease terms on FHA-insured mortgages of $12,000 or less, taking into account the general effect of such action "upon conditions in the building industry and upon the general economy." [97]

As described in the President's Special Message and in the 1954 *Economic Report*, Burns proposed giving the President discretionary authority to vary terms in both directions:

> The way to avoid the inflationary influence of excessively liberal mortgage credit terms at certain times, and to help offset unfavorable developments by an easing of terms at other times, is to make provision for permissive adjustments in the conditions on which credits may be insured or guaranteed. To some extent these influences on the construction industry may be exercised through general monetary and credit measures. But the specific device of varying the terms and conditions of mortgage financing will ordinarily be more effective, since it goes directly to those aspects of the loan contract—the down-payment requirement and the repayment period—to which borrowers are most sensitive. . . . It would be desirable to broaden the area of permissive action by authorizing the President to regulate, within appropriate statutory limits, the maximum loan-value ratios, terms to maturity, and interest rates that may be carried by FHA-insured and VA-guaranteed loans of all types.[98]

Grebler notes that "this was the first time in about twenty years of housing legislation that the principle of administering major federal credit programs in such a manner as to help maintain economic stability was clearly enunciated in governmental policy." [99] That Congress did not see fit to grant the authority appears not so much as a rejection of the Administration arguments as a reluctance to increase presidential discretion and a recognition of the housing industry's aversion to a potentially restrictive force on its activities.

Although the permissive adjustment proposal may be viewed as distinctly the Council's contribution (and only a shadow of what Burns wanted),[100] it by no means constituted the extent of the

Council's concern over housing. In a process typical of policy formulation as a whole, the Council also provided information and ideas that gave both impetus and shape to the President's proposal to create a secondary mortgage market. The proposal as it ultimately appeared in the President's Special Message of January 25 represented the gradual and constant interweaving of strands of ideas from countless sources, of which the Council was one.

During the fall of 1953, the proposal was being developed concurrently by both the Advisory Committee's Subcommittee on Housing Credit Facilities and the Council's ABEGS Task Force No. 7 on Strengthening the Financial System and Increasing its Contribution to Economic Stability. The subcommittee itself was composed of three mortgage bankers, George L. Bliss, A. R. Gardner, and Aksel Nielsen, Richard G. Hughes of the National Association of Home Builders, Robert Patrick of the Bankers Life Insurance Company of Des Moines, and Norman P. Mason of the William P. Proctor Company, North Chelmsford, Massachusetts. Included on the Task Force were Albert Koch, Chairman, Raymond Saulnier, also of the Council staff, and Ralph A. Young, Director of the Federal Reserve's Division of Research and Statistics. In addition, the Council's Task Force No. 1 on Home Modernization and Repair Programs was interested in it from the viewpoint of providing financial aid for the improvement of existing structures. Active concern fanned out beyond the Council and the Advisory Committee to include the White House, the Federal Reserve, the VA's loan guaranty operation, and various components of HHFA.

The net result of the many-sided involvement was an intricate, often spontaneous interchange of ideas, the origins of which become largely undeterminable in a maze of memoranda and correspondence, drafts and redrafts, telephone calls, and conferences. T. B. King, Assistant Deputy Administrator of the VA's loan guaranty program appeared before the Advisory Committee's subcommittee, as did Walter W. McAllister, Chairman of the Home Loan Bank Board, Saulnier of the Council, and Guy E. Noyes and Winfield W. Riefler of the Federal Reserve Board. Various ideas for a secondary mortgage market came to Task Force No. 7 from such sources as the VA and the Home Loan Bank Board. On temporary loan to the Council from the Federal Reserve Board, Koch had no difficulty in maintaining constant contact with his home-based colleagues, Young, Noyes, and Riefler, the last two of whom served on Task Force No. 1. Within the Council, Robinson Newcomb, Achinstein, Saulnier, and Koch not only shared ideas with one another but joined as informants and interpreters, reporting to Burns and maintaining touch with such officials as P. N. Brownstein of the VA and Neil J. Hardy, who tripled as HHFA Assistant Administrator, a director of FNMA, and Executive Secretary of one of the Advisory Committee's subcommittees.

The proposal that emerged from this web of contact and association was more a product of consensus than of compromise between basic conflicts. Task Force No. 7 commented favorably to Burns and ABEGS on the establishment of a privately financed mortgage discount exchange that would contribute to economic stability by providing an active mortgage market. The *Economic Report* made a similar proposal and stressed that "the proposed agency should be financed with private funds to the greatest extent practicable." [101] The President's Advisory Committee proposals went into more detail and included the recommendation to abolish the Home Loan Bank Board. The principal differences between the Council's proposals and those of the President's Advisory Committee appear to center on the matter of the Treasury's supporting the market if and when necessary, a proposal that the Council favored and a majority of the Advisory Committee opposed. The main aim of the secondary mortgage market proposal as expressed in the President's Special Message was to provide more adequate credit facilities by reorganizing FNMA, liquidating its $2.5-billion portfolio, and creating a market dominated by private financial intermediaries. Regarding Treasury support, the President endorsed the Council's position by recommending that "the President should be enabled to authorize FNMA to borrow directly from the Treasury for the sole purpose of purchasing certain kinds and types of insured and guaranteed loans when the President determines such action to be necessary in the public interest." [102]

Compared with its largely subordinate role in the development of the tax program, the Council appears to have participated more directly and more as an equal in the various aspects of the housing program. Without denying the primary and dominant contribution of the President's Advisory Committee, the Council was apparently able not only to contribute to this Committee's thinking and, through it, to the program itself, but also to add a significant proposal of its own. It was able to provide an approach of overall economic welfare that softened the underlying conservatism of both Committee and Administration. The Council's ability to participate lay in two reciprocal factors. On the one hand, the Council "knew" housing, and, on the other hand, the agencies concerned with housing needed this knowledge. As an official of the time commented, "because of Saulnier, the Council was able to reassert itself in the housing area."

Saulnier's expertise in the mortgage banking area was complemented by Koch's general monetary and Federal Reserve viewpoint, Achinstein's familiarity with government economic operations, and Newcomb's long experience with government public housing and construction activities. In their roles as Council leaders in the two Task Forces concerned with aspects of housing, these four had access to the operating agencies involved—namely, HHFA, VA, and the Federal Reserve Board—as well as to the Advisory Committee itself. Moreover, Koch, Achinstein, and Newcomb were experienced Washington careerists not reluctant to link inside analysis with outside advice. And Saulnier, by virtue of his consulting experience with Federal Reserve and Agriculture, was no less cognizant of the ways of bureaucracy. It appears obvious that these men were thoroughly familiar with departmental thinking, and consequently their overall perspective enabled them to make suggestions and shape proposals. This strength of knowledge and disposition to operate were reinforced the following year by the addition to the staff of Leo Grebler, one of the foremost economists in housing.

For their part, HHFA and the Loan Guarantee Division of VA were not agencies traditionally strong in authority, vigorous in operation, or impervious to clientele pressure. Neither HHFA nor VA had Cabinet status; neither Administrator Cole nor Administrator H. V. Higley of VA were leaders of the Humphrey stamp. As a member of Congress, Cole had opposed federal housing programs. HHFA and especially its constituent, FHA, had long been under attack on administrative grounds. The President's Advisory Committee's Subcommittee on Organization of Federal Housing Activities in the Federal Government was tactful but clear in its criticisms of confusion of responsibilities, of operating activities of the Administrator's office, and other incompatible functions.[103]

These factors, combined with the Administration's assumption of responsibility characterized more by reluctance than enthusiasm, meant limited White House acceptance of the housing agencies and little sympathy for their problems. Channels to the President were not clear. Donovan's report that the President gave "enthusiastic" support to the 1954 housing program was diluted by including Eisenhower's own comment that "when the government was drawn into such activity, . . . it must approach it 'with jaundiced eye and a good microscope.' " [104] Consequently, to the proponents of housing, Burns and the Council became welcome allies who, with their combined expertise in housing, concern for general economic welfare, and access to the President, were able to keep the housing operation from withering. As Burns has summed it up, "We had the initiative." [105]

Unemployment Insurance Proposals and the Council as Ally

The Council's impact on housing was repeated in the Department of Labor's proposals to broaden and enlarge the Federal-State Unemployment Insurance System. Hardly a venture that would have been initiated at the specific request of the Republican high command, it had been gestating in the Department's Bureau of Employment Security over the course of three years and was brought to life by members of the Bureau's staff during the process of developing Labor's comprehensive inventory of possible inclusions in the President's 1954 program. In large measure, the proposal owed its emergence in that program to the coincidence of the Bureau's active concern for employee security with both Burns' belief in unemployment insurance and his search for ways to improve built-in economic stabilizers.

At a meeting in October, 1950, the Bureau of Employment Security's Federal Advisory Council, made up of "outstanding representatives of labor, management, and the public who are especially familiar with employment problems," [106] unanimously resolved that "in those states where, in a significant number of cases, the maximum [level of employment benefits] is operating to prevent payment of benefits in line with the principle of 50 per cent of wages, the maximum limit on weekly amounts should be raised to permit this principle to operate." [107] At the same meeting, it was also recommended that states extend the duration of benefits to at least twenty-six weeks a year. In the 1950–52 environment of Korean War mobilization, controls, inflation, and full employment, the Committee's recommendation languished, being nurtured neither by compelling need nor by pressure from any interested source.

Interest in unemployment insurance was revived, however, in the fall of 1953 by such activities as the American Assembly conference on "Economic Security for Americans." Its comprehensive findings pointed to the fact that approximately one-third of the nation's work force was not covered by unemployment insurance, which in turn underscored the desirability of broadening coverage.[108] In noting that most state unemployment insurance laws paid benefits averaging "considerably less than 50 per cent of previous earnings" for a relatively few weeks in any twelve-month period, it suggested an increase in the duration of coverage.[109] It also raised questions regarding the various states' ability to operate independent unemployment insurance systems and whether or not the federal government should embark upon any loan or grant program to states who had exhausted their own resources.[110]

As the similarity of these concerns to those of the Federal Advisory Council suggests, the American Assembly conference was pulling together and publicizing current thinking rather than breaking new ground. The facts and figures and pros and cons of various possibilities thrashed out in this conference formed the backbone of the ideas already being developed by the Bureau of Employment Security. As Clarence Long, Chairman of the Council's Task Force on Revision of Unemployment Compensation System, has put it,

The set of proposals was well digested by the time the Council got to it. It was in large part a matter of the Department of Labor's initiative and represented something they had worked on for some time. All we did was boil it down and add a few refinements, but it was essentially a Department of Labor creation.[111]

When, as a Labor Department official recalled, Burns consulted
James P. Mitchell, the new Secretary of Labor, regarding recommendations to be included in the 1954 *Economic Report*, the unemployment insurance proposal was in final form and ready for
promotion. Organized labor favored extension of coverage, and
Mitchell was reputedly anxious to push this particular program.
Hence, Burns, who, from his knowledge of business cycles, was
familiar with the theory and facts of unemployment insurance, once
again served as the welcome ally. As he has recalled,

The proposals of the Bureau of Employment Security were welcome but
also old stuff to me. The major fact is that I kept urging on the President,
on Jim Mitchell, on Humphrey, Weeks, ABEGS, and others the need for
liberalizing the unemployment insurance program. If the Bureau of Employment Security had not made its explicit proposals, I would have made
proposals like them. Details aside, I kept making them long before I saw
what the Labor Department sent down. Moreover, I tried to build up
support for these proposals in the business community as well as within
the Executive by constantly urging that improved administration must
go hand in hand with liberalization. I rather doubt if the Labor Department by itself could have accomplished much in 1953 or 1954 on this
problem.[112]

As if to underscore the significance of the Council's assistance, the
proposals for broadening unemployment insurance as part of the
President's program had their major presentation in the 1954 *Economic Report*. The basic recommendations were (1) to enlarge the
unemployment insurance program to include approximately 10 million additional workers—most notably, 2.5 million federal civilian
employees; (2) to shorten the experience-rating period; (3) to suggest that states "raise these dollar maximums so that payment to the
great majority of beneficiaries may equal at least half their regular
earnings";[113] (4) to urge states to increase the potential duration of
unemployment benefits to twenty-six weeks; (5) to permit federal
loans which do not bear interest to states whose reserves are near
exhaustion; and (6) to encourage efficient administration.[114]

Although much of the credit for the inclusion of the proposals in
the President's program must in fairness go to Burns and to such
professional staff as Long, their contributions to the development of

the specific content of the proposals were minor. What these men did do was not to provide ideas but, as Burns' statement emphasizes, to produce the necessary encouragement and support for what others had proposed. In short, they served an essential catalytic function. With particular expertise available at both the presidential appointee and staff levels, the Council used the power of its acceptance in the Eisenhower Presidency and of its role as spokesman for economic conservatism to gain favor for a series of proposals, not of tremendous importance in the overall program, not of priority in terms of Republican objectives, but of importance to the particular department representing the interests of labor. In a current period of growing unemployment, the Council minimized the New Deal social welfare aura by stressing adequate unemployment insurance as "a valuable first line of defense against economic recession [helping] . . . to curb economic decline during an interval of time that allows other stabilizing measures to become effective." [115] That these particular proposals would probably not become effective in time to help the immediate situation did not negate their long-term value.

At the same time, the Council's weight was also sufficient to checkmate Labor's interest in increasing the minimum wage above the existing level of 75 cents an hour. To Burns, "an effective minimum wage should cover millions of low-paid workers now exempted." [116] Extension was one thing but increase something quite different. As noted in the 1954 *Economic Report,* Burns feared the adverse effect on economic recovery:

A minimum does not protect the inadequately rewarded worker if it is too low. On the other hand, it may not benefit him if it is too high as to push up the whole scaffolding of wages and of costs of doing business, thus leading either to inflation of prices and the worker's own living costs, or to elimination of the less efficient employers and workers. Yet the ability of the employer to absorb a high minimum wage is limited. Indeed, the low-pay industries of today are often those earning modest profits, having limited opportunities to increase productivity, and containing firms easily squeezed out of business by rising costs.[117]

Mitchell, for his part, had committed himself to seek a minimum wage increase in speeches during the fall before the CIO convention and the UAW Full Employment Conference. Implying that the lines of dispute had not been sufficiently drawn to allow or force a decision, the 1954 *Economic Report* studiously avoided any recommendations in this area and concluded two pages of general discussion with the postponing statement that "The Secretary of Labor is continuing his intensive canvass of this highly complex problem and is consulting with appropriate groups. At the proper time recommendations will be made to Congress." [118] A year later, in a last-minute decision made at the White House the night before the presses on the 1955 *Economic Report* had to be locked up, the President accepted Burns' recommendation for an increase to 90 cents as opposed to $1.00 favored by Mitchell and $1.25 sought by the unions.[119]

These sketches of the Council's participation in proposals covering tax reform, housing developments, and unemployment compensation reveal the extent and nature of its involvement in the President's 1954 program—a program, it will be recalled, of immense diversity and scope that attempted to reconcile welfare liberalism with economic conservatism. By no means do they represent the breadth of the Council's involvement in the full range of proposals having economic significance. However, as illustrations, they do reveal Burns' constant attempt to increase the adaptability of the President's essentially long-term program to the potential demands of the unfolding economic situation. Partly in anticipation of the economic developments as he foresaw them, partly as a fulfillment of the government's recognized economic responsibilities, Burns offered proposals, refinements, and reinforcements that reconciled his own convictions with those of the Eisenhower Administration.

Inasmuch as the annual messages were about to be delivered and the President's program was about to be transferred to the other end of Pennsylvania Avenue, the Eisenhower Administration's major attention could and did shift to dealing with the gathering recession. To reverse the tide would be a prime Administration objective for the first six months of 1954. The part the Council was to play in this effort was foreshadowed by the content and tone of its first *Economic Report*.

V. COUNTERING THE
RECESSION OF 1953–54

In the 1954 *Economic Report* President Eisenhower struck notes of confidence and reassurance that a serious depression was not on the way, notes that were similar in tone to those struck in both his State of the Union Message and his Budget Message. As drafted by Burns, the *Economic Report* emphasized the solid accomplishment of the American economy and the promise of a "great opportunity before the American people." [1]

The upsurge of production and employment, which has been sustained with but brief interruptions in the United States for about a dozen years, continued in 1953. New records were established in industrial activity, employment, and the disbursement of incomes. Unemployment reached the lowest level of any peace-time year in recent decades. The average level of prices was remarkably steady. The fruits of expanding production and enterprise were shared widely. Perhaps never before in their history have the American people come closer to realizing the ideal of high and expanding employment, without price inflation, than in 1953. But some sections of industry, notably farming, failed to participate in the widespread prosperity. The index of consumer prices inched a little higher in spite of some decline in food prices. And economic activity, taken as a whole, receded somewhat toward the close of the year. [2]

The settling of economic activity in the latter half of the year was attributed to inventory adjustment to current sales "and little else." [3] On behalf of the President, Burns concluded with "some confidence" that the adjustments would not become cumulative and pointed to well-maintained investment outlays, sound financial institutions, ample credit, the nonspeculative nature of recent prosperity, and the effectiveness of built-in stabilizers.[4] Moreover, "the resourcefulness of individual enterprise and the new horizons that have recently opened up for the consumer will serve our economy well in the more normal environment that, it may be hoped, will be ours in the years ahead." [5]

Such optimism enabled Burns to concentrate on the economic segments of the President's program. Under "Pathways of Strength," he could introduce "bold steps to protect and promote economic stability" and to "stimulate the expansive power of individual enterprise."[6] In this manner tax reforms, housing proposals, and unemployment compensation were indicated as some of the steps that would lead "Toward a Stronger Economy." [7] As an accompaniment to his analysis and recommendations, Burns concluded with a statement that the Administration's free-enterprise approach was "the Basis for Progress." "The arsenal of stabilizing weapons" would be available but applied only on behalf of "reasonable stability." The Administration's emphasis would be upon providing a favorable environment for the full range of individual and entrepreneurial effort.[8]

Not only did the latest economic data confirm Burns' analysis and approach, but the first Republican administration since 1929 was anxious to play down the possibility of a recession and to give a promising account of its economic stewardship while underscoring the contrast with the previous administration in the approach to that stewardship. Moreover, Humphrey's dictum stated in the Cabinet meeting of January 15, 1954, that "prosperity depended more upon the confidence of all the people than upon any particular government measures other than removal of impediments to individual initiative" [9] limited the scope of possible countercyclical action. It is probable, too, that Burns' outlook enhanced the Administration's chances of staying on the offensive by urging concentration on the programs the Administration had spent months preparing rather than advocating the defensive battling of recessionary trends. With conviction founded on his knowledge of business cycles, Burns could conclude that the President's program was "not a legislative program of emergency measures, for the current situation clearly does not require one." [10]

Agreement was expressed by a number of economists testifying before the Joint Committee on the Economic Report.[11] Martin Gainsbrugh, chief economist of the National Industrial Conference Board, emphasized that four of the eight leading economic indicators used by the National Bureau of Economic Research were pointing "sideward, if not up." Alvin Hansen considered that, on the basis of $71 billion of federal expenditures for fiscal 1954, it is "plausible to hope that a cumulative spending collapse is unlikely." Dexter M. Keezer of the McGraw-Hill Publishing Company reported that "American business, as a whole, is planning to spend more for new plants and equipment in the first quarter of 1954 than in any first quarter on record. . . . We have found no evidence of extensive cutbacks in anticipation of business recession." Two weeks before, General Motors had announced its plan to invest $1 billion in its two-year expansion program.[12]

If analytical prognostication about the future was reassuring and optimistic to some professional economists, the outcry over the current situation based on public welfare and political considerations was not. At the same Joint Committee hearings, Walter Reuther of the CIO predictably protested the 3.09 million unemployed, the one out of twelve jobless in Detroit, the 10 percent drop in industrial production, and the steel industry's operating at 74 percent of capacity:

How does the *Economic Report* explain the drop of 1 million jobs and the fact that production in the fourth quarter of 1953 was no better than the fourth quarter of 1952 and actually $7 or $8 billion below last spring?

This is all described as a mere "corrective process" which will provide a more durable basis for business enterprise. Corrective process, indeed. What's corrective about the waste and misery of joblessness? I'd like to see the boys who wrote that one take the show on the road and explain to the million or more who've lost jobs just what's "corrective" about their status.

We believe, and we believe this sincerely, that the most serious aspect of our problem is the political indifference, the kind of calloused complacency which we think certain people in responsibility are taking toward this unemployment problem.[13]

In the same mood of concern and protest, Reuther continued by attacking the tax reform measure on anticyclical grounds:

Clearly, then if you want to turn this thing around you must see that major emphasis must now be placed on strengthening consumption. . . . Our basic economic problem in 1954 simply is not one of furnishing some new, special incentives for business investment. Can anyone seriously believe that we'll overcome this downturn this way? [14]

On the same subject, Gerhard Colm, who had gone from the Keyserling Council staff to the National Planning Association, pointed to the *Economic Report's* failure to demonstrate that present taxes were obstructing investment or that the proposed tax changes would substantially increase investments under conditions then existing.[15]

As the statistics for January, February, and March revealed steadily increasing unemployment, the President was under mounting pressure to act—to hold a conference on unemployment, to initiate public works programs as a spur to consumer buying before the recession became cumulative. In February, Democratic Senator Paul Douglas wrote the President, "A look at the present economic situation indicates, in my judgment, that the time for action is here. At least we should take some initial effective steps to counteract the downward trend." [16] By February, Republican Congressmen began to worry about the fall elections. The political climate was warmed by epithets of "fear deal," "prophets of gloom and doom," "trickle down theory," and "What's good for business." But, as Donovan has noted, "until worst came to worst [the President] continued to ride the squall as his fiscal and economic advisers urged, relying on the economy to right itself with the stimulus of tax reductions, freer credit, liberalized social welfare measures and, above all, confidence by businessmen, home builders, investors and consumers." [17] By the Cabinet meeting of March 12, the President was deadly serious and insisted upon preparedness to act at any moment. "Humphrey, calm as a cucumber, as usual, advised the President against any radical action that could not easily be cut off." [18]

Throughout the build-up of pressures and counterpressures, the Council was both a participant and a witness. The estimate of a mild recession and the awareness of the heightening public concern over unemployment converged on the Council's charts and in the minds of its personnel. As the institutional embodiment of the Chief Executive's responsibilities under the Employment Act, the Council would be the recipient of much of the popular as well as professional credit or blame for accelerating or postponing recovery, for prescribing the right or the wrong treatment. Personally and as part of the presidency, the Chairman and his staff shared with the Administration the pressure, the spotlight, and certainly the motivation to end the recession.

Burns continued to brief the President in weekly conferences and attempted to keep departmental officials informed through attendance at Cabinet meetings, discussions within ABEGS, and constant informal contact. The substance, method, and ultimate impact of the Council's operations were largely determined by its own cautiously optimistic analysis of the economic situation. Its impact was also affected by the noninterventionist convictions of Humphrey and by the President's own general predilection toward economic conservatism, as well as by the separate views and operating independence of the many departmental centers of authority over what Eisenhower referred to as the "formidable . . . arsenal of weapons" available for maintaining economic stability. As summarized in the *Economic Report* they included credit controls administered by the Federal Reserve, Treasury debt management policies, presidential authority to vary the terms of mortgages carrying federal insurance, flexibility in budget administration, supports for agriculture, modification of the tax structure, and public works.[19]

Despite their inclusion in the arsenal, Burns considered public works to be of little use as an immediately effective counterrecessionary weapon. To mobilize, to fuse, and to bring to the firing line such a weapon was too long a process, at least for the battle looming in early 1954. According to Burns, "only as a last resort" should countercyclical emphasis be put on large public works programs.[20] Unfortunately, fear of recession and interest in public works went together in the popular mind, and, like it or not, the Council was associated with the readying of the public works weapon.

Planning for Public Works

Applying public works programs is quite different from planning for them. Available evidence suggests that as early as the spring of

1953, Burns was actively interested in the latter. One of his first moves upon coming to Washington was to secure the services of Robinson Newcomb for work in this area. On July 9, the Budget Bureau informed departments and agencies that, in preparing the fiscal 1955 budget, they should anticipate new construction starts "consistent with a less restrictive budgetary policy" [21] by developing plans for authorized high-priority projects.

In testifying before the Joint Committee on the Economic Report in February, 1954, Assistant Budget Director Rowland Hughes submitted material that referred to a Budget Bureau study regarding public works and flexibility in the budget "prepared last summer . . . at the request of the Council of Economic Advisers." [22] Hughes also remarked "Then we have also and are cooperating actively with the Economic Council in their analysis and preparation of the projects which are good and which should be kept on the shelf, so to speak." [23] One of the original Task Forces organized in September was devoted to public works planning. It was staffed in part by Fisher, Long, and Newcomb, who were the Council's experts on resources, employment, and public works, respectively.

Chapter 10 [24] of the *Economic Report* made much of the work that had been accomplished in accumulating project drawings and specifications, in preparing blueprints, in assembling agency six-year construction programs, and in starting work on a continuous inventory. It stated that "proposed projects are being sifted and classified according to their size, type, location, status of plans, urgency and other practical criteria." Although the major emphasis was on long-term planning to conserve natural resources and to meet the needs of a "dynamically evolving economy," there was also a clear undercurrent of countercyclical considerations, indicating an awareness and anticipation of the possibility of immediate needs. If adequate engineering studies and blueprints existed, public works expenditures could promote stability. If necessary, "Federal public works could be stepped up by one-half within a year. . . . Many small Federal projects . . . can be started upon short notice or terminated promptly."

Heading the *Economic Report*'s list of public works needed "to keep abreast of the economy" was an enlarged program of public roads: "The total annual expenditure required to provide an adequate road system within a decade is apparently over 8 billion dollars, which compares with a current outlay of about 5 billion." [25] Although not mentioned, the context of the chapter implied that such an expenditure would provide both an investment stimulus and a recession cushion. Reportedly, Burns believed that the impact of highway investment was much greater than that of most public works expenditures. Improved public roads had a multiplier effect— of encouraging community subdivisions, of creating suburbs, of developing stores and shopping areas. It was presumably with both this and the recession in mind that Burns supported the increase in the highway construction budget for fiscal 1955 and also the Federal Aid Highways Act of 1954, which was believed to be the largest highway bill ever passed.[26]

Neither the *Economic Report* nor the President's other two annual messages had made specific recommendations regarding federal aid to highways beyond requesting authorization for an expanded program. This vagueness suggests that ideas and differences on this particular phase of the President's program had not been worked out by the start of the new year. The President's urging of an enlarged highway program in his February 10 press conference was interpreted as a subsequent Administration endorsement of the McGregor Bill, which, when approved in May, authorized almost $2 billion additional federal support to state public road programs during fiscal 1956 and 1957. Burns' interest in the investment aspects of public roads was to become more pronounced in 1955 in connection with the work of the President's Advisory Committee on a National Highway Program, headed by Lucius Clay.

By February, consideration of the long-term investment potential of public roads and of public works in general had given way to concern about immediate recession. The focus of attention and pressure from the unions, the public, the press, and Congress was on launching a frontal attack of broad-scale public works on rising unemployment. Within the Administration, the focus was on planning such an attack *if* circumstances warranted. July 1 was the tentative date by which the government would be prepared to act. Eisenhower had asked Burns to coordinate the reports on departmental plans for public works projects.[27] Donovan's accounts of Cabinet meetings during February, March, and April indicate that the Council was moving ahead rapidly on plans that might be needed, while Humphrey maintained that public works would be appropriate if the other antirecession operations then in progress should fail to turn the tide. At the same time, the President was telling his press conference that, in Donovan's words, "the time had not yet arrived when a slam bang emergency program was needed." [28] At Burns' suggestion, a special public works planning group was added to the Council staff. Starting in April, John S. Bragdon and, later, George A. Deming devoted full time to perfecting public works plans for projects at both federal and state levels. Their operation subsequently developed into the Office of Public Works and was housed in the White House.

In the end, no program of additional public works was undertaken for countercyclical reasons, and the so-called shelf of public works projects apparently existed more in name than in fact. Public works considerations had a more psychological than practical impact. In a very real sense, the amount of popular attention focused on public works was disproportionately large compared with the Administration's expectation of implementing them. Despite pressure from the unions, Congress, and other sources and despite the debate within the Cabinet, there appears to have been little real disposition within the Administration to bring public works out from the antirecessionary arsenal. In fact, the Administration sought to avoid additional expenditures in this area if at all possible. Although Burns was more willing to consider limited increases than was Humphrey, he did not advise use of the weapon. His own economic analysis indicated that such a counterattack would not be necessary.

Nevertheless, the considerable planning, concern, and attention centering on public works did give an impression of the government's awareness of its responsibility and of its willingness to act if conditions demanded. The New York Times wrote of "wide works plans drawn for crises, . . . ready to roll within weeks whenever Eisenhower decides action is necessary . . . if [he] triggers for action." [29] Moreover, the Council was regarded both publicly and within the government as the agency most responsible for public works—for what was developed and for what was being held in readiness.[30] James Reston felt justified in writing of the Council's ABEGS as an "important, if obscure" body charged with drafting "anti-slump" plans to combat "rolling adjustment when and if it reaches the danger zone." [31] The Council had the planning experts; the President had designated Burns as the coordinator of the Administration's antirecession activities, which, of course, included public works. Owing to the specific nature of their respective activities, of their institutional standing, and of their clientele interest, none of the operating agencies with programs in the public works area could develop an overall campaign. Coordination of the Bureau of Yards and Docks, the Public Building Service, and the Forest Service, to name a few, would have to come from the outside.

The Council's prominence in the public works area was indirectly underscored by the introduction of the Douglas-Bolling Bill, which, if passed, would have been known as the Public Facilities Act of 1954.[32] Its purpose was to provide for more effective planning, coordination, and programming of public works under the centralized responsibility of the President. It would have required the annual *Economic Report* to include specific information regarding needed public facilities, federal policy, and legislative recommendations.[33]

As early as March 19, Burns began to report favorable economic trends to the Cabinet.[34] Although the increasing unemployment figures and hence the heightening sense of public urgency lagged behind these trends by two months or more, the Cabinet became less inclined to embrace public works programs with each succeeding report. If, in the President's metaphor of "arsenal of weapons," public works was the artillery of massive retaliation and therefore not suitable in the situation, other available weapons more mobile, more limited, but more immediate in their effect were appropriate.

Fiscal and Monetary Encouragement

On March 24 Eisenhower told his press conference that there was no need then for drastic aid to business, but rather a "crying need" for action on his legislative program.[35] Despite his encouraging report of a week before, Burns gave the Cabinet on March 26 a list of possible countercyclical steps that could be taken: alter tax-depreciation policy, modify Federal Reserve monetary requirements, liberalize terms on government-guaranteed mortgages, and step up the rate of government domestic procurement.[36] Burns reported at the next Cabinet meeting that the situation justified executing these recommendations, and the President agreed that these things should be done "without delay" to the degree that executive authority existed.[37]

These simultaneous concerns of late March over both the delay in congressional action on the President's program and the need to execute countercyclical recommendations underscored the inseparability of the present from the future. Not only did much of the President's program have both immediate and long-term significance but congressional reaction to the program was significantly influenced by the short-term situation.

In no issue was this inseparability more apparent than in regard to tax policy. The year had opened with the effectuation of the much heralded and pre-destined $3-billion reduction in personal income taxes and of the expiration of the excess profits tax estimated to mean almost another $2-billion reduction in federal revenues. Offsetting this $5-billion reduction by the $1.3-billion increase in Social Security contributions that also went into effect on January 1 produced a net loss to the Treasury of $3.7 billion, estimated on a full-year basis. The further reduction of the $1.4 billion proposed in the Administration's tax reform measure would bring the total to $5.1 billion, indeed a large amount to a deficit-conscious administration—and not the whole story. The expiration of excise taxes on gasoline, tobacco, alcohol, and automobiles, and the reduction in the 52 percent corporate income taxes, all of which were scheduled to go into effect on April 1, would increase the reduction another $3 billion to produce a grand total reduction of $8.1 billion.

As indicated previously, the Administration's tax reform measure was under heavy attack for aiding business rather than the consumer and for giving relief to the stockholder rather than the wage earner. The appearance as well as the fact of favoring corporations rather than general consumers raised objections among Congressmen of both parties who, among other things, were mindful of the forthcoming congressional elections. It mattered little that these reform measures contained "the seeds of important future revenue gains to be reaped from the economic growth they will stimulate." [38] The clamor for prompt action to stem the recession served to sharpen the attack. The Administration was consequently very sensitive to the short-run vulnerability of its long-term proposals. It recognized the urgency of aiding the economy; at the same time, it was determined not to increase deficits any more than absolutely necessary. The very fact that no action was taken on Burns' first proposal to the Cabinet to liberalize depreciation allowances—an administrative step that would not have required congressional approval—suggests the predicament of the Administration.

Action did have to be taken, however, to avert the expiration of the excise tax and the reduction of the corporate income tax, both scheduled for April 1. In seeking extension of the former and postponement of the latter, the Administration was obliged to accept as an alternative either the proposal of Speaker of the House Joseph W. Martin, Jr., to reduce by 10 percent (approximately $1 billion) the excise tax on luxury items (such as the jewelry made in the Speaker's home district of Attleboro, Mass.) or the proposal of Democratic Senator Walter F. George to increase personal exemptions from $600 to $800 in 1954 and from $800 to $1,000 in 1955. As emphasized by Humphrey, the former was the lesser of the two evils: "We will vigorously oppose blanket increases in exemptions that will throw us back into substantial deficit financing which cannot be justified at the present time and which we have been working so hard to overcome." [39] Not only would accepting the luxury excise tax cut lessen the increase in the deficit, but it would make the reform proposals more palatable and—most important for the short run—it would benefit the consumer at a time when a fillip to purchasing power was needed. As Burns recalled, "We felt that the cut might not be a bad idea for countercyclical reasons. Moreover, you have to be careful not to erode away the income tax base." [40] Three days before the cut became effective, the New York *Times* reported that the "President's economic advisers expect a substantial rise in consumer buying next month to end the downtrend in the Nation's economy . . . predicated on the anticipated $1,000,000,000 cuts in excise tax legislation now before Congress." [41]

In the final analysis, the Administration endured a $1-billion drop in luxury excise revenue in order to retain $3 billion of revenue from other sources, thereby achieving a net gain of $2 billion. This same $1 billion served also as the price for killing the more drastic personal exemption proposal and for helping to gain congressional approval of the $1.4-billion tax revision measure. Even this measure did not survive unscathed, for the reduction contained in the dividend and exclusion feature of the proposal was modified from what the Administration had originally requested. As the President conceded, "Sometimes it was necessary to swallow castor oil along with the sweet coating," [42] or, in the words of an Administration official, "They put one over on us."

In this instance Burns was in the position of endorsing on counter-recessionary grounds a decision that was dictated by the prime goal of reducing the deficit. His best contribution was in sharing the Administration's unalterable opposition to the personal exemption proposal and in pointing out that one of the consequences of letting the luxury excise tax cut go through would be a $1-billion boost to the economy. In addition, he concluded that the $3-billion boost that would have resulted if the April 1 reductions had taken effect as originally scheduled would have been excessive. For the fact of the matter was that, when the tax reductions that were enacted became effective on a full-year basis, they totaled $7.4 billion, or $6.1 billion when net of the $1.3-billion increase in Social Security payments. Such reduction was a fiscal policy development of major significance for an economy that in 1954 was endeavoring to regain the path of economic progress.

On the monetary policy front, countercyclical activities got off to a much earlier start. Commencing with its open-market purchases in May and June, 1953, the Federal Reserve Board carried out a policy of credit relaxation that continued for over twelve months. In July, 1953, reserve requirements for member banks were reduced and further open market purchases were conducted in September, October, and December. In the spring of 1954, the Federal Reserve lowered the rediscount rate first from 2 to 1¾ percent and then from 1¾ to 1½ percent. In late June, it lowered reserve requirements from 22 to 20 percent for demand deposits of central reserve banks, from 19 to 18 percent for those of reserve city banks, and from 13 to 12 percent for those of county banks. Required reserves for time deposits were cut from 6 to 5 percent in all banks. It was estimated at the time that the lowering of reserve requirements would release approximately $1.5 billion of reserves and create a potential expansion of $9 billion.[43]

With the exception of the action taken in May, June, and July, 1953, to ease tension in the financial markets, the Federal Reserve's steps to ease credit appear to have constituted the most important series of measures adopted consciously for countercyclical purposes. Grebler, for example, attributes the sharp increases in home building in 1953 and 1954 not to a change in demand, but to these steps.[44]

Throughout these actions Burns was in frequent touch with Chairman Martin of the Federal Reserve Board. In messages from the President that he initiated, in his visits to Martin's office, and in Martin's visits to his office, Burns did not hesitate to prod the Federal Reserve to relax its monetary controls. Nor did Burns hesitate to attempt to influence Martin through Humphrey.[45] There seems little doubt that, on behalf of an administration wanting to exploit monetary means to recovery, Burns earned a measure of success through his constant urging and encouragement. On June 14, for example, the Federal Reserve was reported to be resisting "Administration feelers" to lower rediscount rates,[46] yet only a week passed before the Federal Reserve did ease the credit situation, not by the rediscount route but by lowering reserve requirements.

An evaluation of the amount of influence the Council had on monetary policy during the period may be particularly difficult to determine. Nevertheless, the Council does appear to have played an essentially auxiliary role, largely limited to confirming and accelerating what the Federal Reserve itself determined to be appropriate countercylical action. Except with regard to debt management operations, the nation's monetary policies have been primarily the responsibility of "The Fed." Operating largely as a self-contained institution, it was practicing the independence it had won just three years previously, an independence accepted by the President and generally expected by Congress. In terms of resources, the Federal Reserve had a large staff of economists, one that was as knowledge-able of current trends and as confident of its own analysis and con-viction as was the Council. Although the Federal Reserve was represented on ABEGS, Martin was not a member of the Cabinet. Moreover, the characteristically limited external activity of the Council staff inhibited extensive Council–Federal Reserve contact. Koch's temporary assignment to the Council staff on loan from the Federal Reserve and Lusher's "Tuesday Group" served as two of the strands of contact that did exist at the staff level. Under these cir-cumstances, the locus of the creative as well as ratifying portions of monetary policy decisions remained well within the Federal Reserve.

On the related matter of varying the terms of housing credit as a countercyclical weapon of almost immediate impact, the Adminis-tration was less active. Available evidence suggests that Burns made relatively little headway with the recommendation Donovan reports he made to the March 26 Cabinet meeting to liberalize terms of gov-ernment-guaranteed mortgages. Influence with HHFA and a hand in developing the housing portion of the President's program did not extend to producing any actual easing of mortgage terms during the 1953–54 recession. If, as a former associate has alleged, "Burns pushed hard as hell" on the easing of mortgage terms for anti-recession reasons, his efforts met with success in the acceptance of major provisions of the housing program aimed at long-term growth and stability of the economy. But he was unsuccessful in achieving the implementation of any specific countercyclical action in early 1954. According to Grebler,

Legislative and administrative actions affecting housing credit specifically were relatively minor factors in the expansion of home building in 1953–54. There was no deliberate effort by the Executive Branch to use the governmental programs to stimulate residential construction as a means of cushioning the business recession.[47]

True, only a limited stimulant was available, but even that appar-ently was not applied. The President's discretionary authority, granted in the 1953 Housing Amendments, to ease terms on FHA loans on houses valued at $12,000 or less was not used. The most that Burns seemed able to do was administrative in nature. He has recalled, "We urged HHFA and VA to accelerate their processing of loan applications. We got them some money to hire some more people." [48]

Although the peak of the housing boom, in which nonfarm housing starts rose from a monthly total of 65,800 units in December, 1953, to 116,500 in June, 1954,[49] was reached before the bulk of the President's housing proposals were enacted into law in August as the Housing Act of 1954, the *expectation* of more liberal terms based on the proposals undoubtedly gave a psychological boost to the boom. Financial intermediaries, builders, and prospective home owners were encouraged not only by easier credit conditions but also by the prospect of continued support for housing expansion. The Council's contribution to the proposals themselves and the emphasis given to their value as available antirecession weapons in the *Economic Report* and throughout the early months of 1954 entitled the Council to share the credit due the Administration for this encouragement. This still was not as impressive an achievement as if Burns had been able to gain acceptance for his proposal to liberalize terms under existing authority made to the Cabinet in March. His inability to gain this acceptance must in large measure be attributed to Secretary Humphrey's determination to minimize government intervention and avoid increasing the risks of larger deficits. Support of Burns' position from such Cabinet discussion participants as Harold Stassen [50] was hardly enough to clear the Humphrey hurdle that lay astride the path to the President's approval.

Stepping Up the Rate of Governmental Expenditures

To help the Administration meet its recovery objectives, Burns and his Council undertook a good deal more than planning public works, prodding the Federal Reserve, and facilitating the quicker processing of loan applications. One of Burns' more interesting activities was his attempt to have the rate of expenditures within prescribed budget totals accelerated. The nature of this proposal differed considerably from that of undertaking more public works projects involving the expenditure of federal funds *in addition* to those already in the 1954 budget or anticipated for the fiscal 1955 budget. Projects already in the budget were presumably projects of demonstrated need; they were planned, anticipated, and perhaps already begun. The variable in Burns' proposal was the matter of scheduling, and the counterrecessionary potential lay in the possibility of accelerating the production schedule in order to step up the rate of public spending. Such budget flexibility, or "administrative flexibility in the Budget," was defined in the 1954 hearings on the *Economic Report* as "those actions which can be taken by Federal Government officials either to speed or slow down Federal expenditures within existing laws and without new appropriations from the Congress." [51]

In the summer of 1953, the Budget Bureau informed Burns that by presidential action the rate of government expenditures could be increased by at least $3 billion a year—$2 billion from the accelerated operation of the wholly owned government corporations and $1 billion from government programs in which scheduling could be tightened.[52] Whether a $3-billion increase could, in fact, be realized would depend upon the circumstances operating at the time acceleration was attempted. For, as Caplan has written, "The effectiveness of budget flexibility is geared to the kind of forces in operation at the time it is needed, and the nature of the forces is partly dependent upon the kind of budget flexibility available at the particular time." [53] Much of the emphasis given to the planning of public works, particularly to those projects coming under the jurisdiction of the federal government, appeared attributable to Burns' interest in budget flexibility as a countercyclical weapon. As the unemployment increases continued into the spring of 1954, such a weapon—far less cumbersome than public works—had possibilities of both effectiveness and acceptance.

Eisenhower's response on March 19 to suggestions made at a Cabinet meeting by Humphrey and Vice-President Nixon that federal projects scheduled for the future should be started immediately was to instruct Burns to expedite the Council's work on possible courses of action. Thus, by the time Burns urged acceleration at the meetings of March 26 and April 2, the idea had already gained a vital measure of acceptance. Secretary Weeks immediately urged "faster action" on the program to build tankers, a suggestion that was endorsed by the President.[54]

Six weeks later at the Cabinet meeting of May 14, Burns presented the idea of undertaking a stepped-up expenditures program for the last quarter of fiscal 1954 and the first quarter of fiscal 1955. He argued that such acceleration of the rate of expenditures would have a favorable antirecession effect without increasing budget totals. As interpreted by a Budget Bureau official, the supporting reasoning was essentially as follows: Even in normal circumstances summer is often a time of economic slump. Business must not confuse the seasonal with the long-term. Therefore, we must "step up" government expenditures, which will aid the economy, fill the normal summer dip, and boost the long-term recovery that will start in the fall. We must expedite the benefits to the public. This can be done within the overall expenditures planned for fiscal 1954 and 1955. We should not jeopardize long-range objectives for national welfare by eschewing short-range expenditure acceleration. The President directed that expenditure for "worthwhile" projects where funds were available be accelerated. Projects requiring legislation or supplemental appropriations, however, were to be excluded and, because no publicity was being given the step-up, Congress was not to be requested to expedite its action on regular appropriations, supplementals, or enabling legislation already requested.[55] These restraints indicate that, although the principle of step-up was accepted, there were considerable differences of opinion about the specifics of its implementation.

Burns' ideas for step-up included military purchases, repair and modernization of new buildings, construction of atomic energy installations, and the building of small bridges and forest roads.[56] At the Cabinet meeting of the following week he suggested that the industrial potential and employment needs of Group 4 ("depressed") areas be recognized in the awarding of contracts, without, of course, violating the basic specification that awards go to the lowest qualified bidder.

Following the Cabinet's acceptance of Burns' proposal, the Budget Bureau prepared an internal report on various government activities that had some potential for being stepped up for varying lengths of time. This report contained a master list of forty-five items for possible acceleration that conceivably could boost federal spending by something over $1 billion, of which approximately three-quarters would be in defense outlays, by September 20, 1954.[57] Such an acceleration would be accompanied by a deceleration during the remaining three quarters of fiscal 1955. In early July, departments and agencies were requested by the Budget Bureau to submit plans of how items under their jurisdiction could possibly be completed more rapidly.

Unfortunately, it is not possible to assess accurately the impact of the step-up decision as an antirecessionary device, for, although a certain amount of acceleration was in fact accomplished, there was no retrospective analysis of the degree to which any of the forty-five items were actually stepped up or of the effects thereof. A study of the impact of these specific actions would have been of great value in analyzing their strengths and weaknesses under the particular circumstances and in providing guidelines for future recessionary situations. Burns wrote in late 1957 that "the rescheduling of expenditures for the fiscal year 1955 was delayed in execution and became effective when no longer needed." [58] As an example of this, Secretary Weeks announced to the press in late July that contracts not normally awarded for six months would be placed immediately. In this connection he mentioned shipbuilding and airport construction. In a related but separate program there would also be an approximately $100-million five-month acceleration of highway apportionment to the states.[59]

Regardless of the largely unknown and perhaps inconclusive results, the credit for the initiation of step-up activities must go to Burns. Apparently it was his idea, an idea that he and public works expert Newcomb had considered well before the recession gathered headway, that was included in the Council's public works planning and that Burns himself sold to an Administration which in all probability would not otherwise have embraced it. Although concentrated on the expenditures of the Department of Defense, the multi-agency nature of step-up activities enabled the Council to assume an initial leadership role.

From the vantage of hindsight, commentators remarked that both Burns and Humphrey must have realized that acceleration would increase total expenditures. Despite a degree of flexibility, the cumulative effect of such factors as expenditure commitments, administrative delays, production lead times, and clientele interests would inevitably lead to some increase. Therefore, Burns' proposal and Humphrey's apparent acceptance of step-up may be viewed as a measure of the former's determination to counter the recession as best he could and of the latter's willingness to rationalize such action within the confines of hard-and-fast principles of budget balancing and debt reduction. Under the pressure of circumstances, Burns could exploit, albeit modestly, Humphrey's ability to "give a little." Although it may be, as Lewis suggests, that Burns greatly overestimated the flexibility of public works outlays,[60] the failure to review the step-up program leaves hidden any specific information regarding its actual effectiveness. The question remains unanswered whether or not acceleration was, in fact, accompanied by an increase in expenditures. These inquiries, however, do not nullify the conclusion that the program was Burns' most innovative contribution to the Administration's activities aimed at conquering the recession.

The Voice of Conservative Confidence

In late May and early June, Burns was presenting such increasingly optimistic reports on recovery to the Cabinet that by its meeting of June 11, the Cabinet was able to throw off the sense of urgency that had hung over it since early February.[61] By July, the Council's *Economic Indicators* showed improvement on numerous fronts. Unemployment was continuing the decline that had commenced in April, and the average work week of factory production was climbing. New construction remained at a monthly rate of above $3 billion during June, while new housing starts regained their level of the preceding year. Stock prices reached new highs in late June. Despite a slight drop in disposable income, consumer spending increased during the second quarter, while savings decreased from 8 to 7.1 percent of disposable income. During May, consumer prices, though increasing for food and housing, remained stable in other areas. The rate of inventory disinvestment appeared to be decreasing and the industrial production index was estimated to have increased for the first time since the preceding July. Overall economic activity as measured by the GNP declined an estimated $1.2 billion on an annual basis from the first to the second quarter of 1954 compared with a $6.3-billion drop from the fourth quarter of 1953 to the first quarter of 1954.[62]

August proved to be the trough of a mild recession that, according to a 1958 analysis, started from the peak of thirteen months before and that registered a decline of 1.5 percent in GNP from 1953 to 1954 as measured in constant prices.[63] The Federal Reserve steps to ease credits coupled with the Treasury's tax reductions and limited borrowing operations did much to counter the $10.5-billion drop in federal expenditures from the fourth quarter of 1953 to the second quarter of 1954, to support a high level of personal consumption expenditures, and to stimulate investment. The impetus of other important developments, outside the limits of discretionary Administration moves, accomplished the rest—the automatic operation of built-in stabilizers, the high level of demand for fixed investment, the increase of state and local expenditures, and the contribution of net foreign investment.

In his review of the recession contained in the 1955 *Economic Report*, Burns was able to write, "By the late summer of 1954, a broad foundation had . . . been laid for industrial recovery." [64] By the first quarter of 1955, the forces of recovery had carried GNP measured in constant dollars beyond the peak established in the second quarter of 1953.

In general terms, the impact of the Burns Council on the policies adopted and actions taken to conquer the recession was to reconcile Republican conservatism with the Administration's countercyclical responsibilities. Through its activities, the Council achieved a modification and liberalization of Administration views—not as much as a revision, but an updating to modern circumstances. As Holmans remarks, "The economic policies of the Eisenhower Administration suggest that the Republicans have indeed learnt a great deal since 1933." [65] The general policy statements in the Burns *Economic Reports* represent Administration sanction of commitments exceeding those which probably Eisenhower and more certainly Humphrey would have volunteered on their own initiatives. "My Council," Burns has said, "had a philosophy that gave the President's program unity." [66] This was a philosophy rooted in "tenets [that] are basic and inseparable": the relative efficiency of competitive markets, compared with government directives, for organizing production and consumption; widely shared confidence as a prerequisite to the generation of jobs and income; maximum encouragement to and minimum interference with the private economy on the part of the federal government; reliance in anticyclical policy upon indirect influence on private behavior rather than direct control; federal government collaboration with the states in promoting research and providing public facilities; and federal assistance in cooperation with states and localities in helping "less fortunate citizens" with problems of unemployment, illness, old age, and blighted neighborhoods.[67] Built-in stabilizers, continuing large government expenditures, and the commitment behind the Employment Act none the less may have been the hard coin of government support underlying Burns' concern for confidence. Yet confidence was itself a valuable psychological stimulant to growth and stability, and Burns injected it wherever possible as a complement to indirect fiscal and monetary measures and as an alternative to massive countercyclical action. Both to and for the Administration he was the voice of conservative confidence.

Burns' inductive economics reinforced policy objectives and provided an excellent analysis of unfolding developments. In concert with the Council's small degree of reliance upon forecasting and the government's ability to effect stability, the Council's inductive economics was thoroughly consistent with conservative policy objectives of noninterference, reduced expenditures, and balanced budgets. Except for underestimating the reductions in government expenditures for fiscal 1954 and allegedly overestimating administrative budget flexibility, the Council correctly assessed the mildness of the recession and provided an informational basis for appropriate Administration policies. Economists with Treasury, Federal Reserve, and Commerce, as well as with the Joint Committee on the Economic Report, were all in essential agreement, but the same views expressed by the President's economists were particularly reassuring. Through Burns, the Council kept the President and the Cabinet informed; through ABEGS, chaired by Burns, the Council accomplished the same thing with departments and agencies. To the President, Burns provided constant and expert counsel; to the departments he conveyed an overview of recession developments and governmental countermoves that transcended particular departmental operations and outlook. To clients and professional colleagues he was an analyst of economic phenomena without peer. As Achinstein recalls, "No one could match him in the skillful use of statistical data." [68]

The significance of the Council's performance at the general policy level was not duplicated, however, at the level of specific activities. The Council may well have been the major architect of the Administration's policies that were undertaken for countercyclical reasons, but these policies did not represent the developments of major countercyclical impact. Aside from recognizing its role as architect, its leadership in creating a climate of confidence, and its prodding on various countercyclical fronts, it appears reasonable to conclude that, one, the Council's influence on the federal government's actions of tax reduction and monetary easing which most significantly contributed to recovery was minor and, two, those instances where its influence was significant involved actions that did not bulk large in recovery impact. This conclusion does not argue by implication that the government's programs specifically undertaken for recovery reasons were inadequate or otherwise wrong or that the Council would not have urged and the government undertaken other action had the situation been different. Rather, it attempts to portray the significance of the Council's contribution in the perspective of what actually occurred.

However great may have been their countercyclical significance the $5-billion tax cuts that went into effect on January 1, 1954, were not devised as stimulants to recovery from the 1953–54 recession.

The reduction in personal income levies was in accordance with tax legislation enacted during the Korean mobilization; its implementation required no action by the Eisenhower Administration. Similarly, the excess profits tax would have expired automatically the preceding July had not the Administration successfully pressed Congress to extend it another six months as a means of easing the critical deficit situation. It was fortuitous that both these reductions as well as the off-setting $1.3-billion increase in Social Security contributions became effective at a time of declining activity. "The way is clear" statements made during the fall of 1953 by Secretary Humphrey at Burns' urging and later echoed by President Eisenhower and others appear as confirmation for countercyclical reasons of what had been initiated by the previous administration and could not—practically speaking—be reversed. Given the importance attached to maintaining the confidence of the business community, these reassurances that the reductions would go through none the less may well have been successful, as indicated by the climb in stock prices that commenced in early October.

As previously indicated, the $1-billion reduction in luxury excises was a legislative rather than an executive measure. Countercyclical considerations were no doubt joined in the minds of Congressmen by reactions to portions of the Administration's tax reform proposals and by election-year interests. Burns favored the cut for recovery reasons, but his support was complemented by the Administration's necessary acceptance of it in order to avoid a larger deficit that would have resulted from the exemption-increase alternative or from the other tax changes originally scheduled for April 1. The potential contribution of the luxury excise reduction to recovery was as much a rationalization as an objective behind the Administration's accepting with no more than token resistance what it did not suggest in the first place.

As for the revisions involving a tax reduction of $1.4 billion, they were indeed supported by Burns. More than Humphrey he recognized and argued on behalf of their having short- as well as long-run economic impact. An awareness of the immediate recession presumably played a part in approval of proposals by Congress in the summer of 1954. The recovery was in full swing, however, by the time that the reductions involved could take effect. In other words, the Council had a supporting hand in an important measure that in its subsequent impact did not contribute to the immediate recovery.

It does not negate the benefit of the Council's prodding with regard to Federal Reserve recovery actions to recognize that they were rooted in a highly self-contained and insulated decision-making process. Although Burns no doubt encouraged a variety of steps to accelerate aid to particularly hard-hit industries and areas,[69] the benefits, such as they may have been, from the step-up program he had initiated came after the recovery had started. The considerable planning that went into public works was accomplished under the Council's leadership, but, as already noted, they never went into action in this particular antirecession war.

If the Council's contribution to specific policies appeared to be more peripheral than basic, more catalytic than creative, more in decision modification than in decision-making, it nevertheless gave these policies economic and political viability and increased their adaptability to both long-range and immediate economic developments. It was within the confines of Administration policy, defined both by him and for him, that Burns took the initiative by suggesting various specific measures and by continually pressing against the policy of restraint—testing it, trying for more active interpretations within its limits and, in the process, keeping the makers and executors of economic policy conscious of their opportunity for contributing to the nation's economic well-being. In the context of major programs and actions, each modifying contribution appears relatively minor, for it brought little change in basic content. Yet, viewed in series, they totaled an assortment of essential refinements for which the Administration was grateful. In short, by accurately analyzing economic trends, counseling justified caution, modifying inactivity, and by coordinating—at the President's request—the Administration's antirecession campaign, Burns enabled the first Republican administration in twenty years to lead the nation out of a mild recession and to forge an acceptable link between Eisenhower's economic conservatism and his welfare liberalism that did not violate the Employment Act.

For its accomplishments, Burns and his Council reached a high-water mark of prestige and acceptance. A fitting accolade came from the President, who, when the 1953–54 recession crisis was over, reportedly turned to Burns and said, "Arthur, you'd have made a fine chief of staff during the war." [70] As the professional economics adviser and business cycle expert, Burns was almost a hero—a symbol of recovery and sound economic conservatism. The generally antiintellectual approach of the Administration made this adulation all the more remarkable.

Throughout the period, Burns enjoyed full rapport with the President. He was particularly relied upon for the specific policy planning that marked the Administration's interest in public works. But also the President liked and trusted him as a personal adviser accepted without reservation, whose scholarly yet confident manner was a welcome leaven to an entourage heavily weighted by men of wealth and experience in practical affairs. As expressed by one observer, "The President needed him; he was the one egghead among a crew of millionaire business men; he had an effective bedside manner."

As a reflection of his acceptance by Eisenhower, Burns was similarly accepted as a member of the Administration's top policy set consisting of Hauge, Adams, Humphrey, and Dulles. During the recession period, Burns was a regular participant in Cabinet meetings and succeeded in developing and maintaining informal contact with a large range of Administration officials.

Although they reportedly got along well enough personally and although each was essentially conservative within their respective milieus of industry and economics, their backgrounds, their orientations, and the nature of their relations with the President were entirely different. The operating world of industry opposed the intellectual environment of teaching and research. The operating responsibility of one opposed the advisory responsibility of the other. Eisenhower's considerable acceptance of and dependence upon Burns, the adviser, could not compete with the dependence upon the personal and institutional strength of Humphrey, the imposing Secretary of the Treasury. Childs concludes that Humphrey was the most influential member of the Eisenhower Administration.[71] A Council staff member of the time regarded the Secretary of the Treasury as the government's strongest economist.

It was primarily from Humphrey that Burns experienced the

dominant and the most persistent opposition to his countercyclical recommendations. The opposition was not absolute, nor did it apply with equal fervor to all issues, for both men sought the nation's economic recovery. Although Humphrey accepted the principle of compensatory fiscal policy, it was such a reluctant acceptance that his tolerances for approving specific countercyclical actions were limited. Within the confines of these tolerances Burns did find room "to prod and stiffen" Treasury's stand on reduction in tax revisions and to persuade Humphrey to announce that the tax cuts would go through as scheduled. On the other hand, if, as Burns contends, the Cabinet deliberately blurred the draft of the public works chapter in the 1954 *Economic Report* on public works planning, Humphrey must have taken a leading part. The Administration's failure to liberalize housing mortgage terms makes Burns' reported recommendation for such action appear as an unsuccessful attempt to exceed tolerances. The failure to alter depreciation allowances would appear to fall in the same category. Humphrey's coolness to step-up no doubt contributed to the delay in getting it started and to its limited nature.

These observations do not mean, however, that Burns, during either the 1953–54 recession or subsequent periods of his chairmanship, vacated his own convictions for those of Humphrey. What they do suggest is that Humphrey frequently constituted the highest, and sometimes the unassailable, hurdle standing between Burns' recommendations and their implementation, that these differences were often more than those of detail and emphasis, and that Burns—in accepted advisory fashion—adjusted his advisory operations and expectations accordingly. Available evidence clearly indicates that Burns advised in terms of his analysis of economic conditions and objectives, that Humphrey at times sought his advice, and that upon occasion the President accepted Burns' viewpoint over that of Humphrey. As Burns recalls, "We fought hard at times and each lost some battles to the other." [72] Apart from one known instance (not during the 1953–54 recession), both Burns and Humphrey were prudent enough to avoid obliging the President to choose between them.

Differences with Humphrey notwithstanding, the general acceptance of the Council within the Administration and the Council's recognized success in dealing with the recession enabled Burns to achieve his goal of restoring the Council as the respected center of economic advice and counsel within the Presidency. If the Council's public image was held by some to have been tarnished during Keyserling's chairmanship, it was generally considered refurbished to a new luster during the first year of Burns' regime. As a Council staff member remarked, "Burns rehabilitated government economists."

The operational counterpart of the Council's success was that its functioning centered on Burns. Burns and the Council were synonymous; there was little separate identity of the other members and less of the staff members: "I believed that the staff functioned primarily to advise me; it was not supposed to go about selling programs." [73] His own strong intellectual traditions made him skeptical of staff members whose training represented other schools of thought;[74] he did not rely upon them for economic evaluation and judgment.

As a result, Burns played things close to his vest: "He did not let his staff know what he thought." His working associations of any degree of intimacy appear to have been limited to a few staff members like Achinstein, who as a colleague of many years served as something of a confidential assistant, and Saulnier and Shere, each of whom reportedly acted occasionally as informal chief of staff.[75] Consequently, the staff was not likely to become involved in policy deliberations but received assignments that were essentially requests for data and information denuded as much as possible of policy overtones and interpretations: "I would at times assign antirecession and anti-inflation projects at once so as to hide my own thoughts; I wanted objective thinking from the staff." [76] It was not unusual for Burns to make essentially the same assignments to more than one staff member, or to have two work together on one project as a means of exposing varying viewpoints as well as checking for accuracy. By this means, Burns could obtain the benefit of, for instance, Lusher's considerable knowledge and understanding of economic developments without Lusher's GNP interpretation, of which Burns was distrustful. In addition, there was a heavy reliance on routine assignments such as preparing monthly and weekly reports on economic developments and keeping track of legislation of economic significance.

For some members of the staff, this assiduous avoidance of policy involvement was thoroughly in keeping with their own views of what they should be doing. As one has recalled,

I was satisfied before taking the job that I would differ little from Burns about basic issues of policy in my own field of economic stability and that my primary responsibilities would be analytical rather than advisory. Although we might differ on matters involving income distribution, housing, social security, and the like, I would not be working on problems where such issues would be involved even implicitly. I believe that such an approach was typical of the people temporarily recruited from universities.[77]

Others, who were non-Keynesians and who were concerned with economics, "not some social philosophy," chafed under his impenetrability; they wanted to help Burns but found it hard to know how to do so.[78] For still others, more anxious to enter the fray of policy-making, the constraints, enforced objectivity, and prescribed assignments almost in the manner of "research assistantships" were frustrating and degrading. A number would credit Keynes' theories with having more utility than that of a mere "apparatus" or "filing case." Lusher may have been the most outspoken Keynesian, but he was not a minority of one. Some staff members, like Achinstein, Lusher, and Newcomb, had sufficient government experience to favor a more positive approach to policy involvement than did Burns.

Intentions perhaps to the contrary, Burns was by no means entirely impervious to these attitudes; he could not be and still retain a loyal staff. Nor could he maintain completely the staff's isolation from considerations of policy. The staff reportedly had little hesitancy in disagreeing with Burns and were frequently outspoken in their disagreements. He reportedly responded to staff criticism by toning down the free enterprise approach in the opening chapter of the 1954 *Economic Report*, which, in its first draft, is said to have resembled laissez-faire economics as might be interpreted by the National Association of Manufacturers.

Outside contacts made through the ABEGS Task Forces inevitably involved some policy involvement by the staff. This was particularly true of Lusher's "Tuesday Group," which, as an informal gathering of senior professional economists from the Budget Bureau, Treasury, Commerce, Labor, and the Federal Reserve, considered such matters as expenditure and revenue estimates and economic assumptions underlying the annual Budget and State of the Union messages. A number of its members participated in a conference at Princeton University on antirecession policy that was organized by the National Bureau of Economic Research at Burns' request and from which a series of papers were published.[79] If, as has been suggested,[80] Burns was less anti-Keynesian when he left the Council than when he arrived, the three-year experience on the firing line of advising the President must share the credit for the change with a staff that was relatively liberal in its economic orientation.

To some degree, differences between Burns and the staff and within the staff itself were supplemented by a division between the full-time government career economists and the temporary academic consultant group. The separateness was reinforced by the inability of the consultants to develop a continuing participation in Council activities or a running association with their Council brethren. Although an amicable apartness, such things as differences in salaries thought to be favorable to the academicians reportedly constituted minor irritations. These various rifts did not necessarily mean a formality or rigidity of day-to-day activities and relationships. Organization of work in terms of major areas of economic activity did not preclude informal access and communications within the staff itself and between the staff and the Council members. Burns was "Arthur" to virtually everyone. Staff meetings were held quite frequently, even if seldom at the intended weekly intervals.

The preparation of the annual *Economic Report*, although involving external contact, was primarily an internal project dominated by Burns. Following discussion between Council members and staff in late October, Burns would write "from scratch" the initial draft of the major chapters. Thus, for the 1954 *Economic Report*, he wrote the initial drafts of the chapters pertaining to "Performance of American Economy," "Government Policy in a Year of Change," "Pathways to Strength," and "Dealing with Economic Instability."

Chapters on particular aspects, such as "Role of Government in Economic Progress," "Reforming the Tax Structure," "Government Aids to Housing and Finance," and "Economic Relations with Other Countries," were initially drafted by other Council or staff members under the coordinating direction of Jacoby. They were all then rewritten by Burns. Only in the appendices did Burns forego rewriting in favor of editing and careful review. The same pattern of Burns' dominance was followed even more rigorously in subsequent *Economic Reports*.[81]

The staff contribution was primarily in providing information and data and then reviewing the drafts. Their memoranda of comments on the final draft would be sifted through a Reports Review Committee made up of staff members—Achinstein, Shere, and Stocking in 1954—and the more significant observations of the committee would be passed on to Burns. Interdepartmental clearance apparently was superficial and in two stages—general discussion of the contents and recommendations of the *Economic Report* in ABEGS meetings and a review of drafts distributed in galley proofs with a deadline for comments that precluded extensive change. Review by the Budget Bureau was more extensive in order to assure conformity with the Budget and State of the Union messages. The focus of White House review, done principally by Hauge, was on the "Letter of Transmittal," in which the President summarized his *Economic Report* in three or four pages. The 1954 letter, for instance, was the joint effort of Hauge and Jacoby.[82] The *Economic Reports*, as they finally emerged, bore the Burnsian stamp clearly evident both in the contents and in the excellence of the expository prose.

The restrictive nature of internal operations and the constraint of policy involvement carried over into external operations as well. In March, 1953, Burns was new to the Washington scene. With respect to the bureaucratic environment in which he found himself, he has been described as "a babe in the woods, but he caught on fast and became a shrewd and first-rate operator." Another has said, "He quickly learned what the President's interests were, who the influential people were, and what battles to fight and avoid." [83]

Burns conferred with President Eisenhower on a regularly scheduled weekly basis until the President's heart attack in September,

1955. Although, of course, not the only contact with the President, these Monday morning conferences, also attended by Hauge, served two major purposes: to brief the President on current economic developments and needs and to increase the President's grasp of economic affairs generally.[84] In addition to contact growing out of particular operating problems, Burns would often meet informally over the luncheon table with Adams and Hauge or Humphrey and Dodge, as well as with Chairman Martin of the Federal Reserve Board and Treasury Under Secretary Marion Folsom. His negotiating tactic was not to rush in or quickly volunteer his views but to save his fire until he knew it would count. If what he supported was going to occur, he would not climb on the bandwagon but would conserve his own reserve of obligations owed him for issues still in doubt.[85]

Burns was, in fact, the only member who spoke publicly on behalf of the Council. He alone testified before Congress and on economic policy questions normally did so in executive sessions. Reminiscent of Nourse's views, Burns did not wish to endanger his objective advisory relationship with the President. His request that no transcript be made of discussion led to disputes with Chairman Douglas of the Joint Committee on the Economic Report in 1955 and 1956.[86] Virtually all Council relations with the White House were funneled through Burns with the other Council members only "occasionally" joining him in meetings with the President or conferring with aides.[87] No member of the staff dealt directly with any presidential aide, much less with the President.

As economic adviser to the President, Hauge constituted an important part of the Council–White House link. Despite the seeming overlap and potential conflict between this position and that of Burns, the two tasks were essentially complementary rather than overlapping. As economic troubleshooter, Hauge fielded the great variety of immediate problems which constantly came to the White House such as appeals for tariff increases on Swiss watches and pressure for changes in the Benson farm price support program. Burns would be informed of the problem, but he and, through him, the Council normally would not take part unless the matter involved economic analysis of the type the Council was organized to do. "I regarded the Council as the economic intelligence center of the Administration," [88] Hauge has commented.

Burns also assumed the major share of Council relations with the executive departments as a whole. During the early months of his incumbency ABEGS became his principal means of developing departmental associations:

I was new to government; I didn't know my way around or have contacts. I relied upon it at first as the vehicle for getting the Council established, developing contacts, getting in on things. I organized it in the early fall of 1953 to consider broad objectives of public policy and how they should be achieved.[89]

Over the recession period, ABEGS with few exceptions met weekly, relying on only a very general agenda and keeping no minutes. Although composed of top-level operating officials of major departments having programs of economic significance, ABEGS had no coordinating function but served merely informational and communicative purposes. For these purposes, it appears to have been reasonably successful: "It was for Burns a line of intelligence; he kept attendance up and was both wise and smart enough to use it as a way of keeping in touch with operating people, not just economists." [90] As one such person recalls, "It gave Arthur ideas." It helped him keep the President informed of what was going on within the departments, of what was likely to come to his attention. To Hauge, "Probably its greatest contribution was in giving the agency people some sense of the overall economic effects of their actions—greater perspective, greater integration." [91]

As originally organized, ABEGS was equipped with an Auxiliary Staff Committee and a series of interagency Task Forces. The former was made up of senior staff assistants of ABEGS members, who were supposed to brief their principals on various issues and to review and analyze proposals made to the Board. However, this group soon became superfluous and died a quiet death. The Task Forces appear to have been more useful during the early years, at least to the Council. Headed by a senior member of the Council staff and composed of representatives of appropriate agencies, each Task Force tackled a particular problem, such as federal credit aids to construction, unemployment compensation, tax revisions, or means of strengthening the financial system.[92] Task Force chairmen initiated and carried out most of the work, while the other members provided background material. The final report, however, would reflect the Burns viewpoint.[93]

Although Task Force reports included recommendations that might ultimately find their way to ABEGS, the work of the Task Forces was more informational than executive. Their chief value was in serving as a more specific extension of ABEGS's intelligence activities; they brought information to the Council and also provided a working level foothold in a number of agencies. In addition, they gave those Council senior staff members who served as Task Force chairmen a degree of policy involvement that did not normally come from other assignments.

In the latter years of the Burns chairmanship, ABEGS deteriorated in activity and usefulness and was not subsequently revived. Despite its demise, Burns has apparently retained his belief in the potential of such a group, for he has proposed that there be established an Economic Policy Board to function in economic matters in much the same manner that the National Security Council does in the area of defense. More elaborate than ABEGS, it would involve representation at the Under Secretary level of the primarily economic policy agencies as well as regular meetings of the President with agency heads.[94]

Although Council staff members kept in touch with agencies concerned with their respective areas of research and analysis, relatively few appeared to maintain contacts that were more than essentially informational. The more active association and collaboration in cases such as Nicholls with Agriculture, Long with Labor, Koch with the Federal Reserve, and Lusher with his "Tuesday group" stand out as atypical. This does not mean that regular contact was ruled out, for, as Hauge has commented, "If he was a good man and known, he got around, was accepted, and carried weight in the departments with which he dealt." [95] The point is that the staff was in no sense outgoing; its contacts regarding professional matters were closely controlled by Burns. Those contacts that the staff members maintained were used primarily as a means of gathering information and carrying out prescribed missions. Initiative and discretion were limited, proselytizing excluded.

Burns served as chairman of the Council for some two years beyond the period of the 1953–54 recession; in fact, he served for two years more than he had planned.[96] Starting in late 1954 and extending until his resignation after Eisenhower's reelection in November, 1956, Burns directed the Council in its participation in a number of economic policy areas. The more notable of these included taking the lead in preparing programs of anti-inflation activity beginning in late 1954, developing new programs of assistance to the chronically depressed areas out of which emerged the Area Redevelopment Administration in 1961, promoting federal aid to highway construction, initiating the Cabinet Committee on Small Business, and encouraging government agencies concerned with compiling statistics in their efforts to improve their statistical programs.

Following his resignation, Burns returned to Columbia and became President of the National Bureau of Economic Research. He was succeeded in the chairmanship of the Council by Saulnier, who had been elevated from the staff to Council membership in April, 1955. His position as a Council member in turn was filled by Paul W. McCracken from the University of Michigan. Joseph S. Davis from Stanford, who had been appointed to the Council in 1955, completed the Council membership. Except for somewhat less close relations with the White House, the Saulnier Council appears to have followed operational patterns similar to those of its predecessor. The period of Saulnier's chairmanship, covering all of Eisenhower's second term, was the longest chairmanship up to that time. It was marked, in economic terms, by the inflation that began to emerge in early 1956 and extended to the third quarter of 1957 and by the short recession that began in late 1957 and extended into the second quarter of 1958. Government economic activity was of a relatively passive nature. The continuation of budget deficits and the threat of inflation comprised the major concerns of this period. These were precisely the concerns that, symbolizing a conservative tradition, were carried over into the first new administration of the 1960s.

VI. 1961—THE YEAR OF
CONTINUING TRADITION

After the election of 1960, John F. Kennedy and his entourage wasted no time in launching the final stage of his long preparation for the presidency. The glittering generalities and hypothetical issues of campaign rhetoric now evaporated before the reality and complexity of specific problems and opportunities. Deadlines, dilemmas, and pressures underscored the fact that decisions would have to be made and leadership resources committed.

Kennedy's Inaugural Address had made abundantly clear his primary concern for world peace, yet he was also fully aware of the press of national issues. Communist intransigence in Berlin and elsewhere, the simmering Cuban caldron, the needs of developing nations, to say nothing of the deteriorating balance-of-payments situation, were all problems that had to be considered in the light of such national concerns as defense, civil rights, and economic growth. The economic downturn provided a compelling immediacy to the objective of "getting the country moving again." To deepening unemployment was added the ever-present fear of inflation and the threat of increased labor-management strife.

Clearly, these were not new crises or issues; indeed, they had in varying degrees of intensity plagued both Kennedy's postwar predecessors. Yet Kennedy believed that these matters were uniquely crucial to the times at hand. James MacGregor Burns quotes Kennedy's conviction that the 1960s would be "far more demanding and dangerous, 'the age of change and challenge has come upon us. . . . The next year, the next decade, in all likelihood the next generation, will require more bravery and wisdom on our part than any period in our history.'" [1] To the manifold problems and issues of his age, Kennedy was to apply concepts of office and to bring types of assistance different from those used by his predecessors. If Truman bore the burden of the "buck that stops here" and Eisenhower was the peacemaker, then Kennedy might be called the source of activity. "I'm no Whig," Burns quotes him as saying in 1959. "[The President] must serve as a catalyst, an energizer, the defender of the public good and the public interest against all narrow private interests which operate in our society." [2] From the White House, as from a command post, would issue strategy and tactics for everything from containing the cold war, battling for and with civil rights, and providing jobs to ultimately winning the next election.

To the multiple challenges of national and world affairs Kennedy would apply a brand of leadership at once rooted in his own experiences and reflected in the values of his generation. Nineteenth-century idealism would give way to twentieth-century "pragmatism." Pragmatism as the art of the practical would not be devoid of values, nor would it be derived from them. Rather, conviction and commitment would grow out of rational analysis of fact and experience. Feasibilities and priorities would support rather than rely upon ideology. Manipulations would join, if not supersede, the persuasive force of ideas. Intelligence, administrative competence, an impressive knowledge of the details of public issues, an acute sense of timing and political reality would all be combined with boundless energy, directness, and crisp decisiveness in reaching acceptable solutions to national and international issues. Realism and courage unencumbered by emotion, along with ability and initiative, would bring new science to the art of politics. They would also bring new progress in the quest for national achievement and world peace.

Such qualities were at the same time characteristics and criteria. They characterized the President and the immediate staff that fought the four-year election campaign with him, and they served as important criteria in the selection of persons to fill the major operating and advisory positions of the Kennedy Administration. Theodore C. Sorensen as Special Counsel, Myer Feldman and Lee C. White as his assistants, P. Kenneth O'Donnell, Lawrence F. O'Brien, and Ralph A. Dungan as general political assistants, and Pierre E. G. Salinger as Press Secretary all reflected the President's own values and methods. Yet by virtue of make-up and association these men undoubtedly contributed to as well as reflected the emerging style of the new Administration. The leading newcomer, McGeorge Bundy, who would assume such an important role in White House operations, surely fitted the mold, as did Walt Rostow and, to a lesser degree in an ambiguous but important liaison role, Arthur Schlesinger, Jr. Even aside from his unique position, Robert Kennedy as Attorney General certainly blended into the picture. The application of similar criteria seems evident in the appointment of men such as David E. Bell, Dean Rusk, Douglas Dillon, Robert S. McNamara, Stewart Udall, Orville L. Freeman, and Arthur J. Goldberg—all able men of twentieth-century youth, vigor, and practicality.

No incongruity with the pattern appears in the appointment of Walter W. Heller as Chairman of the Council of Economic Advisers. That Heller had not met the President until the preceding October but had been highly recommended by a number of people including Paul A. Samuelson, who was reputed to have been Kennedy's first choice, is common knowledge. Heller was selected on the basis of Kennedy's standards of ability; he arrived and plunged into work in the Kennedy milieu. Instead of the lengthy delays that had attended the Truman appointment of Nourse and Keyserling and the Eisenhower selection of Burns, Kennedy included Heller among his initial pre-inaugural appointments. Such promptness indicates not only the importance attached to securing adequate staff assistance as quickly as possible but also demonstrates the importance of matters economic and Kennedy's intention of dealing with them actively. In a statement drafted by Neustadt and Bell, both of whom were experienced in the ways of the presidential bureaucracy (Democratic style), Kennedy commissioned the Council "to return to the spirit as well as the letter of the Employment Act." The economy was to be treated not

in narrow terms, but in terms appropriate to the optimum development of the human and natural resources of this country, of our productive capacity and that of the free world. . . . Under Dr. Heller's direction, I expect the CEA to take its place as a key element within the Presidential Office. I believe we can make a major contribution to the successful organization of the Presidency and by revitalizing the Council of Economic Advisers we shall fill a gap in the staff services available to the President.[3]

For his part, Heller hoped that he could "serve the President-elect in developing policies that will bring the economy back to its full potential."[4] Few could find fault with these generalities, which symbolized potential agreement on basic objectives of economic policy.

Forty-five years old at the time of his appointment, Heller shared the energy and drive of his new chief and associates across Executive Place. His academic background and experience fitted him admirably for work on the New Frontier. He did his undergraduate work at Oberlin College and earned his M.A. and Ph.D. at the University of Wisconsin. After serving during World War II as a financial economist with the Treasury Department, he embarked upon a career of teaching and research in economics at the University of Minnesota, where his work also included significant operating experience in public finance. He was associated with the U.S. Military Government in Germany in 1947–48 as Chief of Internal Finance and was a member of the ECA mission on German fiscal problems in 1951. In addition to acting as consultant to the Minnesota Department of Taxation, he was tax adviser to Governor Freeman. Heller also served as consultant to or committee member of a number of organizations including the UN, the Committee for Economic Development, and the U.S. Census Bureau. He collaborated in the authorship and editing of economic publications, contributed to various journals, and testified extensively before committees of Congress. His orientation was to economic operations rather than to economic reflections. In order to serve on the Council he took leave from his position as Chairman of the Department of Economics of the University of Minnesota.

As a sign of the times, Heller, too, was soon reported as claiming to be a pragmatist.[5] Yet the pragmatism in Heller's economics appears to be different from that of the President and his immediate associates. Heller's pragmatism embraces rather than excludes an a priori philosophy or ideology. Perhaps reflecting the theme of welfare and social responsibility associated with John R. Commons, who for many years strongly influenced the teaching of economics at the University of Wisconsin, Heller sought not merely a reduction of unemployment but the development of "social capital" primarily through greater investment in education and training. Consequently, Heller's primary concern appeared to be with substantive policy objectives, that is, with policy application rather than with economic theory or theoretical analysis. He endorsed an active concept of government responsibility; he had confidence in the public sector of the economy, and he emphasized the relative efficacy of fiscal (as opposed to monetary) policy. His convictions harmonized with the full employment concept of the Employment Act; a sense of action and a realistic awareness of policy execution attuned him to Kennedy pragmatism. He approached his assignment on the New Frontier equipped with demonstrated economic expertise that was charged with ideology and practicality.

To complete the Council, Kennedy, acting in characteristic fashion, persuaded Heller's choices of Kermit Gordon and James Tobin to accept Council membership. The President-elect telegraphed Tobin from Palm Beach on December 23 and Gordon from the Hotel Carlyle headquarters in New York on January 5. Both appointments were announced that day. At the time of his appointment Gordon, then forty-four, was on leave from an economics professorship at Williams College and was directing the Ford Foundation's Program in Economic Development. He had completed his undergraduate studies at Swarthmore with highest honors in economics in 1938 and, following studies at Oxford as a Rhodes Scholar, in 1940–41 did graduate work in economics at Harvard. He served with OPA in 1941–43 and afterwards was associated with the economic affairs office of the State Department, first as special assistant, then as consultant. He had been on the Williams faculty since 1946. When Gordon became Director of the Bureau of the Budget in December, 1962, his position on the Council was taken the following May by John P. Lewis. Lewis, it will be recalled, had served with the Council as a staff member during the Keyserling period.

Prior to returning to the Council he had joined the economics faculty at the University of Indiana.

James Tobin, at forty-two the youngest of the triumvirate, was educated at Harvard and received his Ph.D. in 1947. He had joined the faculty of the Department of Economics at Yale University and was appointed Sterling Professor of Economics in 1957. He was also Director of the Cowles Foundation for Research in Economics. Among his colleagues he had gained a reputation in the fields of statistical method, econometrics, and economic theory. In 1955 he received the John Bates Clark Award, which is given no more often than every two years to an economist under forty in recognition of his contribution to economic knowledge.[6] Tobin's prior government service had been as an associate economist with OPA and WPB in 1941–42 and as a consultant to the Federal Reserve Board, 1955–56. He had written several memoranda on economic policy for Kennedy in 1960 before the latter's nomination. In August, 1962, Tobin returned to Yale and his position on the Council was assumed by Gardner Ackley, who was then forty-seven years old. A professor of economics on leave from the University of Michigan, Ackley served from 1940–46 with OPA and OSS and in 1951–52 as Assistant Director of OPS; in 1964 he succeeded Heller as the Council's sixth Chairman.

The new triumvirate had its first meeting as Council-to-be in Gordon's apartment in New York City on the night of his and Tobin's appointments. Although the new Council inherited ten staff economists from the outgoing Saulnier Council, many of these would be leaving during the ensuing weeks and months. A staff was re-created around Arthur Okun from Yale, Robert Solow from the Massachusetts Institute of Technology, and David Lusher, the veteran holdover from the previous Council. These presidential appointees and staff members together constituted the undermanned nucleus of professional economists who, after feverish preparatory activity in December and January, took on the task of advising a President born in their century and into their generation. Sworn in a week after the Inauguration, the new Council immediately commenced to fulfill the larger role expected of a revitalized body—that of being part of a revitalized national government.

First Things First and All at Once

Swept along by the new brush of change and businesslike activity of the Kennedy Administration, Heller and his colleagues were soon caught up in the same pressures and deadlines as the President. In an atmosphere reminiscent of Washington in the early days of the New Deal, they shared an enthusiasm and a sense of dedication with new associates throughout the Executive Office Building, in the White House, and extending deep into the federal bureaucracy. As they settled down to the specific task of advising (that is, producing), they found themselves faced with four problems or challenges, which, even if viewed as priorities, demanded simultaneous attention:

1. The Council had to meet the immediate demand for analysis and advice regarding the recession. Doing this involved not only decisions concerning specific countercyclical steps to be taken but also the initial testing of economic policy, the establishing of precedents and values, and the taking of positions that would govern future issues.

2. Since the Council was seriously short-handed, an adequate staff had to be assembled quickly. Staffing presented problems not only of recruiting qualified economists but also of pressing against budget ceilings.

3. As an agency almost completely reconstituted at the political appointee level in personnel and outlook in a new administration, the Council had to reestablish its relationship with the other offices with which it would have to, or would want to, deal and which were themselves adjusting to new friends and foes.

4. Perhaps most important because of its impact on the other three problems, the Council had to establish and articulate its own philosophy regarding national economic policy. Granted, this would evolve in the daily pressures of informing the President, developing analysis, taking on commitments, making assignments, drafting and redrafting, but a reasoned statement could not long be postponed; the first public testimony before the Joint Economic Committee was barely five weeks away. Such an articulation would not be so much

a hard-line commitment as a major step by the Council in getting its bearings for its own convictions and conduct.

As had been the experience of the Council of almost eight years before, Heller and his colleagues were quickly drawn or pushed to the center of the stage by the immediate economic situation of early 1961. Within three days of their taking office, the President would deliver his State of the Union Message. After the brief and overriding eloquence of the Inaugural Address, specifics and priorities were awaited by idealists and pragmatists alike. Consequently, the Council shared in the weekend drafting of a statement, the first portions of which would deal with the state of the economy, balance of payments, and necessary public expenditures for the public welfare. New information and analysis had to be worked in with existing ideas and arguments. Proposals had to indicate initiative, leadership, and cooperation with the Hill. Wording had to strike a balance between commitment and leeway for choice of alternatives not yet discussed or agreed upon. Although the President might say that domestic problems "pale when placed beside those which confront us around the world," [7] unemployment steadily mounting to almost 7 percent of the civilian labor force gave the message special urgency. The drafting of the State of the Union Message constituted the first of many hectic races or what perhaps might more accurately be described as the first leg of a marathon to be run in the weeks and months ahead.

Perhaps nothing typified for the Council the pressure and excitement of those early days more than the special message to be delivered on February 2 on a "Program for Economic Recovery and Growth." Scheduled for delivery four days after the State of the Union Message, it was hammered out in Heller's office in several successive sessions which lasted until 4 A.M. Although Sorensen and others in and out of the government contributed to it and although the President revised it in part, the message itself and the program it described were almost entirely the work of the Council. As a quick sprint it gave the Council not only an immediate challenge to its abilities and convictions but also an opportunity to establish itself with the President, the White House staff, the Budget Bureau, and the operating agencies. Moreover, the race had hardly begun.

Four days later would follow a message on gold and balance of payments, then, in quick succession, one on national resources on February 23 and another on the federal highway program on February 28. The Council participated in the preparations for all these in varying degrees. At the same time it had to stake out the main dimensions of its own forthcoming testimony to the Joint Economic Committee on March 6, that is, its support of the President's emergency program, its analysis (at least by implication) of the last Eisenhower-Saulnier *Economic Report*, and its statement of national economic policies. And throughout these major undertakings it bombarded the President with requested and volunteered memoranda of ideas, analyses, and recommendations. It also threw itself into the formulation of specific countercyclical operations.

These formulations were rooted in two related but distinct factors: (1) the relative mildness, in strictly economic terms, of the recession along with the likelihood of an upturn within six months and (2) the diminishing rate of economic growth as reflected in the increased frequency of recession and decreased strength of recovery. The basic strength of the upward trend in government expenditure and the expected increase in consumer expenditure might soon stall and reverse the inventory reduction that was once more viewed as the culprit of the recession. These factors, however, seemed ineffectual against a decreasing rate of economic growth and a rate of civilian unemployment that had jumped in the peak periods of July, 1953, July, 1957, and May, 1960, from 2.4 to 4.2 to 5.1 percent, respectively.[8] Following the slide of the last half of 1960, it stood at 6.8 percent seasonally adjusted in December.[9]

The social and political significance of persistent unemployment compelled a reversal of both the short-run situation and the long-term trend. Reversal was a major campaign promise; steps toward its achievement were among the initial postelection moves. As President-elect, Kennedy had commissioned a number of task forces to deal with aspects of the problem within the framework of national economic policy. One was concerned with depressed areas and chaired by Senator Douglas, another focused on tax reform and was headed by Stanley S. Surrey, and a third, chaired by Samuelson, was concerned with the depressed state of the economy.

Of the three, the last was perhaps the most generally significant because of its broad application to both recession and growth. The resulting task force report was not long, nor was it the result of lengthy investigation and deliberation. Rather it was a crash project prepared in a great hurry by task force members who, as professionals generally well known to one another, worked informally wherever they could most conveniently meet—at The Brookings Institution in Washington or in hotel rooms in St. Louis sandwiched between sessions of the annual meeting of the American Economic Association. Although written almost entirely by Samuelson himself, the report bears the thinking and views of the other task force members: Gerhard Colm, veteran of many national economic policy-making campaigns and elder statesman of the "full potential" school, Henry Fowler, who would soon be Under Secretary of the Treasury, Otto Eckstein of Harvard, who was Technical Director of the Joint Economic Committee's Study of Employment, Growth, and Price Levels in 1959, and Joseph A. Pechman of The Brookings Institution, along with Tobin and Heller of the Council-to-be.

Entitled "Prospects and Policies for the 1961 American Economy," the report promptly struck the Administration's basic theme of concern for the immediate recession and chronic slackness and for the increased activation of our economic potential:

One cannot realistically expect to undo in 1961 the inadequacies of several years. . . . The goal for 1961 must be to bring the recession to an end, to reinstate a condition of expansion and recovery and to adopt measures likely to make the expansion one that will not after a year or two peter out at levels of activity far below our true potential. Indeed, policy for 1961 should be directed against the background of the whole decade ahead. Deliberate slack for stability is not a policy open to responsible government.[10]

Its prescriptions of "First Line of Defense Policies" included increasing expenditures by the pushing ahead of necessary governmental programs "on their own merits," improving unemployment compensation, stimulating residential housing construction, and innovating monetary policy with the setting of low interest rates on long-term bonds and high interest rates on short-term maturities. This innovation, soon to be known as the "twist" policy, was designed to encourage domestic investment and at the same time both attract foreign capital and stem the outflow of American funds. The "Second Line of Defense Policies" focused upon a temporary tax cut of 3 to 4 percent through reductions of withholding deductions, to start in March if necessary and with authority granted to the President to extend cuts for a second or third three- or six-month period but not beyond the end of 1962. The emphasis was clearly on a temporary measure if short-term circumstances warranted it:

With the continued international uncertainty and with new public programs coming up in the years ahead, sound finance may require a maintenance of our present tax structure, and any weakening of it in order to fight a recession might be tragic. Even if it should prove to be the case that growth makes reduction of tax rates possible in the long run, that should be a decision taken on its own merits and adopted along with a comprehensive reforming of our tax structure. (Various tax devices to stimulate investment might also be a part of a comprehensive program designed to eliminate loopholes, promote equity and enhance incentives.) [11]

Released on January 5, two weeks before the Inauguration and almost a month before the President's Economic Message, the report constituted the future administration's foremost public expression of specific proposals up to that time. These proposals represented a new approach set forth under the name of one of the nation's leading economists. Specific and innovative in both fiscal and monetary aspects, the proposals set the stage; they constituted the models or points of reference in the subsequent choice of policy alternatives. In the early weeks of the Kennedy Administration, they silhouetted opposing concepts of economic thought and action, concepts held or at least unopposed by those who would decide.

Over a week before his installation as Secretary of the Treasury, Douglas Dillon responded to the Samuelson Report by announcing that he had no present intention of recommending a tax cut, thereby jeopardizing a balanced budget and the serious balance-of-payments situation, nor did he endorse the recommendation of giving the President temporary authority to adjust tax rates. He did, however, favor tax reform and indicated tentative support for repeal of the deduction-and-credit feature on dividend payments, withholding taxes on dividends and interest—"if a practical system could be worked out"—and tightening up on overseas investments. He was "open minded" on the possibility of revising depletion allowances.[12] Without providing details, he told the Senate Finance Committee that specific tax reform proposals would be made by April 1 but that long-term cuts should await budget surplus.[13]

Indeed, it was the concern for balanced budgets and the balance-of-payments problem that colored the new Administration's early economic policy thinking. Kennedy's State of the Union Message previewed forthcoming specific proposals for short-run stimulation and acceleration that were rooted in Samuelson's "First Line of Defense Policies"; it mentioned "tax incentives for sound plant investment" but said nothing about a tax cut or discretionary authority for changing taxes as mentioned in the "Second Line." It revealed a major concern over the prospect of budget imbalance in both 1961 and 1962:

Nevertheless, a new Administration must of necessity build on the spending and revenue estimates already submitted. Within that framework, barring development of urgent national defense needs or a worsening economy, it is my current intention to advocate a program of expenditures which, including revenues from a stimulation of the economy, will not of and by themselves unbalance the earlier Budget.[14]

The same basic theme came through strongly in the President's February 2 message on economic recovery and growth. He acknowledged both the campaign promises made and the economic advice received by speaking of reversing the downward trend in the economy, narrowing the gap of unused potential, and abating waste and misery and at the same time maintaining reasonable price stability. Yet he pledged his Administration to a budget that would be balanced over the years of the economic cycle and to policies that would not contribute to inflation. The measures he was taking and proposing on behalf of recovery did not threaten this pledge; they did not include tax reduction. In his discussion of ways to promote long-term economic growth and stability, he observed that "today, most industries have the facilities to produce well above current levels. They lack only customers." But then he gave a preview of a forthcoming proposal to modify the income tax laws to provide not additional customers but additional incentives for investment in plant and equipment.

This suggestion was accompanied by proposals to strengthen the nation's education, health, research, and training activities, to improve the development and conservation of natural resources, and to solve the problems of productivity and price stability through effective labor-management relations.[15] At his news conferences both the day before delivering his special economic message and a week later, President Kennedy indicated that he did not favor a tax cut, that he was not convinced that Congress would entertain such a proposal, that a cut would limit the government's ability to go ahead with other programs of possibly greater long-run use, and that he would have another look at the economy in April.

Thus, in February, 1961, when the leading economic indicators showed no sign of reversal except for slight upturns in average weekly hours of work and seasonally adjusted unemployment and when business inventories had dropped $3.7 billion between the third and fourth quarters of 1960, the Administration appeared to accept the Samuelson Task Force's "First Line of Defense" proposals but not the "Second Line." The Administration acknowledged some of the letter of the proposals but little of their spirit. Although there was much journalistic discussion as well as labor union pressure on behalf of a temporary tax cut to meet the short-term emergency, there was apparently very little prospect of such a move within the Administration. Dillon was opposed to it for reasons of maintaining revenues and minimizing deficits in the face of rising expenditures. Kennedy was likeminded and also was concerned about inflation and the asked-for "spirit of sacrifice," and he did not want to jeopardize other parts of his program. He foresaw the likelihood of international events forcing an increase in defense expenditures and wished to avoid any tag of fiscal irresponsibility.[16] That the Task Force's tax proposals were in its "Second" rather than "First Line of Defense" suggests that its members were far from insensitive to the President's antipathy. Only on the Council was there unanimity concerning temporary tax reduction. But the odds against it were overwhelming, and the alternatives of increased expenditures appeared adequate. The best the Council could do was to seek qualifications in the Administration's balanced-budget commitment.

Under this commitment there was consequently no reaching for basically new economic policies. The Council therefore sought to reverse the immediate downturn through a variety of largely conventional discretionary measures, such as acceleration of procurement and construction programs, acceleration of the payment of tax refunds and veteran's life insurance dividends, expansion of loan programs to farms and small businesses, easing of bank and mortgage credit terms, distribution of surplus food (in part through the food-stamp program), expansion of the state Employment Services operations, and the promotion of export trade through the Export-Import Bank. In addition, the Administration requested that the Congress enact measures that would, among other things, extend unemployment insurance benefits, enlarge the unemployment compensation system, improve aid to dependent children, and increase Social Security benefits—this last reportedly being a proposal of Heller's. Congress acted favorably on all but the unemployment compensation measure and also passed Administration proposals to provide for increased minimum wage, area redevelopment, housing, emergency feed grain, agriculture lending programs, federal aid to highways, natural resources development, airport assistance, aid to education, and other related measures.[17]

All these steps were important. They indicated initiative and determination to effect a reversal as quickly as possible, and, although it cannot be said that they alone caused the upturn of the second half of 1961, they presumably contributed to it. They did not, however, constitute an attack on the challenge of long-term growth or decisions on how to do so; there was as yet no test of the prevailing orthodoxy of basing economic policy upon objectives of a balanced budget and anti-inflation defense.

In the midst of participating in the Administration's counter-cyclical activities, the Council strove mightily to add to its own staff. Opportunities and demands for analysis and advice were increasingly beyond its manpower. The short-handed staff of professional economists serving on a regular or consultant basis could not be expected to endure the pace indefinitely, yet recruiting additional staff presented problems. There was, first of all, a great demand for bright, able New Frontiersmen throughout the government; economists, lawyers, journalists, political scientists were all being sought

by everybody from Secretary of Defense McNamara to Peace Corps
Director Shriver. Second, it was difficult for qualified economists,
who were in short supply and who constituted the most likely prospects for staff recruiting, to leave their teaching and research posts
in the middle of an academic year. And third, there was, for some, a
measure of uncertainty whether or not service with the Council
would benefit their careers. Respect for Heller and the response to
Kennedy shared by many intellectuals throughout the country did
not entirely blot out convictions that the Council had not yet proved
itself.

If recruiting difficulties were not bad enough, lack of funds added
to the problem of procuring the additional manpower needed. It
quickly became obvious that fulfillment of objectives envisioned by
the President and his Council would be impossible without staff
over and above what was permitted under the salary ceiling
($345,000 annually) of the Employment Act, which was based on
salary rates long since superseded by federal pay raises. Consequently, the President requested that the ceiling be lifted so the
staff complement of 1948–52 could be regained. In letters to the
Speaker of the House and to the President of the Senate, he pointed
out that "Problems of international economic policy as they relate
to these goals [full employment, economic growth, reasonable price
stability] are demanding an increasing share of this Council's attention. . . . I am also asking the Council to take on additional responsibilities. . . . The Council will be unable to discharge its duties
without an increase in its personnel budget." [18]

When passed by Congress in June, the amendment removed the
ceiling entirely, but not until the Council succeeded in obtaining a
supplemental appropriation in the following September was it able
to move ahead with further staff acquisitions. In testifying on behalf
of the supplemental, Kermit Gordon illustrated the Council's plight
by pointing out that the Council had not been able to prepare a
basic study on the positions and problems of small business and that
a study of capital investment requirements of long-term economic
growth, which had limped along, was now forced to mark time for
lack of sufficient personnel. [19] To augment his hard-pressed staff,
Heller made extensive use of consultants, who for short periods of

time or on a part-time basis applied their expertise to specific projects of active concern to the Council. Born of immediate necessity in early 1961, the practice of hiring consultants was extensively used throughout the period of Heller's chairmanship.

At the same time, the Council was endeavoring to establish its relationship throughout the Executive Office and with the agencies and departments with which it dealt. Off and running with other members of the New Frontier, the Council experienced a sense of welcome assistance and mutuality of interests. Heller's previous experience in the Treasury, his orientation toward program as opposed to theory, his breadth of acquaintance among government economists, and his testifying experience on the Hill enabled him to move about with a minimum need of introduction. There seems to have been no difficulty in establishing close working relationships with Dillon in the Treasury, Bell in the Budget Bureau, or Sorensen in the White House. Heller's relations with the President were reportedly cordial if not particularly intimate. His relations with Secretaries Arthur Goldberg of Labor and Luther Hodges of Commerce were more institutional but still were professionally cordial. The external relations of the Council established through its chairman were reinforced by the ready acceptance of Tobin and Gordon as well as of a number of the early staff members who were either well known in government or who quickly learned their way around.

In the significant congressional area, Heller wasted no time in establishing cordial relations between the Council and the Joint Economic Committee. He knew of the testifying issue between Chairman Nourse, the Committee, and Keyserling in 1947–48. He was well aware of the subsequent feud over testifying between Arthur Burns and Paul Douglas when the latter was Committee Chairman. He recognized the potential sources of argument and unfriendly questioning from such Committee members as Chairman Patman and Representative Curtis of Missouri. "Our concern," he told the Committee during his first presentation on March 6, "is with the over-all pattern of economic policy." The concern carries with it

a responsibility to explain to the Congress and to the public the general economic strategy of the President's program, especially as it relates to objectives of the Employment Act. This is the same kind of responsibility that other executive agencies assume in regard to programs in their jurisdictions. . . .

In Congressional testimony and in other public statements, the Council must protect its advisory relationship to the President. We assume that the Committee does not expect the Council to indicate in what respects its advice has or has not been taken by the President, nor to what extent particular proposals, or omissions of proposals reflect the advice of the Council.

Subject to the limits mentioned, members of the Council are glad to discuss, to the best of their knowledge and ability as professional economists, the economic situation and problems of the country, and the possible alternative means of achieving the goals of the Employment Act and other commonly held economic objectives. In this undertaking, the Council wishes to cooperate as fully as possible with the Committee and with Congress in achieving a better understanding of our economic problems and approaches to their solution.[20]

As important as the testimony was to the Council in establishing more harmonious relations with the Committee, it was even more important as an opportunity to set forth conceptual foundations of economic policies that both interpreted and stepped ahead of expressed presidential thinking. After all, the Congress and the nation wanted to know what the views of the President's economists were, and the economists wanted to set them forth for public, congressional, and Administration edification. Basically, Heller was suggesting that if, as agreed, economic recovery is not only a cyclical problem but also one of chronic slack, if the gap between what we can produce and do produce (at the time estimated to equal $500 for every American household) is increasing, if the renewal rate of capital stock is slowing down, and if the balance-of-payments problem is persisting, then existing policies and concepts may be neither appropriate nor adequate. Although he urged adoption of the "twist" monetary policy, first suggested two months earlier by Samuelson, and also advocated easier credit terms for housing, Heller focused his principal attention on fiscal policy. Speaking of automatic stabilizers, he noted, first of all, that

under present conditions and tax rates, the "built-in" flexibility of the Federal budget offsets between 25 and 30 percent of the drop (or increase) in GNP, with approximately one-half of the offset coming from corporate taxes, and most of the rest from the various social security programs. Second, welcome as the built-in stabilizers are when the economy contracts, they are a mixed blessing when it expands. As soon as business conditions take a turn for the better, we can expect the Federal tax system automatically to cut into the growth in private income. When the economy again reaches the boom phase, this drain of private incomes will serve as a desirable restraint on inflation. But up to that point, it tends to slow down the recovery process. Third, because economic growth automatically broadens the tax base, the revenue raising power of the Federal tax system has been rising relative to expenditures. . . . In other words, the relative growth of revenues in recent years brings the budgets into balance substantially below full employment at current levels of Federal expenditure and tax rates. In the absence of tax cuts, large expenditure increases, or a substantial worsening of the economic situation, only modest deficits are likely to develop. . . . Indeed, recent fiscal trends make clear that full recovery with the present tax structure would generate substantially more revenue than is required by the President's proposed program, thus leaving a generous margin for retirement of debt and restraint of inflation. Whether this margin is consistent with the achievement of full employment cannot yet be determined.[21]

In addition to outlining the dysfunctions of the existing stabilizers, Heller fired a shot at what a year later was to be called a "myth" and also injected an idea that was to become a major pillar of economic policy:

The success of fiscal and budget policies cannot be measured only by whether the budget is in the black or in the red. The true test is whether the economy is in balance. Only an economy which is realizing its potential can produce the goods and create the jobs the country needs. If at the end of this year the unemployment ratio is still near 7 per cent, our fiscal policies would have to be viewed with great concern, even if there is little or no deficit in the budget. On the other hand, if we have succeeded in reducing the unemployment ratio and expanding output significantly by year's end, we will be on our way to the goals of a stronger economy and the restoration of budgetary strength.[22]

In summarizing policies for economic growth, he urged that a larger share of the nation's resources be allotted to the expansion and development of human skills and physical capital. Education and research were as important as plant and equipment. Natural resources must be conserved as well as developed.

Such explorations into the new frontier of economic policy were not bold adventures beyond the horizon of Administration thinking. Indeed, a foretaste of Heller's analysis had been presented in 1959 in a comprehensive Joint Economic Committee study led by James W. Knowles and Otto Eckstein.[23] Much that Heller said was well within range: emphasis on growth, endorsement of accelerated expenditures, the willingness to seek temporary tax reductions if circumstances warrant, the reliance on tax incentives to stimulate investments. Essentially they were probes toward acceptance of new concepts for the reaching of acknowledged objectives. They were not specific recommendations in an action document that had to be accepted or rejected but rather ideas to be cultivated within as well as outside of the Council, to be tested against opposing ideas in the arena of issues and events. To omit any reference to the idea of a permanent tax reduction did not deny the arguments of tax drag in potential support of such an idea. Heller's analysis was part of the developing process of his own thinking as well as being one of his early lessons to the President and to the public on the possibilities of economic policy; as such, it attempted to anticipate the future.

Tax Reform: Step One

At the very time that the Heller Council was gaining momentum as a presidential advisory body and the Administration was trying to turn or to help turn the immediate recession tide, Secretary Dillon was preparing to unveil the Administration's promised tax reform proposals which would be of significance to long-term economic growth. On April 20, at the height of the Bay of Pigs crisis, President Kennedy sent to the Congress in the form of a special message his proposed "first steps" toward the broad objective of tax reform "the result [of which] should be a tax system that is more equitable, more efficient, and more conducive to economic growth." [24]

He proposed, first, an investment incentive measure that would provide "the largest possible inducement to new investment which would not otherwise be undertaken," and, second, a series of measures designed to remove some of the defects and inequities in the taxation of both domestic and foreign income. Although the investment incentives would entail a revenue loss of $1.7 billion a year, the proposals to close loopholes would result in an offsetting gain in revenues, "thus no net loss of revenue is involved in this set of proposals." The measures of the second step of income tax reform would follow in the next year: "Their purpose will be to broaden and unify the income tax base and to review the entire rate structure in the light of these revisions." [25]

The origins of the Administration's interest in tax reform and hence in these "first step" proposals are in large measure traceable to a comprehensive set of hearings on income tax revision conducted in 1959 by Wilbur D. Mills, the Democratic Chairman of the House Committee on Ways and Means. Encouraged by the concerns and ideas of nongovernmental lawyers and economists that had percolated up to him and aided initially by two like-minded congressional economists, Norman Ture on loan from the Joint Economic Committee and Gerard M. Brannon of the Ways and Means staff, Mills wished to inquire into

the opportunities for constructive reform of the Federal Tax System, . . . the immediate objective [of which] is reduction in tax rates without sacrificing revenues required for responsible financing of government.[26]

His specifications for appropriate revisions revealed concern for the proliferation of special exemptions, deductions, and other provisions benefiting particular groups that were eroding the tax base and thus raising problems of equity among the tax-paying body politic:

Tax reform must seek, among other things: (1) a tax climate more favorable to economic growth; (2) greater equity through closer adherence to the principle that equal income should bear tax liabilities; (3) assurance that the degree of progression in the distribution of tax burdens accords as closely as possible with widely held standards of fairness; (4) an overall tax system which contributes significantly to maintaining stability in the general price level and a stable and high rate of use of human and material resources; (5) a tax system which interferes as little as possible with the operation of the free market mechanism in directing resources into their most productive uses; and (6) greater ease of compliance and administration.

The present income tax system, Chairman Mills pointed out, is criticized as failing to achieve these objectives.[27]

Of considerable depth and scope, the hearings, papers, and discussions generated political as well as professional interest in reform and hence led to a nascent commitment "to do something." Of particular significance to the determining of what to do was the fact that among the approximately 400 witnesses were experts from colleges, universities, and research organizations who were to participate in the development of both the 1961 and subsequent proposals, either as members of the Kennedy Administration or as outside consultants to it. Not the least of these were Heller, Surrey, Harvey Brazer, and Mortimer Caplin. Surrey was destined to head President-elect Kennedy's task force on tax policy and then to become Dillon's Assistant Secretary for Tax Policy. Brazer was to become Surrey's Deputy Assistant Secretary and Director of the Treasury's Office of Tax Analysis, and Caplin was to become Commissioner of Internal Revenue.

In addition, there was Pechman, then of the Committee for Economic Development and more recently of The Brookings Institution. As an acknowledged tax expert, he had frequently served as consultant to government agencies, including the Council and Treasury; he was a Council staff member in 1954–56, and he was to be a principal participant in the development of the 1961–62 tax proposals. Richard Musgrave, at that time at Johns Hopkins and now at Princeton, was another witness who subsequently served as a Treasury and Council consultant on Kennedy tax proposals. Another witness, E. Cary Brown of Massachusetts Institute of Technology, is credited with the major part in developing the key investment incentive proposal and, with Musgrave, wrote the original draft of the President's tax message.

Although the ideas that emerged throughout the hearings were splintered and sometimes conflicting, they were none the less representative of the drive for reform by a large segment of tax professionals. Among participants such as Heller, Surrey, Pechman, Musgrave, Brazer, and Brown, there was a consensus and continuity of views that countered the policies of then current or former Eisenhower officials, many of whom also testified or submitted written statements. The interest of professionals in creating a case for tax reform and then selling it to receptive leaders of Congress is reminiscent of the genesis of the Employment Act fifteen years earlier. Their hearings provided more than a forum for the expression of emergent tax reform thinking; they sparked the 1960 Democratic campaign platform as well as the reports and the specific proposals that were to follow in both 1961 and 1962.

As its prescription for a tax policy that would contribute to economic growth, the Democratic party platform promised to close loopholes, reform inequitable depletion allowances, repeal special considerations for recipients of dividend income, reduce deductions for extravagant business expenses, and improve tax collection. Kennedy had advocated a review of depletion allowances on 104 commodities in his first television debate with Nixon. He envisaged a $700-million to $1-billion gain through closing tax loopholes and urged revision of personal and corporate rates and of depreciation allowances to spur growth.[28] The anti-Republican tenor of these statements was consistent with the substance of the Mills hearings, as was the omission of any recommendation for a tax cut. Economists such as Heller, Samuelson, and Galbraith, who were reported to have counseled Kennedy during the campaign, were apparently advising in parallel terms of tax revision within existing revenue limits accompanied by sustained expenditures for needed public programs.

The President-elect's establishment of the Surrey Task Force on Taxation appears as a natural sequel both to the Mills hearings and to the campaign commitments. A member of the Harvard Law School faculty, Surrey had for a long time been in the forefront of tax reform. As with the Samuelson Report, the Report of the Surrey Task Force was a "crash project" pushed through in three weeks of the hectic postelection, pre-Inauguration period. Like Samuelson, Surrey was aided by a small group of economists and lawyers active in tax reform. They included Musgrave, Caplin, Ture, Brown (as a consultant), and Adrian DeWind, a New York attorney who had specialized in tax matters and who had served as Chief Counsel (with Surrey as Special Counsel) on the House Ways and Means Subcommittee on Internal Revenue Administration in 1951–52.

The Report itself was submitted to the President shortly before Inauguration. Apparently out of respect for congressional sensitivity to its constitutional preeminence in tax matters (particularly that of Representative Mills), the Report was, unlike the Samuelson counterpart, never made public. Salinger did indicate, however, that it covered major areas of tax measures to encourage economic growth by permitting higher levels of private capital formation, correcting existing abuses and inequities, strengthening enforcement, eliminating or lessening the preference aspect of estate and gift taxes, and, where appropriate, reducing tax rates.[29] An internal document, it formed the basis of the Treasury tax reform proposals that had already been heralded by Secretary-designate Dillon.

Thus, tax reform was part of the economic policy cargo that the Kennedy ship of state stowed aboard as it prepared to put to sea. Those who had had a hand in its preparation over the many preceding months and who were also about to sign on as crew hoped it would fit in with other proposals of countercyclical and economic growth significance. Because of the immediate recession, long-term reform proposals were inevitably and prominently coupled in public discussion with short-term tax reduction possibilities, thereby underscoring what was to remain a complementary, even if not always a congenial, association. The guarded reference to an appropriate tax reduction only served to increase the policy and political intensity of the association. As in the early months of 1961, when the Treasury staff was busily preparing specific proposals and drafting the promised presidential tax message, recession fears could focus attention on, and provide support for, tax reform, but its intended impact was on long-term growth, not short-term recovery. Reform had been motivated by other than strictly cyclical considerations.

The President's special tax message as drafted in Treasury in collaboration with the Council and the White House was a fitting "first step" tribute to the work that had been initiated almost two years before. In language reminiscent of the Mills Committee and of the testimony of Heller, Surrey, Pechman, Musgrave, and others, Kennedy complained about the accretion of preferential treatment and at the same time indicated the pressures that were upon him:

Of course, some departures from uniformity are needed to promote desirable social or economic objectives of overriding importance which can be achieved most effectively through the tax mechanism. But many of the preferences which have developed do not meet such a test and need to be re-evaluated in our tax reform program.

It will be a major aim of our tax reform program to reverse this process by broadening the tax base and reconsidering the rate structure. The result should be a tax system that is more equitable, more efficient and more conducive to economic growth.[30]

In a passage reminiscent of his February 2 speech on economic recovery, the President acknowledged that "high capital investment can be sustained only by a high rising level of demand for goods and services" but then, in the sentences immediately following, emphasized the contribution the investment incentive itself could make "now" to the antirecession efforts, increased employment, and exports. Benefits would accrue in the form of increased expenditure in the capital goods industries, additional employment in these industries, and creation of more jobs in the consumer and service industries growing out of the demands of these additional wage earners, adding up to the total increase of an estimated half-million jobs.

The investment incentive itself that would cost the government an estimated $1.7 billion in lost revenues would take the form of tax credits ranging from 6 to 15 percent of expenditures for different categories of investment in new plant and equipment. The counterpart measures to increase revenues by something over $1.75 billion broke down into three areas: tax treatment of foreign income, correction of structural defects, and improved tax administration. By the elimination of foreign "tax havens" and by a general tightening of tax provisions governing income earned abroad, the Administration hoped to reduce the balance-of-payments deficit and to increase revenues by approximately $250 million annually. The first of the proposed structural corrections was a 20 percent withholding of taxes on interest and dividend income, much of which went unreported each year. This would not be a new tax but would, through more effective collection, increase revenues by $600 million a year. The second was a repeal of the 1954 provision which excluded from income the first $50 of dividends received and provided a 4 percent credit against taxes on such dividend income in excess of $50. The President argued that the exclusion and credit feature was a "dead end" and neither encouraged equity investment nor properly met the "double-taxation" factor as originally argued. Repeal would increase revenues by $450 million a year. The remaining revenue-increasing proposals concerning expense accounts, the sale of depreciable business property, and earnings from cooperatives and mutual fire and casualty insurance companies would increase revenues by an estimated $450 million or more.

The tax administration proposals included the establishment of taxpayer account numbers (originally proposed during the Eisenhower Administration) in order to take advantage of automatic data processing developments, increased audit coverage, and closer reporting of inventories, the manipulation of which had been a method of tax avoidance. As final measures, the President also recommended that the existing corporate income and excise taxes be extended for another year, that the existing net 2-cent tax rate on aviation gasoline be extended to include jet fuels, and that after fiscal year 1962 this rate be increased at the rate of ½ cent yearly "until the portion of the cost of the airways properly allocable to civil aviation is substantially recovered by the tax." [31]

Despite the importance that the Administration attached to the proposals, their reception in Congress was something less than enthusiastic. Chairman Mills, who was a prime instigator of reform to broaden the tax base, was himself cool to further preferential treatment to business in the form of the investment incentive measure. Moreover, particular interests represented by business leaders, lobby groups, and individual congressmen strongly opposed various specific reform proposals. There was generally greater preference for further accelerated depreciation measures in the manner provided for by the 1954 Code than for the incentive proposal. The prospect of stricter treatment of travel expenses and the establishment of withholding on interest and dividend income evoked particularly vehement opposition. As a result, despite months of extensive hearings and lengthy considerations during the summer of 1961, the House Ways and Means Committee was unable to draft a bill, much less report one out. Despite Administration urging to the contrary, the Committee shelved the April proposals.

With the first step stymied, Under Secretary of the Treasury

Henry Fowler indicated in October that the major reform planned for 1962, that is, the second step, would be dropped in favor of another effort on the first. Consequently, the staffs of both Treasury and the Joint Committee on Internal Revenue Taxation reworked both the incentive and reform proposals during the fall of 1961, in effect, modifying both the revenue-losing features of the former and the revenue-producing features of the latter.

As a "first step" the incentive and structural reform measures did not seriously challenge the prevailing economic views of 1961. On the contrary, they confirmed them. The investment incentive credit itself was innovative; it was carefully designed to take effect as the economy moved into full employment, yet it assumed the primacy of investment relative to consumer expenditures as the crucial activator of economic growth. In holding to such an assumption, a Democratic administration was turning its back on the traditional tax policy of its party in favor of the accepted views of the previous administration. Quite apart from this traditionalism, however, the structural reform proposals did constitute an attempt to reverse the trend of tax policy and tax code development and thereby give meaning to the criteria of tax breadth and equity. Regardless of their ultimate outcome on Capitol Hill, the significant fact is that the loophole-closing, base-broadening reform proposals put into concrete form as presidential recommendations many of the ideas espoused by economists and lawyers. In combination, the two measures of incentive and reform were expected to carry one another on their respective coattails. The cost of the investment incentive took the form of broadening the tax base; the businessman's consolation for the tax increase in the latter was in the benefit of the former. To the hoped-for satisfaction of many voters, congressmen, and administrators, there would be no net loss of revenue. For the economy there would be redistribution of expenditures into more productive channels, that is, investment.

Such was the continuing tradition. Against it the Council could do little in regard to the tax proposals. It could endorse the structural reforms, but, in an environment of a new Administration attempting to wend its way between world pressures, domestic economic stagnation, and legislative opposition, the Council could not strike out for innovation and expect to survive, much less succeed. The dominance of prevailing views was by no means restricted to the tax salient. The emerging recovery at home and the Berlin crisis abroad provided further rationalization for their potency and acceptance, at the same time washing out possible challenges of contrary analysis and advocacy.

Continuing Tradition: "Strictly in Balance"

In spite of their importance the spring and summer deliberations over specific tax measures constituted a sideshow attracting the specialized attention of experts in the Treasury and Congress, members of the Ways and Means Committee, and affected interests. The primary focus of government and public attention was on other, more dramatic, arenas that provided action of major economic and national security significance.

On the national scene, the economy was waging its expected and heartening comeback. GNP appeared to have "bottomed-out" in the first quarter of 1961 at an annual rate of $500.8 billion, which was a shade better than had been expected. More encouraging, July estimates for the second quarter indicated an increase to $515 billion. In the dynamic area of gross private domestic investment, private investment increased an estimated $8.2 billion (seasonally adjusted annual rate), and total business inventories, which had been liquidated at an annual rate of $4 billion in the first quarter, were accumulated at a rate of $2.5 billion in the second quarter, a reversal of $6.5 billion.[32] Although these and other measures of the economy pointed to increased prosperity, there was, however, little consolation in the level of unemployment, which stood at 6.8 percent. Even worse, the good signs of recovery were overshadowed by the darkening world outlook.

As if to give prescience to President Kennedy's concluding comment in his State of the Union Message that "there will be further setbacks before the tide turns," overseas crises and deterioration framed every scene. Continued strife in Southeast Asia, the Congo, and North Africa, the abortive Cuban invasion, and the successful Russian space orbit were jarring experiences for a new Administration valiantly trying to organize and settle down while conveying to a worried public its own confidence in its ability to cope with all contingencies. After the shock of the Bay of Pigs, Krushchev's constantly increasing pressure on Berlin loomed as the major counterforce to peace and national security, the major drain on leadership resources, and the major permeating influence on decisions and priorities.

Aside from the overriding urgency of "turning the tide," the economic significance of these developments was that, just when the Administration wanted to invest in domestic programs as ends in themselves as well as on behalf of recovery, it had to increase defense expenditures. The improving picture at home decreased the pressure for countercyclical action at the same time that overseas developments increased the pressure of potential inflation. The requested increases of $3.4 billion in expenditures and $5.2 billion in obligational authority over the Eisenhower budget for fiscal 1962, which the President sent to Congress in late March, were not the end but the beginning of increased expenditures and larger budget deficits. Although the President well understood the effect of such increases, it was the complementary nature of recovery and increased defense spending that dominated the economic thinking of mid-1961.

The President's Special Message to the Congress on Urgent National Needs, delivered in person on May 25, reflected the impact of these forces. At the time dubbed the "Restate of the Union Message," it followed its predecessor in emphasizing "the extraordinary times and challenges that lie beyond our shores." Kennedy wished to promote "the freedom doctrine"—and this meant additional expenditures for economic assistance and information activities, along with "free world" and national defense. He also served notice of expanding civil defense, disarmament studies, and space exploration.

In his call to action he was, at the same time, forced to put a damper on "Economic and Social Progress at Home." He could point with a sense of accomplishment to the gathering recovery and to the improved balance-of-payments situation, yet for persistent unemployment only a new manpower development and training program could be promised and for wage-price stability only labor-management restraint hoped for. In the face of returning prosperity and requests for additional funds for defense and space, the President was obliged to postpone until 1962 the public works proposals of Senator Clark upon which both Gordon and Heller had worked. In addition, he asked Congress to go slow, "to refrain from adding funds or programs, desirable as they may be, to the Budget, to end the postal deficit—through increased rates—to provide full pay-as-you-go highway financing, and to close those tax loopholes earlier specified." This was indeed in the spirit of sacrifice and fiscal responsibility. It was as if the luster of the blessings promised by the host of countercyclical steps taken earlier in the year had, in the light of recovery and national security pressure, become dimmed.

Ten days later, on June 4, the President conferred with Premier Krushchev in Vienna. The accumulating pressures on Berlin were capped when Krushchev's *aide-memoire* demanded that Berlin be made a free city; otherwise, Russia would negotiate a peace treaty with East Germany with which both West Germany and the Allies would henceforth have to negotiate. This threat was hammered home not two weeks later with a warning that the peace treaty would be signed not later than December 31. For the first time since Korea the prospect of global war took on an awful immediacy. For the six weeks from mid-June to late July the tension accelerated, with charges and countercharges among the chief adversaries, with consultations among allies, with the desperate flood of refugees from East Berlin, and with feverish consideration of mobilization measures within the Pentagon–White House–Capitol triangle.

Heller, Dillon, Bell, and others joined with White House advisers in urgently considering ways to finance the Berlin build-up. Consensus, not compromise, was the objective. Given the prospect of a defense budget significantly increased beyond what was already contemplated, it is small wonder that the possibility of a tax increase should be added to the actions under consideration. The possibility made inevitable the question about its likelihood at the President's July 19 press conference, to which he replied, "The judgment on taxes and on expenditures will be made in the light of what will produce the best economic situation for the United States in the coming months. We will make it clear at the time that we complete our review and announce then, as to what exactly we propose on taxes." [33]

The reality of the possibility became apparent two days later, when the New York *Times* carried a front-page report that the Treasury recommended to the President that taxes be increased to meet the additional spending of an estimated $2 billion required by the Berlin crisis.[34] The Washington *Post* on the following day credited the proposal to Secretary Dillon, Budget Director Bell, and Chairman Heller, as the President's "top three fiscal experts." By its account, the alternatives under consideration were a lifting of the personal income tax in every bracket by two points effective January 1, 1962, or by lifting the tax one point and also raising the tax on corporate profits from 52 to 53 percent.[35] The discrepancy in the attribution of the origin of the proposal is less important than the indication that it was being actively considered and would have to be rejected or accepted by the time the President addressed the nation on July 25. When and where the proposal actually originated is less significant than the nature of the deliberation and the outcome.

Support for a tax increase followed three main lines of argument. First, the theme of sacrifice, struck during the Inaugural Address and frequently upon subsequent occasions, provided the necessary psychological justification, particularly if, as part of the build-up, thousands of young men were to be called away from civilian homes and pursuits for military service. An emergency tax hike might well arouse a complacent nation, more concerned with summer vacations than with Berlin, to an awareness of national peril. It might also indicate the seriousness of our intent to the Russians. Second (and of more political significance), there was the fear of the charge of fiscal irresponsibility. Conviction of its potency demanded continued integrity of the dollar at home and abroad. Spending programs already being considered by the Congress could not be jeopardized; a tax increase might help things along. And third, there was the fear of inflation. It appeared that the deficit for fiscal year 1961 just ended would be $3.9 billion higher than originally expected and $1.7 billion more than the March estimate. In addition, there was the likelihood that the deficit for fiscal year 1962 would exceed $5 billion. Additional defense expenditures of from $2 to $3 billion would only make matters worse. The developing recovery eliminated the conventional rationalization for continued deficit financing. Along with increased expenditures it threatened price and wage stability. The prospect of mobilization-inspired scare buying added an unwelcome stimulus to this line of reasoning.

At the time of the President's press conference on July 19, these arguments were judged to represent the consensus of the White House advisers, Secretary of Health, Education and Welfare Abraham Ribicoff, Secretary of Labor Goldberg, Secretary Dillon, and Attorney General Robert Kennedy.[36] In clear opposition were Walter Heller and the Council. To them a tax increase on top of a rate structure already regarded as a severe drag on an up-swinging economy would snuff out prematurely the accelerating recovery. A defense expenditure increase of the size contemplated would not risk inflation, and the increase would both spur the economy and help generate additional tax revenues. Moreover, it was unlikely that Congress would surrender an inch of its prerogative to levy taxes by giving the President temporary authority to increase taxes. If the threat of a deficit imperiled the Administration's legislative program, thrusting a tax-increase proposal upon a fully occupied Congress would imperil it even more. In the final analysis, a tax increase could only be justified by a full-mobilization shooting war, and for that Congress could act as quickly as a bill could be printed.

What had started as an urgent search for alternative methods of financing turned into a tense debate over increasing taxes. On Thursday, July 20, one day after the President's news conference, it was assumed that Kennedy had all but decided "to seek a $2 billion increase." [37] The following day Kennedy's tentative decision was telephoned to Heller, who was in Texas on a speaking engagement. Tobin in Washington registered the Council's objections, and Heller took up the cudgels upon his return to Washington the following morning. It appears that by this time Dillon, who was reported to have been a proponent of a tax increase, shifted his position and supported Heller along with Bell.[38] The hold-out support for the tax increase reportedly came from Ribicoff, who stressed the spirit-of-sacrifice and fiscal-responsibility arguments and who wanted to avoid opposition to domestic welfare and foreign aid programs.[39]

White House advisers Sorensen and Bundy, who presumably initially favored an increase, appeared in the latter stages to be neutral if not unenthusiastic.

The debate continued over the weekend of July 22 as the drafting of the President's message proceeded both at the summer White House and in Washington. On Saturday, Wilbur Mills telephoned Kennedy to register his opposition to increased taxes and warned of the impact of a request upon foreign aid and welfare programs.[40] That the President's own mind was not completely made up on the tax question itself or on related aspects of economic policy is indicated by the fact that he conferred over the weekend by telephone with a number of his advisers, including Heller. Moreover, Seymour Harris flew with the President to Hyannis on Friday, and, at the suggestion of Heller, Paul Samuelson returned with him on Monday. Reportedly [41] the latter pressed hard against a tax increase. Monday was consumed in a last-ditch series of meetings that extended into an evening session at the White House.[42] It terminated with the participants in the debate having to wait until the next day, the day of the speech, to know the President's decision.

In the speech itself, economic policy was at best subordinate to the overriding issue of Berlin: "We seek peace, but we shall not surrender." The major part of his listeners' attention, emotion, and thought of survival was focused on the President's declaration of policy in Berlin and on his announced intention to enlarge the armed forces, expand the nation's military might, and embark upon a fallout-shelter program. For the economics of the crisis, he put a $3.454-billion price tag on new defense budget requests, saying, "The Secretary of the Treasury and other economic advisers assure me, however, that our economy has the capacity to bear this new request." After summarizing the recovery developments of the last quarter, he concluded,

This improved business outlook means improved revenues: and I intend to submit to the Congress in January a budget for the next fiscal year which will be *strictly in balance*. Nevertheless, should an increase in taxes be needed because of events in the next few months to achieve that balance, or because of subsequent defense crises, those increased taxes will be requested in January.[43]

Thus, the arguments against the specific proposal to increase taxes proved compelling. Recovery must not be restrained. Defense expansion could be absorbed without risking inflation. But the arguments used in favor of the increase were not to be denied; their force was applied to another discretionary area of fiscal policy—the budget for the fiscal year of 1963. In a very real sense, the price for not increasing taxes became the commitment to balance the budget. Such a commitment, especially when made almost twelve months in advance of the year involved, was far more significant than the refusal to raise taxes. It in no way jeopardized the immediate defense build-up, and it removed an almost certain threat to other Administration programs then before Congress. To the beneficiaries of federal programs it provided a reminder of the spirit of sacrifice. In creating a spirit of frugality, it provided assurances of fiscal responsibility to conservatives at home and bankers abroad. At the same time, by substituting a future stricture on spending for an immediate tax increase, it exchanged a threat to the recovery in 1961 for a brake on possible inflation in 1962. Notwithstanding frequent reinforcement by Secretary Dillon during the fall, the commitment to a balanced budget was revocable should defense needs require acceleration into full mobilization. In the final analysis, the commitment constituted an explicit endorsement of underlying economic views— in time of prosperity the budget should be balanced. The recovery of mid-1961, gathering more momentum than at first expected, provided circumstances that could not be denied. If the budget could not be balanced next year, when could it?

To Heller, the decision not to raise taxes was a battle won. The commitment to balance the budget was a far more important battle lost. To avoid raising taxes did nothing to the existing taxes which were stunting economic growth short of full employment. To impose a budget-balancing stricture on programs for the next fiscal year (that is, until July, 1963), did nothing toward building the "human capital" in which Heller was so interested through education, training, and decreased unemployment. It did nothing toward realizing the nation's economic potential. Given the commitment *and* the expanding defense expenditures *and* the deficits likely for fiscal year 1962, fiscal year 1963 would be a lean year for domestic programs.

These were the ramifications that concerned Heller in the Berlin crisis deliberation. The outcome meant a "yes, but" reaction to his expansion analysis and advice. The Administration, or, more properly, the President, accepted in principle Heller's thesis of growth to counteract the underlying weakness in the nation's economy; he understood and accepted the argument against a tax policy too restrictive to boost the growth rate. Yet in this particular application, tradition survived. Under circumstances of returning prosperity and crisis, it thrived.

Return to the Spirit

The immediacy of Berlin and the prospect of a balanced budget may have constituted two of the Council's most pressing midsummer concerns, yet they were far from its only ones. There was much, much more to the serious game of advice than a particular set of decisions. After all, the President had asked the Council to play a broader role than it had in the previous administration, "to return to the spirit as well as the letter of the Employment Act." After all, there were many facets to Heller's goal for the Council of helping to develop "policies that will bring the economy back to full potential." If the President wanted to move on many fronts, so did Heller; if the President had a thirst for information and a willingness to be educated, if he sought conflicting advice in its raw unreconciled form, Heller's Council would respond. If conflicting advice was competitive, his Council would compete. If three Council members and a small professional staff were off and running in January, they were still running by the end of the year, along with additional colleagues and a corps of part-time consultants. As John Lewis was to comment two years later, "I thought Keyserling worked hard until I saw Heller." [44] Yet such was the pace of the 1961 New Frontier.

Once the recovery began to blossom, the immediate focus on countercyclical policies expanded into considerations of such challenges as economic growth, wage-price stability, manpower development, the plight of the cost-squeezed consumer, and the future of small entrepreneurs among corporate giants. Developing technology led to studies of its impact on the economy, of conservation of natural resources, and of the direction of research and development. The balance-of-payment problems not only required constant attention but seemed to serve as a springboard to a whole host of international economic considerations, not the least of which was the international monetary system and its liquidity problem. The overriding concern for peace in a troubled world led to studies of the economics of disarmament and defense cutbacks. Concern on these many frontiers of policy meant a great outpouring of studies, memoranda, and position papers, much of which went directly to the President, to the White House staff, to interested agencies, or to interagency committees needing vehicles and sounding boards for their deliberations and consensus. These multidimensional concerns influenced the Council's own composition and operations; it ramified into its participation in a variety of specific issues in 1961, such as the Transportation Bill, the trade expansion program, the Housing Act of 1961, and overall planning.

Reportedly instigated by Sorensen and Feldman in the White House, the Transportation Bill was an effort to move in on a program that had originated in the Department of Commerce under Sinclair Weeks but from which little had emerged.[45] Kermit Gordon and Charles Taff, the Council's staff consultant on transportation from the University of Maryland, participated in an informal task force headed by Clarence L. Martin, Jr., Under Secretary of Commerce for Transportation. They played a leading part in the development of the proposed legislation, much of which was actually drafted in the Council's offices. Because the bill involved both financial assistance to and economic regulation of the transportation industry, it was a politically sensitive matter to Commerce (particularly the Bureau of Public Roads). Correspondingly, the Interstate Commerce Commission and the Urban Renewal Administration of HHFA, as well as the relevant committees of Congress and the Council as Administration spokesman, wanted to assure equitable treatment of surface, water, and air carriers, not to mention shippers, travelers, and affected communities. The Council, representing the President and having the least at stake institutionally, fulfilled the drafting and arbitrating roles.

With a lesser degree of active participation, Gordon also joined in the drafting of the Trade Expansion Act, which for the most part was handled from the White House by Howard Peterson.[46] Gordon's involvement in the Housing Act of 1961 centered in his role as chairman of an *ad hoc* committee on housing credit.

Planning was not so much a specific substantive issue as a policy and managerial concept that achieved renewed relevance under the aegis of maximum employment, production, and purchasing power. If there was to be full utilization of the nation's resources, especially of its labor force, and if the economy was to develop to its full potential, then some rational consideration had to be given to the direction of the government's economic policies and to its own activities that contributed some 20 percent to GNP. Full potential was a goal, and the reaching of it required planning and conscious coordination or at least an awareness of the cost of noncoordination. Considering their relatively higher growth rates, the Administration could not ignore the economic planning being developed within the Common Market countries. Despite obvious institutional and political differences, the operation of France's Commissariat du Plan was of particular interest to the Administration.

Under these circumstances, the Council made a modest and tentative proposal for one possible instrument for more rational economic planning, the "full employment budget" which was originally linked in the 1940s with Gerhard Colm. Seeking to develop interest and cooperation on the part of American business, Heller in October, 1961, presented a model for "full employment perspective . . . as a basis for government and business planning" to a group of technical consultants of the Business Council's Committee on the Domestic Economy.[47] As a "conditional decision model" indicating possibilities rather than forecasting, it was supposed to guide government and business action toward achieving a high utilization economy. Shortly thereafter Heller told the National Planning Association at the establishment of its Center for Priority Analysis that fulfillment of such a goal involved the proper allocation of resources and hence the establishment of priorities and determination of cost-benefit relationships. Heller's concern for planning was complemented by that of Bell, who as Director of the Budget Bureau, was interested in planning for rational, coordinated, long-term commitment of government resources. It was from this managerial view-point that he urged departments and agencies to develop five-year budgets, out of which could be prepared the annual budgets on which the Congress still insisted.

Planning as a procedure was one thing; as a substantive policy objective it was something else. At the presidential level, planning was more a matter of academic concern than a basis for concrete action. The Business Council representatives were reportedly cool to what struck them as a device for more direct government involvement in their decisions and activities. For an analysis of the Heller Council, however, the outcome of its interest in planning in 1961 is less significant than the evidence it supplies of the Council's initiative and of its aggregative approach to full employment economic policy. Along with its analysis and advice on the full range of economic matters concerning the Chief Executive, the case reflects the Council's characteristics stemming from its composition as well as demonstrating its internal and external operations.

By the end of its first year, the Heller Council had accumulated a staff of nineteen professional economists in addition to the services of another nineteen economists [48] retained on a part-time consultant basis. Taken as a whole, the professional staff was essentially a group of young, recently-trained academicians who were by and large without prior government experience but who were eager to apply on a temporary basis their expertise to the manifold challenges of the New Frontier. As a measure of their professional objectivity, it is unlikely that they would have responded to a call from a Burns, a Saulnier, or, hypothetically, a Milton Friedman under a Nixon Administration. Nor is it likely that they would have been asked. They were primarily Keynesian with a heavy quantitative orientation. The average age of the fourteen newcomers (that is, excluding Mrs. Furlong, Miss James, Kaplan, Lusher, and Stettner), was thirty-two. Eleven had completed Ph.D. degrees since 1956. Two, Richard E. Attiyeh and Sidney G. Winter, Jr., had not completed their doctorates at the time of their appointments. Eight came directly from faculty positions: Barbara R. Berman from Harvard University, Rashi Fein from the University of North Carolina,

Richard Nelson from Carnegie Institute of Technology, Arthur M. Okun from Yale University, Lee E. Preston and Lloyd Ulman from the University of California at Berkeley, Vernon W. Ruttan from Purdue University, and Robert M. Solow from the Massachusetts Institute of Technology. Three joined the Council staff almost directly from their doctoral studies: Charles A. Cooper from the Massachusetts Institute of Technology, Richard N. Cooper from Harvard University, and George L. Perry from the University of Minnesota. Of the remaining two, Leroy Wehrle came directly from an operating assignment with the U.S. government in Laos and Sidney G. Winter, Jr., was recruited from the RAND Corporation. Attiyeh, Nelson, Wehrle, and Winter had been recent graduate students at Yale University. Only two, in addition to Wehrle, had had prior government experience: Miss Berman had served four years as an economist with the Bureau of Labor Statistics, and Fein had been a Bureau of the Census statistician for a year.[49]

Of this group of fourteen, eight were to leave in 1962 and six in 1963. Stettner, from the previous Saulnier staff, was also to resign in 1962 to accept a position with the Organization for Economic Co-operation and Development (OECD). Okun, Solow, Perry, and Ulman were to return to the campuses from which they had come, while Miss Berman and Richard Cooper were to accept new appointments at Brandeis and Yale Universities, respectively. Fein was to accept a position at The Brookings Institution, and Charles Cooper and Winter were to join the RAND Corporation, to which Nelson was to return. Ruttan was to join the Rockefeller Foundation operation in the Philippines, and Wehrle was to return to Laos to take on a succession of two new assignments with the U.S. Mission there. Many of this original staff, however, were to form the nucleus of "alumni" who were to continue to associate with the Council. Both Coopers, Fein, Nelson, Perry, Preston, and Ulman were to serve as consultants in subsequent years; Okun was to become a Council member.

Although the nineteen part-time consultants were retained to supplement the new and active permanent staff, more significantly their expertise and experience were needed on an *ad hoc* basis dealing with the variety of particular problems with which the Council was concerned. Association with the Council was hardly a new experience to Henry Briefs, Burton Klein, Pechman, or Schultze, who would soon join the Budget Bureau as an Assistant Director. Charles Taff and Robert Triffin had also worked with earlier Councils. Samuelson was no newcomer to the Kennedy economic policy-makers. The others, including Kenneth J. Arrow, Martin Bronfenbrenner, James Duesenberry, and Eckstein, were established professionals available for specific and part-time assignments with the Council. On the basis of salary figures and estimates for fiscal years of 1962 and 1963 and assuming salary levels generally comparable to those of the full-time staff, it is apparent that these consultants constituted approximately 10 percent of the Council's professional resource.[50]

From the Council's staffing experience of 1961 there emerged a three-fold staffing pattern: the career professionals, such as Lusher and Kaplan along with statisticians Miss James and Mrs. Furlong, the academic professionals, who comprised the largest group but served for short periods of time, and the consultants, who came and went in accordance with both their own academic schedules and the Council's special projects or its *Report*-writing season. It was as if the first group were the distance runners who pounded away in a year-after-year stride, the second group were the sprinters who ran at a sixty-hour-a-week pace for a year and who then retired to benefit and recoup, and the third group were the individuals who dominated the field events. All did their bit, all served as essential teammates for the Council members who coached, captained, and ran with them.

And as the teams or combinations of the same Council varied from time to time, so did the emphasis of the Council's work and the nature of its operations. The balance between continuity and Council experience, on the one hand, and new blood and outside views on the other had a bearing on the pace the Council could maintain, on the combination of issue-events in which it could participate. Large-scale turnover may have provided the Council with a corps of bright well-trained individuals and subsequently of campus-based disciples, but it also posed a constant problem of recruitment, and it necessitated constant shifting of assignments, breaking in of new people, and renewing of outside contacts. The Council's transient character affected personal relationships among the staff; stints of Council experience often led to new positions, new associations, and new professional interests. These were all staffing matters with which Heller grappled during the first year. It was out of them that he fashioned the Council's method of operating.

Under Heller's active direction, the Council members as a group were the center of activities. They were the initiators and coordinators; each had his particular area of activity. In addition to general leadership, Heller handled fiscal and monetary matters as well as education and welfare. Tobin concentrated on theory and overall economic analysis and the international monetary and balance-of-payments fields. As indicated above, Gordon became the chief projects or operating man. There was no formal division of the creative and analytical aspects of the Council's work between the Council members and the professional staff. Policy consideration was not the province of presidential appointees alone. Their responsibility for determining or articulating the Council's position on particular issues did not preclude staff members from researching on their own initiative, arguing, or drafting; indeed, all such activities were expected of them and by them.

The approximate division of work among the Council members was not matched by a parallel trifurcation of the staff. Rather, there was a fluid matching of individual areas of interest and competence with the particular fields of economic policy in which the Council was active. This matching meant a localizing around such poles as balance of payments, international economics, defense and disarmament, economic growth, manpower, consumer economics, natural resources, the economics of technology, and research and development.[51] But assignments shifted with priorities and pressures. "Lead guys" for one project would not necessarily fill the same role on the next. Competence was expected in more than one or two related areas, and special skills were contributed to the work of the Council as a whole, particularly at *Economic Report* time.

Under such arrangements, the informality, characteristic of the Council since the days of Nourse, took on a particularly youthful, collegiate, and somewhat hectic air as Heller drove them from project to project. There was no formal chain of command. Presidential appointees, "whizz kids," and consultants were soon on a first-name basis. Working contacts between staff and Council members were direct and frequent. Although Okun and Solow occasionally filled roles as fourth and fifth Council members, their standing was transitory and dependent upon the issues and projects of the moment.

The pervasive association and mixing that characterized internal operations, however, did not carry over to its external affairs. By no means entirely, but for the most part, external operations were handled by the Council members themselves and to a far lesser degree by senior staff men such as Solow, Okun, and Lusher. Considering the newness to Washington of so many of the young staff, this situation was not surprising. Informal association and exchanges of information with counterparts in other agencies, particularly in the Budget Bureau, was one thing, but representing the Council on committees and work groups was something else. This limitation of inexperience notwithstanding, a Council that had flung itself into a wide range of activities on behalf of the Chief Executive and that wished to continue the good relations established in January found itself committed to the time-consuming occupation of developing and maintaining a wide range of contacts not only with the President and the White House but also with Congress, departments and agencies, foreign governments, and leaders of business, labor, agriculture, and the economics profession. As the description of "Council Activities" in the 1962 *Economic Report*[52] makes clear, this occupation took the form of extensive direct contact and participation in a wide variety of standing and *ad hoc* committees.

The Council's contacts with the President were for the most part maintained by Heller, who reportedly never encountered any difficulty arranging an appointment when he so desired. Periodically Kennedy would meet with the Council members as a group or with any combination of two or with Gordon and Tobin individually. On particular occasions, he also conferred with Okun and Solow. Much of the White House association focused on Sorensen, Myer Feldmen, and Carl Kaysen. As had been determined by the President at the time of Heller's appointment, there was no counterpart to Gabriel Hauge or Donald Paarlberg, who served as White House economist and intermediary.

The most regularized contact between the Council, the Budget Bureau, and the Treasury grew out of the so-called "Troika" (or "Triad") group. This committee was suggested by Heller and, composed of Dillon, Bell, and Heller, it met regularly to assemble for the President the latest possible picture of the economy and the budgetary-revenue situation. One of its major "exercises" was the preparation each fall of the budget and revenue estimates for the coming fiscal year. The Troika arrangement of the presidential appointees was extended to two subordinate levels of second- and third-level officials of the three agencies who collaborated in the preparation of data for their principals. In more or less constant touch throughout the year, they assumed some of the nature of Lusher's by then defunct "Tuesday Group." Lusher himself was one of the Council participants in the Troika group.

A result of this arrangement was a closer association between the respective departments—one that was not limited to Dillon, Bell, and Heller but that penetrated into their respective staffs. As individuals these three apparently had a more congenial relationship than had Burns, Humphrey, and Dodge. All were Kennedy men by conviction and nature; all were realists. During 1961 Dillon most closely reflected (and contributed to) the President's economic thinking, at the same time enjoying a social rapport with him not experienced by the others. If Bell experienced a closer relationship with the President than did Heller, it grew out of the massive and constant governmentwide concerns of operating policy characteristic of his Bureau. The respective advisory, managerial-budgetary, and fiscal operations of Heller, Bell, and Dillon led not to basic conflict but to different shadings of emphasis on priorities, strategies, and tactics.

Reflecting the fiscal emphasis of Kennedy's economic policy, the Council's relations with the Federal Reserve Board were cordial and frequent but less active than its relations with the Treasury and the Budget Bureau. When monetary policy was an active factor, Troika was expanded into the "Quadriad" to include William McChesney Martin, but, as the Council's 1962 *Economic Report* was to indicate, this enlarged group met only "periodically" with the President to review monetary developments, issues, and policies.[53] One particular area of association centered in international monetary affairs. Martin was a member of Heller's delegation to the Economic Policy Committee of OECD. Over time, Martin may have developed a greater commitment to full-employment objectives. His concern for stability was respected and in large measure shared by the President. Federal Reserve Board interest rate policies and open market operations were not at variance with Administration views during 1961, but "the Fed" continued to operate largely on its own.

Relations with the White House and participation in the Troika and the Quadriad were only part of the Council's external operations. It was fully involved in a proliferation of committees, work groups, and task forces that crossed agency lines, linked with other governments, or involved the UN. Council participation in interdepartment committees ranged from membership in the Economic Growth Study Committee to the Special Advisory Committee on the Statistical Abstract. Reflecting the perceived importance of international economic policy, the Council was involved in such activities as the Interdepartmental Committee of Under Secretaries in Foreign Economic Policy. Heller, Tobin, Gordon, and Solow all became involved in the work of OECD and the economic policy operations of the UN.[54]

Relations with Congress and with nongovernmental groups were as important but not as extensive. The Council followed up its initial presentation to the Joint Economic Committee with subsequent testimony in April and again in June on international exchange and payment matters. Tobin testified before the Senate Committee on Banking and Currency in support of the Administration's "Truth-in-Lending Bill." [55] In addition to the October meeting with the Business Council already described, the Council met briefly with the Economic Policy Committee of the AFL-CIO. An overworked Council had little opportunity to do more. Far more significant in the informal and day-to-day sense were the individual and informal contacts with professional colleagues at The Brookings Institution, the Committee for Economic Development, and the National Planning Association.

The internal and external operations of the Council sooner or later focused on the preparation of the President's *Economic Report* as the annual statement of the President's stewardship of the nation's economic welfare and the Council's interpretation of that stewardship. Even as the Administration turned in the fall of 1961 to the specific fulfillment of the commitment to a balanced budget for the fiscal year of 1963, so did the Council. The legislative review and budget mark-up sessions in the White House and Budget Bureau were matched by the Council's own mobilization efforts to create a document "setting forth" existing and needed "levels of employment, production, and purchasing power," the "current and foreseeable trend," a review of economic conditions, and a program with recommendations for carrying out policy objectives of maximum employment, production, and purchasing power.[56] It was the Council's maiden *Economic Report to the President*, and its preparation was approached with care and thoroughness.

Care and thoroughness were collaborative undertakings. Major content emphasis was determined by Heller with Tobin and Gordon, but consultants and staff members such as Solow all had a hand in conceiving, drafting, reviewing, and redrafting. The final product was indeed a Council document. As the Council members of two years later were to tell the staff preparing the 1964 *Economic Report*, "We want most staff members to devote a respectable share of their time from now on to planning, collecting, and analyzing materials, and drafting major pieces of the *Report*."[57]

The approximate division of work was essentially vertical; that is, the major sections or chapters were divided among groups, each of which developed and put together their respective portions into approximately final form. The method was in marked contrast to the more centralized and horizontal Burns approach, whereby information and analyses were gathered by the staff but the final drafting was done almost entirely by Burns. Undoubtedly, the *Economic Report of the President* and the Council's own *Report to the President* encouraged this relative delegation and participation characteristic of the Heller Council. Admittedly, the drafting of the former, which was a policy rather than an analytical document, was done primarily by collaborating with Sorensen in the White House and to a lesser degree with Tobin and Gordon. Whereas the President's part of the *Economic Report* went through a formal clearance with the major departments and agencies concerned, the Council's own *Report to the President* made the rounds for comments and suggestions but with no commitment to formal clearance. The Treasury, for instance, subjected both portions to careful scrutiny.

Given the recovery that by late 1961 was exceeding expectations, the *Economic Report's* recounting of the year's economic developments posed no great problem; it was viewed as a success story, and the Council could deal with it in a straightforward manner. Forecasting the future was something far more difficult. The policy objective of promoting economic growth offset by the commitment to balance the budget made it difficult to perceive what the future held in store; it made it difficult to explain fulfillment of both growth and balance; and it was difficult to develop positive policy recommendations for "maximum employment and production."

The Council's resolving of their dilemmas would not be revealed until January 20, 1962, nine days after the President's State of the Union Message and two days after the Budget Message. In a sense, the pressures and problems of putting together that first *Economic Report* symbolized the accomplishment of the Heller Council for its first year. Wrapped up in it were the realities of returning to "the spirit as well as the letter of the Employment Act." Responding to the call of the New Frontier, the Council had been aggressive in its establishment, tactful in its operation, and prodigious in its output. It had kept a receptive and knowledgeable President abundantly supplied with information, interpretations, and ideas. In the hard, cold measure of impact on specific economic policy decisions, it registered significant accomplishment: winning liberalization of Social Security benefits as a countercyclical move, helping to shape transportation and trade bills, aiding in the development of the monetary "twist" policy, helping to keep mortgage rates down, developing the rationale of the wage-price guideposts, and gaining reversal of the Berlin tax increase decision. For these alone, the 1961 Heller Council must be regarded as successful and worthy of recognition as a body of expert economic presidential advisers.

Despite these accomplishments, however, despite the fact that Kennedy shared Heller's basic economic objectives, understood modern economics, and accepted in principle his Council's analysis and advice, the Administration did not surrender its underlying traditional economic policy assumptions and values. To what degree such a hold was balanced between the Administration's or Kennedy's own convictions, on the one hand, and the recognition that the public and Congress had to be led, on the other, is hard to say. But, based on the commitment to balance the budget for the fiscal year of 1963 alone, it is apparent that the Council's chief had not yet made the break. Perhaps in terms of the Council's relative inexperience, the parallel newness of the Kennedy Administration, the events of the year at home and abroad, it would have been premature to expect a development of such magnitude. Whether or not the Heller Council's destiny lay permanently in important but piecemeal, rather than in fundamental, successes would depend upon the next year's combinations of pressures and opportunities, of beliefs and circumstances.

VII. TAX REDUCTION AND THE NEW TRADITION

The Council started 1962 by having to live with the extremely clear articulation of continuing tradition it had helped to draft. In fulfillment of the commitment to balance the budget for fiscal year 1963, made at the time of the Berlin crisis, the President's State of the Union Message, his Budget Message, and his *Economic Report* all spoke of continued growth, high employment, and price stability, but in a voice of restraint. The three documents charted a course between the Scylla of recession and the Charybdis of inflation. To have cleared one in 1961 meant not foundering on the other in 1962; a balanced budget was to be the North Star:

The Federal Government is expected to operate in 1963 with some surplus. This is the policy which seems appropriate at the present time. The economy is moving strongly forward, with employment and income rising. The prospects are favorable for further rises in the coming year in private expenditures, both consumption and investment. To plan a deficit under such circumstances would increase the risk of inflationary pressures damaging alike to our domestic economy and to our international balance of payments. On the other hand, we are still far short of full capacity use of plant and manpower. To plan a larger surplus would risk choking off economic recovery and contributing to a premature downturn.[1]

The President could contemplate in his *Economic Report* the attainment of a $600-billion GNP in 1963 and the development of opportunities under " 'maximum' use of productive capacity now lying idle and capacity yet to be created," he could describe an economic growth rate of 4½ percent "within our range of capabilities during the 1960s," he could speak of further help to "our low income fellow citizens" and of the need to balance "our international transactions," and he could go so far as to hold out the prospect of a GNP of $570 billion for 1962. These possibilities were, however, all limited by the constraints of a budget "appropriately paced to the expected rate of economic expansion." The well-tempered balance that would yield a surplus of $500 million also would be just "vigilant" enough to restrain inflation without inhibiting sustained recovery and just "flexible" enough to stimulate the economy should recovery fall short of expectations.[2] By implication, the existing tax structure would sustain, not restrain, consumption and investment.

The bywords in economic policy recommendations thus became "effectiveness" and "stability" rather than "expansion" and "potential." "A Program for Sustained Prosperity" as providing "defense-in-depth against future recessions"[3] consisted of standby tax reduction authority, standby capital improvements authority, and a strengthening of the federal-state unemployment compensation system. None of these defenses represented proposed additions to the new budget; all were based on a "trigger" principle of springing into effect if appropriate economic conditions developed. Although the proposed standby tax reduction authority was expressed in the general terms of Employment Act objectives, the conditions activating the capital improvement authority and unemployment compensation were expressed in terms of specific changes in unemployment statistics. The standby tax reduction authority proposals had first been broached in the Samuelson Report of the previous year. Standby public works programs had long been part of the standard set of countercyclical considerations. Though rejecting a public works program urged by Senator Joseph Clark the preceding May, Kennedy promised to include some form of Clark's ideas in the Administration's 1962 program. A similar unemployment compensation proposal had been ignored by the first session of Congress, which now was asked to implement it.

Other "measures for a stronger economy" focused on strengthening the nation's financial system (largely in the form of an exhortation to consider the July, 1961, recommendations of the Commission on Money and Credit which the *Economic Report* endorsed, coupled with recommendations for the demonetizing of silver), developing the nation's manpower through enactment of the Manpower Development and Training Act and the Youth Employment Opportunities Act (both originally submitted in 1961), as well as revitalizing the U.S. Employment Service, tightening the Welfare and Pension Plans Disclosure Act, and "strengthening our tax system." [4] The last suggested measure was essentially a restatement of the April, 1961, modified tax proposals resulting from the House Ways and Means Committee's scrutiny and review during the preceding summer and fall.

The key investment credit feature of the modified proposals had been simplified to an 8 percent credit against the tax for gross investment in depreciable machinery and equipment instead of the originally recommended rates of 15, 10, and 6 percent depending upon the amount of increased investment. Consistent with the original proposals, the entire package of investment credit and structural reform in the new version would involve no net revenue loss. As in the cases of previous summaries of tax proposals, the President asserted that a major tax revision would soon be forthcoming:

Later this year, I shall present to the Congress a major program of tax reform. This broad program will re-examine tax rates and the definition of the income tax base. It will be aimed at the simplification of our tax structure, the equal treatment of equally situated persons and the strengthening of incentives for individual effort and for productive investment.[5]

Taken as a whole, the budget and proposed economic programs were the President's, the products of his convictions and those of both Secretary Dillon and the President's immediate staff. These products had the endorsement of Budget Director Bell and presumably the acquiescence, though unenthusiastic, of Goldberg and Hodges. The White House's reputed acceptance of Heller and respect for his views were overwhelmed by the combined force of political pressures and program commitments. Heller could not compete with the gravitational pull of the surviving economic tradition, which held, even if perhaps reluctantly, the President and, it was assumed, legislators and voters. Thus, the President's preview of coming attractions gave scant recognition to the analysis that unfolded on subsequent pages of the Council's *Annual Report to the President*. The President's *Economic Report* to the Congress and the nation, which was an exposition of policies, preached growth while recommending stability; the Council, in its analytical *Annual Report* to the President, Congress, and the nation, supported stability while justifying growth—and both these *Reports* were between the covers of one document. The Council's analysis argued for full recovery and full utilization of resources; it proposed the standard of a full-employment surplus.

Objectives of maximum employment ("or to put it the other way round—minimum unemployment") and full production underpinned the Council's program for 1962.[6] Unemployment of 4 percent was a "modest" goal for stabilization policy alone.[7] The production focus was on the gap between actual and potential, which in the first quarter of 1961 was figured as $51 billion and in the last quarter as $28 billion (annual rates).[8] The production potential for 1962 was estimated at $580 billion.[9] Looking ahead even further, "a full utilization economy in 1963 would provide nearly 72 million civilian jobs and generate an estimated $600-billion GNP (1961 prices)." [10]

Although the projected $570-billion GNP for 1962 proved to be overly optimistic, the annual rate of growth of 11 percent at current prices for the preceding three quarters [11] made the attainment seem entirely possible at the time it was proposed. In fact, "a somewhat higher figure is likely if the Congress enacts promptly the Administration's proposed tax credit for investment." [12] What is more, if balanced expenditures and revenues (with a slight surplus) materialized and supported continued prosperity, price stability, and balance of payments improvement, then the $570-billion GNP became something of a necessity. The Council's analysis of prospects enabled it to rationalize budget balancing as prudent and the standby measures as appropriate insurance. Given on one hand expenditures based upon necessary governmental activities and, on the other, "the blindly symmetrical" effects of the built-in stabilizers within the tax system, "discretionary budget policy, e.g., changes in tax rates or expenditure programs, is indispensable—sometimes to reinforce, sometimes to offset, the effect of the stabilizers." [13] Standby authority covering capital improvements, temporary tax reduction authority, and unemployment compensation would provide the necessary discretion and flexibility.

Support for the Administration's standby proposals as well as for the investment incentive tax proposals that would be taken up again by the Congress did not preclude the Council's putting its major emphasis on economic growth and, in doing so, focusing attention on consumption:

Faster economic growth in the United States requires, above all, an expansion of demand, to take up existing slack and to match future increases in capacity. Unless demand is adequate to buy potential output, accelerating the growth of potential is neither an urgent problem nor a promising possibility.[14]

It is the preeminence of demand "now and in the years ahead" (as Heller was to tell the Joint Economic Committee) [15] that underlies first the emphasis on a feasible growth rate of approximately 4.5 percent per year for the decade, and secondly, investment in human resources, technological progress, plant and equipment, natural resources, and housing.[16]

The most potent supporting argument for recovery and growth was the concept of the full-employment surplus based upon the companion concept of the national income accounts budget. The former is defined as "a measure of the restrictive or expansionary impact of a budget program on over-all demand." [17] The latter represents a classifying of federal transactions in accordance with national income and product accounts for the economy. Because its operations within the national income accounts framework allows for comprehensive analysis of the economic impact of federal fiscal policy, it is becoming an increasingly important complement to the conventional administrative budget and the consolidated cash budget. The administrative budget is essentially a legal instrument referring to the allocation of funds and is more a management than an economic tool. It operates on a cash basis; net loan and credit transactions are included, but trust fund transactions, which in 1962 approached $25 billion per year, are excluded. The consolidated cash budget is also computed on a cash basis but includes both net credit transactions and trust fund transactions along with congressional appropriations. Although its consolidated measure of cash transactions with the public make it more valuable for economic analysis of fiscal policy than the administrative budget, its failure to distinguish, for example, between spending and lending transactions limits its usefulness. The national income accounts budget concept shows federal receipts and expenditures on an accrual basis; it includes trust fund transactions and excludes net credit transactions that, although economically significant, can more appropriately be treated as aspects of monetary and credit policy. Such a concept excludes transactions that affect liquidity rather than current income; it distinguishes between expenditures for goods and services and transfer payments and, by computing corporate income and tax payments on an accrual rather than cash basis, it permits fiscal policy analysis that realistically recognizes corporate spending decisions.

As a measure of restrictive or expansionary impact of budgetary programs, the full-employment surplus concept provides a basis for analyzing both existing and proposed policies. Concerned with the impact of discretionary programs rather than with that of automatic stabilizers, the concept distinguishes between the restrictive or expansionary effect of a given fiscal program under varying economic conditions on one hand and the restrictive-expansionary aspects of possible fiscal program alternatives under given or desired economic situations on the other hand. The concept subjects economic policy alternatives to measures of the ratio of actual to potential GNP ("utilization rate") as well as to measures of budgetary surplus or deficit as a percentage of potential GNP. Although not a perfect measure, because it does not reflect changes in the composition of the budget, the full-employment surplus concept establishes criteria for evaluating the impact of possible changes in federal expenditures and tax rates both on the economy as a whole and on private demand. Consequently, the concept is far more than a passive measuring device but, in conjunction with the national income accounts budget, constitutes a rationale for justifying expansionary policy.[18]

The Council's *Economic Report's* explanation of the concept suggests what might have happened if the economy had been operating at full employment. The underlying assumption is that, generally speaking, "one budget program is more expansionary than another if it has a smaller full employment surplus."[19] By implication, the *Economic Report* asks whether there can be too large a full-employment surplus and, if so, whether current budget policy is too restrictive. Given the Council's emphasis on the gap between actual and potential GNP, its long-standing concern for the underlying weakness of the economy, its equally constant attack on blindly symmetrical tax policies, and the tentative nature of its forecasts for 1962, particularly regarding inventories and investment, the well-hedged answer to both questions is "yes":

As the economy returns to the full employment track, the full employment surplus will need to be kept from growing indefinitely, and perhaps be reduced. The choice—or rather the division, for it is unlikely to be an "either-or" matter—is between reductions in tax receipts and increases in government expenditures, whether Federal, State or local. A pragmatic decision will almost certainly involve both. It is unlikely that the most urgent unmet needs of the population will lie all in the area of private consumption or all in the areas traditionally allotted to public consumption and investment. Undoubtedly much of the reduction in the full employment surplus should be channeled directly to private purchasing power, just as most, by far, of present consumption spending is in private hands. The choice of a balance between public and private expenditures is an important choice for society. It should be made consciously through the normal democratic processes. And it should be made by weighing the urgency of alternative uses of resources, rather than by appeal to simple slogans on one side or the other.[20]

The Council's explicit analysis and implicit advocacy of the full-employment surplus concept did not constitute recommendations that would have to be acted upon by the Kennedy Administration. Nor was the Council's exposition an attack on the President and his commitment to a balanced budget for fiscal 1963. Rather, the thesis was an attack upon the concept of balanced budgets as the objective of economic policy and, as such, provided concepts which could justify an unbalanced budget through an increase in expenditures, a tax reduction, or combinations thereof. Given the Council's convictions, the standby recommendations—billed as the Council's proposals to the President—were indeed pale shadows of what it would have preferred to fight for. Still, unfolding developments of 1962 would in their exposure of the lag between "conventional wisdom" and necessary action, thrust largely unanticipated challenges and pressures upon the Council's views, at least unanticipated so soon.

The Pause That Refreshes Not

Consideration of the President's economic prospects and programs for 1962 had scarcely been dropped from editorial comment and the hearings agenda of the Joint Economic Committee when the recovery of 1961 began to sputter. Early March readings by the Council and Department of Commerce showed that although GNP for the fourth quarter of 1961 had increased $16.4 billion (annual rates at current prices), the rates of gross private domestic investment and of inventory accumulation had both slowed down. Weekly hours of work had declined slightly; housing starts for November, December, and January had declined relative both to immediately preceding months and to the same months of the preceding year; and the balance-of-payments deficit had increased during the fourth quarter although at a slower rate than in the third quarter. Little comfort could be found in the slight decrease of 0.2 percent in unemployment during February.[21]

At both his March 7 and 14 press conferences, the President had to field questions about "the slowdown in our recovery":

And I think that we should wait till—let the winter go, and let's see what happens in February and March, then we can make a judgment as to whether there is a recovery.[22]

No, I stated to [the labor leaders] that, of course, we were not as happy about January, that the figures in January were not as high as we hoped they would be. The preliminary estimates we've got now for February indicated that February is much better. . . . I think we should wait.[23]

Despite admonition to the public to wait, private concern within the Administration over the debilitating calm became sufficiently acute to spur action. The area redevelopment proposals were before Congress, the standby public works measure had gone to the Hill on February 19, and appeals by the President for action on improving unemployment compensation had twice been made during the month. At the urging of Heller and labor leaders the Administration also rushed to the Congress a draft amendment to the standby public works measure calling for a capital improvement program that would make $600 million immediately available to some 958 eligible labor surplus areas.

While encouraging these measures, Kennedy and Secretary of Labor Goldberg were conscious of the inflationary peril and urged steel workers and management to act with restraint in their contract negotiations. In effect, exerting their personal and institutional prestige on behalf of the public interest, the two men had been endeavoring to develop an era of cooperation between traditional adversaries by having both parties agree to a noninflationary contract. Letters from the President to industry leaders in the preceding September, the tying of wage increases to productivity in accordance with guidelines developed by the Council, and the Administration's constant kibitzing on negotiations reflected a deep concern for labor-management peace and price stability, particularly in the economy's bellwether steel industry.

The sudden and totally unexpected announcement by U.S. Steel of $6-a-ton price increase on April 10, barely two weeks after the noninflationary wage settlement, jarred the Administration to its foundations. Betrayed, it thought, it could do nothing on behalf of its prestige and the nation's welfare but apply swiftly and without compromise its awesome resources of presidential leadership, investigative powers, and contractual leverage. By all accounts, Walter Heller and the Council were leading participants in the development of the seventy-two-hour campaign that forced U.S. Steel to rescind its price increase.[24] The President's economic advisers helped to determine the strategy of trying to persuade major steel producers such as Inland, Armco, and Kaiser to hold the price line. Based in part upon the Council's earlier analysis of the steel industry, it joined with Labor Department economists in developing within the first twenty hours following U.S. Steel's announcement the Administration's economic argument that, contrary to U.S. Steel's contention, a price rise was not necessary.

As summarized in a subsequently completed Council "White Paper," the arguments focused upon the recent and predicted stability of labor costs, the decline in the price of raw materials, the adverse impact of recession and underutilization—and not of labor costs, as U.S. Steel contended—on profits, and the disadvantages of raising prices as a means of financing capital improvements. The White Paper also argued that, if prices were raised, the steel industry's position vis-à-vis domestic and foreign competition would worsen, the balance of payments deficit would increase, economic stability would be threatened, federal budget expenditures would increase, and the likelihood of reducing unemployment among steel workers would be reduced.[25] McConnell may rightly attribute "the real power" in the steel price struggle to the market place,[26] but it was the power of the Presidency, the articulation of which was strengthened by expert economic advice regarding the market place, that brought about the reversal by U.S. Steel's Roger Blough on Friday, April 13.

Barely was this struggle over than the market break of late May thrust another crisis upon the nation and the Administration, forceably reminding another administration of the crash of 1929. Confident of its own analysis, the Kennedy Administration could argue that plummeting Dow-Jones averages reflected not weakness in the economy or in the government, not reaction to government meddling, but rather a recognition that the government and the nation were winning a battle against inflation and that the stock market prices were too high relative to both earnings and overall price stability. Yet, the steel crisis and the market break together, occurring within a six-week period, laid bare business distrust of government, particularly a Democratic government headed by a Kennedy who was not so conservative after all. The two events shattered a chilly calm of cooperation with business that Kennedy had been trying hard to improve upon. The crisis brought to the fore once again the thirty-year-old issues of government interference in business affairs and of government's role in the economy.

Crises and acrimony deepened the gloom and frustrating discontent that pervaded the spring of 1962. True, the steel wage settlement had in effect been ratified, and April opened with modest indications of resumed recovery. But the reports of new records in personal income and industrial activity could not hide the revelation that the increase in GNP for the first quarter had dropped to $6.8 billion annually from $16.4 billion for the preceding quarter.[27] Many of the individual increases, as welcome as they were, were less than they had been during the 1958–60 recovery. Moreover, unemployment at 5.5 percent of the civilian labor force was virtually unchanged, the balance-of-payments deficit for the 1961 fourth quarter was larger than originally estimated, and, as unreliable as they might be, stock prices were continuing to decline. With prospects of a $570-billion GNP and of a reduction to 4 percent unemployment evaporating, economic expectations were not being met. The combination of economic doldrums and business-government antagonism inevitably would cause some form of reappraisal of events and attitudes, which, for Kennedy's Administration imbued with his style of confidence and pragmatism, would be more searching than agonizing. Economic pauses do not refresh; they dull and waste and weaken.

The fact that postwar economic cycles had been progressively less impressive in their recovery and more frequent in their oscillation, largely regardless of government policies, cast doubts upon the validity of assumptions underlying those policies. The knowledge in June that fiscal 1963, far from being in balance, would instead probably close with a $4-billion deficit caused by a short-fall of revenues magnified these doubts. The persistence of unemployment, bad enough as an economic statistic but far worse in terms of human suffering and lost votes, spurred a search for alternatives. The success of and competition from Western European and Japanese economies developing under quite contrary policies and values were suggestive; their favorable balances of payments with us were compelling. The hostility of the business community with which Kennedy earnestly desired to cooperate in the interest of economic growth and stability provided a final note of exasperation.[28]

It is small wonder then that, in his commencement address at Yale on June 11, Kennedy should have asked for a sophisticated examination of the myths about big government, fiscal policy, and mutual confidence between government and business.[29] Drafted in large part out of material prepared by the Council, which had developed an unofficial "myth kit," the speech was a high point of presidential efforts to substitute understanding and reappraisal for hostility and rigid bias. During May and June, Kennedy attempted to explain his Administration's position and its need for cooperation with business groups. A White House Conference on National Economic Issues in mid-May, a Brookings Institution conference for business executives in early June, and a meeting in Washington with business executives, including Roger Blough of U.S. Steel, right after the Yale speech, were but three of the President's forums. Kennedy's exchange of correspondence in July with David Rockefeller as published in *Life* appears as another chapter in a dialog that, it was hoped, would be continued.[30] That dialogs and concern for myths did not continue to be publicly articulated seems less significant than the fact that these matters were broached at all. It was the probing of basic thinking that was important; it was the emergence in June of tax policy as the primary weapon against economic stagnation that was to test new thinking.

The Day Taxes Were Cut

Tax policy came to the fore, not suddenly but gradually during the winter and spring of 1962, pushed by the forces of circumstance, experience, and a newly emerging set of values. More specifically, realization of the potentiality of tax policy as a leading weapon against unemployment and stagnation grew out of the tax reform activity of the previous eighteen months, the success and failure of economic policies over the same period, and the growing preference for tax reduction as well as reform over other fiscal and monetary alternatives. Although analytically separate, reduction and reform were operationally intertwined in their impact upon one another and upon the nation's economy.

For its part, tax reform was on the agenda for 1962 regardless of events; it was both a "first-step" holdover from the previous year and a promised comprehensive "second-step" revision for that year. It will be recalled that the original proposals upon which the House Ways and Means Committee refused to act the preceding summer had been worked on during the fall and early winter by staff members of the Joint Committee on Internal Revenue Taxation in cooperation with Treasury specialists. Adoption of the resulting modifications had been urged by the President in his annual messages, and the House Ways and Means Committee resumed its action on the measure early in the new year. By March 13, the Committee had approved the main features of the proposals by a vote of 18 to 7 and had reported out a bill to the House a week later. In a letter of congratulations to Chairman Mills, Kennedy summarized the benefits of the measure in terms of recovery, growth, and balance of payments, and also warned that rejection

would mean a loss of gold as our industries fail to keep pace with their modernized overseas competition—a loss of jobs as our economy fails to grow—and a loss of revenue, resulting in further budget deficits, as we fail to achieve full employment before another recession, or fail to collect fair taxes on every kind of income.[31]

Although passed by a vote of 219 to 196 by the House in late March, the bill's treatment was more tortuous in the Senate, where Senator Byrd, as Chairman of the Finance Committee, registered his opposition to the bill by refusing to handle it.

The Treasury tax staff also had in the works two other reform projects, one to establish new guidelines for computing depreciation on equipment and factories and the other to develop the relatively comprehensive second-step tax reform measures. Charged by law with maintaining "reasonable" depreciation rates, the Treasury, as a spur to investment, liberalized the depreciation guidelines for textile manufacturers in 1961. In 1962 it undertook the preparation of new rates for other areas of production. Of the two actions, comprehensive tax reform was the more significant and the more heralded. Secretary Dillon reiterated in January and periodically throughout the spring his promise to propose sweeping tax reforms for 1963 to be presented to Congress later in the year.

In addition to focusing attention on the progress of the tax reform measure in the Senate, the disappointing economic developments of the spring gave new impetus to the possibility of tax reduction. Appealing in its own right as an immediate lift to the economy, tax reduction was an increasingly preferred alternative to expanding public works expenditures. Besides being too slow a process to be beneficial as an antirecession device, increasing expenditures were thought likely both to be inflationary and to grow into long-term commitments to continuing expenditures. Moreover, to propose increased expenditures was to evoke opposition to the programs they would finance or to encourage the sponsoring of pet projects that lay outside the Administration's program priorities.

Not wishing to jeopardize the outcome of Senate deliberations on the reform measure, Dillon had consistently played down the prospects for tax cuts. Early in the year he had hedged to some 600 congressional aides by speaking of a "modicum of tax reduction" and allowing that "maybe this could be the case." [32] He reportedly argued against reduction within the Administration on the basis that economic forces, other than tax stimulus, were sufficient both to stem recession and reignite recovery. More convinced of the need of tax reduction and more bullish over prospects of its acceptance, Heller kept expounding both within government circles and publicly the validity of its underlying rationale. A week after the steel-pricing controversy, he told a regional conference of the U.S. Chamber of Commerce in Los Angeles that the revised depreciation guidelines and investment incentive then before the Senate were the beginning not the end of tax revision. Anticipating the comprehensive tax revision program that would restore the tax base and adjust income tax rates, he foresaw the possibility of a tax cut:

And given the great growth potential of our economy—which, operating at full steam, adds as much as $5 to $6 billion a year to tax revenues without any change in tax rates—the prospect for eventual net tax reduction should not be ruled out. Bearing on this prospect will be questions of budgetary policy as well as the economic question of whether *levels* of taxes—not just their *structure*—are consistent with the levels of consumption and investment required by the American economy for full employment and faster growth. These are open, not closed, policy questions in Washington today.[33]

Heller's reports to the President of the achievements of European economies and of the apparent willingness of European governments to embrace deficits with confidence and success provided examples and encouragement.

The submission to Congress on May 8 of a draft and technical explanation of a bill to give the President the standby authority to reduce taxes temporarily as requested in his *Economic Report* appears as a low-key endorsement of the idea of tax reduction. True, the bill had virtually no chance of enactment. Had it not been for the earlier commitment to the proposal and for the economy then being stalemated, the bill probably could not have mustered sufficient importance for the Council and Treasury to commit the necessary resources to do the legwork, drafting, and clearance. To one of the drafters of the President's covering letters to Sam Rayburn and Lyndon Johnson, the bill's relative insignificance was revealed in the acceptance of the draft without change. Indeed, a later comment was, "I don't believe the Secretary gave it a second thought, and the White House took it lock, stock and barrel—that never would have happened with something of importance." [34] Yet, there was enough support and tacit endorsement by the President to push the standby authority bill to the Hill as grist for the mill of economic recovery, as fulfillment of a commitment, or possibly as a trial balloon on behalf of tax reduction.

The steel-price conflict and the stock-market break added both emotion and urgency to considerations of the investment incentive tax proposal because, coupled with Treasury's depreciation revision, they provided a possible "something for business" rapprochement between the Kennedy Administration and the nation's industrial, commercial, and financial leaders. The Administration was thinking in terms of a "balanced" bill in which the revenues lost from the presumably welcome investment incentive credit would be offset by the revenue increases derived from the unwelcome structural reforms. However, although the rapprochement factor might strengthen congressional support for the investment credit proposal, it would at the same time strengthen resistance to the structural reform proposals.

By June, the economic pause and the complex of surrounding circumstances forced tax policy to the center of the stage for presidential consideration and decision. To the degree that the Dow-Jones gyrations were believed accurately to reveal economic ill health, the idea of a tax cut assumed prominence. President Kennedy led off his June 7 news conference with the clearest statement to date of his thinking and his proposals. Echoing earlier reports by the Council, he struck for tax reduction by declaring that the existing tax structure exerted

too heavy a drain on a prospering economy, compared, for example, to the net drain in competing Common Market nations. If the United States were now working at full employment and full capacity, this would produce a budget surplus at present taxation rates of about $8 billion this year. It indicates what a heavy tax structure we have, and it also indicates the effects this heavy tax structure has on an economy moving out of a recession period.[35]

Such a lesson, Kennedy indicated, was taught by the feeble recoveries after the 1958 and 1960 recessions. After endorsing the investment incentives measures already before Congress and the depreciation revisions shortly to be issued, he looked ahead to the next year:

A comprehensive tax reform bill which in no way overlaps the pending tax credit and loophole-closing bill offered a year ago will be offered for action by the next Congress, making effective as of January 1 of next year an across-the-board reduction in personal and corporate income tax rates which will not be wholly offset by other reforms—*in other words, a net tax reduction.*[36]

This promise of things to come was followed by a reiteration of other fiscal measures already proposed as necessary assistance to the nation's economy. The President would not, however, provide details of his proposal nor commit himself on the possibility of recommending a cut before the next year. "Of course, this is our best judgment at this time . . . if new circumstances brought a new situation, then we would have to make other judgments." [37]

To inaugurate current deliberation and future commitment on tax reduction and reform was to subject to reexamination a whole series of policy and operating premises. True, such reexamination had been brewing for some time, but the more immediate concerns magnified it into a project of major significance for the Administration. Such magnification alerted the entire complex of interests and institutions that participate in tax policy formulation and that would be affected by the results. The more likely the prospect of basic and comprehensive tax policy revision, the more far-reaching and persistent would be the participation in the development of the revised policy, the more tax matters would take priority over other issues needing attention, attack, or support, and the more apparent would be the clusters of viewpoints along the continuum from all-out endorsement through collaboration, indifference, and competition to all-out opposition.

To describe the existing tax structure as restrictive was to emphasize the primacy of growth at the risk of endangering stability, a risk not universally acceptable. To link reform with reduction was to underscore their substantive and strategic interdependence, the precise nature of which had not been determined. To promise across-the-board reduction was to declare that stalled aggregate demand needed both consumer and investment incentives, a declaration leading to conflicting recommendations by labor and management. To talk of *net* reduction was to admit by implication the likelihood of increased deficits, the mere hint of which provoked ire from the nation's capital to the voter hinterlands.

At the level of operations, a prospective change in the expenditure-revenue relationship forced consideration of its ramifications into the full span of government programs. Any change would affect the government's ability and willingness to alter expenditures for defense, scientific, overseas, and domestic programs; it would influence debt management policies and the stabilizing force of monetary policy. To alter arrangements within the components of the revenue side would affect such specific government objectives as aiding particular industries and categories of individuals, maintaining fair competition, and shifting the distribution of income. Any change would affect the nature of the tax base, aspects of equity, and incidence between categories and subcategories of corporate and personal income. Another area affected would be the reliance upon exemptions, deductions, and credits as means of relief for the taxpayer. Of course, the nature of tax administration and enforcement would show the impact of any alterations.

It was small wonder then that the battle area grew from separate engagements over revision, reduction, and standby authority into a general tax war and that the number and variety of combatants, hitherto largely limited to the Treasury and the House Ways and Means Committee, increased to a more general mobilization. In addition to administrators and legislators, there were growing ranks of concerned lawyers and economists, accountants and collectors, entrepreneurs and executives, editors and lobbyists. All were alerted; all joined up under their particular banners varyingly equipped with statistical analyses, memoranda, testimony, draft legislation, propaganda artillery, and inside intelligence.

The Hill salient was dominated by Mills, whose views would be crucial to any ultimate decision. Who else better symbolized the constitutional power of Congress to "lay and collect taxes, duties, imposts and excises"? Mills, his Ways and Means Committee, its staff, and the staff of the Joint Committee on Internal Revenue Taxation could be neither ignored nor outflanked. Long convinced of the need for reform to broaden the base and close the loopholes, Mills was far from convinced of the need for reduction. He had no desire to jeopardize reform by encouraging reduction. He had taken no steps to consider the President's standby reduction authority proposal. The transfer to the Senate of the investment incentive measure and the other surviving components of the original 1961 tax reform proposals in no way diminished Mills' overriding influence.

Senator Byrd's opposition was even less qualified, since he had little interest in reform, and reduction of taxes without reduction of expenditures was inconceivable. His refusal to manage the Senate's consideration of the reform proposals then before it removed Byrd from the line of the battle but apparently not from the infighting. In his absence, Senator Kerr assumed responsibility for the Senate's consideration of the bill. The Senate's reception of the various provisions was anything but hospitable. As demonstrated by the protests from restaurants and hotels against the proposed restriction of business expense deductions, pressure from the affected interests was aggressive and tenacious. The day before the President's news conference, Republican Senators Morton, Carlson, and Dirksen urged that the bill before the Senate be put aside in view of Administration plans for comprehensive reform in 1963.

Under the circumstances, prospective support for reduction appeared unlikely. Only Hubert Humphrey proposed an immediate tax cut as a stimulant to the hesitant economy. The President knew well that even within his Administration support for reform *and* reduction was not unanimous and that antipathy to the latter, however qualified, was firmly based in that institution most powerful in determining tax policy, the Treasury. Addressing a meeting of financial writers in New York two nights before the President's news conference, Secretary Dillon enunciated his version of Administration policy:

I'm glad to hear such talk [about income tax reduction] as a stimulus to the economy. To me it portends a sympathetic reception to the overall income tax reform on which we have been working since last year and which was promised by the President in his tax message a year ago last April. . . . Naturally, any reduction will cost the government revenue and will bring with it the need to broaden the base of our tax structure so as to offset the reduction in whole or in part. . . . It [the tax reform program] will not be a hasty ill-considered reaction to the gyrations of the stock market.[38]

Undoubtedly aware of the President's thinking and the influence of the pressure he was under and the advice he was receiving, Dillon's concern nevertheless focused upon reform, the maintenance of revenue, and the tax views of Congress. Opportunity for comprehensive reform was contingent upon the fate of the tax measures then before the legislators. With variations and permutations, these measures were also direct and indirect concerns of members of his department. Within Surrey's office, Brazer had mobilized a staff of twenty-five economists and statisticians who were divided into groups concerned with international taxation, business taxation, personal taxation, excise taxation, and revenue estimation. As Director of Surrey's Office of Tax Legislation, Donald C. Lubick had a staff of some fifteen lawyers concentrating on the legal and legislative aspects of tax matters. These were the two staffs that had worked out the details of the 1961 reform proposals largely developed by Musgrave and Brown. The Lubick and Brazer staffs had worked with their congressional staff counterpart on modifications for 1962 and subsequently had kept tabs on the measure as it went through the House and on into the Senate. These same Treasury staffs, comprising the nucleus of the Administration's tax expertise, both prepared the depreciation schedules, soon to be published, and developed the comprehensive and climactic tax proposals. Hard at work for eighteen months, their influence was weighted with experience, numbers, and full-time application. In addition, the two groups were aided by a score of part-time consultants such as Pechman, Musgrave, Eckstein, Brown, Carl Shoup of Columbia, and Melvin I. White of Brooklyn College.

Nor was tax policy the concern solely of the analytic and legal staffs. Caplin's Bureau of Internal Revenue, as administrator of the tax laws, was also involved in a supporting role. Moreover, tax policy had to meet standards of tolerable consistency with other Treasury operations. Robert Roosa and Dewey Daane, Treasury Under Secretary and Deputy Under Secretary for Monetary Affairs, respectively, were concerned with the impact of taxes on debt management. Henry Fowler, as Under Secretary, shared Dillon's overall concern but primarily from the political point of view. Such consensus as there was focused on reform more than on reduction. There was interest in reduction but predominantly as a supporting rationalization for reform.

As of June, at best a small minority thought net reduction warranted consideration as an end in itself. Any thought of reform *and* net reduction had to be tempered by the estimates of congressional reaction. The debt ceiling and the worrisome balance-of-payments situation combined to chill enthusiasm for reduction. This enthusiasm would have to be generated by officials and persons relatively unburdened with operating responsibility for solvent financial management. The impetus would not come from Martin and the Federal Reserve Board, which, like Treasury, was concerned over economic stability. The Board was cooperating with the Treasury Department in the operation of the "twist" policy of maintaining high short-term interest rates to stem the outflow of capital and low long-term rates to aid domestic investment and growth. In the view of both institutions, to cut taxes without reducing expenditures was to invite inflation.

Support and encouragement for reduction of taxes came in part from the Departments of Labor and Commerce. Secretary of Labor Goldberg, by personal conviction and because of the pressures on him, was sensitive to continued high levels of unemployment and would favor steps that would increase disposable income for the nation's workers and cut down on unemployment. Secretary of Commerce Hodges, who as Governor had done so much to advance the development of North Carolina, was less concerned about deficits than about avoidance of recession. At the time of the stock market break in late May, he alone of the Cabinet members urged an immediate cut in personal and corporation taxes along with the announcement of new depreciation allowances. Yet, because of their respective major tasks, neither department had the opportunity nor the resources to push the cause of reduction in any sustained way. Both had other matters demanding their attention and that of the President. The two Secretaries did talk to the President, which helped the cause, and they made speeches, which also helped, but these actions were of secondary importance.

It was primarily within the Executive Office of the President that tax reduction had its sustained support, and the principal if not the sole impetus continued to come from the Council of Economic Advisers. In a sense standing between the Council and the Treasury, the Budget Bureau was not necessarily opposed to tax reduction, but, concerned about the expenditure of appropriated funds for authorized purposes, it shared Treasury's sensitivity to deficits. According to one observer, "Dave Bell agreed with Heller but concern for expenditures and efficiency made it difficult to provide active support." In early June, Bell shared Dillon's public optimism for an upturn in the economy exceeding expectations during the remainder of 1962.[39] Involved with a host of particular activities that make up the President's program, the Budget Bureau staff could react more enthusiastically over expenditure increases than revenue decreases. For its part, the White House staff seemed less concerned with tax policy substance than with reflecting the President's views of the matter, whatever they might be, easing the pressures upon him, and considering the political ramifications of possible alternatives. As Richard E. Mooney describes Sorensen, "He is more concerned with success, pitfalls, and failure than with content for its own sake."[40]

The inspiration and rationale of analysis and advice for tax reduction were generated primarily from the Council's office on the third-floor southwest corner of the Executive Office Building. The five-year lag in economic growth, the failure to achieve the fulfillment of economic potential, the drag characteristic of the existing tax structure, the reliance upon balanced budgets as the *sine qua non* of national economic policy had all been hallmarks of Heller's criticism of domestic economic policy. Emphasis on increasing consumer demand, increasing the nation's investment in human capital, loosening the tax structure, and evaluating fiscal policy in terms of full-employment surplus became equally well known as Heller prescriptions. Growing out of these, particularly the last, was the concept that smaller surpluses or larger deficits created by appropriately reduced income taxes could be a worthwhile price to pay for the prosperity, and, ultimately, budget surplus that would be generated by the increased income derived from the reduced taxes. Although not publicly acknowledged as a tenet of Administration policy in the spring of 1962, such a fiscal policy was part of the rationale within the Administration. And the President, in his speech at Yale, went so far as to acknowledge that "Obviously deficits are sometimes dangerous—and so are surpluses." [41] "Even at Treasury," according to James Reston, "distinction is being drawn between deficits caused by a tax cut and deficits as a result of new spending." [42]

The economic pause and surrounding circumstances of June not only supported Heller's position but added a dimension of urgency to his argument. It was a dimension, however, that cut both ways. Though encouraging the idea of a tax cut "now," the very emphasis on current circumstances made the cut dependent on the latest vicissitudes of the economic indicators. Thus, by concentrating on the immediate situation rather than the long-term objective, the right objective was linked with not entirely the right reason. Moreover, in the debating during June, a permanent cut was confused with a temporary "quickie" cut, which Heller did not want except under the aegis of the standby authority proposal already submitted. Consequently, although the immediate situation partially validated the argument for tax cuts on the basis of recovery, to stress the countercyclical need "now" was to ignore the underlying long-term rationale of growth. And to stress the latter was to lose the support of the anticyclical worriers and to risk the opposition of the budget balancers, who could justify a tax cut only in terms of obvious and immediate recessionary danger. It was premature to argue publicly for present increased deficits as a cost of future budget surpluses. Under these somewhat damned-if-you-don't-and-damned-if-you-do conditions Heller pressed for a cut "now" if possible but, if necessary, later rather than not at all. Time was on his side.

The force of Heller's advocacy of tax reduction was strengthened by his having the support of his fellow Council members and staff, who also favored an immediate cut and one not encumbered by association with tax reform. By the same token, the Council's interest in tax reduction was channeled away from involvement in the specifics of reform by the very nature of its professional resources. Heller and Tobin, along with Okun, Solow, and others of the Council staff were active in the economic analysis of various specific tax reform proposals rather than in the development of the proposals themselves. A staff member commented that they had no direct counterpart to Brazer, that is, no tax-structure man, except in so far as Heller was one; and he was involved in too many other things to play the part of the tax expert.

The strength of its lack of staff resources was that the Council was obliged and able to focus on tax reduction more than on tax reform, to consider basic tax policy and not details, and to analyze such policy in terms of its impact upon other economic issues, and vice versa. Tax reduction and reform were but two related means to the end of national economic welfare. Defense and nondefense spending programs were others. Trade expansion, which was occupying much of Kermit Gordon's time, was still another and was linked to the new impetus given to international affairs. Success of a trade expansion program would depend upon and at the same time contribute to economic growth at home. In all these areas the Council analyzed and advised, drafted and redrafted, cooperated and competed, while maintaining its constant watch on the nation's functioning economy.

The strength of the breadth of the Heller Council's involvement was that it reflected precisely the breadth of economic policy pressures and opportunities facing President Kennedy. This parallel heightened the receptivity to its advice by a President troubled by the spectre of stagnation and seeking new answers to persistent questions. At the same time, the wide area of its involvement provided the Council with an entree to the other primarily economic agencies whose advice the President was also receiving; that is, the Treasury, the Budget Bureau, and the Federal Reserve Board. With the Troika of Dillon, Bell, and Heller, and, more inclusively, the Quadriad of these men with Martin, lay the responsibility of reconciling as much as possible their respective views on tax policy and of developing reform and reduction proposals acceptable to the President. With them too lay the privilege of pressing their own advice on aspects about which they could not or would not agree but from which the President would have to make a choice.

It was not only the top echelon who participated in this process of cooperation and competition so basic to decision-making operations. The supporting ranks of Surrey and Brazer in Treasury, Schultze and Cohn in the Budget Bureau, and Capron and Smith in the Council, not to mention the range of colleagues in their own and related agencies, contributed importantly to the process. That those in Treasury would have the prime authority and responsibility for developing specific contents by no means ruled out offense and defense from other quarters. Indeed, the participants were not limited to government bureaucrats, for experts from such organizations as The Brookings Institution, the National Planning Association, the Committee for Economic Development, and the universities were also brought into or attracted to the fray. Nor was the process fought as a battle or played as a game strictly within formal confines of meetings and memoranda, speeches and position papers. Rather it overflowed into the informal bureaucratic channels of telephone calls, luncheon conversations, car-pool debate, and rumor circulation. Tax policy competed with trade expansion and even aid to education, medical care for the aged, and youth employment for the energies and abilities of scores of public servants operating from both ends of Pennsylvania Avenue. Whether full-time or part-time, whether as elected or appointed career officials, many were directly or indirectly associated with tax policy activity and inactivity during the weeks of June, July, and the first half of August.

During those warm summer weeks the Administration avoided open commitment for or against a tax cut. In the five news conferences between his Yale speech on June 11 and his television address to the nation on August 13, in which he announced his intention to cut taxes in 1963 but not before, the President did little more than sidestep leading questions and to reiterate that a firm decision would have to await conclusive economic developments one way or another. In the meantime, he urged favorable action on both the tax revision measures, which were receiving unsympathetic treatment in the Senate, and the standby tax reduction proposal, which remained buried in the House Ways and Means Committee. Over the same period, Dillon, Bell, and Heller were also relatively noncommittal in public statements, although Dillon did again register his opposition to cuts in 1962 before the Senate Finance Committee.[43]

For the most part, what open debate and deliberation there was came from sources other than the executive branch. From the Senate, Hubert Humphrey urged an immediate cut; he believed that one could be approved by the Congress, and he announced periodically, following appointments with the President, that the chances of a cut being recommended were improving.[44] On the Republican side, Senators Case, Javits, and Keating also favored an immediate cut. Against these were Senators Byrd, Williams of Delaware, Kerr, Robertson, and even Paul Douglas, a Democrat often regarded as a liberal economist. For his part, Wilbur Mills remained equally unenthusiastic for a cut. He held closed hearings in late July and early August apparently with the intent of killing any possibility of reduction at that time. There is no evidence that arguments for a cut, reputedly from people such as H. Ladd Plumley of the Chamber of Commerce, Colm of NPA, Pechman of Brookings, Stanley Ruttenburg of the CIO, and R. L. Johnson of the Farmers Union in any way changed Mills' mind.

Perhaps the most noteworthy support came from two sources that could hardly be expected to agree. Both the AFL-CIO and the Chamber of Commerce urged immediate cuts, although in different sectors of the economy and for different reasons. The union sought cuts in personal income primarily in the lower brackets; the Chamber favored cuts in the upper brackets and in corporate income as aids to investment. As a supplement to the union appeal, Walter Reuther in mid-July also urged a reduction of $5 billion and barely two weeks later one of $10 billion.

Although such talk and deliberation was outside the Executive Branch, the impact of these points of view nevertheless registered. They created pressure for action, they revealed or confirmed the reactions that could be anticipated from given courses of action, and they helped set up some of the parameters of acceptable solution.

Events themselves, such as they were, contributed additional determinants. The delays and compromises in the passage of the tax revision bill hardly bode well for prompt congressional action on tax reduction requests, to say nothing of more comprehensive reforms. Trade expansion and other "must" legislation could not be delayed. The establishment on July 12 by Executive Order of the new depreciation schedules, the first revisions since 1942, gave an immediate lift to the economy by its promise of $1½-billion annual savings affecting 70 to 80 percent of the total value of industrial equipment being utilized. In the meantime, the July economic indicators showed the economy making some gains which, though hardly enough to call an upsurge, were enough to weaken the drive for a reduction.

It was in this environment that the Administration inched toward a decision in its own deliberations. The continuous process of consideration, discussion, and speculation was punctuated by three meetings of the chief participants from Treasury, Budget, and Council with the President. The first was held in early July (the transcript of the President's July 5 news conference refers to the President's discussion with Dillon "this week" [45]) but was not publicized, the second was the well-publicized meeting of July 13, and the third was held on August 8, five days before the President addressed the nation. Of these meetings the second appears to have been the most important. It included morning, luncheon, and afternoon sessions during which Kennedy apparently conferred first with the advocates of tax reduction, that is, Secretary Hodges and Under Secretary Gudeman of Commerce, Secretary Goldberg of Labor, David Bell, and the three Council members, who then were Heller,

Gordon, and Ackley. In response to the President's suggestion to Heller that it would be good to have the views of economists who were somewhat removed from the immediate premises in Washington, Paul Samuelson and Robert Solow of M.I.T. were brought in especially for the meeting. This group presumably argued in favor of proposing an immediate permanent cut "now." They would have said in effect: "Both the immediate and long-term economic situation calls for a cut. Never mind the other factors for, regardless of them, the nation will be better off with a reduction in the long run anyhow."

The President lunched with business leaders who reportedly had varying views on the timing of a cut. During the afternoon he conferred with the opponents, namely, Dillon and Mills. Dillon emphasized the possibly adverse effect of a tax cut on the balance of payments; both stressed the impact of a tax cut proposal upon reform plans and other legislation and discussed pessimistically the likelihood of such a proposal being accepted by the Congress.[46]

In the end, the only action taken was to postpone the decision until August, when the July economic data would be available for analysis. The decision not to seek a tax cut "now" as announced on August 13 was for all practical purposes reached in July, and the third meeting on Friday, August 8, was at best a ratification of that decision as well as a preparation for the final announcement by the President. His address was prepared over the weekend, with Sorensen and Heller working with the President up to 30 seconds before he faced the cameras.[47]

The address itself was an elaboration of what the President had told his news conference nine weeks previously. It summarized the accomplishments of the Kennedy Administration and recited the basic arguments for the cut—the five-year lag in the economy, the relative growth of the Western European and Japanese economies, the persistent gap between progress and potential, and the drag of the current tax structure:

For these reasons, this Administration intends to cut taxes in order to build the fundamental strength of our economy, to remove a serious barrier to long-term growth, to increase incentives by routing out inequities and complexities and to prevent the even greater budget deficit that a lagging economy would otherwise surely produce. . . . And the right time for that kind of bill, it now appears in the absence of an economic crisis today—and if the job is to be done in a responsible way—is January 1963.

Such a bill will be presented to the Congress for action next year. It will include an across-the-board, top-to-bottom cut in both corporate and personal income taxes. It will include long-needed tax reform that logic and equity demand. And it will date that cut in taxes to take effect as of the start of the next year, January 1, 1963. . . .

The billions of dollars this bill will place in the hands of the consumer and our businessmen will have both immediate and permanent benefits to our economy.[48]

The significance of the President's statement thus seems fourfold: (1) it stilled the turmoil over a tax cut "now" by indicating there would be none, (2) it reaffirmed earlier pronouncements that the Administration would be seeking congressional approval of net tax cuts for 1963 in 1963, (3) it signified a break with the past in terms of governing economic philosophy, and (4) it signified a victory for Walter Heller and his Council. Although August 13 could be viewed, as it was by Nossiter, as "The Day Taxes Weren't Cut," [49] it is equally plausible in terms of these four points to view it as the day that taxes were cut.

On economic grounds, the decision not to seek a tax cut in August does appear as a failure to act. Not only was the economy generally faltering, but the doldrums of that period provided the best possible illustration of the five-year lag and weak recovery which were precisely the conditions a net reduction would help to correct. Most accounts indicate that the President accepted the arguments and evidence, that his desires and instincts said "cut." If the President felt this way, why the delay in the reduction? Why not "now"?

As Nossiter and many other commentators clearly recognized, Kennedy was restrained by other noneconomic factors. Mills was strongly opposed to immediate reduction because of the lack of clear indications of recession and because such a step would deny an essential sweetener for the structural reforms in which he was primarily interested and which had yet to be presented to Congress. Further, Mills felt that imposition of the tax cut without accompanying reduction in expenditures would increase the risk of inflation. Without Mills' support, no tax legislation was possible. The slow and tortuous progress of the 1962 revision dulled any remaining optimism that a bill could be passed quickly. Furthermore, to push the tax cut would jeopardize other priority legislation by risking a fight within Congress at a highly inappropriate time. Although Dillon favored cuts in the next year (the nature and extent of them yet to be determined), he was strongly opposed to any immediate cuts for reasons paralleling those of Mills. The likelihood both of a sizable deficit instead of a modest surplus for fiscal 1963 and a congressional refusal to enact a postal rate increase for additional revenue made the prospect of further deficits stemming from a tax reduction all the more unwelcome. Martin's distaste for deficit financing and the power of the Federal Reserve to react to its use by raising interest rates were an additional restraint. A few enlightened sophisticates might not be worried about deficits, but the general public was, and in an election year this was an important consideration. Kennedy wished to meet the criteria of fiscal responsibility as applied by the general public and by the business community both at home and overseas.

Consequently, not to seek an immediate cut was to accept the validity and predominance of essentially noneconomic factors, that is, the realities of the immediate political situation. This acceptance represented the convictions of Dillon and Surrey and hence was the essence of their differences at this time with Heller and his colleagues. By the same token, to commit the Administration to seek cuts with reforms the next year was to fix a terminal period for bowing to such noneconomic factors; the commitment signified acceptance of the economic considerations justifying the cut. To argue on August 13 that taxes should be cut seems far more important than the refusal to cut them at that particular time. The public commitment to traditional concepts of balanced budgets, accepted as valid for years, enunciated by the President almost exactly twelve months previously, and reiterated in the presidential messages at the start of the year, had its effect upon specific policy alternatives in August. To justify future tax reduction, as the President did, by identifying tax policy as the most potent weapon available for achieving long-term growth and by criticizing the current structure for inhibiting such growth was to have the Administration break with the past by establishing a new tradition.

The period from August to January served as a time of mourning for old values. Although there was no apparent reexamination of basic economic policy at the time of the Berlin crisis, during the last half of 1962 there was such a reappraisal inspired by the spring reports of the faltering economy, the steel pricing and stock market crises, and the accumulating evidence of upward economic progress under contrary policies in Western Europe and Japan. It was the new thinking resulting from the reassessment that cropped out in bits and pieces at news conferences and was evidenced in the Yale speech, the call for a dialog between business and government, and finally in the August 13 address. New foundations for economic policy had been erected on the New Frontier.

In view of the Council's constant espousal of what was both said and implied, the presidential commitment to tax reduction is essentially a victory for Heller, his fellow Council members, and his staff colleagues. The Council articulated the basic philosophy that, validated by the events of 1962, was finally accepted by the Administration. In this atmosphere of the new philosophy, Heller's testimony before the Joint Economic Committee five days before the President's speech constituted the Council's first delineation of the precise bases for what would be proposed in January, 1963.

The Commitment Fulfilled

"Walter Heller worked like a beaver on that testimony," [50] recalls Pechman. Once the decision not to seek an immediate tax cut had been reached, Heller's efforts were directed less toward a hope of last-minute reversal than toward the campaign beyond. The major focus of his presentation on August 8 was upon the values and issues that would shape the January tax proposals. His summary of the record of gains since the first quarter of 1961 and his description of the mixed nature of the prospects for the near future were preparatory arguments for the "fundamental measures of tax reduction and tax reform":

Unless adverse economic developments require earlier action, no decision has been made on the size, composition, and timing of a recommended tax reduction. But the basic case for easing the net tax drain on the economy, as well as the broad principles which should guide tax reduction, are reasonably clear in the light of our unsatisfactory economic experience of the past 5 years.

A reduction in net tax liabilities of both consumers and business spurs the economy's advance toward full resource utilization in three important ways: First, it increases the disposable income of consumers . . . the so-called "multiplier effect." . . . Second, by bolstering sales and pushing production closer to capacity, tax reduction stimulates investment in inventories and in plant and equipment, the so-called "accelerator effect." . . . Third, by reducing the Government's share of business earnings, tax reduction improves profit margins and increases the supply of internal funds available for investment.[51]

Heller then set forth a series of considerations intended as relevant to the subsequent determination of the size, composition, and timing of tax cuts:

1. The longer-term need for reducing the excess of Federal revenues over Federal expenditures that would be realized at full employment. . . .

2. Any short-term need that may exist for overcoming temporary deficiencies in consumer and investment demand.

3. The necessity of combining individual and corporate income tax reduction in the manner best suited to stimulating both consumption and investment, to support both markets and incentives.

4. The appropriate relationship to the projected reform of the tax structure, a reform designed to improve equity and remove the artificial tax barriers or concessions that divert resources from their most efficient uses and thus impair our rate of economic growth.

5. The invigorating effect of tax reduction on the economy and the resulting "feedback" of revenues to the Federal Treasury. . . .

6. The monetary policy being pursued. . . .[52]

When we look ahead instead of backward, it is the size of the job yet to be done that demands attention and commands action: the continued hardship, inequity, and waste of unemployment; the excessive amounts of unused industrial capacity; the unsatisfactory pace of economic expansion in 1962; and the remaining gap in our balance of payments. My statement today has put its emphasis on this unfinished business of economic policy. The uncertainties of current economic developments and prospects underscore the urgency of that unfinished business.[53]

This then was the platform from which the Council would attempt to influence the development of specific tax reduction measures. As had been the case in the preceding months, this platform would form the main line of reasoning for analysis and advice with which the Council could bombard the President and Sorensen, thereby helping to shape White House thinking and indirectly that of the Treasury. Similarly, the platform would continue to be the basis of Council participation in the development of specific proposals. In the Council's work with Goldberg, and later Willard Wirtz, in Labor, Bell in the Budget Bureau, Hodges in Commerce, to say nothing of Dillon, the platform would be the dominant frame of reference. In the other aspects of economic policy, it would identify the Heller approach.

Related to but also coincidental with the launching of the tax campaign was Kennedy's establishment, in late August, at Heller's recommendation, of the Cabinet Committee on Economic Growth. Designed "to coordinate Federal activities and policies in this field and to advise the President on steps to accelerate the growth of the U.S. economy," [54] it was composed of the Secretaries of Treasury, Labor, and Commerce, the Director of the Budget Bureau, and the Chairman of the Council, who would act as Chairman. As a committee to take the initiative in developing growth policies, the Cabinet Committee provided an important vehicle for Heller in the hammering out of the tax proposals.

Such a formal arrangement was, however, no substitute for the constant inside analysis and outside contact that had to be carried on at the Council and staff levels. Significantly, such involvement was not so much in conflict with the needs of other areas of Council analysis as they were mutually beneficial. For example, the tax effects on balance of payments depended upon analysis and knowledge previously developed. So it was with trade expansion, area development, and other areas. As for the likely nature of tax reduction itself, by mid-September it was generally expected that the drop for the personal income tax rate would be to about the 15-to-65 percent range from the then existing 20-to-91 percent range and that the corporate rate would drop from 52 percent to 47 percent. Yet the specifics within these general limits were not known outside of the Treasury, even if they were agreed upon inside that department. There was conjecture but little certainty about Treasury ideas for structural reform. "We know," said one senior Budget Bureau official at the time, "that they are working on some $30 billion of ideas but we don't know what ones."

In fact, as of mid-September, Treasury was itself uncertain as to what structural proposals it wanted to make. The development of the proposals was far more complex than originally anticipated. Work had started in the fall of 1961, when Brazer joined Surrey's staff. Preliminary studies had been undertaken, consultants had prepared analyses and recommendations. A set of proposals had been drafted by July, 1962, but apparently the draft had not been sufficiently developed to be released. The extension of congressional consideration of the 1962 revision into the fall necessitated constant follow-up by Surrey's staff and hence a stretch-out of its work on the 1963 proposals.

Despite the absence of public pronouncements, Treasury's basic views were well known, and the speculation over the nature of its proposals was fairly uniform. In addition, testifying before the Joint Economic Committee in August was no less a platform for Dillon than for Heller. Fundamental similarities were matched by fundamental differences. Dillon, like Heller, recognized "the margin between our productive potential and the current rate of business activity," but the primary solution was not in increasing consumer demand but in encouraging investment—"in fuller and more effective use of our unmatched human and physical resources." Domestic and foreign markets are important but secondary, their expansion ultimately dependent upon the expansion of investment. Like Heller, Dillon sought constructive use of the taxing power, but, as expressed in terms of problems, his approach differed:

(1) Our tax structure has placed a heavy burden on the productive investment so vital to the growth process. (2) The current rate structure siphons off so large a fraction of the increased income generated by business recovery that forward momentum is dissipated before full employment and full utilization of industrial capacity can be reached. (3) Overly high rates of individual income tax interfere with the economic process. Energies and resources are diverted from the business at hand and concentrated on minimizing tax burdens through the use of a patchwork of special deductions and exclusions, built up over the years to lighten the burden of our onerous rate structure. (4) Our tax system today lacks provision for flexible and timely adjustments to meet swiftly developing changes in the overall level of economic activity.[55]

This emphasis on investment led Dillon to a review of the advantages to be derived from the new depreciation guidelines already established and the investment incentive still before the Senate.

Dillon shared Heller's conviction that a tax structure was needed that would both increase consumer demand and provide new incentives, but he did not publicly endorse the full-employment surplus concept. Instead, Dillon felt that the tax structure should provide "for an appropriate surplus of revenues over expenditures when the economy is operating at acceptable levels of employment and plant utilization." Although he recognized the consequent need for tax reduction to achieve an acceptably operating economy, "tax reform is just as important," and by implication far more so. Dillon's and Heller's area of closest agreement was their acceptance of increased deficits as "a necessary downpayment on economic growth," although Dillon appeared to have in mind something relatively mild and temporary. At least, however, Dillon accepted the prospect of a net reduction.[56]

In part the Heller-Dillon differences reflected different philosophies, but they also reflected different institutional and operational restraints. Dillon did not have the same governmentwide viewpoint as Heller had but was guided by the institutional responsibilities and perspectives of a major department. Dillon was therefore obliged to accept the demands of money management operations, of balance-of-payment problems, and of the limitations of debt ceilings. The criterion of program feasibility was as potent an argument as the hardship of national unemployment. The impact of congressional response on what Dillon proposed and opposed gave a pragmatic hue to his convictions and strategies. During the summer of 1962 he was obliged at one and the same time to develop preliminary support for the forthcoming 1963 program and to argue in favor of the investment incentive credit bill upon which the Senate was then deliberating not too favorably. He could not alienate what support he had for the bill by being too specific or extreme about the program.

As it turned out, congressional consideration of the 1962 program was a bottleneck to the development of the 1963 proposals until the program became law in mid-October, almost eighteen months after it had been first proposed by the President.[57] Final acceptance of the investment incentive feature was by no means an easy matter and was attributed to an unlikely coalition of loyal Democrats who agreed to support the Administration and conservatives from both parties who favored benefits for business. The statute provided for an investment credit of 7 percent, which, when added to the new depreciation guidelines, would increase the flow of internal funds by over $2 billion a year [58] and also would permit tax treatment comparable to that received by foreign competition.[59] However, the elimination or watering down of many of the proposed structural reforms in response to a variety of pressures transformed the proposal from a bill through which revenue would be increased to an act which resulted in a net loss of revenue.

Once the incentive measure was passed, the Treasury tax analysis and legislative staffs at last could turn full-time attention and resources to the 1963 reform proposals. The panel discussions that had been started in the spring with a number of consulting experts were resumed. Comptrollers, accountants, lawyers, and economists from industry, unions, and universities inserted their ideas and contributed their expertise to the thinking for the future. Surrey recalls, "We sought their judgment on policy issues and on the technical aspects of such matters as depletion allowances, capital gains and many other items." [60] Starting in October and extending into mid-November, specific proposals prepared by the Brazer and Lubick staffs were subject to item-by-item review and final development in a series of internal Treasury meetings. The meetings were called by Dillon, and he with Under Secretary Henry Fowler took an active part in the proceedings with Surrey and his staffs. Concerned primarily with structural reform, the meetings involved no participation on the part of the Council, the Budget Bureau, or the White House. Both creative solutions of problems and the initial ratification of decisions necessitated by specific reform proposals were thus accomplished within the Treasury. However, these prescriptions had yet to be exposed to an appraisal in terms of the counterbalancing effects of tax reduction.

The first exposure came in mid-October, precisely when the Administration was "eyeball to eyeball" with the Soviets over their arming of Cuba with offensive missiles. The President and his entourage were totally immersed in this crisis, political campaigning had temporarily been abandoned, the presidential concerns for domestic matters had been put aside. Nevertheless, the President's Cabinet Committee on Economic Growth took up the basic issue of the entire tax program—namely, the amount of deficit to be sustained through tax reduction. At its first meeting the Committee moved to have a staff paper prepared on the impact of taxes on full employment. The paper was to be written by Brazer and, as he recalls it, the topic was originally suggested by both Fowler and Heller. The paper was not intended to be an official Treasury document or a position paper that the Committee would be expected to endorse. Rather, it was to be a vehicle for discussion on a subject relevant to the Committee's mandate. Nor was the paper intended to be a defense of tax reduction as such but rather one of a series of papers on determinants of economic growth. Other papers were prepared dealing with such topics as the impact of civilian technology, education, and science.[61]

Although he did not disagree with the contents of Brazer's paper as such, Fowler was sufficiently concerned over its possible impact on the support of Mills and other members of the Ways and Means Committee for the tax proposals then being developed that he reportedly wished to avoid its presentation. He was out of town when it was put on the agenda, however, and the paper was brought up for discussion at the Cabinet Committee's meeting on October 26. The meeting was held in Heller's office and, in addition to Heller and Brazer, was attended by Dillon, Fowler, and Dewey Daane of Treasury, Bell and Schultze of the Budget Bureau, Richard Holton of Commerce, Secretary Anthony Celebrezze and William Cohen of Health, Education and Welfare, and Secretary Wirtz and Seymour Wolfbein of Labor, with William Capron of the Council staff acting as secretary.

The paper itself was not so much an original treatment of taxes and economic growth as a presentation of arguments for tax reduction that had been developed over the months by Brazer himself as well as by the Council and other proponents of reduction. After describing deficit implications for various alternative combinations of high and low income and consumer relief with investment incentives, Brazer concluded that a $10-billion net tax reduction would be consistent with objectives of both growth and stability. His conclusions were similar to those of the Council and he arrived at them by essentially the same reasoning.

Although conceding the possibility of a net reduction and hence a deficit increase, Dillon had been reluctant before the meeting in his concession and noncommittal as to the specific composition of such a reduction. Throughout 1961 and well into 1962 Treasury had not opposed tax reduction as such but viewed it primarily as a supporting rationalization for reform rather than as an end in itself. As late as the spring of 1962, Dillon had reportedly been holding out for a tax reduction of small enough proportions to be balanced by contemplated revenue-producing reforms of the same magnitude. As the 1961 recovery began to fail in the early months of 1962, however, as the projections of a small surplus for fiscal 1963 grew fainter even before the year started, and as the appeal of a tax cut grew in May, June, and July, the certainty of a deficit for fiscal 1964 through necessary reductions became generally even if privately accepted. Dillon could talk in New York on June 4 of tax reduction compensated for in whole or in part by reform, and Kennedy could talk in Washington two days later of net reduction, but behind the words were disagreements and uncertainties only as to how much the reduction would be. Early spring estimates of $2 billion grew to $5 billion by mid-June. By fall, Brazer's justification in terms of $10 billion would have been a surprise only to those unfamiliar with the emerging situation.

What was generally appreciated, however, had to be firmly recognized within the Administration. The January deadline for presenting proposals was fast approaching, a multitude of tax policy and operational questions were yet to be answered, and expenditure programs had to be determined for the next fiscal year. With decisions on all of these matters directly influenced by deficit considerations, some determinations of just how large a cut would be permitted could no longer be delayed. The combination of circumstances made it necessary to obtain some indication from Secretary

Dillon as the chief architect of whatever specific proposals were to emerge. The continued slack in the economy, the continued opposition of Mills to any cuts that would jeopardize reform, and the continued worry over balance of payments and overall economic stability all combined to create an atmosphere of uncertainty and unease. To this atmosphere the Cuban crisis contributed an element of dramatic tension.

The minutes of the Cabinet Committee's meeting reveal that there was extensive discussion of the relationship between the size of the tax cut and a full employment surplus. Out of the discussion grew (1) "substantial support" for a full-employment budget surplus that would be close to zero or possibly slightly below, that is, a deficit; (2) "considerable agreement" that the tax cut at the upper range proposed by the "Treasury paper" would be of approximately the right size; (3) "some strong feeling" for quick action on a sizable cut for 1963 with possibly the bulk of it coming sooner rather than later in the year; and (4) unanimous agreement that the objective of full employment be pursued as quickly as possible.

The formal outcome of the discussion was a report that was forwarded to the President six weeks later, on December 1. Although it also dealt with matters of civilian technology, education, and manpower, the lead-off topic of the report was taxation. The report recommended a $7- to $12-billion net reduction in taxes "as quickly as possible," a major reduction in rates for all income brackets, and a revision of the income tax base through such modifications as depletion allowances and other provisions governing the taxation of natural resource industries "to permit efficient allocation of resources and rate reduction larger than otherwise possible." The report was signed by Dillon, Under Secretary Edward Gudeman of Commerce, Wirtz, Bell, Heller, and Capron of the Council in his capacity as Executive Secretary of the Cabinet Committee.[62]

Seen in perspective, the paper and meeting represent a confirmation and recognition of a gradually emerging consensus accepting sizable tax reduction. Although only two of many such representations that doubtless can be identified regarding this issue, they had the effect of committing Dillon and Treasury to the support of substantial reduction. Many had felt that the Treasury, through aversion to increased deficits, preoccupation with reform, or both, had been dragging its feet on reduction. To have Brazer as one of the few in Treasury favoring reduction be the man to justify reduction was to apply an appropriate bit of leverage on Dillon. Fully aware of the significance of commitment, however, Dillon would not have permitted Brazer to deliver the paper and would not have attended the meeting himself had he not already been moving toward a change of attitude. "There is no doubt in my mind," Brazer recalls, "that the paper and discussion had an impact on Dillon's thinking, but the change of mind was gradual, not sudden." [63] To the degree that Dillon's view was changed by it, the meeting's consensus modified a position he had taken before the Joint Economic Committee in August; at the same time it established him in a position from which he would not be expected to retreat, yet one that would allow him to maintain leadership and control over tax program development.

The discussion of the Brazer paper is a significant consideration in two additional respects. First, it illustrates the policy initiative and involvement of professionals, in this case economists such as Brazer, Heller, and colleagues in both agencies. This involvement and initiative transcended formal discussions and levels of responsibility and resulted in a policy creation role that spanned weeks of informal association. Secondly, the episode illustrates the half-creative, half-catalytic role in the decision-making process of advisory groups such as the Cabinet Committee on Economic Growth. The Committee served Heller as a means for exchanging views and developing a consensus favoring tax reduction as one method of achieving economic growth. Surely both Heller and Fowler were aware of the possibility of a breakthrough with Dillon. In another way, the group afforded a means of reaching an understanding without formal alignments and attendant identification of winners and losers. In their respective roles, Heller and Brazer could take pleasure in establishing the principle of significant tax reduction, which Dillon in turn was able to acknowledge.

Acceptance of the principle of significant reduction by no means constituted a formal commitment to any specific course of action;

important questions of the relationship of reduction to reform and of the content of specific reform measures were left unanswered. But, at least, by establishing the principle, these questions were moved to the top of the decision-making agenda.

The issue of the relationship of reduction and reform broke into two parts: (1) the substantive aspect of whether the cut should be made all at once or be spaced out over a period of time, and if the latter how, and how it should be tied to revenue-producing reform and (2) the tactical problem of how closely integrated and inter-dependent should be the reduction and the reform portions in their presentation to Congress. The reduction could be granted all at once or stretched out in increments, depending upon the desired impact on the economy and the revenue needs of the Treasury. "One-shot" or incremental cuts could be phased with reform measures. Assuming, for example, the aim of a $10-billion net reduction including a $2-billion package of reforms, an $8-billion cut could be sought in 1963 with no reforms established, and the remaining $2 billion could be obtained the following year by combining $4 billion of additional reductions with $2 billion of revenue-producing reforms. Such an arrangement could be spelled out in one bill and so promoted by the Administration in Congress, or it could be presented as two different bills, thereby separating reduction from reform and removing any support or impediment that one might give to the other. Thus, there were available a number of alternative combinations of reduction and reform and the legislative establishment thereof.

Given both the state of the economy and the desire to stimulate long-term growth quickly and strongly, Heller favored maximizing across-the-board reductions to take effect in 1963 and seeking legislative approval of such cuts independent of reform. Throughout the fall deliberations he argued within the Administration for a substantial cut in 1963, preferably of at least $7 or $8 billion out of a total cut of $10 to $12 billion, with the rest being reserved for a second-stage program combining further tax reduction with substantial tax reform. In a speech delivered to the President's Labor-Management Committee in November, Dillon in no sense pulled back from his acceptance of reduction, and he echoed Heller's advocacy to the same group on the preceding day of applying the major portion of cuts to individual rates. However, Dillon would not be more specific than to indicate a willingness to make some cuts early in 1963 and to link the remainder with the reforms to broaden the tax base which were to come later.[64] Furthermore, he would not deal with any reductions apart from reform unless economically necessary.

Dillon's arguments for a minimum cut in 1963 were buttressed by the paradox of a new Budget Bureau forecast of a $7.8-billion deficit for fiscal 1963 accompanying a mild upturn of the economic indicators. The Labor-Management Committee in its own final report went considerably beyond Heller's position by advocating a $10-billion tax reduction early in 1963, clearly stipulating that "thorough revision of the tax system should not be permitted to postpone action on the urgently needed reduction of tax rates." [65] The President indicated in his November 20 news conference that there would be no immediate resolution; that tax matters would be discussed "in the next ten days" but that there would be no further information until early January.[66]

While debate continued over the content and timing of the cut as well as over the tactics for its presentation, the tax experts in Treasury were attempting to complete the development of the Administration's reform proposals. Surrey, Brazer, Lubick, their colleagues, the corps of part-time consultants, and Dillon comprised the reform ideologists who sought to create an improved tax structure. Dillon had assumed office talking of comprehensive reform, Surrey was the natural choice for developing a reform program, and the prospect of such a development is what attracted Brazer to Washington in the first place. Disagreement over specifics, countless revisions and compromises, to say nothing of the peripheral interest of such Treasury officials as Daane, Roosa, and Caplin by no means detracted from unanimity on the basic dimensions of the program.

Developed apart from those of reduction, the new reform proposals were intended to expand on the limited reforms originally proposed in April, 1961 (and so recently passed) and to make good on the long-term objectives of tax policy. By such measures as altering the depletion allowances for oil and other resources, tightening up treatment on capital gains, and establishing a capital gains tax at death the reformers hoped to close tax loopholes, achieve a greater degree of equity across the range of taxpayers, simplify tax administration, and, at a more ultimate level, aid economic develop-ment. An overriding consideration in the development of specific proposals was a judgment of their acceptability to Mills.

If nothing else, witnessing the long-extended process of getting the 1961 revisions through Congress in 1962 gave the Treasury tax staff a realistic measure by which to estimate what might be feasible in 1963. The Treasury staff was aware that pressures would surely develop from the complex of special interests, but, as one who was involved recalls, "We tried to play it straight rather than politi-cal." [67] According to Surrey,

Of course we were concerned with the feasible, but feasible in terms of what we considered necessary and appropriate to recommend, not just what would be acceptable in the end. We knew we would get beaten on some items and would have to compromise others, but we considered it important to present the issues. A capital gains tax at death was an academic matter two years ago, and it wasn't accepted now, but at least Secretary Dillon was talking about it today before the Senate Finance Committee and pointing out the merits of the proposal.[68]

Under the circumstances, there was no point in proposing the imposition of a tax on income from municipal bonds. Knowing that such senators as Robert Kerr would most certainly block any exten-sive revision of the oil depletion percentage allowances, the staff labored to develop a more acceptable minimum. Their interest in such tax reduction as was to be proposed was in large measure contingent upon their estimates of its impact on reform.

The Council, notwithstanding its concern for basic economic philosophy and its promotion of substantial tax reduction, had vir-tually nothing to do with the development of the reform proposals. "We didn't participate; we just reacted," recalls a staff member. Council communications with Treasury in the area of reform were strengthened fortuitously by individuals who served as consultants to both. Pechman, for example, worked on capital gains proposals with both agencies.[69] For the most part, the Council stuck to "second-level generalities," that is, analyses of tax-cut and reform combinations, tax incidence, and other economic ramifications of changes in the tax area. The Council was in no sense opposed to reforms as such. It was skeptical about the feasibility of the tax on capital gains at death on political and strategic grounds but supported it anyhow. Heller and a number of his colleagues had shared in much of the early development of an approach to broadening the tax base; they would have liked to play a more intimate part in the preparation of the reforms. But, in the converse of the Treasury's position, the Council's concern for reforms was contingent upon their substantive and strategic impact upon tax reduction.

After Thanksgiving the tempo accelerated as decision-making on deficits, reduction, and reforms led to a steady stream of meetings, memoranda, and telephone conversations among experts, Administration officials, and politicians. Dillon and Heller concentrated on their respective concerns for reform and reduction. While the Treasury's reform proposals were being completed, Dillon pressed within the Administration for a combination of reduction and reform that would produce a minimum deficit. He reportedly appealed in writing to the President for a reduction in expenditures from $98 to $96 billion for fiscal 1964.

At the same time Heller showered the President and the public with analyses, speeches, and articles justifying tax reduction,[70] while he and Ackley, the latter having replaced Tobin in August, were attempting to pull together the President's and the Council's annual *Reports*, both of which would involve far more than tax policy. Gordon's transfer to the Budget Bureau to replace Bell, who in turn was leaving to head the Agency for International Development,[71] left the Council short-handed at its busiest time. To help out, Council "alumni" such as Tobin, Okun, and Solow, all of whom had resumed their academic careers, returned to active duty over the Christmas holidays to assist in the preparation of the *Economic Report*. Although the full depth and breadth of economic policy were involved in the presentation of the *Economic Report*, the tax program would still be the dominant element. Consequently, aided by consultants such as Musgrave and Pechman, those of the staff who had been closest to tax developments over the preceding months turned to drafting for government and public consumption the formal analysis of the impact of the Administration's tax proposals. Whatever their specific features might be, reduction and reform had to be related to other governmental programs and to the nation's economic welfare as a whole.

It was the working out of this very relationship that brought the White House and the Budget Bureau more directly into the final stages of the development of the tax proposals. The President's State of the Union Message and his Budget Message did far more than represent January speech deadlines; the preparation of the two speeches compelled the fitting together of the Administration's 1963 budgetary and legislative programs, of which tax proposals would be a part. Revenue-expenditure estimates could not be accurately set until proposed changes in income tax rates were agreed upon and their establishment within fiscal 1964 assumed. Prepared expenditures for defense, space, transportation, education, and many other areas, all of which were going through final mark-up sessions within the Budget Bureau, were directly affected by the outcome of the tax deliberations. Priorities within the Administration's legislative program and strategies for its presentation to Congress hinged upon the content of the tax proposals and the strategy governing *their* presentation.

Such interaction and interdependence meant an almost constant association between officials and professionals within the Executive Office and between it and the Treasury. Many of those involved made up the various levels of Troika, which had little to do with the tax proposals as such but which, as a Treasury-Budget-Council group concerned with expenditures and revenues, facilitated communications on tax-related matters and developed the rationale for tax proposals then reaching their final form. A number of these persons dealt with Sorensen, Feldman, and White in the White House, to whom tax proposals were but one concern.

Activity and final deliberation within the more immediate presidential arena were matched by an increasing amount of general interest and comment over the forthcoming tax proposals from persons both in and outside of the government. Whether attempting to influence the outcome, to react on behalf of clients or constituents, or merely to be heard, protests and encouragement reflected mixtures of fear of recession, old orthodoxy, and new views. One school spoke out for immediate tax cuts primarily at the lower- and middle-income levels, independent of, and therefore not endangered by, reforms and later far-reaching reforms possibly coupled with subsequent step reductions in personal and corporate income taxes. In varying degrees this school included Secretaries Hodges and Wirtz, Senators Humphrey and Javits, the AFL–CIO, CED, and some economists, such as Gerhard Colm. Another school sought to avoid or at least to minimize cuts, to focus such cuts as were made on corporate taxes, and to make the cuts contingent upon reduction in expenditures. Senators Byrd and Kerr, former President Eisenhower, Raymond Saulnier, who preceded Heller as Council Chairman, and Dan Throop Smith, who, it will be recalled, was George Humphrey's tax adviser in Treasury, were among those who argued along these lines.

In addition a third school was made up of men whose convictions aligned them with the former group but whose traditional values placed them in the latter school. Countering traditional business views and the anti-Administration feeling that still smoldered after the steel-price encounter, this third school emerged with a clear if qualified acceptance of tax reduction and a concomitant acceptance of budget deficits. At the time, M. J. Rossant of the New York *Times* wrote of the "softening" of the business community's traditional credo of budget balancing. He mentioned Thomas S. Lamont, Allan Sproul, Henry Ford, Jr., and Thomas J. Watson, Jr., as among those who endorsed cuts and intentional deficits and had faith in the economy's ability to handle inflation as it arose.[72] The questioning of myths had apparently not been entirely limited to the New Frontier. Aware of competitive business progress in Europe, these men could subscribe to the views of European economists and delegates to OECD favoring liberal tax cuts and deficit financing. The emergence of this fresh body of opinion from members of the business "establishment" was not lost on a President who had soon to go to both the people and Chairman Mills with his program.

On December 15, President Kennedy spoke to the members of the Economic Club of New York about his tax program. In this, his first public statement on taxation since his August 13 speech, he went well beyond both the familiar arguments against the restrictive tax structure as it then existed and the equally well-known objective of personal and corporate income tax reductions, increased incentive, and improved equity. As a preview of things to come he defended deficits—temporary deficits, to be sure, but deficits all the same—not as necessary burdens of recession but as the best means, even in times of relative prosperity, to achieve full employment:

An economy hampered by restrictive tax rates will never produce enough revenue to balance our budget just as it will never produce enough jobs or enough profits.

In short, it is a paradoxical truth that tax rates are too high today and tax revenues are too low, and the soundest way to raise the revenues in the long run is to cut the rates now. . . . I repeat: our practical choice is not between a tax-cut deficit and a budgetary surplus. It is between two kinds of deficits: a chronic deficit of inertia, as the unwanted result of inadequate revenues and a restricted economy; or a temporary deficit of transition, resulting from a tax cut designed to boost the economy, increase tax revenues, and achieve—and I believe this can be done—a budget surplus. The first type of deficit is a sign of waste and weakness; the second reflects an investment in the future.[73]

These arguments begged the questions of how much deficit and how temporary; they said nothing precise about the sorts of tax cuts. Yet Kennedy's statements did make clear to a notable congregation of "doubting Thomases" the Administration's rationale for the tax program then being thrashed out "down in Washington," which would be spelled out in detail a month hence.

The final deliberations took place in Palm Beach. The four-man review team of Sorensen, Gordon, O'Brien, and Heller, which had been working over the 1963 program during the preceding four months, flew to the Kennedy headquarters in Florida on the day after Christmas. Dillon, Fowler, and Surrey of Treasury and Feldman of the White House accompanied them in order to participate in the final ratification, rejection, or modification of the proposed tax reform-reduction program. At this meeting final decisions were reached on the permissible limits of the deficit likely to result from reductions, the nature and extent of reductions, the precise relationship of reduction to reform, the components of the reform package, and the strategy of the program's presentation to the Congress.

Economic forecasts for calendar 1963 and fiscal 1964 clarified uncompromisingly planned budget totals, revenue alternatives, and the resulting deficit. Necessary expenditures for defense and space programs combined with the favorable impact of tax reduction on economic growth to make a sizable deficit both necessary and desirable. But Kennedy felt that a deficit exceeding the record $12.4-billion peacetime deficit of 1959 might jeopardize the tax cut in Congress. Consensus having been reached on both the size of reduction necessary to get the economy moving again and upon the basic division of the cut between individual and corporate taxes, the major remaining issue was how much of the cut could be applied in 1963 and how much extended into subsequent years. Prospects of inadequate economic improvement without sizable cuts strengthened Heller's arguments for concentrating more of the reduction in 1963, but, as he concedes, "the budget deficit ceiling argument prevailed —along with sound fears of exceeding inflationary speed limits— and President Kennedy upped the 1963 scheduled cut by only about half a billion." [74] Only by spacing the tax cuts could the ceiling not be exceeded. The Herlong-Baker bill, already introduced in Congress, proposing tax reduction in five steps, buttressed the spacing approach favored by Treasury.

Heller had sought a relatively loose alliance between reduction and reform in the crucial issue of to what degree and in what manner they should be associated. However, reforms were so important to Treasury and the danger of rejection of important changes thought to be so great that some support from a connection with reduction was considered essential. Treasury was obliged to reverse its original position of favoring cuts primarily as a supporting rationalization for reform and attempt to attach reforms to the coattails of reduction, which had become firmly established as an end in itself.[75] Large cuts warranted by short- and long-term economic circumstances provided desired rationalization for counterbalancing reform. Indeed, Mills' prime interest in reforms alone became instead Mills' opposition to reduction without reform. A major factor in final deliberations before its presentation was the assessment of

Mills' reaction to the entire tax program. To gain his support, Under Secretary Fowler journeyed to Arkansas to assure him of the Administration's intent to hold the line on expenditures, link reduction with reform, and pace reductions over a number of years.

After the Palm Beach meeting, final refinements of the tax presentation were left up to Treasury. The remaining joint undertaking by Treasury, the White House, the Budget Bureau, and the Council was their preparation of the President's articulation of what had been developed in fulfillment of his televised commitment five months before. The agencies had already agreed on what each would be responsible for in preparing the President's State of the Union, Budget, and Special Tax Messages and the *Economic Report*.

In the State of the Union Message delivered on January 14, the President announced his intention to propose to Congress reductions totaling $13.5 billion, $11 billion of which would come from reduction of individual rates and $2.5 billion from reduction of corporate rates. These amounts were to be achieved by reducing individual income tax rates from a 20-to-91 percent range to a 14-to-65 percent range and by reducing the corporate tax rate from 52 percent to the pre-Korean 47 percent level. In order to keep these reductions "within the limits of a manageable budgetary deficit," Kennedy proposed phasing cuts over a three-year period starting in 1963. On the basis of the annual rates the 1963 reduction would amount to $6 billion. These reductions would be coupled with "selected" reforms or "structural changes" that would begin in 1964 and that would yield $3.5 billion in offsetting tax revenues, producing a net $10-billion reduction in tax liabilities. In addition, budgetary receipts would be increased $1.5 billion by gradually shifting the tax payments of large corporations to a more current basis: "This combined program . . . is a fiscally responsible program—the surest and the soundest way of achieving in time a balanced budget in a balanced full employment economy." [76]

The Budget Message delivered three days later further explained the deficit situation by predicting a $11.9-billion deficit, or half a billion under the ceiling of $12.4 billion, on the basis of the administrative budget, a $10.3-billion deficit on the more comprehensive consolidated cash basis, and a $7.6-billion deficit on the basis of the accrual-type national income accounts. The Budget Message revealed that the immediate impact of the proposed reduction would be to reduce fiscal 1964 revenues by approximately $5.3 billion, but, considering the increased revenues resulting from more current tax payment by corporations *and* the spur to the economy provided by the reduction, the net revenue loss would in fact be an estimated $2.7 billion.[77]

It was for the President's *Economic Report* released on January 21 to reveal that the reduction would not go into effect until July 1, the previous messages having referred only to "this calendar year." Consistent with its theme of economic growth, the *Economic Report* pointed out that the $8 to $9 billion of additional consumer income resulting from the tax reductions would swell into a flow of some $16 billion of additional consumer goods and services.[78] Under a heading "Fiscal Policy for Full Employment and Growth," the Council's *Annual Report* provided far more detailed and comprehensive economic justifications for both the reduction and reform aspects of revision than did the President's *Economic Report*. In support of the latter, it briefly reviewed the weaknesses of the present system from inequities to discouragement of investment incentives but said nothing about the reforms themselves: "To eliminate in a single step all forms of unjustifiable special treatment is not feasible. But the President's program will make decisive progress in this direction." [79]

President Kennedy's Special Message to the Congress on Tax Reduction and Reform, which was delivered on January 24, provided the missing information about the reforms. It too described the need for reduction and reform and the resulting benefits to the economy and the taxpayer. The section on "Proposals for Rate Reduction," with the proposals themselves by then well publicized, filled in the details of the phased personal and corporate rates reductions while emphasizing the resulting benefits of increased consumption, additional production incentives, and stimulation for small businesses. "The Proposals for Structural Revisions" started off with relatively noncontroversial measures designed to relieve hardship and encourage growth: liberalized standards and child-care deductions, favorable tax treatment for older people, allowances for moving, deductions for charitable contributions and research and development, and provisions for income averaging.

It was the measures described in "Base Broadening and Equity" that revealed the nature of the reform proposals. The first was to put a floor of 5 percent of adjusted gross income under itemized deductions. The section also proposed tightening up on deductions for minor casualty losses, charitable deductions, sick pay, and group term insurance premiums. The request for the repeal of the 1954 dividend and credit exclusion which had been voted down in 1962 was resubmitted. Revision of depletion allowance rates was not proposed, but in place of such revision the section requested a tightening of provisions regarding excess deduction carry-over, grouping of properties, capital gains on the sale of mineral interests, and the use of foreign tax credits to offset U.S. tax liabilities. The final group of proposals centered on revision of capital gains taxation with particular attention given to a tightening of computational and definitional loopholes, the transferring of certain categories of income from capital gains to ordinary income classifications, and taxation of capital gains at death.

Although recognizing congressional, that is, Chairman Mills', prerogative in the matter, Kennedy wished to make clear the Administration's commitment to reduction *and* reform:

The entire tax revision program should be promptly enacted as a single comprehensive bill. . . . Tax reduction and structural reform should be considered and enacted as a single integrated program. . . . The reduction in the top rate from 91% to 65%, which in itself is a major reform, cannot be justified if these other forms of preferential tax treatment remain. . . . To the extent that erosion of our tax base by special preferences is not reversed to gain some $3.4 billion net, Congress will have to forego—for reasons of both equity and fiscal responsibility—either corporate or personal rate reductions now contained in the program.[80]

Presumably drafted in Dillon's Treasury and endorsed by Mills, these statements reveal the dependence of reform upon reduction. Whether as commitments these statements would stick, whether as requirements of Congress they would be accepted, only time and the legislative process could tell. The provisions themselves were subject to the same tests. By January 24, 1963, the proposals for reduction and reform had left the Executive Branch for another and very different arena of cooperation and competition, not to return for thirteen months. What had been created by officials and experts under the direct aegis of the President as something desirable and necessary was next to be reviewed and reworked by legislators and experts whose words and deeds represented different pressures and opportunities, different stakes in creating change and maintaining the *status quo*.

Conclusion and Epilogue

If the delivery of the President's Special Message on Taxation completed the development of the proposals as proposals, what conclusions can be drawn regarding the contribution of the Heller Council to that development? In this specific case, what difference did the Council make? What does its contribution to tax revision as one area of economic policy suggest regarding the overall significance of its performance?

There seems little doubt that the Heller Council developed and gained acceptance for the economic philosophy upon which the tax program was built. The sterility of the five-year lag, the gap between progress and potential, the resistance to improvement of unemployment, and the drag of the wartime tax structure constituted the elements calling for change. Tax reduction, expansion of consumption relative to investment, deficit based upon full-employment surplus, and applications of both multiplier and accelerator concepts made up the countering elements on the basis of which answers to the call would be developed. Together the elements comprised a compelling leitmotif repeated throughout the development of the program. Based on a combination of Keynesian analysis, a Commons interest in human welfare, and a New Frontier sense of purpose, the resulting composition was given its first public try-out before the Joint Economic Committee in March, 1961. After its second presentation in the January, 1962, *Economic Report*, the piece was refined, expanded, and played with increasing frequency—both publicly and privately—throughout the year. Ignored at first, it gradually became acceptable and was then adopted as part of the

Administration's repertoire with its most notable performance in the 1963 *Economic Report*.

As for the tax program itself, the Council had virtually no hand in the development of the reform proposals. The Council lost its battle for proposing a tax cut in the summer of 1962; it failed in its effort to avoid spacing the 1963 program reductions over three years and to have reduction proposals considered unencumbered by reform measures. In short, the program was basically that of the Treasury. The Council, by its argument and education, however, sold the idea of tax reduction on its own merits and having brought the idea through the consideration of whether or not to seek cuts, the Council then shaded the contents of some of its specific aspects. The $10-billion net reduction approximates what Heller had in mind and although the reductions were spread over three years rather than concentrated in one, smaller initially than Heller had advocated, applicable later than he thought appropriate, and more tightly bound to reform than he thought wise, Heller's arguments very likely saved the reductions from being even more thoroughly compromised. This influence meant in turn that the Administration accepted a larger deficit than it originally had had in mind. Furthermore, the Council's persistent pressure for tax relief for the consumer probably caused the proportion of tax reduction to be larger for the individual than for the corporation and larger for the lower and middle brackets than for the upper brackets than originally had been envisaged.

In expounding its views, the Council educated not just the President, Congress, and the public, but also Treasury. It is reasonable to conclude that Treasury architects accepted the Council's viewpoint to the degree that they felt possible by the time the tax proposals had reached the final stage of ratification. It is also reasonable to assume that "liberals" within Treasury, such as Brazer, would not have been able to modify Treasury's stand without outside help from the Council. In other words, Treasury's final tax proposals represented a balance between Heller and Mills, between reduction and reform, that would not have been the same had there been no Heller. The sense of accomplishment that Heller and his associates may have had over the ultimate passage of a bill involving an

$11.5-billion net reduction may have been tempered by both the delay in its passage and the fate of the reforms that the Council too had favored. But at least the Council's economic arguments on behalf of reduction appear to have won general political acceptance. To the reformers in Treasury went the bitter pill of seeing proposed structural reforms designed to increase revenues by $3.5 billion whittled down by the legislative process to reforms producing only an additional $300 million.[81]

As demonstrated by the Administration's tax program, the primary significance of the Heller Council is that it was the most important single creative force in the development of a new approach to economic policy. As the Employment Act of 1946 ratified the government's responsibility for the nation's economic welfare (and hence its acceptance of Keynesian principles), the tax proposals of 1963 signaled the policy-maker's recognition that expenditure-revenue combinations leading to deficits can be a constructive force in economic growth. Policy thinking became more consistent with economic thinking. A new tradition was established. The Council analyzed, advocated, articulated, and gained acceptance for new economic values, new techniques of economic analysis, and new concepts of fiscal policy as a positive contributor to national economic well-being. As recognized in subsequent paragraphs, the Council's was not a solo performance, but among its peers the Council took a lead which it did not relinquish; it persuaded, cooperated, and competed with tact and effectiveness.

Of parallel significance is the fact that the Heller Council won Kennedy's acceptance of its views. It is quite a turnabout for a President to commit himself to a balanced budget one year and defend a voluntarily incurred deficit the next. Heller provided the President, who was above all else a pragmatic politician, with an economic force or model against which, on economic matters, political or noneconomic forces could be measured.

My own belief is that the Council, primarily in the person of its Chairman, encouraged Kennedy to develop a sophisticated economic philosophy which he had not previously possessed and, in so doing, transformed an instinctive conservative into a conscious liberal. It is impossible to say how much of this transformation was a matter of Heller's actually changing Kennedy's mind, that is, his convictions, on economic policy and how much was a matter of strengthening his willingness to champion publicly Keynesian full-employment economics that he may already have privately accepted, regardless of the political consequences. The first refers to his thinking and the second to his strategy; Heller apparently affected both. The conservatism that Kennedy preached in 1961 appears to have been synonymous with the conservatism he thought. The first half of 1962 was marked by a conflict between the public stance he felt obliged to take and the developing shift in his thinking. His espousal of tax reduction in the latter half of the year reflected a return to relative coincidence between his thinking and his public advocacy.

Correspondingly, in the beginning the Council was more tolerated than successful. Subsequently, it was more successful in principle than in practice, but ultimately it was successful on both counts. This progression in turn indicated a growing acceptance of the Council for its views and also for its competence. The Heller Council was part of an Administration that valued competence highly and penalized incompetence with exclusion. The Council made the grade with Kenneth O'Donnell and Lawrence O'Brien as well as with the President. Such acceptance was translated into generally harmonious relations with the Budget Bureau, the Treasury, the Federal Reserve, and the wide range of other agencies with which the Council dealt. Such disenchantment with the Council as there was appeared to come primarily from the antigovernment businessmen who thought the Council did too much [82] and segments of the labor phalanx which objected to the Council's putting less emphasis upon larger expenditures than upon tax reduction and also to the Council's attempt to cultivate business groups.

The significant impact of the Heller Council is important in itself, but the explanations for it are no less important. At the risk of oversimplification, four separate but related reasons for the Council's impact emerge:

1. The faltering in early 1962 of a recovery started barely twelve months before, another in a series of postwar falterings, enhanced the Council's arguments with acceptance and urgency. The persist-

ence of the balance-of-payments problem forced a close examination of cause and effect, to say nothing of a search for new approaches. The success of the "twist" policy of high, short-term and low, long-term interest rates gave an indication of what experimentation might accomplish. The postwar prosperity and relatively greater rate of economic growth of competing countries provided convenient and tempting examples of advantages to be derived from economic planning and liberal deficit policies. The refusal of Congress to accept expenditure increases, as initially favored by Heller, obliged both the Council and the Administration to turn their attention to tax reduction.

2. The Council had in Kennedy a remarkably receptive and educable President. He was at the time the first President of the United States and only world leader born in the twentieth century willing to grasp and work with modern economics. His concept of the Presidency, his style of political leadership, and the issues with which he was attempting to deal encouraged, even forced, him to make full use of the Council. Kennedy's pragmatic responsiveness to unfolding developments at home and abroad, his rapport with intellectuals, and his impatience with the pace of public affairs in general and of Congress in particular combined to yield a unique receptivity to the Council's views as well as harmonious working relationships.

3. As a Budget Bureau colleague remarked, "Heller was lucky in his Secretary of the Treasury." Despite the fundamental difference in orientations between Heller's emphasis on growth and Dillon's on stability, they were both able men in their respective roles. Each could understand and respect the views and responsibilities of the other. Each apparently had a very high regard for the ability of the other. Their differences, as important as they were in, for example, the tax proposals, were more in terms of emphasis than of principle, of timing than of content. Heller was thought to be more ebullient than Dillon, who was known for his calm reserve, but each was able to communicate with the other, to cooperate on a broad variety of projects, to adjust to the views of one another and—more important —to those of the President. Such an association did not rule out competition, but it did mean competition in compromise rather than in divisive conflict. This creative variety of competitive relationship

extended to the staff levels of the Council and Treasury and also to the other components of the Kennedy Administration led by men such as Bell and then Gordon of the Bureau of the Budget and Martin and his Federal Reserve. Between like-minded men of considerable ability there existed in their work a spirit of rapport and mutual assistance essential to the Council's achievement and to its assistance to others.[83]

4. The Heller Council was in 1961 and 1962 a strong Council composed generally of very able, well-led, aggressive, amazingly hard-working, and productive professionals. The Council was able to capitalize on the experiences of its predecessors and from the developments in economic knowledge, in improved statistical data, and in advanced quantitative analysis. Under Heller's driving force, the Council became a round-the-clock scout on the New Frontier.

In short, the Heller Council was in harmony with its times. In an era of change, the Council advocated change, change that spanned economic, social, political, and technological developments, change that was as tidal as civil rights and as explosive as Cuba. The Council too was in a hurry; to be passive and conventional in public policy was to be out of tune.

Part of the anguish over Kennedy's assassination is the belief held by many that he was beginning to break out of the detached uncommitted approach to issues of which James MacGregor Burns had written only four years previously [84] and of which some of his own lieutenants complained in the summer of 1962. "If we only knew what he really wanted," they would say. It is not too great a tribute to suggest that the Heller Council was one of the contributors to the emergent breakthrough. On November 22, Heller was part of a delegation led by Secretary of State Rusk en route to Japan to develop more effective economic arrangements with that nation. He was working with Dillon, Martin, George Ball, and McGeorge Bundy on promoting international monetary reforms. Heller had received permission to proceed with the development of the antipoverty program, upon which Robert Lampman of the Council staff had done the preliminary work. Although under attack, the Council's guides to wage rates were established as a major factor in labor-management wage negotiation. In part coincidental with, in part an outgrowth of the Council's contribution to the 1963 tax program, the guidelines represent a new breadth and depth of policy involvement achieved by the Council and encouraged by Kennedy.

After the assassination, Heller developed close working relationships with President Johnson. However, after almost four years of sixty-to-eighty-hour weeks, he resigned in November, 1964, to return to the University of Minnesota. The Council chairmanship was assumed by Gardner Ackley. To fill not only Ackley's place but also that of John P. Lewis, who had resigned earlier in the year to take a position with AID in India, Johnson appointed Arthur Okun of Yale and formerly of the Council staff and Otto Eckstein, a frequent consultant to the Council from Harvard. To these professionals and their colleagues has gone the responsibility of advising a far different President and an increasingly different Administration on ways to achieve "The Great Society."

VIII. THE POLITICS OF ECONOMIC ADVICE

The determination of the overall significance of the Council's performance in terms of its impact on economic policy and its fulfillment of or deviation from original expectations should be possible if the activities of the Council under three separate chairmanships are considered from a point removed from the parade of events, issues, and decisions that constituted them. A description of the characteristics of the Council's advisory function which explains its performance should likewise be feasible. For the accomplishment of both tasks, however, comparisons between the Keyserling, Burns, and Heller Councils as each of them functioned under different Presidents and in response to different situations become not ends in themselves but means directed toward an evaluation of the Council's part in the American Presidency.

The Council's Performance

As the symbol of the President's responsibility for the nation's economic welfare and as a source of specific economic knowledge, the Council of Economic Advisers has emerged as the government's economic ideologist. It is a source of ideas and information rather than a force in execution and coordination. Characterized by an expertise that is essentially substantive rather than derived, the Council has helped more in policy formulation and analysis than in management. It has brought to the policy-making environment at the presidential level a body of knowledge that is as pervasive in its coverage as are the President's political responsibilities. In these terms the Council has aided presidential leadership. Each of the Councils studied went beyond factual analysis and advice (important as these were) to provide the rationale for the economic policies of the respective administrations. The exposition of each Council's rationale in everything from its annual *Report* for the President to congressional testimony, from prepared speeches to spontaneous conversation, has provided the models or sets of standards, that is, the objectives and values, by which specific government economic policies were designed and evaluated and by which deviations toward other values and objectives have at least been recognized. Keyserling's analyses and recommendations became the standard for early Korean mobilization policies. Burns, it will be recalled, regarded his Council's philosophy as giving a sense of continuity to the policies of the Eisenhower Administration. Heller's analysis of economic stagnation and its causes constituted the rationale for an emerging new tradition.

As the economic conscience for its administration, each Council served as educator, spokesman, and catalyst. The articulated analysis and advocacy of each was for the edification of the President, other advisers, and leaders in the Administration and Congress, as well as interested nongovernmental segments of the public. Burns' weekly sessions with Eisenhower, Keyserling's and Heller's memoranda to Truman and Kennedy, respectively, were essentially educational. In its annual *Reports*, each Council spoke to as well as for the President, summarizing both what it had been hammering at in the year just passed and what it sought for the year to come. In these *Reports* all three Councils floated trial balloons that soared or burst, that helped to convince—but not necessarily commit—the President. Truman was Keyserling's addressee for arguments on behalf of the Council's desired role in the "Economics of Defense." In the same manner, Burns sought acceptance for countercyclical principles from Eisenhower, and Heller's emphasis upon the gap between actual and potential production in the 1962 *Economic Report* was addressed to Kennedy and, perhaps even more, to Dillon, Mills, and others whose support the President needed.

The Keyserling, Burns, and Heller Councils all had a liberalizing effect upon their Presidents, which in turn created a difference in the President's outlook, his priorities, and his handling of economic policy problems. Liberalization has been on the side of activity rather than inactivity. In trying to extend Fair Deal liberalism, Keyserling carried the Truman Administration somewhat beyond its own relatively liberal tendencies but not as far as Keyserling himself would have liked. In trying to gain acceptance of government countercyclical responsibilities, Burns moderated traditional Republican thinking but presumably not as much as he would have desired. In trying to spur economic growth, Heller accelerated and helped to complete Kennedy's public break with accepted tradition but not as quickly as he had hoped. Explicitly and implicitly, the Councils have represented their Presidents in the development of particular decisions, such as Blough's participation in the Treasury–Federal Reserve accord, Burns' damper on an increase in the minimum wage, and Gordon's coordination of the drafting of the transportation bill in 1961.

As ideologist, the Council has been associated with a full range of specific economic policy issues. Yet, relative to the roles and contribution of others in operating agencies, it has acted less often as an integral participant in the decisions surrounding specifics than as a creator, sounding board, or facilitator. The Council's frequent identification with a particular decision as an economic policy issue, its pronouncements on policies, and its participation in drafting messages have often belied the specific development that has gone on in relevant departments. The experience of the three Councils suggests that in the cases where the Council has had a relatively deep impact on specific program development, the issues have spanned a number of operating agencies or the Council's expertise has represented the relevant body of knowledge.

By the same token, the Council's frequently peripheral impact on the specific content of particular decisions has often belied its contribution to the climate in which the decision was made. The significance of the Council's impact on particular issues has consisted most often in the churning of issues, in bringing them to the decision state, in promoting the rationale, in helping to gain presidential approval, and so affecting the outcome. Such was the significance of Keyserling's sense of urgency, Burns' concern for confidence, and Heller's arguments for growth. Granting the impossibility of untangling the complexity of the decision-making process or of measuring with certainty what might have happened had there been no Council, the case studies indicate that the Council's performance has, in fact, made a substantial difference.

In effecting differences, the Council has been, not always but usually, on the side of promotion rather than restraint. Distinct from the Budget Bureau's traditional "No,"[1] its reaction has typically been "Go." Its successes have derived from getting things started or changed, and its failures from being unable to prevent things from being undone or delayed or stopped. During the first six months of the Korean crisis Keyserling strengthened the opposition to Baruch's arguments for full control and Symington's moves toward full mobilization. Similarly, in 1951 Keyserling failed to counter the Administration's adherence to partial mobilization led by Wilson. Probably there would have been no study of budget flexibility nor any preparation of public works plans, much less a subsequent step-up effort, had it not been for Burns' anticipation of the 1953–54 recession. As a Budget Bureau commentator put it, "We probably spent more and did more through the government than we otherwise would have—with Arthur as well as with Leon." Probably also the Kennedy Administration would not have been so willing to embark upon new economic policies, nor so soon, had not the Heller Council forcefully presented its analysis of recurring recession to both the government and the nation. As Keyserling tried to stiffen the Treasury's position in relation to the Federal Reserve Board in 1951, so Burns stiffened Humphrey's stand in the 1954 tax program, and Heller stiffened Dillon's willingness to accept tax reduction on its own merits in 1962.

Expectations Revisited

The performance of the Council, the nature of its impact, and the difference it has made assume greater significance when considered in terms of fulfillment of or deviation from original expectations. As seen in Chapter 1, the Council was set up with the hope that it would (1) help to prevent postwar depression, (2) interpret the Employment Act according to either the "maximum employment, production and purchasing power" or the "promotion of free enterprise" interpretation of the Act's policy statement, (3) fulfill a planning function in accordance with one or the other interpretation, (4) provide expert advice objectively, and (5) function as a presidential institution.

A CHANGE IN OBJECTIVES. Contrary to original expectations, not preventing deep depression but controlling inflation and encouraging economic growth have become the Council's major economic policy objectives. Consequently, although the Council has analysed and advised concerning recession, its more enduring preoccupation and primary frame of reference have centered in achieving and reconciling the two objectives just mentioned. Compared with the Depression of the early 1930s, the recessions of 1948–49, 1953–54, 1957–58, and 1960–61 were mild and of short duration. According to Wilfred Lewis, real GNP declined 2.3, 3.7, 4.3, and 2.2 percent, respectively, and the declines lasted two, four, two, and three quarters, respectively.[2] All declines were reversed within thirteen months, with unemployment not exceeding 8 percent of the labor force.[3]

Variation in the relatively active sector of inventory investment rather than a major breakdown in postwar economic functioning appears to have been the cause of the recessions. Immediate postwar demand, built-in stabilizers, and recognition of the government's responsibility symbolized by the Employment Act all contributed to preventing depressions of deep and epidemic proportions. As both Brown and Lewis conclude, discretionary fiscal policies played a secondary role in achieving economic stability.[4] Without in any way depreciating the unemployment and hardships which accompanied them, none the less the recessions might be looked upon as temporary halts in a twenty-year march of prosperity.

Under the circumstances, the general price rises of 1947–48, 1950–51, and 1955–57, initially created by the combination of prewar depression and wartime expansion, replaced fear of postwar depression as the dominant factor in economic policy deliberations.

Keyserling was burdened with concern over inflation throughout his association with the Council; his offensive on behalf of economic expansion met with resistance largely because inflation was thought to be the accompanying price.

Desire to control inflation through reduced expenditures and balanced budgets were the primary ends and means determining the acceptance or rejection of Burns' countercyclical recommendations. Besides exerting an inhibiting effect on countercyclical activities, fear of inflation led to various proposals for amending the Employment Act to include an explicit commitment to fight inflation, for example, by Burns in his speech before the American Statistical Association in September, 1962. Only when emerging price stability coincided with another mild recession and the national elections of 1960 did fear of inflation give way to the more positive issue of economic growth. As a political slogan, "getting the country moving again" rang with validity in the midst of sagging economic activity and reports of comparatively greater growth abroad.

Although less emphasis was placed on the mobilization of resources, what Keyserling had initially espoused as economic expansion was subsequently accepted as economic growth. Yet the fear of inflation—legacy of the late forties and fifties—still exerted a restraining force on the growth policies advocated by Heller, a force that was not lifted until the economic pause of mid-1962 made tax reduction and the prospect of temporarily increased deficits a worthwhile investment in both growth and stability.

DIFFERENT POLICY INTERPRETATIONS. The expectation of differing interpretations of the Employment Act has been an expectation fulfilled; each Council has clearly chosen one interpretation or the other. There is no difficulty in ascribing the "maximum employment, production, and purchasing power" interpretation to the Keyserling and Heller Councils nor the "free competitive enterprise" interpretation to the Burns Council. With or without explicit reference to the Act's policy statement or to its requirements of the Council, each has adopted one or the other as means to the objectives of economic prosperity. Apart from distinctions in basic interpretation, however, the qualifications in actual application of one interpretation have reflected tacit recognition of the other, and, consequently, the differences have been in priorities and emphases rather than in mutual exclusiveness of principle.

Whereas the Keyserling and Heller Councils were concerned with growth in terms of optimum use of the nation's economic resources, the Burns Council was concerned with growth in terms of improvement over the past. To the former groups the "gap" referred to the distance from the present to the potential; to Burns, it referred to the distance from the present to the past. Colm illustrated this distinction in his testimony before the Joint Committee on the Economic Report in 1955:

In a period of rapid increase in the labor force and in labor productivity, it makes a great difference whether existing levels of employment, etc., are evaluated against past levels or needed levels. For instance, by comparison with the past one can come to the conclusion that 1954 "will go down in history as one of our most prosperous years" (President's Economic Report, p. 11). By comparison with needed levels, it becomes apparent that 1954 was a year in which production was about $20 billion below a level corresponding with satisfactory employment.[5]

In the first *Economic Report* prepared under his direction, Keyserling had President Truman say, "Our economy can and must continue to grow. . . . Our immediate goal for 1950 should be to regain maximum employment. . . . This would mean about 61 million civilian jobs." [6] Burns, in his first effort, had Eisenhower say, "Our economic goal is an increasing national income, shared equitably among those who contribute to its growth, and achieved in dollars of stable buying power." [7] And Heller in his, had Kennedy claim under a banner of "Goals of Economic Policy" that "the unfinished business of economic policy includes . . . the achievement of full employment and sustained prosperity without inflation [and] the acceleration of economic growth." [8] The difference in the choice and shading of words is the important one of means-ends relationship. All three Councils wanted both growth and stability, but to Keyserling and Heller optimum growth was at once both an end in itself that required governmental activity and a means to stability. To Burns the achievement of stability and growth through minimum government interference and the cultivation of confidence carried increasing growth as the standard of progress.

None of the three questioned the primacy of private enterprise; each accepted the basic validity of countercyclical policy. Keyserling and Heller would not dispute Burns' counterrecessionary principles of prompt, coordinated, and sensitive preventive action if and to the degree necessary, but they would differ on what conditions constituted "necessity" or what constituted the best mixture for preventive action. Although subsequently more willing to favor decreased revenues, Heller's similarity to Keyserling's preferring expanding expenditures for both short- and long-term purposes stands in contrast to both anti-inflation measures and minimum governmental activity in the private economy as emphasized by Burns. Under roughly comparable recession situations, Heller appeared more willing than Burns to have the government undertake compensatory action, but less willing to rely upon built-in stabilizers which, in fact, he thought should be changed. Whereas Heller favored tax incentive for increased consumption, Burns advocated incentives for greater investment. Monetary policy was considered a more dynamic force relative to fiscal policy during the Burns period.

The Keynesian emphases of Keyserling and Heller were distinct from the inductive emphasis of Burns. Greater reliance was put upon aggregate analysis and long-range forecasting during the Keyserling and Heller periods. A more literal interpretation was given to the Employment Act's requirement of analyzing existing and needed policies for maximum employment, production, and purchasing power. Both Keyserling and Heller, however, used the analytical techniques favored by Burns and exhaustively studied the various economic indicator series associated with the National Bureau of Economic Research. By the same token, Burns may have avoided publishing quantitative projections in the widely distributed annual *Reports*, but he certainly made all sorts of forecasts and utilized long-term Keynesian projections as part of the "inside" process of analysis and advice:

For internal purposes the Council utilizes and makes all sorts of quantitative estimates. It seems unwise, however, to publish near-term estimates that rest heavily on assumptions and conjecture, and that is bound to be the case with numerical "goals" or "targets." The use of such estimates by the President in his Economic Report would not render a useful service to the nation.[9]

The differing interpretations of the Employment Act were reflected in each Council's analysis and advice and in the content and format of its respective annual *Reports*. The following chapter discusses the part these differences also played in shaping the relations between the Council and the President and in determining the unique aspects of each Council.

INCREASED ACCEPTANCE OF PLANNING. The distinction between the two different interpretations of Employment Act policy have been merged with the expectation concerning the Council's planning function. Planning as the rational anticipation, development, and coordination of policies and programs in terms of overall objectives has not reached the degree feared by the "free-enterprise" advocates nor has it matched the hopes of the "maximum-employment" advocates. Yet, under both maximum-employment and free-enterprise interpretations, there has been in the intervening years a perceptible shift toward a concept of comprehensive planning of both substantive and managerial significance. Increasingly, anticipation of myriad specific needs and possibilities has been viewed in terms of a specific rationale and an organized set of policy objectives. Increasingly, the managerial coordination of agency programs, separate in their resources, impact, and supports, has become an economic planning process, defined by Elliot as "the process of preparing programs for future action in relation to objectives, instruments and issues in which 'economic' aspects, roughly and perhaps arbitrarily defined, play an important role." [10]

The continuing attempt to avoid labels of "planning" and "planner" because of their managed-economy connotation may obscure but does not negate the developments of planning in these terms. In effect, these developments modify the conclusions Long reached in 1949 that "Intellectual perception of the need for . . . coordination, . . . has run well ahead of the public's perception of it and of the development of a political channelling of power adequate to its administrative implementation." [11] That Burns was interested in planning less comprehensive and long-range in nature than were Keyserling and Heller does not rule out the conclusion that the

Council has been both a participant and a beneficiary of the gradual *de facto* legitimacy accorded planning as part of the advisory function.

The crucial aspect of the Council's involvement in planning is its application of its central function of developing policy rationale and ideas to the providing of standards and models for the future as well as current economic policies that comprise the Administration's economic plans. There has been no attempt to develop or implement, on behalf of the President, single-strategy planning or comprehensive governmental direction of economic activity characteristic of current European planning efforts. As it has evolved over the years, a presidential plan is not a "bull" setting forth objectives and component details in an unbroken and symmetrical form from White House to field installation, but rather it is a meld of general and specific objectives into an acceptable federation. Consistent with the President's views (which, as his economic ideologist it has helped shape), the Council has advanced the aspect of planning concerned with the determination of objectives and in so doing has improved the meld. Complemented by its extensive economic analysis, the Council has applied its models to a variety of economic policy matters in its year-in-year-out influencing of the President and of others on his behalf.

The Council's emphasis has been primarily on "deductive planning," that is, upon the creation and choice of policy objectives and the determination of more or less ideal component programs for the fulfillment of these objectives. At the same time, the Budget Bureau has, in its budget and legislative program clearance operation, emphasized "inductive planning," that is, the compilation and reconciliation of continuing and proposed component programs, the sum of which becomes overall objectives. Although the Council's view is from the top down and the Budget Bureau's from the bottom up, neither view is or can be taken in its pure form. The Council does and must involve itself in specifics in order to develop, sell, or salvage overall objectives; the Bureau is well aware of overall objectives (many of which it helps to create) in its comprehensive review of past and future governmental operations. The Bureau, however, *must* reconcile specific disparate parts into an operating whole "consistent with the President's program"; the Council need not.

This difference underscores the contrast in functions of planning service to the President. Moreover, it adds to an understanding of federal government planning. Reagan, for one, may complain that the President has no policy-planning staff and that the Council has not achieved the potential of its "authority" to appraise and recommend on behalf of a better "fit" between agency programs and overall economic policy.[12] Such a complaint, however, ignores the dichotomy between deductive and inductive planning. As argued here, the President does have in the Council a policy-planning staff in the creative and conceptual sense of future policy. He has in the Bureau a policy-planning staff in the sense of coordinating future policy operations. As their close working relationships indicate, the two are interdependent, but they are not the same.

It is in the sense of being a model that the *Economic Report* has become an important planning document. The *Report* is not an action instrument serving as a link between the departments, the President, and the Congress in the legislative, budgetary, or executive processes. Instead, it is an informational and promotional document that both reviews the past and previews the future, that in its analysis and rationale "sets the sights" of economic policy. It contains very little that is new or unacceptable to the relevant departments and nothing that is specifically contrary to the expressed views of the President. Its recommendations are not firm commitments to act—even less so now than during Keyserling's chairmanship, when, according to Lewis, who served with both the Keyserling and Heller Councils, the President's *Economic Reports* were "indispensable engines of consent":

Keyserling worked for consensus among departments. What was said and not said was important. If an issue appeared, it meant that the issue had gone through the wringer; if not, it hadn't. That meant Truman had not tried or not been able to knock heads together. As comprehensive as the budget [was], it went through a great review and clearance process; not so now. Consensus is more informal.[13]

Normally, economic policy recommendations have their principal articulation in the Budget Message or the State of the Union Message or, frequently, in special presidential messages. Although major economic proposals are normally described in the *Report*, the descriptions themselves tend to be general and introductory and to serve as complements to major presentations elsewhere and to the Council's economic analyses contained in its *Report* to the President. Nevertheless, as summary descriptions flanked by both recitations of policy objectives in other messages and economic analyses, the President's *Report's* recommendations oblige the congressman, to say nothing of the departmental administrator, to view his program interests in the full perspective of the Administration's economic policies, or, at least, make it more difficult to avoid seeing the broader picture.

The Council's planning function did not emerge immediately but rather evolved as part of the evolution of the advisory function. The peacetime planning envisaged by Keyserling in the late 1940s for postwar prosperity and inflation control was, in terms of acceptance, premature and hence rejected. Its first significant acceptance came under circumstances of emergency or specific application. Although lacking adequate testing, NSC 68 none the less contributed a general set of national security objectives and values that formed a recognized basis for separate actions. So too did Keyserling's early recommendations and urgings regarding Korea, although they were exhortations and distinct from formal and specific commitment. Wilson's Defense Mobilization Order No. 4 had an even more specific guideline effect. The elaborate preparations and processing behind Eisenhower's 1954 program had all the earmarks of a planned campaign. Burns' inductive economics by no means excluded short-term planning for stabilization purposes. In fact, such planning was consistent with the views of the father of inductive economics, Wesley Mitchell, who in the 1930s endorsed public works, slum clearance, and economic planning and was himself a member of the National Planning Board during the Roosevelt New Deal period.[14]

That Burns' considerable efforts at developing public works plans had only a partial application in the 1954 step-up program did not invalidate the value of the plans nor detract from Eisenhower's appreciation of their existence. That the planning activities of the Burns Council were not more extensive was at least in part due to there being less government activity for which plans were needed. Heller's support of tax reduction as one step toward maximum utilization of our national resources was not in the direction of general planning as such, for reduction would have the effect of increasing the proportion of economic activity subject to nongovernmental planning and of decreasing the proportion subject to governmental planning. However, his concern over unemployment, excess capacity, stunted growth, unfavorable balance of payments, and frequent (even if mild) recessions led to analysis and advocacy on behalf of objectives which did constitute an impetus for and dependence upon overall planning.

In fact, the jump from relatively specific, emergency, and short-term programming to more comprehensive planning of governmental programs received perhaps its biggest boost in the acceptance, during the Kennedy Administration, of the basic policy objective of accelerated economic growth. By Administration interpretation, growth involved projections into the future in terms of potential, the anticipatory nature of which required forward planning. By its complexity, the development of growth policy into specific objectives and subobjectives meant the necessary determination of standards and values of compromises and relationships that in turn affected international, defense, and domestic policies. The very development and interdependence of governmental programs, of which economic growth has been but one objective, has demanded a greater degree of planning operations; they have forced a more centralized determination of objectives and priorities, of allocation of limited resources, of minimization of overlap and conflict. Reconciling means and ends has meant greater significance of the President's program as *his* program and hence both a greater need for and a greater expectation of his programming initiative and creativity.

The increased recognition of the need for planning has been both complemented and supported by its increased feasibility, that is, the increased availability of techniques by which effective planning can be developed. Enormous strides in the development of information sources and quantitative analysis have made possible more complete, thorough, and up-to-date diagnoses of the nation's economic health; they have improved the understanding of relationships among different economic phenomena. These developments have in turn been aided by the revolution in computer technology and its derivatives of data processing and operations research.

The whole field of "management science" has focused on communications, rational decision-making, and program evaluation. The operations of Troika and Quadriad have undoubtedly facilitated understanding and consensus among principal economic policy-makers. The development of "performance," or "program," budgeting has supplied additional impetus to efficient and coordinated programming of widely varying activities. The Budget Bureau has encouraged departments to develop budget projections that stretch three, four, and five years into the future. The advances in program analysis and review within the Defense Department, which accounts for half of federal expenditures, have provided example, encouragement, and—through interdependence of operations—pressure for planning throughout the government. Few departments are without some form of recognized planning operation responsible for both anticipation and evaluation. As analytical and managerial techniques contributing to more effective policy development and execution, these developments have not only facilitated planning but also weakened much of the philosophical and operational opposition to it.

The net effect of these many-sided developments has been increased general political and popular acceptance (which Long had found lacking) of the President's planning responsibility as part of presidential leadership and of the Council's planning function as part of that leadership. This acceptance by departments, the Congress, the public, and the President himself has often been more implicit than explicit, partially rather than fully understood, and unconsciously rather than consciously embraced, but it has developed all the same. The advances over the planning that existed in 1949 have not been in the name of planning or in fulfillment of some ideal concept of planning; far from it. They have, however, reflected the pragmatic responses to the demands for increased governmental services efficiently supplied. The limited nature of the advances tend to reflect the impact of political independence and substantive diversity upon services to be planned rather than philosophical or emotional reactions to planning as such.

The evolution of the Council's planning function is related to its deviation from the remaining expectations concerning its advisory objectivity and its institutional nature.

PROFESSIONAL OBJECTIVITY PLUS. The expectation that the Council would provide expert advice in a professionally objective and passive manner has been not so much unfulfilled as significantly complemented. Analysis of the Keyserling, Burns, and Heller Councils indicates that the President has received expert advice; moreover, he has received objective advice in the sense of complete information and honest appraisal. As this analysis has so far indicated, however, the advice has not been objective in the literal meaning of the word—that is, detached, impersonal, and unprejudiced. Rather, the Council's objectivity has been within the framework of governing economic and policy values—or objectivity within subjectivity not instead of it.

With some exceptions, the Council has met Nourse's mandate that it "piece together a complete and consistent picture" of the nation's economy and that it "interpret all available literal facts into the soundest possible diagnosis." [15] As examples of exceptions, economists point to the Council's slowness in recognizing the onset of the 1948–49 recession, to the underestimation of the drop in defense expenditures in 1954, [16] and to the overly optimistic GNP estimates for 1962. These errors, however, must be weighed against the far heavier balance of generally accurate estimates of economic advice. Moreover, the validity of these criticisms is at best qualified, since the criticisms are necessarily based upon the Council's public statements and the critics cannot know what the Council may have revealed to the President and other policy-makers privately nor distinguish clearly between information that the Council develops and information that reflects not analysis but decisions in which economic and noneconomic factors had to be reconciled.

Its alleged lapses notwithstanding, the Council has by its analysis and advice over the full range of national economic policy strengthened the quality and rationality of economic decisions. It has drawn information from a variety of sources in and out of the government. It has provided and, in a sense, imposed upon the President a more comprehensive running account of the nation's economy than he had ever had previously. Although its preoccupation with current economic policy has precluded a sustained commitment to research, the Council has benefited from as well as been a spur to research done elsewhere. Keyserling's encouragement of the development of the national economic budget and Heller's development of the related full-employment surplus concept stand as examples of the Council's own innovative efforts. The Princeton conference in 1954 on problems of depression which Burns instigated contributed to the development and understanding of countercyclical policy analysis. Throughout its operations, the Council has worked toward the improvement of economic statistics as indicated in the *Economic Reports,* the monthly *Economic Indicators,* of which over 10,000 copies are distributed each month, and the Council's participation on interdepartmental statistical committees.

Although criticized for glossing over the shifts and inconsistencies of policy formation,[17] the Council's *Economic Reports* have presented informative and nontechnical summaries of national economic developments that have been of considerable educational value both in and outside the government. As Hansen has noted, "On a more technical plane is the notable 1953 Council Report. . . . In a sense this Report is a textbook on the methodology of economic programming."[18] Arthur Burns has noted that "The American people have of late been more conscious of the business cycle, more sensitive to every wrinkle of economic curves, more alert to the possible need of contracyclical action on the part of the government, than ever before in our history."[19]

Although judged by professional peers to be better at some times than at others, the level of competence of the Council's members and staff, particularly as supplemented by outside consultants, has nevertheless been good. And although by no means the master of all specific areas of economic analysis and policy, the Council has none the less emerged as the national center of policy economics and hence is worthy of recognition by the economics profession.

The Council's extension beyond the expectation of strict objectivity has been in its obvious inability either to meet the Nourse ideal of a scientific agency or to avoid policy advocacy. The whole experience of the Council has been one of attempted or achieved active involvement in the development of economic policy. To varying degrees, its energies and skills have been thrown or drawn into the "mix" of both the creative and reconciling phases of the President's political leadership. This involvement "in action" has in effect clothed expertise with a raiment of uncertainty and human frailty: it has armed objectivity with weapons of interests and values. Only subsidiarily were the Keyserling, Burns, and Heller Councils passive or neutral in their advisory function. Advocacy was manifested in their daily activities of policy promotion, presidential education, and agency contact. It was manifested both in the speeches, testimony, and articles of the three chairmen and in the staffing, organization, and operation of the respective Councils. Advocacy was served as a complement to, not a substitute for, analysis.

It is in these terms that the Council *Reports* have been not only instruments of planning and sources of information but, in addition, important instruments of political leadership. They have not, however, been partisan tracts but rather documents oriented to the economic policies and values of the Administration. As one of the President's three annual messages, the *Report* is not unlike a corporate annual report in its portrayal (in as favorable terms as possible) of the year's activities, the accomplishment of the nation's economy, the contributions of government economic policy, and the prospects for future progress. It is precisely with these terms in mind that economists, such as Brown, object to the *Report*'s tone of "omniscience and self-justification." [20] It is in these tones, however, in the specificity or generality of its analyses and projections and in the content of its recommendations, that the Council both aids the President and expresses the Council's political economics. The relatively apolitical 1953 *Report* prepared by a Council serving in a lame-duck status provides an inverse indication of the Council's political orientation.

PERSONAL RATHER THAN INSTITUTIONAL ASSISTANCE. Interpreting the Employment Act, promoting presidential plans and planning, as well as applying politically oriented expertise, have combined to make the Council not a presidential institution like the Budget Bureau as originally expected but rather a personal staff to the President. It has not developed as a permanent entity with bureaucratic formality, specified procedures, and self-sustaining operations. Instead, it has emerged more as a variable group of individuals directly identified with and dependent upon the President.

The strictures of the Employment Act have failed to enforce institutionalization of the Council apart from the President and, if anything, have had a reverse effect. Finding qualified individuals acceptable to the President and, in turn, sympathetic with his views and willing to serve on the Council has proved far more of a hurdle than Senate confirmation. Similarly, congeniality of views between economist and President has been as important a factor in attracting staff members as their expertise has been to their selection. Keyserling's view that confirmation of Council members enhanced their prestige suggests that the legislative control thus applied was less significant than the emphasis placed by the need for confirmation on the personal rather than institutional character of the Council and the importance it gave the member as part of the Presidency. The three-man council form of organization has not prevented direct and individual contact between Council member and President. Reorganization Plan No. 9 has nullified any potential insulation inherent in the committee approach. Budgetary limitations have forced the Council to remain small and informal, preventing any bureaucratic institutionalization, and by denying coordinating capability have insured a role of creative advocacy. The President's *Economic Report* to Congress has not so much driven a legislative wedge into executive policy-making as it has linked the Council to the President by creating a major vehicle for their relationship. By providing a forum for the discussion of the President's economic policies, the Joint Economic Committee's review of the *Economic Report* and the Council's testifying has actually reinforced executive leadership vis-à-vis Congress. With a few exceptions Congress' concern for the operations of the Council has been fairly routine.

In experiencing varying degrees of influence, enjoying varying degrees of acceptance by the President and agencies, the Keyserling, Burns, and Heller Councils made their ways as assemblages of individuals and not of organization men. The chairmen themselves, some of the other Council members such as Blough and Gordon, and a number of the staff men such as Colm, Caplan, Newcomb, Achinstein, Solow, and Okun have identified the Council, not vice versa. As in the case of the Presidency itself, the Council has been shaped in the image of its chairman. Whether creating or reflecting the President's thinking, the chairman has achieved for his Council a compatibility with the President. The virtually complete remaking of the Council with each new administration is indicative of its nonpermanent and noninstitutional character. Positively, it shows the converse—the essentially transitory and personal relationships of the Council with the President.

The Basis of Politically Oriented Economic Advice

The foregoing evaluation of the Council in terms of original expectations and based upon performance in three different situations has attempted to describe the nature and extent of its influence upon economic policy. There remains the companion task of describing the reasons underlying its performance, that is, the cause side of the cause-and-effect relationship. The following analysis elaborates the thesis that the Council's performance as an economic policy ideologist and its fulfillment of some expectations and deviations from others are, broadly speaking, functions of five principal characteristics of the advisory operation: (1) association with the President and his bureaucracy, (2) the operation of political conflict, (3) the pervasiveness of economic policy, (4) the subjectivity of economic analysis, and (5) the competitiveness of advice.

ASSOCIATION WITH THE PRESIDENT AND HIS BUREAUCRACY. The Council has had no choice but, as already described, to become involved in presidential policy and leadership. Under the terms of the Employment Act it has had no identity except as adviser to the President. Everything it has done has been done in the name of the President and the President's program. If, as Sorensen maintains, presidential decision is influenced by "presidential politics," "presidential advisers," and "presidential perspective," [21] then the Council as one set of presidential advisers (and nothing but advisers), has

been linked with decisions, politics, and perspective. Operationally
if not physically, the Council has become attached to the White
House. Its work is part of what Neustadt describes as "the initiatives a President can take"; it belongs to the decisions, agendas,
records, "helping hands," and "grinding stones," things right and
things wrong.[22] As Homan has expressed it, "A proposal made by
the Council to the President is an invitation to him to make a political issue and the Council is no less involved politically because it is
one step removed from the scene of actual political strife." [23] The
Council's interpretative and conceptual advisory operation constitutes the same sort of political creativeness and synthesis as that
attempted by the President but for which he has so little time. Consequently, the Council stands in the center of the arena into which
converge the great multitude of pressures, interests, opportunities,
and problems of national government and from which emerge the
major strands of political leadership.

The Council, however, is obviously by no means alone in its advisory association with the President. By responsibility and initiative, the operating departments are constant in their advice. In
addition to the Council there is, of course, within the Executive
Office of the President the White House staff, the Bureau of the
Budget, and other components such as the National Security Council, the National Aeronautics and Space Council, the Office of Emergency Planning as the residual legatee of ODM, and the Office of
Science and Technology established in 1962. There are in addition,
two operating components, the second of which is of direct interest
to the Council; the Central Intelligence Agency (CIA) and the new
Office of Economic Opportunity established in 1964 to coordinate
the government's antipoverty programs. With the Council they exist
primarily as advisers and assistants to the President. With the Council they comprise the "presidential bureaucracy" as distinguished
from the bureaucracies of other agencies of the federal government.
In their primary orientation to the President, their roots are not in
the large operating departments with separate resources, recognized specialties, far-flung operations, separate clientele, and particular career interests. Rather, their perspective is more nearly
governmentwide; it epitomizes the representative bureaucracy de-

scribed by Long in 1952. With the Council, these components of the Executive Office comprise a presidential "medium for registering the diverse wills that make up the people's will and for transmuting them into responsible proposals for public policy." [24] They reflect a presidential "sensitivity to long-range and broad considerations, the totality of interests affected, and the utilization of expert knowledge by procedures that ensure a systematic collection and analysis of relevant facts." [25] The association with the President makes the medium and sensitivity all the more comprehensive— more so, that is, than those of operating departments or (as Long emphasizes) of Congress.

The educational background of the presidential bureaucracy appears to have been largely in comprehensive disciplines such as in economics, law, and political science. It is true that, among those who have made the federal government their career, many senior analysts and executives have had substantial experience in other segments of the federal government or even with the state and local organizations. Available evidence nevertheless suggests that experience and career development within the Executive Office have constituted their dominant pattern of employment. Economic and budget analysis, legislative clearance, planning, and liaison work have not paralleled or been confined to particular operating programs such as forestry, housing, or defense. Assignments have admittedly involved degrees of specialization toward certain activities and issues but not to the extent of transferred loyalties and motivations. Macroanalysis and advocacy have been preferred to micro-operation and production. The application of professional competence and policy involvement combined at the presidential level have provided more satisfactory fulfillment of career objectives than work at a relatively programmatic level. Top policy review and analysis within the surviving Victorian splendor of "Old State" have provided an atmosphere more closely resembling the unique air of the Presidency than the ordinary ozone of the field installation. Although maintaining a system of governmentwide contacts and associations with operating programs, the presidential bureaucracy is geared to the President's operations and to his deadlines. Its activities have his symbolic coloration. Whether he be a temporary appointee to the Council or a permanent member of the Budget Bureau staff, the presidential bureaucrat is a part of, not apart from, the White House.

THE OPERATION OF POLITICAL CONFLICT. Although the Council's association with the President and his bureaucracy is crucial, it is none the less activated and meaningful only in terms of specific issues. If, as Sorenson concludes, conflict is "the one quality which characterizes most issues likely to be brought to the President," [26] then the Council as a group of presidential advisers is party to the conflict in issues of economic significance. In its varying roles of participant, representative, mediator, protector, and catalyst, it becomes involved in conflicts "between departments, between the views of various advisers, between the Administration and Congress, between the United States and another nation, or between groups within the country: labor versus management, or race versus race, or state versus nation." [27]

In terms of economic philosophy, the Council has inherited the Employment Act's policy conflict. It has been swept up in the generalities and compromises of a statute in which Congress did not resolve conflict so much as give it statutory permanence. Some years ago, Leys wrote that " 'Moral gesture' legislation amounts to an instruction to do nothing specific, but most 'pass-the-buck' legislation is an instruction to resolve the conflict between groups who want definite but rival standards to be legalized." [28] The Council has been faced with the opportunity and problem of living under a piece of legislation that is at once of both varieties. The Council's attempt to receive the "buck" and to give it some concrete interpretation has automatically involved it in the very conflict of "ideas, interests, institutions, and individuals," to use Bailey's terms,[29] that could not reach agreement in the first place. Not only its analysis and advocacy but its methods of operations as well have become parties to the conflict. The passage of time may have mellowed the extent of the conflict, but it has not changed the conflict's basic nature nor diminished the significance of conflict in the Council's operations or in the praise or condemnation it has received for doing or not doing. The pro-and-con reaction to the Nourse-Keyserling feuds, the stretch-out of the Korean mobilization program over the objections of Keyserling, the feet-dragging reaction to Burns' 1954 step-up program, and the breadth of reaction to the 1963 tax revision proposals—to say nothing of the prolonged consideration of it—all attest to the enduring vitality of the ambivalence of the Council's enabling legislation.

PERVASIVENESS OF ECONOMIC POLICY. The inevitability of association with presidential leadership and the dominance of political conflict of which the Council is a part are doubly significant for the Council because of the relevance of economic considerations to such a wide area of governmental policy and operations. Fiscal and monetary policy are not mutually exclusive among themselves, nor do Treasury, Federal Reserve Board, and Budget Bureau monopolize concern for them. They represent broad categories of economic policies that contribute to and draw their significance from such disparate program areas as taxation, housing, foreign aid, international trade and finance, business regulation, defense, labor relations, natural resources, education, and agriculture. Moreover, such seemingly noneconomic issues as civil rights ramify into economic issues as varied as job security and urban expansion.

Where does the Council's potential involvement stop, for example, in the development of federal transportation policies? Both the Burns and Heller Councils were concerned with such an issue. Can objectives of pay-as-you-go financing, maintaining fair competition among different carriers, improving the economic viability of downtown areas, providing better commuting services, and satisfying defense transportation needs be considered apart from one another or from objectives of growth, stability, and decreased poverty? Can the Council rationalize or analyze apart from these considerations or without some form of collaboration with the Interstate Commerce Commission, Treasury, the Bureau of Public Roads, the Defense Department, the Urban Renewal Administration, and the Budget Bureau? Can it ignore the constituencies, views, committee assignments, and seniority of particular congressmen? Can it pass off as someone else's worry the pressures of cement makers, the railroad brotherhoods, beleaguered commuters, city councils, motorists, and so on, ad infinitum? Can it ignore matters of technical feasibility, obsolescence, and innovation?

To all these questions, the answer is "No." The confluence of economic and political aggregates at the presidential level has not delineated any distinct segment or level of government policy for the Council but rather exposed it to the length, breadth, and specifics of federal policy. Its economic analysis, whatever the base in economic theory, reflects the interdependent relationship between interests and institutions which are both initiators and reactors to national economic policy. It seems not without inverse relevance that the Council's relative abstention from involvement in agriculture policy reflects at least in part the considerable isolation of such policy within the Department of Agriculture and its organized clientele.

SUBJECTIVITY OF ECONOMIC ANALYSIS. Association, conflict, and pervasiveness have in turn been complemented by the subjectivity of economic analysis. Economic truth is not unitary; it does not admit of single and objective answers that, by virtue of such attributes, are automatically accepted. Rather, it involves sets of answers that are consistent with some sets of economic and noneconomic consequences, inconsistent with others, and reflective of different values. Sometimes they are automatically or hastily accepted, at other times only after the most careful and hesitant scrutiny. As Arthur Smithies has argued,

Hardly any economic theory can be ideologically neutral. . . . The mere selection of economic problems for investigation involves value judgments. . . . Attempts to draw sharp distinctions between means and ends can be misleading and dangerous. . . . An economic problem of any importance is too complicated for all such judgments involved in its solution to be set out explicitly. An economist who is advising a President on whether or not to employ direct controls in time of inflation must base his advice largely on his views of the importance or unimportance of preserving a free market economy. Those views necessarily involve value judgments.[30]

In reflecting upon his own experience, Burns has written, "Nor can the economist afford to forget that he is rarely able to speak with the impersonal authority of science. Not only is his ability to predict very limited, but in handling issues of policy he is inevitably influenced by his philosophic and ethical attitudes."[31] Aside from any conscious interpretation of the Employment Act, the content and mode of the Council's economic service to the President has constituted an embracing of noneconomic values primarily because the Council's economics have themselves been rooted in values. Even Nourse's scientific objectivity was a reflection of conservative values. As Keyserling had his Wagner, so Burns had his Mitchell and Heller had his Commons. The aggregate projective nature of Keynesian analysis and prescription underpins convictions that government *ought* to be dynamic and active on behalf of national welfare, that it *should* provide a counterbalance to the non-self-regulating economy. The development of quantitative analysis techniques has itself contributed to these political values. The inductive nature of non-Keynesian analysis supports values of a more passive government role—of free (that is, nonregulated) competition, of wealth accumulation, and the preservation of small business. As a value-laden word, "welfare" connotes governmental responsibility to one group and governmental domination to the other. In principle, these combinations of different approaches to economics and different values have not been interchangeable.

The significance of this subjectivity both for the Council as an organization and for the individuals in it is that it has been a source of motivation rather than frustration, a form of security and not danger, and hence a strength and not a weakness. True, some Council personnel have differed in the degree of their willingness to become directly involved in advocacy as distinct from analysis, but this has not detracted from the values that attracted them to the Council and underpinned their analysis. To the Council economist absorbed in the daily process of analysis, of coping with problems and opportunities, of brokering ideas, of meeting deadlines, and of still taking time to think, economics and policy have not been consciously separated but have been naturally combined in a professional, political, and social equilibrium.

Analysis and advice have not gingerly walked some invisible but none the less calculated line between objective economics and substantive policy. Nourse's economic conservatism in a Fair Deal environment rather than his standards of objectivity made it impossible for him to achieve a viable equilibrium—which in turn contributed to his conflicts with his associates on the Council and to his estrangement from the White House. The compatibility of Keyserling, Burns, and Heller with their Presidents and administrations constituted an equilibrium that grew out of a mutual acceptance and understanding of economic and noneconomic values; it was not a compromise between politics and economics. The Council personnel who served as allies to the State Department during the NSC 68 considerations, participated in drafting the Defense Production Act, helped Burns make the National Bureau approach work, developed arguments on behalf of tax reduction were all acting on the equilibrium. Conflict for the professional Council economist has not developed from either political-economic or objective-subjective dichotomies but from consideration of policy values, the means of achieving them, and analyses of specific situations under a given political and economic framework.

THE COMPETITIVENESS OF ADVICE. If a multiplicity of advisers advise the President and his administration on issues characterized by conflict, if such issues are spread over a variety of policies and subpolicies and call forth subjectively based analysis, then advice is bound to be competitive. If the Council members and staff are not neutral regarding their advice, then it is natural that their advice be advocacy and their advocacy be competitive. From its inception, the Council has competed to have its advice considered, to say nothing of trying to have it accepted.

From the Council's viewpoint, the nature of advisory competition can be viewed as threefold:

1. Opposing economic advice, the acceptance of which would mean adoption of policies countering those recommended by the Council. In part this is an issue of economists differing as economists, as, for example, when Federal Reserve and Council economists differ on the relative efficacy of different monetary policy proposals toward the objective of economic growth. In more fundamental terms, it is an issue of economic policy advice being developed in particular and institutional terms. If specific rather than overall policy activates the relations among the President, Congress, the departments, and their respective publics, then such specificity monopolizes the President's leadership resources and fills his chan-

nels of information and advice. Recommendations on decisions to be made on such issues as defense expenditures, foreign aid, balance of payments, collective bargaining, and housing (each of which affects the economy as a whole and is therefore of concern to the Council) are delivered to the President in the package of the department involved, be it Treasury, Defense, State, Labor, or Housing. They are wrapped with the personality of a Marshall, a Humphrey, or a McNamara, insulated with layers of uniqueness, precedent, and constituent interest, and armed with the sponsor's own value-loaded economic analysis. Analysis and advice of departmental perspective, in which the part is allegedly related to the whole, compete with the Council's aggregative analysis and advice, which attempts to apply the whole to the part.

2. Opposing noneconomic advice, which does not necessarily refute economic advice as such but presses for preeminence of other factors of political, military, administrative, or other significance. Presumed production bottlenecks and assessment of the point of maximum danger of Communist aggression rendered Keyserling's arguments for economic expansion irrelevant in Truman's 1951 stretch-out decision. Similarly, in his commitment to a balanced budget in 1961 and his refusal to seek a tax cut in 1962, Kennedy was persuaded by noneconomic advice of the validity of largely noneconomic considerations. At the same time, he accepted the validity of economic considerations in committing his administration to seeking tax reduction in 1963.

3. Other demands upon the President's time and energies. These demands do not offer advisory competition as such but obstruct the transmitting and receiving of advice. In the day-to-day handling of issues and events, the President has limited opportunity to see whom he would like, to summon the Council for contemplative discussion of national policy, or to consider the variety of advice he might like to have. Neustadt sketches a President run largely by the daily pressures put upon him:

A President's own use of time, his allocation of his personal attention, is governed by things he *has* to do from day to day: the speech he has agreed to make, the fixed appointment he cannot put off, the paper no one else can sign, the rest and exercise his doctors order. These things may be far removed from academic images of White House concentration on high policy, grand strategy. There is no help for that. A President's priorities are set not by the relative importance of a task, but by the relative necessity for him to do it. He deals first with the things that are required of *him* next. Deadlines rule his personal agenda. In most days of his working week, most seasons of his year, he meets deadlines enough to drain his energy and crowd his time regardless of all else. The net result may be a far cry from the order or priorities that would appeal to scholars or to columnists—or to the President himself.[32]

If the President has little time for reflecting on grand strategy, he also has little time for reflecting with grand strategists or over what the grand strategists send him. Kennedy's voracity for information of all types was undoubtedly more than met by the quantity and variety of memoranda, reports, and analyses that came to him.

Depending upon the circumstances surrounding the issues involved, the three competitive characteristics exist separately or complement one another; they vary in intensity and therefore in their impact upon the Council.

The source of the Council's competition lies in the formal power and operating involvements of agencies like the Treasury, the Federal Reserve Board, ODM (while it existed), and the Budget Bureau. *Their* direct access to the President, the impact of the immediate situation on *their* operations, and the significance of *their* particular operations in the President's leadership responsibilities therefore all compete with the Council's advisory function. The power behind economic advice is for the most part lodged with the Secretary of the Treasury. His department's functions and traditions make him a preeminent force in fiscal matters. Eisenhower may have welcomed Burns' briefings on economic developments, he may have asked Burns to coordinate countercyclical activities, but he did not attempt to place Burns between himself and Humphrey, nor, according to available evidence, did he directly overrule Humphrey in favor of Burns during the 1953–54 period. By virtue of its independence, the Federal Reserve Board has exerted control over monetary policy. For all intents and purposes, Keyserling was unable to storm these fortresses in order to take a direct part in the reaching of the Treasury–Federal Reserve accord. Heller had to await Dillon's acceptance in principle of the arguments on behalf of tax reduction, and, even when they came, the Secretary's specific proposals were less extensive than Heller had hoped for and were, contrary to Heller's advice, linked with the Treasury's reform proposals. The ODM's policy and operating control of partial mobilization made it invulnerable to Keyserling's advice and criticism.

In addition, the Council has had none of the operating carry-through normally associated with its chief competitor and colleague within the Executive Office, the Bureau of the Budget. Its major functions of budget preparation and legislative clearance make it an essential link in the executive function. They give it unparalleled knowledge of governmental operations, they put it squarely astride the policy-making process, and they enable it to develop a budgetary management hierarchy extending down into departmental and subdepartmental budget offices. The development over the past quarter-century of a Budget Bureau viewpoint has influenced its interpretation of what is and is not "consistent with the President's program." In short, the Bureau is the dominant advisory force within the Executive Office. It does not necessarily smother the Council; often their interests are complementary and their operations cooperative, but its functions give it a measure of power that the Council does not have.

Compared with this array of formal operating power, the Council has no equal powers to bring to the decision-making arena. It may "assist and advise the President," "gather timely and authoritive information," "analyze and interpret," "appraise," "develop and recommend," "make and furnish studies," "make an annual report," "constitute . . . advisory committees," and "consult with such representatives . . . as it deems advisable." [33] It may not, however, require, coordinate, intercede, or accept delegations of authority; it may not impose its will. Executive Order 10161 of September, 1950, in which the Council was permitted to "furnish guides" and "obtain necessary information," and the creation of ABEGS under Burns and of the Cabinet Committee on Economic Growth under Heller stand out as slim façades before a vacant lot of power. Consequently, the Council's formal authority has been essentially passive; there is no expectation on the part of the President or operating agencies that the Council's judgment will necessarily be substituted for theirs. The Council has always enjoyed legitimacy as the President's economic adviser, even when Eisenhower had his own economic assistant in the White House. As a formal part of the Presidency, it has been able to establish and maintain operating relations, but this agency role has done little more than establish the Council as a *de jure* participant in advisory competition. Competitive success has demanded more potent ingredients.

The passive nature of the Council's formal role has obliged it as the President's economic agent to rely upon what reflected power it has been able to gain from him and upon the persuasive force inherent in the application of its expertise. That is, the competitive strength brought by the Council to the decision-making fray has grown out of the accuracy of its expert economic analysis relative to the economic conditions of the time, the explicit or implicit interpretation it has placed upon issues at stake, the appropriateness of the Council's analysis and interpretation to the President's perspective, and the application it makes (or attempts to make) of its analysis and interpretation to the decision-making process.

The analysis of the Council's performance in three particular situations indicates that the Council has experienced significant successes and has made a difference. The Council's powers, however, compared with those of other presidential advisers, have been so transitory, peripheral, and intangible that as a result its competitive position has been consistently weak. Presidential endorsement and persuasion have carried insufficient force to guarantee impact upon economic policy decisions. Indeed, although the President has depended upon his Council, he has depended upon others even more. As Seligman has noted, "Congress may set up a CEA, but it cannot compel the President to seek its advice often, nor listen to it when given." [34] In his summary of pre-1953 Council experience, Robert C. Turner, a former Council member, attributed part of the Council's difficulty in influencing major policy issues to "the problems of muscling in." [35] Sorensen asserts that the President will "pay more attention to the advice of the man who must carry out the decision than the advice of a mere 'kibitzer.' " [36] The expert is normally presumed to be trapped by the narrowness of his own expertise, yet in point of fact the general and aggregative nature of the

Council's expertise tends to hinder its applicability in specific decisions. Ideologies, expert analysis, and advice developed by a small staff and accepted at the general policy level often have difficulty surviving at the level of policy specifics that constitute the bread and butter of presidential leadership.

The net result of the Council's weak competitive position is that it has always been faced with the necessity of creating and maintaining a need for its services, in effect, of nurturing a demand for its supply of analysis and advice. The more its advice and analysis have been directed to the specifics of issues, the more such service has centered upon commitments to action involving one or at most a few operating programs, and the more that action has been hedged with obligation and limited discretion for the operating agency, then even more elastic has been the demand and the greater the resistence to the Council's participation. Conversely, the more circumstances have been marked by such characteristics as basic economic policy significance, policy nascence as compared to precedence, diffused leadership, emergency issues, the need for allies by operating agencies, and interdepartmental coordination, then the more inelastic has been the demand for the Council's involvement.

Truman's absorption during the Korean mobilization with military and international affairs, indirect controls, and decentralized mobilization responsibility created a demand for the Keyserling Council's services and influence that expired when partial mobilization and direct controls coalesced under Wilson's leadership. Burns could serve as leader in public works planning and as ally in the move to enlarge unemployment compensation, but he could be neither in the monolithic tax area nor could he implement his own step-up proposals. Not until economic growth abroad combined with the threat of another recession in 1962 to reveal the inappropriateness of traditional policy thinking (not only to Kennedy but also to advisers like Dillon and Mills) was Heller able to make headway with his arguments. The shift from the Keyserling period of making the *Economic Report* the "indispensable engine of consent" for economic policy recommendations to the articulation of more general and informal consensus, apparently typical of the Heller *Reports*, suggests the relative acceptance for general as distinct from specific advice.

The demand for the Council's services is also affected by the nature of their application. The demand for information and comment, for ammunition and rationalization, for drafting and verbalizing is generally greater (that is, less elastic) than the demand for direct participation in the creative and ratifying steps of decision-making. The relevance of the former as an essential supporting activity is by no means to be denied; in fact, its significance has previously been noted, but the distinction must be made in appreciating the competitive aspects of the Council's advisory activity.

Given the competitive situation, the Council has necessarily been responsive to the kaleidescopic interplay of situational factors. In order to compete, to have their days in court, all three Councils attempted to anticipate issues and opportunities. Early involvement has often enabled the Council to influence issues and decisions before they reach the final ratification stage. In reflecting both its competitive position and the pressures that are upon the President, the Council also has on occasion assumed that half a loaf is better than none; it has tempered both its advice and its methods of operating to what, in the light of its assessment of economic and noneconomic factors, appears to have a reasonable chance of acceptance. It, too, has lived within what Sorensen calls "the outer limits of decision," the limits of "permissibility," "previous commitment," "available resources, time, and information." [37] The Council's reliance upon an interpretive and opportunistic application of its expertise has been inevitable and natural. It is an outgrowth of the environment of presidential association and political conflict, of broad-scale involvement and subjective analysis in which the Council has lived and worked. The Council's performance and operating characteristics have represented the art of the politically possible. In a climactic sense, they have portrayed the relationship between economic knowledge and presidential power.

IX. THE KNOWLEDGE-
POWER RELATIONSHIP

What is the nature of the relationship between the Council as a source of economic knowledge and the President as the head of the national government? How can the *process* of the relationship be characterized? To what factors can the difference between the Council's—that is, the uniqueness of the Council-President relationship from one Council chairmanship to another—be attributed? What is the Council's emerging tradition? The answers to these final questions regarding the Council are in large measure derived from the foregoing analysis, in which the following characteristics were established: the personal nature of the Council's association with presidential leadership and political conflict, the wide range of the Council's involvement in government policy-making, the orientation of its expertise towards policy, and the dependent form of the Council's power as exercised in a competitive environment.

The Nature of the Relationship

For the Council, the relationship between its knowledge and the President's power is one of many relationships, but it is the one of greatest importance to the Council because it is, in fact, the reason for its existence. For the President, the relationship is also one of many. In absolute terms it is important to him; it is accepted, and it is valued. Although it is in relative terms, unique among the

President's advisory relationships, it is not, however, one of his major relationships. The terms most descriptive of the essential relationship between the Council and President are "interdependent" and "variable." The first describes the reciprocal nature of the relationship between respective specialties of expert economic analysis and power-laden political leadership and the relationship between the President's perceived need for the Council and the Council's reaction to that perception. The second term describes the changeable and intermittent nature of the Council-President relationship in its response to the evolving issues, events, and personalities that influence the nature of presidential leadership.

The reciprocity of the Council-President relationship is based upon the paralleling of their concerns and the mutually reinforcing nature of their respective attributes of knowledge and power. As previously recognized, the pervasive nature of the Council's economic analysis matches the nationwide, even worldwide, scope of the President's political responsibilities. Macropolitics and macroeconomics complement one another. The most natural application of the Council's expertise is to presidential problems and opportunities; the whole focus of aggregative analysis is on the national economy. The information, rationale, and advice that the Council gives the President, on both the economy as a whole and on particular issues as they fit into the national picture, strengthen political leadership. In this sense, knowledge is power; knowledge enables the President to enlarge his own specialties of innovation, synthesis, and control. It increases his ability to take the initiative relative to that of the departments and the Congress. The expert information and advice available to the President help him close the gap between the specialized knowledge and sovereignty of departmental programs and responsibilities. At a minimum cost to the President's leadership resources, the Council can speak for him and thereby identify him with what he may want to espouse without being necessarily committed to a particular course of action. In short, the Council strengthens the President's hand; it adds to his coercive power however he may wish to apply it (for example, in the steel-price dispute).

The acceptance of the Council's expertise as the President's economics increases the acceptance of his authority in matters of economic policy, and where applicable it adds economic persuasion to his strategies of influence. In return, the President provides the principal market for the Council's expertise. However circumscribed and tenuous the force of the Council's knowledge, such force is enhanced by affiliation with presidential leadership. Each is strengthened with the special attributes of the other; each can play a stronger role in the decision-making process than would otherwise be the case. That the Council exists for the President does not deny the support its existence gets from him. It is doubtful that Eisenhower's and Kennedy's endorsements of their respective tax programs would have had the political force that they had had it not been evident that each President had understood and adopted the rationale of his economic advisers. It is equally doubtful that the respective Councils would have had significant impact on their President's thinking had they operated with the detachment typical of one of the Council's predecessors, NRPB.

The occasional outward appearances of rejection of the Council's advice—of victory for some other adviser or of noneconomic factors overruling economic considerations—do not so much represent differences of opinion between the President and the Council as they do the existence of different values pressed upon a President who must decide. Reciprocity between expertise and power does not require complete agreement or constant association; rather, reciprocity depends upon the use the President decides to make of the Council and the reaction of the Council to his wishes. Thus, the operations of the Council are dependent upon the value the President attaches to them in terms of his own operations. Sorensen argues that "each President must determine for himself how best to elicit and assess the advice of his advisers."[1] The Council's experience bears out Maass' "tentative requirement" for policy staffs suggested some years ago:

First, the President must personally desire such facilities and must always be fully free to alter or abolish them. . . . A second requirement is that to a considerable extent . . . the policy staff must be flexible as regards both its organization and the permanence of status of its personnel.[2]

In his reflections upon his own experiences, Nourse states that "the success of the Council as an institution, the importance of the place it occupies and the value of its work will be just what the President makes of them." [3] Although the reference is to the White House Office, the following remark by a former Budget Director quoted by Neustadt is similarly applicable to the Council and characterizes its relationship to the President:

"Thank God I'm here and not across the street. If the President doesn't call me, I've got plenty I can do right here and plenty coming up to me, by rights, to justify my calling him. But those poor fellows over there, if the boss doesn't call them, doesn't ask them to do something, what *can* they do but sit?"[4]

In truth, the Council, perhaps more than the White House Office, has succeeded in doing a good deal of independent work, but each chairman has in large measure depended upon his President's view of the Council in directing the type, direction, and extent of the Council's operations. This situation is little influenced by requirements of the Constitution, the Employment Act, other statutes, and custom. Truman's passive acceptance of the Council and his coolness to economics and economists were conditioners of the Keyserling Council's activities as Eisenhower's military concept of staff assistance and his reliance upon a "doctor" to aid his ailing economy were of Burns and his Council. By the same token, Kennedy's thirst for knowledge, his grasp of modern economics, and his style of hard pragmatic analysis shaped the use he made of the Heller Council and of its response to that use.

The interdependent nature of the knowledge-power relationship, the terms of which depend largely on what is acceptable to the President, means that the relationship is also extremely variable. As the President must respond to the developing pressures and opportunities, so must the relationship. It is changeable and intermittent rather than stable and regular. Not only is the relationship active in one crisis and dormant in another but the balances also vary between direct and indirect participation in decision-making, in the different paces and purposes of consultation between the Council, the President, and other members of his Administration, and with shifts in the Council's own operation. In the turbulence of current affairs, it is often the changes in rather than the existence of economic policy issues that activate the Council-President relationship.

The persistence of unemployment and the priority given to its solution by the President and his Administration may be important factors in shaping the President's approach to economic policy, his choice of Council members, and, in turn, the composition and operation of the Council staff. It is, however, the unfolding *changes* in the levels and areas of unemployment that produce either urgency or relaxation on both sides of the relationship. The balance of payments and economic growth in other countries are continuing concerns of the Council on behalf of the President, but it is the *changes* in these areas that set off new questions from the President, that pull his attention from other matters, that propel the Council into some new activity, and that alter its operations and staffing patterns. It is these incremental alterations that set the order of priorities of opportunities and pressures by which both the Council and President work. The degree and importance of changes within areas and the impact of the changes on each other and upon the whole complex of issues facing the President can either effect a major change in Council-President relations or balance out to produce no significant change at all.

The degree of the Council's vulnerability to such variableness is less than that of the White House staff, faced as it is with the alternation of crises and minutae of the President's daily activities. By the same token, the Council's vulnerability is greater than that of the Budget Bureau with its vast coordinating activities and greater still than that of the operating agencies. The variableness of the Council-President relationship is in most obvious contrast to the stable relations the President maintains or is required to maintain with department heads, upon whom he depends to carry out the laws that must be faithfully executed. Although the relationship between the President and the department heads, who are both advisers and executives, is also affected by changing circumstances, the departments have a depth of continuing programs as well as independent strength sufficient for them to sustain and regulate a relationship through the vagaries of current issues. Thus, change does not work the same leverage on the totality of the relationship. Even changes among Cabinet members and the consequent variations in personal relations between the President and his advisers take on the coloration of departmental operations and traditions; they assume some of the same regularity and predictability.

In the final analysis, the interdependent and variable aspects of the relationship between the Council and the President combine to produce a relationship that is moved more by the President's acceptance of the Council than by his dependence upon it. It has become habitual for the President to depend on the Council, but it is because he wants to depend upon it rather than because he has to. The overlap of political and analytical pressures does not necessarily mean that the President will use the Council but simply that its use could be relevant and helpful.

The Relationship Process

The interdependent and variable nature of the relationship between the Council and the President tells us little of how the relationship is maintained; the dependence of the Council upon the President's perception of his need for its services reveals little of the Council's reaction to this dependence. Without denying the Council's dependence upon the President, it can also be concluded that the Council's operations have been determined less by what the President wants the Council to do than by what he does not object to its doing. The performances of the Keyserling, Burns, and Heller Councils reveal that the character of a Council is very much what the Council itself makes it and that, in fact, the Council does much to create and maintain the President's perception of his need for it. The fact that the Council, as an advisory body with no independent power and no independence of program operations, has discretion is essential to an understanding of the process underlying its relations with the President. The nature of this process can be presented in four related propositions.

1. The relationship is maintained primarily through the Council's initiative.

2. The factors that make the Council dependent upon its own

initiative in maintaining the relationship also permit the Council a wide latitude in the choice of its objectives and in the techniques of its initiative. The selection of objectives and of techniques of initiative is determined by the interaction of internal resources, convictions, and conduct with underlying and immediate features of the external political, economic, and administrative situations.

3. The most important technique of initiative is a process of intentional involvement, the degree and nature of which is determined by the Council's objectives and resources as well as the nature of the issue in which it seeks involvement.

4. Involvement is characteristically a process of opportunistic accommodation rather than forceful impingement.

THE COUNCIL'S INITIATIVE. A variety of factors have persuaded the Council that the effectiveness of its operations depend in large measure upon the exercise of its own initiative. These factors have included the relatively asymmetrical dependence of the Council upon the President, the high level of policy generality at which the Council operates, which frequently results in a peripheral role in specific economic policy formulation, and the Council's perennial problem of maintaining a demand for its services. The pervasiveness of its involvement in economic policy and the subjective values supporting its economic expertise, to say nothing of its instincts for organization self-preservation, have given it a willingness and a need to fend for itself. Consequently, the Council has to a large degree been able to set its own sights; it has made its own assessment of its resources in terms of what it has conceived as its objectives, opportunities, and problems, and it has apportioned its resources accordingly.

It has been the Council's initiative in interpreting its function more than the President's delegation that has maintained the relationship of knowledge and power. The President's original appointment of a chairman and two other members, all of whose views have been more or less in harmony with his, and his instructions to them certainly have set the stage of the relationship and of the Council's potential ultimate contribution. These elements may even have thrown the ignition switch, but they have been too general and intermittent to provide sustaining current for an active relationship.

The significance of the Council over time has emerged from relations operated by its own rather than the President's direction. The original Nourse Council would not have gone far on Truman's original marching orders of "now you fellows just keep national income up to $200 billion." The early precedents of the Council could be established by Nourse and subsequently by Keyserling because the President offered no objections. Keyserling's series of monthly and quarterly reports were volunteered, not requested. ABEGS was a Burns creation; the weekly meetings with the President were developed by him. Heller seldom missed an opportunity to inform the President of something that Heller thought appropriate; in large measure, he interpreted the size and nature of Kennedy's appetite for economic information and argument. Certainly, the stimulants of the President-Council relationship have been complementary, but the concern here is to identify the relationship's most important and constant source of energy. It appears to have been the Council.

LATITUDE OF OBJECTIVES AND INITIATIVE. Characterized by a lack of operating momentum—that is, endowed with no formal authority, combined with institutional permanence limited to a maximum of one presidential administration, and committed to only a few command performances other than the preparation of the *Economic Report*—the Council has had little to inhibit its adoption of widely different programs and practices from situation to situation and Council to Council. It has been able to vary the style and degree of its initiative from blatant aggression to defensive avoidance. The same sorts of factors that permitted a Nourse to avoid testifying before committees of Congress for three years permitted a Keyserling to fight for economic expansion wherever possible, a Burns to act with restraint on behalf of conservative and inductive economics, and a Heller to attack existing tax policy prior to the President's public endorsement. The same sorts of factors that have permitted concentration on attempts to participate in formulating policy on grand or limited scales have permitted concentration on factual reporting or on research or on combinations thereof. The same factors that have allowed a Council to risk all have permitted it to risk nothing. These have not been changes of approach or objectives limited to the top level with little significant impact on the professional level but have been basic changes altering the character and operations of the entire Council organization.

These same factors that have allowed the Council initiative and flexibility have extracted their price by making it vulnerable to isolation. The Council has seldom been far from the risk of exclusion from policy formulation, reduced acceptance, frustration, punishment, and insignificance. Certainly, the Council's strategic determinations of its objectives and of its techniques of initiative have been based on necessary assessments of the opportunities and risks presented internally by its own capabilities and interests and externally by its relationship with the President and the Presidency, the prevailing economic philosophy, the bureaucratic environment, and the policy issue at hand. Similarly, determination of objectives and of techniques of initiative have had to be varied in accordance with the more immediate internal and external changes, such as personnel turnover within the Council and sudden or short-term economic and noneconomic developments. In short, the factors adhering to the Council have created the extensive and responsive latitude within which the Council's strategic objectives and techniques of initiative have been determined and executed and the Council's relationship with the President maintained. The Council has been given ample rope with which to make, save, or hang itself.

THE PROCESS OF CONSCIOUS INVOLVEMENT. The Council's major techniques of initiative to maintain the relationship have been those seeking involvement in economic policy affairs; that is, the Council's operations have been more typically motivated by the desire to become involved than to achieve disengagement. The history of the Council can in large measure be seen as an attempt to fulfill this motivation, to offset rather than extend its inherent detachment. Keyserling, Burns, and Heller each endeavored to have their Councils participate in what they considered important. Involvement requiring considerable amounts of time, energy, and emotion has been necessitated by the competitive nature of advice and by the complexity and depth of the economic policy-making process that extends well back into departments and agencies. Depending upon its objectives, the Council's desire has been to link its expertise and convictions to the power centers of decision in order to maximize its impact upon economic policy.

The Council's influence has often depended upon its degree of success in waging an uphill fight to participate in the decision-making process during the formulative stages. Granted that involvement creates the risk of miring the Council in operating details and of burying that which has been one of its chief strengths, presidential perspective, the Council's effectiveness has nevertheless depended upon "getting to the board" and not trying to play solely from its own hand within the Executive Office. Withholding advice or being excluded from advising until decisions have reached the White House for approval has often presented the Council with an already closed issue. Positions have been taken, advisory battles fought and settled, support developed, and commitments made. Although the Chairman occasionally may have preconditioned the President's thinking, the Council's opportunity to influence specific decisions has often shrunk to the job of rationalizing decisons already formed. In other words, there has been a rough correlation between the nature and extent of the Council's influence and the degree to which its involvement has been to formulate policy or to ratify it.

The Council's involvement in particular issues has also depended upon the relevance of its objectives and beliefs to the issue at hand and to the Council's range of discretion. The more anxious the Council has been to shape economic policies in terms of its own economic rationale, the more aggressive and alert it has become regarding opportunities to get to the President, to add permanent staff and consultants in relevant areas, to participate in committees, to consult and be consulted, to associate with fellow policy-makers rather than with technicians. The more crucial a situation has been in national economic terms, such as unemployment or inflation, the more the President has looked to the Council and the more reluctant the Council has been to have decisions take place without its involvement. When the Council has emphasized fact-finding or research, it has adjusted its involvement tactics accordingly; it has focused on different agencies and on different sorts of people; and its pace has changed with the change in pressures and deadlines. But still the Council has sought involvement and not detachment.

OPPORTUNISTIC ACCOMMODATION. The Council's asymmetrical power relationships with its environment and the elasticity of the demand for its services have required that its processes of involvement be characteristically accommodative rather than forceful. The Council's processes have been carried on primarily at the sufferance of the departments and agencies with which the Council has done business. Depending upon its objectives and its assessment of the decision-making situation, the Council has taken advantage of opportunities by being available, by filling vacuums, by purveying expertise, by educating, and by competing with constraint and tact. It has "sold" rather than imposed.

Certainly, accommodation has not meant abject surrender by the Council, for knowledge is not without its intrinsic value, conviction is not without its competitiveness. Advice based on knowledge and urged through conviction carries weight; successful advice helps create its own demand. Expert technical service to an agency has developed into a continuing project, as in the case of the Council's relations with the NSRB in 1950 and with the Labor Department in 1953. Success as an ally to operating agencies that independently are weak in top policy councils has strengthened the Council's impact on program operations. When, in 1954, recession made the revenue aspect of tax policy less significant than its impact on disposable income, the Council was able to move into the middle of the stage with its involvement fully expected. When, in 1962, the commitment to a new tradition was made, the Council, as its prime exponent, was recognized as a leader. When, as exemplified by the Burns and Heller Councils in particular, the Council and the Chairman have been accepted by the President, Cabinet members and aides have listened to what the Chairman has to say; he has been part of top-level informal and *ad hoc* policy groups, and agency representation on Council-sponsored committees has been by high-level political appointees and career officials.

Although these achievements have tended to be cumulative and reinforcing and although they have strengthened the Council, they have not allowed it to exchange the open hand of accommodation for the mailed fist or to exchange persuasion for sanction. In a showdown on a specific decision, whether concerning the decision itself or the question of the participation of particular agencies, the Council has seldom been able to force its way into deliberations;

as in the case of the Treasury–Federal Reserve accord in 1951, Council participation has often not been invited. In these instances, the necessity or advantage for agencies to deal with the Council has been minimized by their direct higher priority access to the President and their vast institutional resources, as well as their clientele support and pressures. The Council has had to adjust to these factors.

Although the adjustment process is common to interorganizational relations, the nature of the process in the case of the Council has been characterized not so much by reciprocity as by the Council's having to take the initiative to fit its objectives and operations to those of other agencies. There has been no evidence that the other major agencies have altered their operations to suit the Council. Thus, the Council has had to accommodate to the other agencies because, relative to them, it has lacked the resources of forceful impingement.

The Consequent Quality of Uniqueness

The description of the nature and process of the Council-President relationship implies that the Council under the different chairmen have been virtually different Councils. In fact, they have. They have been almost as different as have been the presidencies of which they have been a part. Similarities in their responsibilities and functions, in their experience with success and failure, and in the nature of their influence on economic policy do not hide unique aspects of each Council that are important to an appreciation of the presidential advisory function. Because of their respective interpretations of the Employment Act, each of the three Councils studied was recognizably different in composition, in method of operation, and in the way it was received by its administration. Their uniqueness appears to have been greater than the uniqueness of the Budget Bureau under different directors or of the Treasury Department under different secretaries.

The relative stability of the composition of the Keyserling Council, made up as it was of veteran economic analysts was in marked contrast to the temporary service of academicians and part-time consultants that characterized the Burns and, even more, the Heller Council. Whereas the relatively permanent staff of the Keyserling Council was geared to the pace of government operations and to the undertaking of long-term projects, those of the more temporary Burns and Heller Councils were geared more to special projects, with those of long duration being handled by a succession of economists. Experience, continuity, and regularity of pace were in contrast to repeated infusion of fresh viewpoints, problems of operating continuity, and peak work loads for short periods of time. In external operations, Burns' centralized control of relations with the White House, the agencies, Congress, and nongovernmental groups is in marked contrast to the Keyserling pattern of extensive external operations by the other Council members and by staff members as much as by the Chairman. Although external contacts were for the most part maintained by the Council members and one or two senior staff members, the Heller Council's external operations resembled those of Keyserling far more than those of Burns.

No factors had greater influence in creating the individuality of each Council than the differences in each Council's approach to economic analysis, which was manifested by both Council members and staff professionals in the Council's operations. Just as each President wished and was committed by political philosophy to be different from his predecessor, each new Council sought to apply a different economic philosophy and correspondingly different methods from those of its predecessor. Following Nourse, Keyserling wanted to reset the Council's course toward full-employment objectives. Aware of both the problems and the promise of setting precedents for a new agency, Keyserling strove for involvements and operations opposite from those advocated by Nourse. Both Burns and Heller felt the need to revitalize the approach of the Council because, to Burns' eyes, the Council had fallen into disrepute with the economics profession, while, in Heller's opinion, it had not lived up to its responsibilities under the Employment Act.

The differences in composition and approach to economic analysis contributed to differences in working relationships. The informal but recognized delineation between senior and junior staff members, the formality among the Council members themselves, and the

Chairman's balance between direction and delegation in the Keyserling Council were all in contrast to the centralized restraint more typical of the Burns Council. Burns' dominance of his Council, his filtering out of policy considerations from the staff's work assignments, and his cross-checking of the staff work through duplication of assignments were in contrast to the informal crash program policy of the Heller Council. Reminiscent of the activity of the Keyserling Council, the Heller group none the less differed from it in the more equal division of work among the Council members themselves and in the shifting of assignments among the staff. Despite marked similarities in the preparation of the President's *Economic Report*, Heller appears to have made it something more of a joint undertaking in both development of content and in drafting than did Keyserling and especially Burns. Clearance of *Economic Report* recommendations was apparently less detailed under Burns and Heller than under Keyserling. Heller returned to the Nourse and Keyserling practice of separating the President's *Report* and the Council's *Report* into two different documents bound within one cover. Under Burns, the two were combined into one report introduced by a brief summarizing letter of transmittal from the President.

In the process of establishing the economic rationale of their respective presidential administrations and of contributing to particular economic policy decisions, each Council created different reputations and images. All three were aggressive but each in his own fashion. Keyserling, the career New Dealer, pressed the Council's viewpoint with tenacity in an administration which, tentative at best in its embrace of the new advisory body and its ideology, accorded him formal rather than intimate access to the inner circles. Burns, the respected expert on business cycles, articulated modern conservatism and influenced policy decisions in an administration that, thankful for having avoided deep depression, welcomed him as a professional "in house" consultant. Heller as the worldly and whirlwind academician promoted a new economic rationale for pragmatists of the New Frontier, who, recognizing an operator of their own kind, accorded him full membership in their policy-making circles.

The reasons for the differences lie in precisely the same sorts of factors that explain the political quality of the Council's advisory function and the interdependent and variable nature of the Council-President relationship. Each Council has served Presidents of widely differing ideological persuasions and styles, different priorities and concepts of office, and different views of the role of the Council. Each Council has helped create and reflect the environment unique to its administration. The Democratic Fair Deal's wheeling and dealing, its activity and confusion, its social concern for a postwar world, its palace guard—all reminiscent of the Roosevelt era—were quite different from the characteristics of the Democratic New Frontier and very different from the business formality of Eisenhower's "new Republicanism." The significance to the Heller Council of its serving an administration whose twentieth-century leaders accepted and understood the principles of Keynesian economics cannot be overemphasized.

Both the political conflicts and the policies in which each Council became involved were vastly different. The emergency growing out of the Korean War and the apparent proximity of World War III caused fear and pressures for the government and population at large that were different from those growing out of the 1953–54 recession, which were, in turn, different from those that developed in 1961–62. The visceral as well as intellectual reaction to inflation was far different after four years of war production and forced saving than it was after four years of peacetime price stability. Heller was not burdened by Keyserling's problem of the postwar return to normalcy nor by Burns' bugbear of a return to 1929, but neither Keyserling nor Burns had Heller's difficulties with both the internal paradox of sustained prosperity and persistent unemployment and the external competition of relatively rapid economic growth in other democratic countries.

Each Council competed with its advice in the manner it believed possible and necessary, given the complex circumstances obtaining at that time. The crucial difference between the approaches to competition was that the set of strategies and tactics used by Keyserling and later by Heller led to opportunities and risks of commission, while the set used by Burns led to opportunities and risks of omission. The Keyserling Council was part of an active Presidency, and, consistent with its interpretation of the Employment Act, it believed that "maximum employment, production and purchasing power" were not achieved by inside analysis carried on within a suite of offices on the third floor of "Old State." The Council chose to make the most of its environment by participating as aggressively and as comprehensively as possible in an action-packed emergency situation. Consequently, the Council ran the risk of overplaying its hand, of attempting too much, of poaching on the preserves of others, and of creating antagonisms. In part, the Council fell victim of its own choice. Having originally assumed the risks that accompanied opportunity for aggressive participation, the changed situation in 1951 made its decrease in influence inevitable and pronounced. Not having the force to impose its views, the Council could escape neither virtual exclusion by the Administration nor a share in the severe criticism of the Truman Administration.

The Burns Council was not inclined nor did it have the opportunity to function in a manner similar to its predecessor. As part of a less active Presidency, which adopted a more conservative interpretation of the Employment Act, the Council chose to operate as a consultant to the Administration in a gradually evolving and mildly recessionary situation in which minimal governmental direction of the nation's economic life was a primary policy objective. The very practice of limited outside contact and concentration on inside analysis coincided with the free enterprise approach of minimum government activity characteristic of the Eisenhower Administration. Consequently, the Council's basic orientation was toward doing the least necessary rather than the most possible. Its risks were not of doing too much but of doing too little—of being silent rather than protesting, of simply endorsing the *status quo* rather than recommending modification or change, and of inhibiting rather than helping recovery. The success of the Burns Council lay in avoiding these pitfalls. By its own interpretation of the Employment Act and by its analysis of the 1953–54 situation, the Council maintained fundamental agreement with the Administration; it endorsed a basic policy of noninterference while recommending and gaining acceptance for some limited countermeasures.

As with the Keyserling Council, the Heller Council was part of an active Presidency. In choosing to participate aggressively and over a broad area of economic policy, it also ran the risk of over-playing its hand. It did not primarily because it concentrated on developing broad rationale and analysis upon which decisions could be considered and on resisting becoming too enmeshed in specific decision-making processes. It was the combination of an activist philosophy and operations that helped produce a multitude of analyses and recommendations on behalf of the New Frontier.

To be meaningful, these comparisons must be seen in the per-spective of their respective times. Keyserling's aggressiveness and advocacy stood out in part because they were blatant but primarily because they conflicted with the then current expectations that the Council display professional objectivity and passivity. To be for-mally trained as a lawyer rather than as a professional economist, to head a new agency that defended as well as analyzed economic policy, and to expound Keynesian economics made Keyserling and the Council all the more suspect. Burns' restraint was consistent with prevailing values of minimal government interference in eco-nomic activity. A decade after Keyserling, Heller's tactful but equally aggressive activity on many fronts was acknowledged as a natural attribute of professional advice.

Both Burns and Heller benefited from all their respective prede-cessors' experiences. In addition to the advantages of the fresh ap-proach made possible by the complete change in philosophy from the Truman to the Eisenhower Administration, Burns recognized Keyserling's experience by avoiding conflicts between himself and his fellow Council members (Reorganization Plan No. 9) and by centralizing the Council's internal and external operations. The ac-ceptance of Heller's aggressive approach grows not only out of the manner in which he pursued it but also out of the general change in relevant values. Keyserling had already fought a number of battles that did not need to be fought again—the testifying, speech-making, and policy involvement for which he was severely criti-cized were taken as a matter of course in the case of Heller. The consensus favoring an active government, the recognized need to plan and coordinate government programs, the general acceptance of Keynesian principles, the advances in economic analysis, the adoption of economic growth as a legitimate political objective, and, finally, Kennedy's perception of the Council's role all accumulated to make the Heller Council uniquely a synthesis combining maximum benefit from both the experiences of his predecessors and the more general economic policy developments of the previous twenty years.

Conclusion: The Council's Emerging Tradition

The nature of the knowledge-power relationship between the Council and the President, the Council's process of maintaining that relationship, and the uniqueness of each Council combine to indicate the Council's emerging tradition as part of the American Presidency. In the case of the Council, the "right relation of knowledge and power" has become substantive and not procedural, complementary and not conflicting, active and not neutral, and personal rather than institutional. The Council's emerging approach to the advisory function is characterized by pragmatism and variety, by education and subjectivity, rather than by norm and consistency or by coordination and scientific objectivity. The Council has supplied information and analysis, but even more it has articulated the concepts needed for determination and defense of policy. The value of such economic rationale has been gradually recognized and accorded legitimacy by politician and bureaucrat, by economist and layman.

However one feels about the substantive economics of particular Councils and however one judges the importance or value of the Councils' actions, each Council's convictions and conduct will none the less continue uniquely to initiate, facilitate, and rationalize economic policy formulation for its own particular administration. As in the past, the Council's activities will vary from creating a philosophical rationale to providing specialized technical abilities, from recommending specific ideas of its own to promoting those of others, from making formal presentations to the President to kibitzing someone else's hand. As both integral parts and catalysts, these expert activities will be essential to the functioning of leadership and to the process of making policy at the White House level, within the Executive Office, and among various echelons of the operating agencies.

X. CONCLUSION: AN
APPROACH TO ANALYSIS

The evaluation of the Council of Economic Advisers as it functioned as part of the American Presidency in three particular situations raises two concluding questions. Is the Council's performance comparable to the functioning of advice in other bureaucratic settings? If so, does this present study of the Council contribute to a broader understanding of knowledge-power relationships in public and private bureaucracies?

Advice at the presidential summit may be unique; on the other hand, it seems possible that the experience of the Council is the prototype of the advisory function with all attendant problems magnified. Therefore, the Council's differences from the advisory function of other bureaucracies are essentially those of degree rather than of nature. The case for comparability rests upon four general observations that suggest common characteristics of the advisory function:

1. The existence of the advisory function as an identifiable activity in direct support of the person or persons having formal authority and leadership responsibilities is not limited to the Council but is typical of many modern bureaucracies. Advisory offices the primary function of which is to advise their principals on some specific areas exist and act as familar units not only throughout many levels of federal, state, and municipal government but also in countless private, educational, charitable, and military institutions as well. Moreover, in many instances advisory activity is

by no means the private monopoly of inside staffs but, as the Council's experience and the growth of professional management consulting indicate, includes the work of outsiders serving on a temporary or retainer basis.

2. Whatever the bureaucratic setting or work arrangement, these advisory staffs (including the Council) appear to be made up of professional specialists, and the functioning of their advice seems to depend upon the putting to use of a particular form of expertise which is specifically relevant in support of the responsibilities of administrative or executive leaders. Advice from experts does not by nature represent a component part of an organization's productive operation, that is, of its "line." Economics as applied by the Council is but one field of supporting expertise—one that is applied to a variety of settings and also may be used competitively or cooperatively with others in the same setting. Such other areas as law, mathematics, operations research, budgeting, accounting, and journalism illustrate (but by no means encompass) the range of advisory expertise available.

3. The crux of the application of expertise appears to lie, as demonstrated by the Council, in the relationship of the adviser to his principal. This relationship is apparent in the nature of the appointment, physical proximity, pattern of work assignment, personal association, and formal and actual accountability. Differing fundamentally from the situation in operating agencies, the relationship of adviser to principal outranks and at the same time determines all other relationships maintained by the adviser and forms the basis of the nature and success of the advisory function. In whatever way or however the advisory function may be conceived, whoever may be in authority must first of all desire expert advice as an aid to effective leadership—whether that leadership be of a government department, a department store, a research project, or a military campaign. Expert knowledge is viewed by the leader as a complement to power in the interest of fulfillment of organization values and as a contribution to the leader's understanding and control of responsibilities, to his ratification of decisions, and to his individual achievement. Because it is desired and because at the same time it has its own values, the advisory re-

sponse, that is, the side of the relationship possessing the knowledge or expertise, is not passive but contributes to the power side and receives in return some of the values associated with that power. The consequent involvement of the advisory function in the political process seems to be common to the complex of organizational and individual values typical of large-scale operations. The view that advisers as one category of staff specialists have more than passive roles does not so much invalidate the traditional line-staff concept that denies the existence of active involvement by advisers as serve to draw attention to the interaction inherent in the staff-line relationship of knowledge and power.

4. In applying its expertise and maintaining its relationship with the President, the Council went through experiences that can hardly be called unique. Problems of getting started, of interpreting mandates, of building support, of achieving success and surviving failure—all without independent operating responsibility and authority—appear representative of all advisory staffs. It is primarily in shadings of timing, sequence, and intensity that variations appear.

Thus, it is clear that in the sharing of general characteristics of formal existence, dependence upon expertise, significance of the knowledge-power relationship, and types of experience, the Council's performance is both relevant to and comparable to that of other advisory bodies. And if in general this comparability is true, then it should follow that factors relevant to appraising the Council's performance as an adviser to the President should be relevant in considering the performances of other advisory staff bodies.

A basic pattern for analyzing the performance of the Keyserling, Burns, and Heller Councils was found in the expectations originally associated with the Council's being established: (1) helping to prevent a postwar depression, (2) interpreting the Employment Act of 1946 in one of two ways, (3) functioning as a planning agency in accordance with the one or the other interpretation, (4) providing expertise in an objective manner, (5) serving as an institutional part of the American Presidency. The fulfillment of some of these expectations and deviations from others led in turn to discussions both of the bases of politically oriented economic advice (in Chapter VIII) and of the Council-President relationships (in Chapter IX). Thus, to a large extent the original expectations served as the framework for the examination of the Council's functioning. In a similar manner, these same expectations may be looked upon as providing the bases for a general analytical approach conceivably adaptable to other knowledge-power relationships.

By combining the first two, expectations (1) through (4) could be referred to successively as the "advisory objective," the "essential advising activity," and the "nature of expertise." As these three components in many ways reflect and respond to the basic situational environment in which the knowledge-power relationship operates, they should be preceded by another factor identified as the "internal-external environment." As we shall see in the following discussion, these four factors constitute the first phase of the analytical approach and largely determine the second phase, the knowledge-power relationship. The resulting nature of the advisory process follows as the third phase of the relationship. Taken together, the three phases imply a cause-and-effect relationship that may be expressed in the following general proposition: the nature of the internal-external environment operating in a given situation affects the advisory objective, the essential advising activity, and the nature of the expertise, and in conjunction with these components of the advisory function determines the character of the knowledge-power relationship, which, in turn determines the process of the advisory function.

THE INTERNAL-EXTERNAL ENVIRONMENT. Of the factors involved in the knowledge-power relationship, the internal-external environment is the most comprehensively influential. It represents the complex pressures and opportunities growing out of socioeconomic, technological, political, and administrative considerations that devolve upon an administrator and crystallize into the balance of power operating between his organization and its external surroundings. This balance of power embodies the administrator's operation of his authority, persuasion, and sanction in relation to the operation of power available to members of his organization as well as to external associates and clients. The concept would refer to the balance of power existing between the President, his Secretary of the Treasury, and the Chairman of the House Committee on Ways and Means, not merely in the general constitutional and institutional sense but in terms of Kennedy, Dillon, and Mills with regard to the specific issue of tax reduction in 1962. Under comparable conditions of specificity, the concept can refer to the power balance between management and labor or between a firm and its research staff and its customers, competitors, and suppliers.

Within the underlying and immediate dimensions of a particular situation, the balance of power is affected by the nature of the organization objective that activates the balance in the first place. It is affected by the formal structure of power and organization as well as by the informal and intangible aspects of personalities, charisma, and individual values. It also responds to operating concepts of leadership, to the investment and conservation of power resources, and to the applied techniques of cooperation and competition. Little modification is needed to adapt Neustadt's theme of "personal power and politics; what it is, how to get it, how to keep it, how to use it" [1] to a corporate, state, or big-city setting. The scales may be different, but the same sort of balance is sought among the same sorts of complex goals, values, and issues; they function with similar weights of environmental changes, and in turn they contribute similarly to accompanying degrees of conflict and cooperation.

For the leader, the consequent balance of power either requires a "sensitive" application or permits an "insensitive" application of his own power resources. Under conditions of "sensitivity," a potential or actual impingement upon the leader of power from other participating sources as great as his or greater obliges him to be acutely responsive, or "sensitive," to the other sources. To meet demands or to maintain the loyalty of subordinates who have separate clientele support (or pressures), independent financial resources, and needed technical competence, he may be required to sacrifice some of his own objectives or commit a portion of his marginal power reserves. He may at the same time have to strike similar balances with public or special constituent pressures. Often the power balance is pluralistic among voters, legislators, and administrators or among customers, competitors, and suppliers, all possessing resources with which to press their respective claims. A divided board of directors can be as inhibiting to a corporate executive as a narrow margin in the legislature is to an elected or appointed administrator. In these circumstances of "sensitivity," the leader is more the mediator than creator, more on the defense than offense. His strategies and tactics reflect more the short than the long view. His own desires are bound by limited feasibility until the climate improves.

Under opposite conditions of "insensitivity," the leader's power resources under the balance of power are more secure; they may be invested or withheld with relative impunity. Organization components and outside clientele need him more than he needs them, which therefore enables him to do nothing or to maintain an initiative in instituting change, meeting crises, and pushing new programs, products, or services. As actual balance of power situations seldom reach the extremes as hypothecated, the concepts of "sensitivity" and "insensitivity" represent the limits of alternatives either chosen or enforced. Although the effect is in part reciprocal, the internal-external environment as registered by the sensitivity-insensitivity character of the balance of power has an overriding impact upon other determinants of the knowledge-power relationship as well as upon the relationship itself.

THE ADVISORY OBJECTIVE. The advisory objective refers to fulfilling the advisory function in terms of the objectives of the organization. For the organization, the advisory function is one means of achieving those objectives; for the advisory staff, the advisory function is itself an objective. The staff attempts to assist leadership with information, analysis, recommendations, and associated services in accordance with its interpretation of its advisory mandate as expressed in directives, legislation, and verbal and written instructions and its interpretation of organization objectives. Examples are easily imagined; faced with new demands or new technology, a city seeks to develop new sources of water, a toy manufacturer attempts to expand his share of the market, a university endeavors to revise its curriculum—all objectives of varying intensity and ultimateness and of varying immediacy and priority relative to other objectives, yet ones to which the respective advisory functions would respond as contributors to their fulfillment. The federal government's major economic objective in 1946 was to avoid postwar depression; as time went on, this objective was transformed into the twin objectives of stability and growth. Characteristically and consistently in fulfillment of its advisory function, each Council of Economic Advisers attempted to provide the best possible advice in carrying out its interpretation of the government's objectives.

The significance of organization objectives lies in the fact that, coupled with the nature of the external-internal environment, they determine the balance between an advisory objective that is inherently conceptual and one that is inherently coordinative. Keyserling's emphasis on indirect controls, for example, illustrates an inherently conceptual objective in placing a major focus on general policy considerations and approaches. On the other hand, Burns' development of public works plans demonstrates an inherently coordinative objective in its emphasis on policy execution. A conceptual objective leads to the provision of a general rationale for specific policies by the advisory body and, in so doing, indicates that its participation is primarily that of a sounding board, communicator, and facilitator in the decision-making process. The coordinative objective permits the advisory body opportunity to provide specific standards for policy determination and thereby to participate as an integral link in the decision-making process.

The degree of participation based on the conceptual objective depends in large measure upon the proximity of the specific decision at issue to the rationale the advisory body has provided—and the closer the proximity the greater can be the involvement. The participation characterized by the coordinative objective depends in large measure simply upon the requirement that, as part of the clearance process, the issue pass within the adviser's purview. In terms of these alternatives, the adviser's participation is quite different both in intensity and type. In one he is asked to comment on a fully developed proposal and to help develop its rationale for public presentation; in the other, as part of the development process, a proposal is submitted to him in draft form for approval or disapproval. The balance of the advisory objective between these two extremes of concept and coordination affects the nature of the essential activity of the advisory body, but it must be made clear that to establish conceptual objectives as opposite of coordinative objectives by no means invalidates the distinctions between staff offices that coordinate and those that advise. Rather, in view of the fact that the advisory function is not entirely passive, an attempt is here made to portray the alternative type of activity in which it is possible for the advisory body to participate.

THE ESSENTIAL ACTIVITY. The essential activity refers to the primary means for carrying out the advisory function within the decision-making framework. The balance between conceptualizing and coordinating objectives influences a similar balance between the activities of planning, control, and evaluation. Such activities are interdependent, but they are different in emphasis and not equally appropriate for the advisory function's different types of participation in decision-making.

Informing, analyzing, and recommending are meaningful primarily in terms of these activities. Planning, both long-term and short-term, attempts to reconcile objectives and goals that are based on aspirations and potentials with forecasts based upon commitments, resources, and precedence. Plans are either deductive in the sense of providing general models or specific single strategies into which operating components are more or less expected to fit, or inductive in the sense of their summing up component parts to comprise an articulated plan. Plans as general models may or may not be followed precisely; deviations do not invalidate them, for they serve primarily as something to shoot for. Plans as single strategies are more rigid; they press for conformity and assume rationality from major to subordinate parts of a program. Plans may cover all organizational operations, or they may be limited to a particular operation such as finance, marketing, manpower, or organization.

Control builds on planning; it attempts to make good on plans, but its emphasis is less on the future and more on the immediate. It is synonymous with coordination in the sense of each person or unit of an organization being informed as to the planned behavior of the other for the reaching of accepted goals.[2] It presumes a co-incidence of organizational means and ends and attempts to provide both motivating and inhibiting forces essential to a balance of compliance and initiative.[3] Control applies techniques not only of planning but also of such processes as budgeting, scheduling—for example, the Program Evaluation and Revue Technique (PERT)—maintenance of performance standards, reports, and inspections.

Evaluation as the third activity focuses on the past; that is, it makes comparisons over time and considers performance in terms of organization plans or other measures, such as standards of profitability, market quotas, trends of past years, rate of turnover, and wage-price guidelines.

Although analytically separate, these three activities blend into an advisory function that (depending on which activity is emphasized) tends to be either more abstract or more operational, thereby reflecting the conceptual or the coordinative advisory objective. That is, the emphasis of activity is either on the side of planning—of the future, of goals, of general models, and of evaluative standards of potential—or on the side of control—of single strategies, of forecasts and commitments, of evaluative standards of precedence and projections. Although these activities reflect the objectives of the advisory function, the precise character of the activity is also influenced by the nature of the expertise involved.

THE NATURE OF THE EXPERTISE. The nature of the expertise comprises the character of the body of knowledge involved, the applicability of the expertise to the organizational objectives and to the advisory objective and activity, and the professional or bureaucratic orientation of the expertise.[4]

1. The body of knowledge may be self-contained, that is, a science based on objective criteria or verifiable general laws; or it may be dependent and therefore existing as a subordinate application of a more basic body of knowledge or as an integral part of an administrative process. Economics, law, and mathematics are examples of the first; budgeting, accounting, and public relations are examples of the second. Both kinds are equally important as areas of expertise of service to the administrator.

2. The use of expertise depends upon the state of knowledge, that is, the scope and depth of its applicability to the substantive policy issues at hand. The expertise may be pervasive, as is the economics of the Council of Economic Advisers, or it may be specialized, as, for example, an accountant's concern for expenditures and receipts against planned budget totals. The extent of the application is in part determined by the additional factors of the appropriateness of the value orientation of the expertise to the relevant policies, the modernity or obsolescence of available techniques, facilities, and data that the expertise commands as part of its own operation, and the strength of its applicability relative to that of other areas of expertise.

3. Content and application of expertise are in turn dependent upon the capacities and convictions of the expert and upon his views regarding his role in the knowledge-power relationship. Such views include his choice of strategies and tactics in advising and advocating. The expert orientation can be regarded as essentially either professional or bureaucratic.[5] Expertise is normally associated with professions that enjoy varying degrees of recognition and have varying degrees of standards, educational requirements, certifying examinations, and organization activities. To the extent that the expert considers himself and his career linked primarily to his profession, seeks approval for his work by his professional peers, and is neutral to the policy issues on which he is advising, his orientation is essentially professional. Conversely, to the degree that he looks to his employing organization for his job and career satisfaction, seeks approval from his subordinates and superiors as well as from his organization peers, and becomes involved in the policy issues to which he is applying his expertise, his orientation becomes bureaucratic. The part-time consultant would represent an extreme example of the former, and the financial analyst fulfilling a career in one organization would represent an extreme example of the latter. Yet within one organization these orientations are not necessarily mutually exclusive. To a large degree they complement one another, and there are frequently bureaucratic hierarchies of professional orientations within an institution. There is, in fact, a mixture of professional and bureaucratic orientations in every

adviser, but such consideration as career patterns, on-the-job conduct, and turnover experience suggest dominance of one or the other in any given situation.

Taken together, the expertise is, either self-contained or dependent, either pervasive or limited, and either professionally or bureaucratically oriented. To the degree that the Council's experience is typical, the scope of its involvement, its Keynesian or non-Keynesian economics, and the predominantly academic roots of its personnel indicate that expertise characteristics of self-containment, pervasiveness, and professional orientation may tend to go together in an operating situation. Alternative characteristics of dependence, specialized application, and bureaucratic orientation may have a similar affinity.

In summary, it can be seen that the internal-external environment as registered by the balance of power is essentially the given or independent variable. It is the principal creator of the need for expert advice and of the manner in which it is exploited or ignored; it affects the advisory objective and the blend within the advisory activity. In large measure it determines the type of expert who can be attracted to fulfill an advisory role and the way in which he performs in it. To illustrate, a crisis situation which threatens major policy objectives and organization survival while demanding complex technology will evoke a different call for and use of advisory help than will a situation characterized by comfortable evolution, organizational security, and technological simplicity. In the first instance, the advisory function may be coordinative and operational, with its expertise being integrated into organization management. In the latter, the advisory function may be relatively conceptual and abstract, with its expertise being relatively removed from organization management. By the same token, the various components of the advisory function are capable of affecting one another, such as the composition, convictions, and conduct of the available expertise influencing advisory objectives, and vice versa. Moreover, as the advisory function is not passive, it contributes to the "sensitivity" or "insensitivity" character of the balance of power through the relationship it establishes with executive leadership.

Relationship Characteristics and Processes

The foregoing discussion of the four factors comprising the first phase of the analytical approach permits a consideration of the second and third phases, namely, the resultant characteristics of the knowledge-power relationship and the processes of the advisory function. It also permits a description of the impact of the factors upon the relationship and processes.

By applying the terms used above to describe the nature of the Council-President relationship, we can view the knowledge-power relationship as a balance between characteristics of interdependence and dependence and between those of variability and stability. In the first case, the relationship is characterized by either a relatively high degree of interacting and direct reciprocity or by a more remote and institutional relationship. In the second, the relationship is characterized by either a changeable and intermittent relationship, in which typically the expert is accepted by the person in power, or by a relatively static and regular relationship typified by dependence upon the expert by the person in power. In general qualitative terms, the relationship balance can be viewed as being either vague or specific or as being either weak or strong. These balances are in turn affected by other knowledge-power relationships involving the same power and by the concomitant relations between the sources of knowledge involved. For example, the analysis of the Heller Council demonstrated that the relations between Heller and Kennedy were affected by the relations of Kennedy and Dillon, of Kennedy with first Bell and then Gordon, and of Heller with these other three advisers.

The nature of the knowledge-power relationship is not self-determined but is influenced by the balance of power within the internal-external environment as well as by the balances within advisory function components of advisory objective, advisory activity, and advisory expertise. Although the impact of these factors upon the knowledge-power relationship, as well as upon one another, is intricate, full of exceptions, and devoid of precise form of measurement, their particular characteristics and their operating association suggest the following hypothesis: The more the complex internal-external balance of power is "sensitive" rather than "insensitive," the more the advisory objective is conceptual rather than coordinative, the more the essential advisory activity is abstract rather than operational, and the more the advisory expertise is pervasive, self-contained, and professional rather than limited, dependent, and bureaucratic, then the more the knowledge-power relationship is interdependent and variable rather than independent and stable, and the more its impact on decision-making processes is general and peripheral rather than specific and integral.

The more this relationship is characterized by interdependence, variability, and ideological features, the more the processes of the advisory function is characterized by the experts taking the initiative in maintaining the relationship with the leader by accepting a wide latitude in the choice of objectives and procedures, seeking involvement in accordance with those objectives and procedures, accommodating to its environment, and developing a combination of unique values and operations. Conversely, under essentially opposite determining factors, essentially opposite knowledge-power relations will exist and the advisory process will more nearly conform to the contrary characteristics of depending upon precedent and instructions, following an established range of objectives and procedures, limiting its involvement, impinging upon its environment, and in general maintaining the advisory institution's established combination of values and operations.

It is unlikely that there exists a staff advisory office to which the above propositions so baldly stated could actually be applied. It is equally unlikely that all of the determining factors would move in the same direction at the same time with the same intensity or would produce the resulting relationships and processes precisely as predicted. Sensitivity to the balance of power, for example, may be such as to limit severely the advisory function and hence the knowledge-power relationship or, as illustrated in the 1962 tax reduction case, this sensitivity may be precisely the factor that creates the leader's demand for advice, so that potentially peripheral participation is turned into significant participation in the decision-making process.

The validity of the proposition, however, is less important than its attempt to identify factors that appear to determine the knowledge-power relationship and to link into a functional relationship the alternative characteristics of those factors with alternative characteristics of the advisory function. There is no intrinsic value in the factors as set forth; they are not norms but rather parameters that singly and collectively limit as well as influence the relationship. They are not specifications to be met in any idealized way as ends in themselves, because, to varying degrees, they pull against one another. In fact, each actual determinant in an individual situation represents a compromise of opposing features. Professional orientation characteristically may pull against values implicit in organizational objectives. The advisory activity itself makes compromises between planning and control that are meaningful only in terms of the situation in which the compromise is operative. It is a matter as much of minimum inconsistency of one factor to another as of their maximum consistency. An advisory body cannot be expected to coordinate in the sense of control if its mandate is to serve as ideologist; nor can an advisory body advise if the issue in question is outside its field of competence, or if the power balance is so sensitive that every utterance is open to attack. By the same token, the assignment of a temporary professionally oriented consultant may be economical, but it may not be appropriate for a complex problem that requires continuous attention over a long period of time. The successes and failures of the Council were identifiable not merely in terms of its fulfillment or deviation from values implicit in original expectations but also as demonstrated in the uniqueness of one Council to the other in terms of the effectiveness of the different responses of each Council to the different balances of existing factors.

If the experiences of the Council of Economic Advisers are indicative, the knowledge-power relationship implicit in the advisory function is both important and enlightening, and this study of the Council's operations should contribute to a broader understanding of that relationship. It should in all probability suggest an analytical approach that isolates and identifies the operating dynamics and intricacies of the relationship between knowledge and power, adviser and leader.

It is hoped that the analytical approach derived from this study will encourage the consideration of other actual or intended advisory relationships in terms of the complex situational determinants in which they operate. Factors of environment, objectives, activity, and expertise assume significance in relationship to one another and to the knowledge-power relationship in the light of a particular span of time, particular issues, given expertise, and identifiable conflict. The explanation of observable or desired knowledge-power relationships of the advisory function in a given situation may depend upon identification and analysis of these factors.

NOTES

Preface

1. Rossiter, *American Presidency*, p. 25.
2. Homan, "Reflections upon the Council of Economic Advisers," p. 32.

Chapter I. Challenge and Expectations

1. Bryson, "Notes on a Theory of Advice," *Political Science Quarterly*, LXVI (Summer, 1951), 339.
2. Pub.L. 304, 60 Stat. 23, Sec. 4(a).
3. *Presidential Power*, p. 33.
4. *Political Science Quarterly*, LXVI (Summer, 1951), 339.
5. For a more elaborate treatment of approaches to decision-making, see Gore, "Administrative Decision-Making in Federal Field Offices," *Public Administration Review*, XVI (Autumn, 1956), 281–91; Gore, *Administrative Decision-Making*; and Simon, *New Science of Management Decision*.
6. Douglas Dillon, Remarks before the 34th National Business Conference of the Harvard Business School, Harvard University, Boston, Massachusetts, June 6, 1964.
7. The council members and their dates of service are given in the following list:

Name	Position	Dates
Edwin G. Nourse	Chairman	1946–49
Leon H. Keyserling	Vice-Chairman	1946–49
	Acting Chairman	1949–50
	Chairman	1950–53
John D. Clark	Member	1946–50
	Vice-Chairman	1950–53
Roy Blough	Member	1950–52
Robert C. Turner	Member	1952–53
Arthur F. Burns	Chairman	1953–56

Name	Position	Dates
Neil H. Jacoby	Member	1953–55
Walter W. Stewart	Member	1953–55
Joseph S. Davis	Member	1955–58
Raymond J. Saulnier	Member	1955–56
	Chairman	1956–61
Paul W. McCracken	Member	1956–59
Karl Brandt	Member	1958–61
Henry C. Wallich	Member	1959–61
James Tobin	Member	1961–62
Kermit Gordon	Member	1961–62
Walter W. Heller	Chairman	1961–64
John P. Lewis	Member	1963–64
Gardner Ackley	Member	1962–64
	Chairman	1964–
Otto Eckstein	Member	1964–
Arthur M. Okun	Member	1964–

8. Bailey, *Congress Makes a Law*, p. 240.

9. Pub.L. 304, 60 Stat. 23, Sec. 2.   10. *Ibid.*, Sec. 4(c).

11. S. 380, 79th Congress, 1st Session.

12. H.R. 2202, 79th Congress, 1st Session.

13. S. 380, Sec. 3(6).

14. Pub.L. 304, 60 Stat. 23, 3(a).

15. *Process and Organization of Government Planning*, p. 91.

16. *Ibid.*, p. 179.   17. *Ibid.*, p. 192.

18. *President's Economic Advisers*, p. 1.

19. Pub.L. 304, 60 Stat. 23, Sec. 4(a).

20. Telegram from Howard S. Ellis, President, American Economic Association, to Harry S. Truman, Nov. 5, 1949, Harry S. Truman Library.

21. Nourse, *Economics in the Public Service*, p. 107.

22. "Presidential Leadership: The Inner Circle and Institutionalization," *Journal of Politics*, XVIII (August, 1959), 418–19.

23. "The President's Economic Staff during the Truman Administration," *American Political Science Review*, XLVIII (March, 1954), 116.

24. *Journal of Politics*, XVIII (August, 1956), 410–426.

25. Pub.L. 304, 60 Stat. 23, Sec. 5(b).

Chapter II. The Period of Influence

1. *Economics in the Public Service*, p. 114.

2. *Memoirs*, II, 1.

3. *Presidential Power*, pp. 171, 179.

4. *Memoirs*, II, 36–37.

5. Nourse, *Economics in the Public Service*, p. 109.

6. *Ibid.*, p. 103.

7. Silverman, *President's Economic Advisers*, p. 3; *Nation,* August 14, 1946, quoted in Nourse, *Economics in the Public Service,* p. 104n.

8. *President's Economic Advisers,* p. 3.

9. Brigante, *Feasibility Dispute.*

10. *American City,* LIX (June, 1944), 93.

11. Bailey, *Congress Makes a Law,* pp. 46, 110–11.

12. Senator Robert F. Wagner, letter to John R. Steelman, July 15, 1946, Truman Library.

13. Nourse, *1950's Come First,* p. 109 f.

14. H.R. 2756, Economic Stability Act of 1949; S. 281, Economic Expansion Act of 1949.

15. Edwin G. Nourse, "Economic Implication of Military Preparedness," an address before the National Military Establishment Joint Orientation Conference, November 10, 1948, in Nourse, *Economics in the Public Service,* pp. 485–91; for a description of prevailing opinion, see Schilling, "The Politics of National Defense: Fiscal 1950," in Schilling, Hammond, and Snyder, *Strategy,* p. 100.

16. Nourse, *Economics in the Public Service,* pp. 176, 370, 373–74.

17. Silverman, *President's Economic Advisers,* p. 5.

18. *U.S. News and World Report,* April 14, 1950, quoted in Nourse, *Economics in the Public Service,* pp. 376–77.

19. Nourse, *Economics in the Public Service,* p. 280.

20. *American Economic Review,* "Stabilizing the Economy: The Employment Act of 1946 in Operation," Papers and Proceedings of the 62nd Annual Meeting of the American Economic Association, New York, December 27–30, 1949, pp. 144–90.

21. Commission on Organization of the Executive Branch of Government, *General Management of the Executive Branch* (report to Congress, February, 1949), p. 17, quoted in Nourse, *Economics in the Public Service,* p. 455.

22. Nourse, *Economics in the Public Service,* p. 280.

23. Leon H. Keyserling, "Memorandum: Record in Economics Field" and covering note, to Clark Clifford, October 19, 1949, p. 6, Truman Library.

24. Leon H. Keyserling, letter to author.

25. Nourse, *Economics in the Public Service,* p. 286.

26. New York *Times,* May 11, 1950, p. 24.

27. Council of Economic Advisers, "Memorandum: Monthly Report on the Economic Situation," to the President, November 9, 1949, pp. 2–3, Truman Library.

28. *Economic Report of the President,* January, 1950, p. 2.

29. Bailey, *Congress Makes a Law,* pp. 2, 24, 25, 45, 161.

30. *Ibid.,* p. 45.

31. *Ibid.*, p. 65.

32. Charles L. Schultze, interview with author.

33. See Silverman, *President's Economic Advisers*, pp. 11–12; Leon H. Keyserling, "The Council of Economic Advisers' Tasks in the Next Decade," in Colm, ed., *Employment Act*, pp. 66, 71.

34. *Ibid.*, p. 71.

35. Leon H. Keyserling, interview with author.

36. Keyserling, in Colm, ed., *Employment Act*, p. 72.

37. John P. Lewis, letter to author.

38. Roger W. Jones, interview with author.

39. John R. Steelman papers and Clark Clifford papers, Truman Library.

40. For more information see Warren Cikens, "The Council of Economic Advisers: Political Economy at the Crossroads," in Friedrich and Galbraith, eds., *Public Policy*, IV, 102 ff.

41. Gross and Lewis, "The President's Economic Staff during the Truman Administration," *American Political Science Review*, XLVIII (March, 1954), 114–30.

42. Leon H. Keyserling, interview with author.

43. John P. Lewis, letter to author.

44. Grover W. Ensley, letter to Donald Dawson, January 12, 1950, Truman Library.

45. Truman, *Memoirs*, II, 309.

46. For further information see *ibid.*, pp. 294–315; Hammond, "NSC-68 Prologue to Rearmament" in Schilling, Hammond, and Snyder, *Strategy*, pp. 267–378; Stewart Alsop, New York *Herald Tribune*, May 7, 1950, p. 21, and June 23, 1950, p. 17.

47. Hammond, in Schilling, Hammond, and Snyder, *Strategy*, pp. 318–19.

48. *Ibid.*, p. 307.   49. *Ibid.*, p. 343.

50. Nourse, *Economics in the Public Service*, p. 490.

51. Hammond, in Schilling, Hammond, and Snyder, *Strategy*, p. 328.

52. New York *Herald Tribune*, June 23, 1950, p. 17.

53. *Economic Report of the President*, January, 1950, p. 78.

54. *Midyear Economic Report of the President*, July, 1950, p. 2.

55. Truman, *Memoirs*, II, 335.

56. John P. Lewis, letter to author.   57. *Ibid.*

58. *Midyear Economic Report of the President*, July, 1950, p. 46.

59. *Ibid.*, p. 46.   60. *Ibid.*, pp. 4–12.   61. *Ibid.*, p. 48.

62. *Ibid.*   63. *Ibid.*, pp. 43–45.   64. *Ibid.*, p. 48.

65. *Ibid.*, p. 2.

66. Leon H. Keyserling, letter to John R. Steelman, July 5, 1950, Truman Library.

67. H.R. 9176 and S. 3936, Pub.L. 774, 81st Congress, 2d Session.

68. *Presidential Power*, p. 104.

69. *Midyear Economic Report of the President*, July, 1950, testimony of Commerce and Federal Reserve Board representatives before the House and Senate Banking and Currency Committees on the Defense Production Act of 1950, p. 56.

70. Neustadt, *Presidential Power*, p. 104.

71. Council of Economic Advisers, *Economic Indicators*, August, 1950, p. 4.

72. U.S. Congress, Senate Committee on Banking and Currency, *Hearings on S. 3936*, 81st Congress, 2d Session, p. 97.

73. Matthew Hale, letter to author.

74. Richard E. Neustadt, interview with author.

75. Bertram Gross, letter to author.

76. John P. Lewis, letter to author.

77. Benjamin Caplan, interview with author.

78. "Price Control Strategy," p. 103.

79. *Ibid.* 80. *Ibid.*, pp. 48–52, 60–67.

81. Council of Economic Advisers, "Memorandum: Weekly Report on the Economic Situation" to the President, August 17, 1950; August 29, 1950, Truman Library.

82. Thomas B. McCabe, letter to Harry S. Truman, August 10, 1950, Truman Library.

83. Memorandum to Stuart Symington, September 7, 1950, quoted in Ackley, "Price Control Strategy," pp. 111–13.

84. Roy Blough, personal diary.

85. H.R. 8920, 81st Congress, 2d Session.

86. U.S. Department of the Treasury, "Taxation for Defense."

87. Roy Blough, interview with author.

88. Roy Blough, personal diary, entry for July 17, 1950.

89. Roy Blough, interview with author.

90. Council of Economic Advisers, "Memorandum: Special Report on Economic Trends and Policies," to the President, September 26, 1950, p. 7; "Memorandum: Quarterly Report on the Economic Situation," to the President, October 19, 1950, p. 10, Truman Library.

91. David E. Bell, "Memorandum for Mr. Murphy," October 3, 1950, Truman Library.

92. Council of Economic Advisers, "Memorandum: Weekly Report on the Economic Situation," to the President, August 29, 1950, pp. 1, 2; "Memorandum: Monthly Report on the Economic Situation," to the President, September 12, 1950, p. 3; "Memorandum: Special Report on Economic Trends and Policies," to the President, September 26, 1950; "Memorandum: Quarterly Report on the Economic Situation," to the President, October 19, 1950, pp. 9–10, Truman Library.

93. Neil Hardy, interview with author.

94. Leon H. Keyserling, letter to John R. Steelman, September 13, 1950, Truman Library.

95. Council of Economic Advisers, "Memorandum: Special Report on Economic Trends and Policies," to the President, September 26, 1950; "Memorandum: Quarterly Report on the Economic Situation," to the President, October 19, 1950, Truman Library.

96. John P. Lewis, letter to author.

97. David E. Bell, interview with author.

98. Rosenberg, "ODM," pp. 23, 24.

99. *Ibid.*, p. 28.

100. Council of Economic Advisers, "Memorandum: Weekly Report on the Economic Situation," to the President, August 29, 1950, p. 4, Truman Library.

101. *Ibid.*, August 17, 1950, p. 2.

102. Executive Order 10161, September 9, 1950, Sec. 803.

103. Council of Economic Advisers, "Memorandum: Weekly Report on the Economic Situation," to the President, August 29, 1950, p. 3, Truman Library.

104. *Ibid.*, October 19, 1950, p. 10.

105. Council of Economic Advisers, "Memorandum: Special Report on Economic Trends and Policies," to the President, September 26, 1950, p. 10, Truman Library.

106. New York *Times*, October 5, 1950, p. 7.

107. John C. Houston, Jr., "Memorandum for Mr. Steelman: Policy Guidance to Departments and Agencies Operating under Authority of Defense Production Act," September 20, 1950, p. 3, Truman Library.

108. Rosenberg, "ODM," p. 53.

109. "Price Control Strategy," p. 103.

110. John P. Lewis, letter to author.

Chapter III. The Period of Frustration

1. New York *Times*, November 17, 1950, p. 1.

2. *Ibid.*, November 21, 1950, p. 17.   3. *Ibid.*

4. *Ibid.*, November 30, 1950, p. 53.

5. *Ibid.*, December 1, 1950, p. 11; December 3, 1950, p. 53.

6. *Ibid.*, December 3, 1950, Sec. III, p. 1.

7. *Ibid.*, December 5, 1950, p. 1.

8. *Ibid.*, December 5, 1950, p. 28; December 7, 1950, p. 1; December 8, 1950, p. 35; December 9, 1950, p. 6.

9. *Ibid.*, December 8, 1950, p. 47.

10. *Ibid.*, December 11, 1950, p. 1.

11. *Ibid.*, December 11, 1950, p. 20.

12. Council of Economic Advisers, "Memorandum: Further Action on Price and Wage Controls," to the President, December 7, 1950, pp. 1–2, Truman Library.

13. New York *Times*, December 12, 1950, p. 23.

14. *Ibid.*, December 12, 1950, p. 1.

15. "Price Control Strategy," p. 146.

16. *Wall Street Journal*, January 5, 1951, p. 1; January 6, 1951, p. 2; January 18, 1951, p. 1; January 19, 1951, p. 2.

17. "Price Control Strategy," p. 171.

18. *Ibid.*, p. 105.   19. *Ibid.*, pp. 137–39.

20. Roy Blough, personal diary, entry for November 8, 1950.

21. Bertram G. Gross, interview with author.

22. John P. Lewis, letter to author.

23. Roy Blough, personal diary, entry for December 13, 1950.

24. *Ibid.*

25. Council of Economic Advisers, *Economics of National Defense*, p. 18.

26. Roy Blough, interview with author; Ackley, "Price Control Strategy," pp. 231–33.

27. Harry S. Truman, "State of the Union Message," in *Economic Report of the President*, January, 1951; Charles Edward Wilson, radio address, January 17, 1951.

28. White, "Mr. Wilson Goes to Washington," *Reporter*, IV (January 23, 1951), 29.

29. Ackley, "Price Control Strategy," p. 178.

30. Benjamin Caplan, interview with author.

31. U.S. Congress, Joint Committee on the Economic Report, *Hearings on the January 1951 Economic Report of the President*, 82d Congress, 1st Session, pp. 132–47.

32. Leon H. Keyserling, interview with author.

33. "Price Control Strategy," p. 182.

34. Harold Leventhal, interview with author.

35. Gardner Ackley, letter to author.

36. Ackley, "Price Control Strategy," p. 182.

37. Leon H. Keyserling, interview with author.   38. *Ibid.*

39. As in the previous sections, I am indebted for much of the factual information in the following paragraphs to Ackley, "Price Control Strategy," pp. 194–385.

40. Harold Leventhal, letter to author.

41. Franz B. Wolf, interview with author.

42. Council of Economic Advisers, "Memorandum: Monthly Report on the Economic Situation," to the President, February 15, 1950, pp. 7, 8, Truman Library.

43. Council of Economic Advisers, "Memorandum: Quarterly Re-

port on the Economic Situation," to the President, April 6, 1951, p. 17, Truman Library.

44. Roy Blough, personal diary, entry for April 23, 1951.

45. New York *Times*, April 26, 1951, p. 43.

46. Leon H. Keyserling, interview with author.

47. *Memoirs*, II, 44.

48. David E. Bell, interview with author; William McChesney Martin, interview with author.

49. *Economic Report of the President*, January, 1948, p. 86.

50. U.S. Congress, Joint Committee on the Economic Report, *Subcommittee Report on Monetary Credit and Fiscal Policies*, 81st Congress, 1st Session.

51. Council of Economic Advisers, "Memorandum: Weekly Report on the Economic Situation," to the President, August 29, 1950, p. 4, Truman Library.

52. *Economic Report of the President*, January, 1951, p. 142.

53. Truman, *Memoirs*, II, 45.

54. New York *Times*, February 3, 1951, p. 2.   55. *Ibid.*, p. 1.

56. Letter from Thomas B. McCabe to Harry S. Truman, February 7, 1951, Truman Library.

57. Council of Economic Advisers, "Memorandum: Monthly Report on the Economic Situation," to the President, February 15, 1951, p. 9, Truman Library.

58. Rosenberg, "ODM," p. 58.

59. White House press release, February 26, 1951, Truman Library.

60. Roy Blough, personal diary, entry for March 5, 1951.

61. William McChesney Martin, interview with author.

62. Roy Blough, personal diary, entry for March 5, 1951.

63. Roy Blough, interview with author.   64. *Ibid.*

65. Leon H. Keyserling, interview with author.

66. Rosenberg, "ODM," p. 6. I am indebted to Herbert Rosenberg for much of the factual information on mobilization production contained in this section. The interpretations, however, are my own.

67. Roy Blough, personal diary.

68. Rosenberg, "ODM," p. 61.   69. *Ibid.*, pp. 76–77.

70. John P. Lewis, letter to author.

71. Rosenberg, "ODM," p. 111.

72. See Council of Economic Advisers, "Memorandum: Monthly Report on the Economic Situation," to the President, February 15, 1951, and May 17, 1951; and "Memorandum: Quarterly Report on the Economic Situation," to the President, April 6, 1951, Truman Library.

73. John P. Lewis, letter to author.

74. U.S. Congress, Senate Committee on Appropriations, Subcom-

mittee, *Hearings on the Independent Offices Appropriation Bill for Fiscal Year 1952*, 82d Congress, 1st Session, pp. 90–91.

75. Executive Order 10200.

76. Rosenberg, "ODM," p. 71n.

77. *Economic Report of the President*, January, 1951, p. 6.

78. *Ibid.*, p. 68.

79. Council of Economic Advisers, "Memorandum: Quarterly Report on the Economic Situation," to the President, April 6, 1951, p. 9, Truman Library.

80. Leon H. Keyserling, John D. Clark, and Roy Blough, letter to Harry S. Truman, June 5, 1951, pp. 2, 4, Truman Library.

81. U.S. Congress, Joint Committee on Economic Report, *Economic and Political Hazards*, pp. 7, 8, 19.

82. Office of Price Stabilization, Office of Economic Policy, *The Economic Situation and Outlook Review*, No. 1, April 10, 1951.

83. Files of Franz B. Wolf, "Note to Gardner Ackley from Franz Wolf," 1953.

84. John P. Lewis, letter to author; also Lewis, "The Lull That Came to Stay," *Journal of Political Economy*, LXIII (February, 1955), 1–19.

85. John D. Clark, "Draft of Monthly Report," June 7, 1951; "Draft of Monthly Report," September 7, 1951; Leon H. Keyserling, "Memorandum: Comment on Draft of Monthly Report," September 7, 1951; Roy Blough, "Memorandum: Comment on Draft of Monthly Report," September 10, 1951; Council of Economic Advisers, "Memorandum: Quarterly Report on the Economic Situation," to the President, October 15, 1951, papers of John D. Clark, Truman Library.

86. Council of Economic Advisers, "Memorandum: Quarterly Report on the Economic Situation," to the President, October 15, 1951, p. 4, Truman Library.

87. Rosenberg, "ODM," pp. 149–50.

88. *Ibid.*, p. 150.   89. *Ibid.*, p. 153.

90. Director of Defense Mobilization, "Report to the President," December 1, 1951, Truman Library.

91. Rosenberg, "ODM," p. 162.

92. Leon H. Keyserling, letter to author.

93. Rosenberg, "ODM," p. 111n.

94. Burton H. Klein, letter to author.

95. Rosenberg, "ODM," pp. 164–65.   96. *Ibid.*

97. *Ibid.*, pp. 165–67.   98. *Ibid.*, p. 166.

99. David E. Bell, interview with author.

100. Harry S. Truman, interview with author.

101. Roy Blough, interview with author.

102. Council of Economic Advisers, "Memorandum: Quarterly Report on the Economic Situation," to the President, April 21, 1952, Truman Library.

103. Rosenberg, "ODM," p. 69.

104. Council of Economic Advisers, "Memorandum: Monthly Report on the Economic Situation," to the President, February 15, 1951, and May 17, 1951; "Memorandum: Quarterly Report on the Economic Situation," April 6, 1951, Truman Library.

105. David E. Bell, interview with author.

106. Johnson, "Reflections on a Year of Price Controls," *American Economic Review*, XLII (May, 1952), 291.

107. Gross and Lewis, "The President's Economic Staff during the Truman Administration," *American Political Science Review*, XLVIII (March, 1954), 114–30.

108. Leon H. Keyserling, letter to author.

109. Truman announced on March 29, 1952, that he was not a candidate for reelection.

Chapter IV. Inductive Economics for a Republican Program

1. "State of the Union Message," February 2, 1953, *Public Papers of the Presidents* (1953), p. 12.

2. Dale, *Conservatives in Power*, p. 21.

3. *Eisenhower*, p. 163.

4. Arthur Krock, New York *Times*, January 18, 1953, Sec. IV, p. 50. © 1953 by The New York Times Company. Reprinted by permission.

5. *American Presidency*, p. 177.

6. Gabriel Hauge, interview with author.

7. A. F. Burns, *Frontiers of Economic Knowledge*. (See particularly "Economic Research and the Keynesian Thinking of Our Times," pp. 3–26.)

8. *Ibid.*, p. 129.   9. *Ibid.*, p. 10.

10. *Ibid.*, p. 9.   11. *Ibid.*, p. 228.

12. *Ibid.*, pp. 228–29.

13. *Business Week*, July 22, 1961, p. 59.

14. New York *Times*, October 26, 1952, p. 78.

15. Arthur F. Burns, interview with author.

16. New York *Times*, February 12, 1953, p. 10.

17. *Ibid.*, February 17, 1953, p. 18.

18. *Ibid.*, April 6, 1953, p. 29.

19. *Ibid.*, March 7, 1953, p. 11.

20. 67 Stat. 644, "Reorganization Plan No. 9."

21. *Economic Report of the President*, January, 1954, p. 121.

22. *Ibid.*

23. Letter from Arthur F. Burns to Senator Paul H. Douglas, Chairman of the Joint Committee on the Economic Report, February 3, 1956, quoted in U.S. Congress, Joint Committee on the Economic Report, *Hearings before the Joint Committee on the Economic Report*, 84th Congress, 2d Session, p. 690.

24. New York *Times*, March 7, 1953, p. 11.

25. U.S. Congress, Senate Committee on Banking and Currency, *Hearings on the Confirmation of Arthur F. Burns as Chairman of the Council of Economic Advisers*, 83d Congress, 1st Session, quoted in Silverman, *President's Economic Advisers*, p. 16.

26. *Fortune*, April, 1953, p. 116.

27. A. F. Burns, "An Economist in Government," *Forum*, I (Winter, 1957), 4.

28. New York *Times*, March 7, 1958, p. 23.

29. *Ibid.*, November 30, 1953, p. 2.

30. A. F. Burns, *Business Cycle Research*, p. 8.

31. "The Annual Economic Review," *Economic Report of the President*, January, 1953, p. 75.

32. New York *Times*, March 20, 1953, p. 41.

33. W. Lewis, Jr., *Federal Fiscal Policy*, p. 138.

34. Council of Economic Advisers, *Economic Indicators*, May, 1953, pp. 2, 3, 7, 12.

35. Pub.L. 95, 83d Congress, 1st Session.   36. *Ibid.*

37. W. Lewis, Jr., *Federal Fiscal Policy*, p. 139.

38. U.S. Congress, Joint Committee on the Economic Report, *Hearings on the January 1954 Economic Report of the President*, 83d Congress, 2d Session, p. 668.

39. *Ibid.*, pp. 668–69.

40. New York *Times*, May 20, 1953, p. 25.

41. *Ibid.*, June 25, 1953, p. 41.

42. Asher Achinstein, interview with author.

43. *Economic Report of the President*, January, 1954, p. 123. (Italics added.)

44. Arthur F. Burns and Neil Jacoby, "Memorandum," to auxiliary staff, ABEGS, and members of CEA staff, September 29, 1953.

45. New York *Times*, September 13, 1953, Sec. IV, p. 9. © 1953 by The New York Times Company. Reprinted by permission.

46. Arthur F. Burns, interview with author.

47. Donovan, *Eisenhower*, p. 165.

48. New York *Times*, September 27, 1953, Sec. III, p. 1. © 1953 by The New York Times Company. Reprinted by permission.

49. *Ibid.*   50. Donovan, *Eisenhower*, p. 210.

51. Arthur F. Burns, interview with author.

52. W. Lewis, Jr., *Federal Fiscal Policy*, pp. 146–47.

53. "Presidency and Legislation: Planning the President's Program," *American Political Science Review*, LXIX (December, 1955), 980–1018.

54. *Ibid.*, p. 985. 55. *Ibid.*, p. 986. 56. *Ibid.*, p. 992.

57. *Ibid.*, p. 980. 58. *Ibid.*, p. 987.

59. Dwight D. Eisenhower, press conference, January 27, 1954, *Public Papers of the Presidents* (1954), pp. 210–11.

60. U.S. Congress, House Committee on Ways and Means, *Hearings on Forty Topics Pertaining to the General Revision of the Internal Revenue Code*, 83d Congress, 1st Session, 1953, Parts I–IV.

61. *Congressional Quarterly Almanac*, IX (1953), 409.

62. "Budget Message of the President," *Budget of the United States Government* (for the fiscal year ending June 30, 1955), p. M15.

63. Dan Throop Smith, interview with author.

64. *Economic Report of the President*, January, 1954, p. 78.

65. Dan Throop Smith, interview with author.

66. U.S. Congress, Joint Committee on the Economic Report, *Hearings on the January 1954 Economic Report of the President*, 83d Congress, 2d Session, pp. 61, 82.

67. Arthur F. Burns, interview with author.

68. *Economic Report of the President*, January, 1954, p. 77.

69. Arthur F. Burns, interview with author.

70. Dan Throop Smith, interview with author.

71. *Economic Report of the President*, January, 1954, pp. 78–81.

72. Dan Throop Smith, letter to author.

73. *Economic Report of the President*, January, 1954, pp. 78–81.

74. Dan Throop Smith, letter to author.

75. Arthur F. Burns, interview with author.

76. *Ibid.* 77. *Ibid.*

78. U.S. Congress, House Select Committee on Small Business, Subcommittee No. 2, *Hearings on the Effect of the Present Tax Structure on Small Business*, 83d Congress, 1st Session, pp. 299–323.

79. *Ibid.*, p. 301 ff.

80. "Budget Message of the President," *Budget of the United States Government* (for the fiscal year ending June 30, 1955), p. M16.

81. "Presidency and Legislation: Planning the President's Program," *American Political Science Review*, LXIX (December, 1955), 993n.

82. Childs, *Eisenhower*, p. 167.

83. Dan Throop Smith, interview with author. 84. *Ibid.*

85. 63 Stat. 413 (1949), Sec. 2. 86. *Ibid.*

87. Leo Grebler, "Housing Policies to Combat Depression," in *Policies to Combat Depression*, p. 242.

88. Grebler, *Housing Issues*, p. 2.

89. President's Advisory Committee on Government Housing Policies and Programs, *Recommendations*, p. 5. (Italics added.)

90. Special Message from the President of the United States, House Document 306, 83d Congress, 2d Session, January 25, 1954.

91. President's Advisory Committee on Government Housing Policies and Programs, *Recommendations*, p. 15.

92. Asher Achinstein, interview with author.

93. Gabriel Hauge, interview with author.

94. 64 Stat. 798 (1950), Title VI, Par. 2132.

95. Arthur F. Burns, interview with author.

96. Pub.L. 94, 83d Cong., 1st Sess., Sec. 3.   97. *Ibid.*

98. *Economic Report of the President*, January, 1954, p. 84.

99. *Housing Issues*, p. 35, for references on earlier treatment of idea of permissive adjustment.

100. Arthur F. Burns, interview with author.

101. *Economic Report of the President*, January, 1954, p. 87.

102. House Document 306, p. 6.

103. President's Advisory Committee on Government Housing Policies and Programs, *Recommendations*, p. 368.

104. Donovan, *Eisenhower*, p. 174.

105. Arthur F. Burns, interview with author.

106. *Government Organization Manual*, 1953–1954, p. 616.

107. U.S. Department of Labor, Bureau of Labor Standards, Federal Advisory Council, "Minutes of Meeting, October 20, 1950."

108. American Assembly, *Economic Security*, final edition, pp. 40–41.

109. *Ibid.*, p. 141.   110. *Ibid.*, p. 152.

111. Clarence D. Long, interview with author.

112. Arthur F. Burns, letter to author.

113. *Economic Report of the President*, January, 1954, p. 98.

114. *Ibid.*, pp. 96–99.   115. *Ibid.*, p. 96.

116. *Ibid.*, p. 101.   117. *Ibid.*   118. *Ibid.*, p. 102.

119. Clarence D. Long, interview with author.

Chapter V. Countering the Recession of 1953–54

1. *Economic Report of the President*, January, 1954, p. 3.

2. *Ibid.*, p. 11.   3. *Ibid.*, p. 22.   4. *Ibid.*, pp. 71–72.

5. *Ibid.*, p. 13.   6. *Ibid.*, pp. 75–76.

7. *Ibid.*, p. 73.   8. *Ibid.*, pp. 113–14.

9. Donovan, *Eisenhower*, p. 213.

10. *Economic Report of the President*, January, 1954, p. 76.

11. U.S. Congress, Joint Committee on the Economic Report, *Hearings on the January 1954 Economic Report of the President*, 83d Congress, 2d Session, pp. 846, 358–59.

12. New York *Times*, January 20, 1954, p. 1.

13. U.S. Congress, Joint Committee on the Economic Report, *Hearings on the January 1954 Economic Report of the President*, 83d Congress, 2d Session, pp. 722–30.

14. *Ibid.*, p. 725.   15. *Ibid.*, p. 435.

16. Letter from Senator Paul H. Douglas to President Dwight D. Eisenhower, February 19, 1954, quoted in Donovan, *Eisenhower*, p. 217.

17. *Eisenhower*, p. 212.   18. *Ibid.*, pp. 215–16.

19. *Economic Report of the President*, January, 1954, p. 10.

20. A. F. Burns, *Prosperity without Inflation*, p. 34.

21. U.S. Congress, Joint Committee on the Economic Report, *Hearings on the January 1954 Economic Report of the President*, 83d Congress, 2d Session, p. 26.

22. *Ibid.*   23. *Ibid.*, p. 27.

24. *Economic Report of the President*, January, 1954, pp. 103–07.

25. *Ibid.*, p. 104.

26. *Congressional Quarterly Almanac*, X (1954), 499.

27. Donovan, *Eisenhower*, p. 213.   28. *Ibid.*

29. New York *Times*, March 15, 1954, p. 12.

30. *Ibid.*, March 20, 1954, p. 11.

31. James Reston, New York *Times*, March 26, 1954, p. 11. © 1954 by The New York Times Company. Reprinted by permission.

32. H.R. 7766, 83d Congress, 2d Session.

33. U.S. Congress, Joint Committee on the Economic Report, *Hearings on the January 1954 Economic Report of the President*, 83d Congress, 2d Session, p. 520.

34. Donovan, *Eisenhower*, p. 216.

35. New York *Times*, March 25, 1954, p. 1.

36. Donovan, *Eisenhower*, pp. 217–18.

37. *Ibid.*, p. 218.

38. *Economic Report of the President*, January, 1954, p. 79.

39. New York *Times*, February 26, 1954, p. 1.

40. Arthur F. Burns, interview with author.

41. New York *Times*, March 29, 1954, p. 1.

42. *Ibid.*, March 7, 1954, Sec. IV, p. 2.

43. *Ibid.*, June 22, 1954, p. 35.

44. Grebler, *Housing Issues*, pp. 21, 24.

45. Arthur F. Burns, letter to author.

46. New York *Times*, June 14, 1954, p. 12.

47. *Housing Issues*, pp. 28–29.

48. Arthur F. Burns, interview with author.

49. Council of Economic Advisers, *Economic Indicators*, December, 1954, p. 18.

50. Donovan, *Eisenhower*, p. 215.

51. U.S. Congress, Joint Committee on the Economic Report, *Hearings on the January 1954 Economic Report of the President*, 83d Congress, 2d Session, p. 33.

52. *Ibid.*, pp. 33, 34.

53. Benjamin Caplan, "Comment" on David W. Lusher, "The Stabilizing Effectiveness of Budget Flexibility," in *Policies to Combat Depression*, p. 101.

54. Donovan, *Eisenhower*, p. 218.

55. W. Lewis, Jr., *Federal Fiscal Policy*, p. 165.

56. Donovan, *Eisenhower*, p. 219.

57. W. Lewis, Jr., *Federal Fiscal Policy*, p. 166.

58. A. F. Burns, *Prosperity without Inflation*, p. 34.

59. New York *Times*, July 30, 1954, p. 1.

60. W. Lewis, Jr., *Federal Fiscal Policy*, pp. 157, 186.

61. Donovan, *Eisenhower*, p. 221.

62. Council of Economic Advisers, *Economic Indicators*, July, 1954, pp. 2, 3, 6, 9, 12, 15–19, 24.

63. Hickman, *Contraction of 1953–1954*, p. 36.

64. *Economic Report of the President*, January, 1955, p. 16.

65. "The Eisenhower Administration and the Recession, 1953–1955," *Oxford Economic Papers*, X (February 1958), 54.

66. Arthur F. Burns, interview with author.

67. *Economic Report of the President*, January, 1955, pp. 2–3.

68. Asher Achinstein, interview with author.

69. *Economic Report of the President*, January, 1955, p. 18.

70. Donovan, *Eisenhower*, p. 221.

71. Childs, *Eisenhower*, pp. 167–68.

72. Arthur F. Burns, letter to author.

73. Arthur F. Burns, interview with author.

74. Asher Achinstein, interview with author.

75. Bert G. Hickman, interview with author.

76. Arthur F. Burns, interview with author.

77. Bert G. Hickman, interview with author.

78. Asher Achinstein, interview with author.

79. *Policies to Combat Depression*.

80. *Business Week*, July 22, 1961, p. 67; also by former associates.

81. Asher Achinstein, interview with author.   82. *Ibid.*

83. Robinson Newcomb, interview with author.

84. Arthur F. Burns, interview with author.

85. Asher Achinstein, interview with author.

86. U.S. Congress, Joint Committee on the Economic Report, *Hearings on January 1956 Economic Report of the President*, 84th Congress,

2d Session, pp. 535–36, 690–91; Silverman, *President's Economic Advisers*, pp. 16–17.

87. Arthur F. Burns, interview with author.
88. Gabriel Hauge, interview with author.
89. Arthur F. Burns, interview with author.
90. Roger W. Jones, interview with author.
91. Gabriel Hauge, interview with author.
92. *Economic Report of the President*, January, 1954, p. 123.
93. Clarence D. Long, interview with author.
94. A. F. Burns, *Prosperity without Inflation*, pp. 86–87; also "Some Reflections on the Employment Act."
95. Gabriel Hauge, interview with author.
96. New York *Times*, November 14, 1956, p. 1.

Chapter VI. 1961—The Year of Continuing Tradition

1. *John Kennedy*, p. 281.   2. *Ibid.*, pp. 268, 274.
3. New York *Times*, December 24, 1960, p. 5.   4. *Ibid.*
5. *Time*, March 3, 1961, p. 18.
6. Kenneth Arrow and Robert Solow of the 1961–62 Heller staff were also recipients of this award in 1957 and 1961, respectively.
7. *Public Papers of the Presidents* (1961), p. 22.
8. U.S. Congress, Joint Economic Committee, *Hearings on January 1961 Economic Report of the President and the Economic Situation and Outlook*, 87th Congress, 1st Session, p. 10. (The name of the Committee was changed from "Joint Committee on the Economic Report" in 1956.)
9. Council of Economic Advisers, *Economic Indicators*, January, 1961, p. 9.
10. New York *Times*, January 6, 1961, p. 18.   11. *Ibid.*
12. *Ibid.*, January 12, 1961, p. 18.
13. *Ibid.*, January 4, 1961, p. 10.
14. *Public Papers of the Presidents* (1961), p. 22.
15. *Ibid.*, pp. 41–53.
16. James Tobin, letter to author.
17. *Economic Report of the President*, January, 1962, pp. 97–107.
18. U.S. Congress, Senate Appropriations Subcommittee on General Government Matters, *Hearings for the Fiscal Year 1962*, May 24, 1961, p. 788.
19. U.S. Congress, Senate, Committee on Appropriations, *Hearings on the Supplemental Appropriation Bill for 1962*, H.R. 9169, 87th Congress, 1st Session, statement by Kermit Gordon, September 18, 1961, pp. 166–67.
20. U.S. Congress, Joint Economic Committee, *Hearings on January*

1961 Economic Report of the President and the Economic Situation and Outlook, 87th Congress, 1st Session, pp. 312–15.

21. *Ibid.,* pp. 355–57.   22. *Ibid.,* p. 361.

23. U.S. Congress, Joint Economic Committee, *Study of Employment Growth and Price Levels,* 1959.

24. *Public Papers of the Presidents* (1961), pp. 290–303.

25. *Ibid.*

26. U.S. Congress, House Committee on Ways and Means, *Income Tax Revision: Panel Discussions,* press release, May 18, 1959, 86th Congress, 1st Session, p. 2.

27. *Ibid.*

28. New York *Times,* October 14, 1960, p. 21; October 21, 1960, p. 1.

29. *Ibid.,* February 6, 1961, p. 33.

30. *Public Papers of the Presidents* (1961), p. 291.

31. *Ibid.,* p. 303.

32. Council of Economic Advisers, *Economic Indicators,* July 1961, pp. 1, 7.

33. *Public Papers of the Presidents* (1961), p. 516.

34. New York *Times,* July 21, 1961, p. 1.

35. Washington *Post,* July 22, 1961, p. A1.

36. Harris, "Walter Heller: 'Mr. Tax Cut,'" *Look,* XXVII (June 18, 1963), 81 f.; Rowen, *Free Enterprisers,* p. 171.

37. New York *Herald Tribune,* July 26, 1961, p. 21.

38. *Ibid.*   39. *Ibid.*   40. *Ibid.*

41. *Business Week,* January 27, 1962, p. 78.

42. *Nation's Business,* May, 1964, p. 369.

43. *Public Papers of the Presidents* (1961), p. 537. (Italics added.)

44. John P. Lewis, interview with author.

45. U.S. Congress, Senate Committee on Commerce, *Report on National Transportation Policy.*

46. Bauer, Pool, and Dexter, *American Business,* p. 76.

47. *Business Week,* October 14, 1961, p. 34.

48. *Economic Report of the President,* January, 1962, p. 196.

49. American Economic Association, *1964 Handbook.*

50. U.S. Congress, House Appropriations Committee, *Hearings on the Treasury, Post Office Department, and Executive Office,* 87th Congress, 2d Session, p. 776.

51. *Economic Report of the President,* January, 1962, p. 196.

52. *Ibid.,* p. 196 f.   53. *Ibid.,* p. 197.

54. *Ibid.,* pp. 197–98.   55. *Ibid.,* p. 199.

56. Pub.L. 304, Sec. 3, 79th Congress, 2d Session.

57. Walter W. Heller, "Memorandum for the Professional Staff, Initial Assignments for the 1964 Annual Report," October 10, 1963.

Chapter VII. Tax Reduction and the New Tradition

1. "Budget Message of the President," *Budget of the United States Government 1963*, pp. 8–9.
2. *Economic Report of the President,* January, 1962, pp. 3–13.
3. *Ibid.,* p. 17.   4. *Ibid.,* p. 25.   5. *Ibid.,* p. 27.
6. *Ibid.,* pp. 40–56.   7. *Ibid.,* p. 48.   8. *Ibid.,* p. 49.
9. *Ibid.,* p. 50.   10. *Ibid.,* p. 53.   11. *Ibid.,* p. 63.
12. *Ibid.,* p. 62.   13. *Ibid.,* p. 71.   14. *Ibid.,* p. 108.
15. U.S. Congress, Joint Economic Committee, *Hearings on the January 1962 Economic Report of the President,* 87th Congress, 2d Session, p. 47.
16. *Economic Report of the President,* January, 1962, pp. 108–43.
17. *Ibid.,* p. 80.
18. *Ibid.,* pp. 77–78; *ibid.,* January, 1965, p. 63; Committee for Economic Development, "Fiscal and Monetary Policy for High Employment; A Statement on National Policy by the Research Committee of the Committee for Economic Development," 1962, p. 29; Commission on Money and Credit, *Money and Credit,* pp. 141–42.
19. *Economic Report of the President,* January, 1962, p. 80.
20. *Ibid.,* pp. 142–43.
21. Council of Economic Advisers, *Economic Indicators,* March, 1962, pp. 1, 7, 9, 12, 18, 22; New York *Times,* March 10, 1962, p. 25.
22. *Public Papers of the Presidents* (1962), p. 197.
23. *Ibid.,* p. 227.
24. For interesting minute-by-minute accounts of the episode, see Hoopes, *Steel Crises;* McConnell, *Steel and the Presidency;* New York *Times,* April 23, 1962, pp. 1, 25.
25. Hoopes, *Steel Crises,* pp. 172–86.
26. McConnell, *Steel and the Presidency,* p. 115.
27. Council of Economic Advisers, *Economic Indicators,* April, 1962, p. 1.
28. Hoopes, *Steel Crises,* pp. 229, 246–47; pp. 222–60 are also relevant. See also Rowen, *Free Enterprisers.*
29. *Public Papers of the Presidents* (1962), pp. 470 ff.
30. "A Businessman's Letter to JFK and His Reply," *Life,* July 6, 1962, pp. 30–34.
31. *Public Papers of the Presidents* (1962), p. 262.
32. New York *Times,* January 27, 1962, p. 9.
33. Walter Heller, "Prospects and Policies for Economic Growth," excerpts from an address to U.S. Department of Commerce Regional Conference, Los Angeles, April 19, 1962.
34. Harvey Brazer, interview with author.

35. *Public Papers of the Presidents* (1962), p. 457.

36. *Ibid.* (Italics added.)   37. *Ibid.*

38. New York *Times*, June 5, 1962, p. 67.

39. *Ibid.*, June 1, p. 1.

40. "Economic Oracles of the New Frontier," *New York Times Magazine*, August 4, 1963, p. 62. © 1963 by The New York Times Company. Reprinted by permission.

41. *Public Papers of the Presidents* (1962), p. 472.

42. New York *Times*, June 6, 1962, p. 40.

43. *Ibid.*, June 14, 1962, p. 27.

44. *Ibid.*, July 11, 1962, p. 18; July 18, 1962, p. 1.

45. *Public Papers of the Presidents* (1962), p. 540.

46. New York *Times*, July 13, 1962, p. 1.

47. Walter Heller, interview with author.

48. *Public Papers of the Presidents* (1962), p. 616.

49. "The Day Taxes Weren't Cut," *Reporter*, September 13, 1962, pp. 25–28.

50. Joseph Pechman, interview with author.

51. U.S. Congress, Joint Economic Committee, *Hearings on the State of the Economy and Policies for Full Employment*, 87th Congress, 2d Session, p. 115.

52. *Ibid.*, pp. 115–16.   53. *Ibid.*, p. 119.

54. *Economic Report of the President*, January, 1963, p. 160.

55. U.S. Congress, Joint Economic Committee, *Hearings on the State of the Economy and Policies for Full Employment*, 87th Congress, 2d Session, p. 664.

56. *Ibid.*, pp. 663–66.

57. H.R. 10650, enacted as Pub.L. 87–834, 76 Stat. 960, October 16, 1962.

58. *Economic Report of the President*, January, 1963, p. 18.

59. *Public Papers of the Presidents* (1962), p. 787.

60. Stanley Surrey, interview with author.

61. William Capron, interview with author.

62. Minutes summarized by permission of Gardner Ackley.

63. Harvey Brazer, interview with author.

64. New York *Times*, November 16, 1962, p. 1.

65. *Ibid.*, November 15, 1962, p. 28.

66. *Public Papers of the Presidents* (1962), p. 837.

67. Harvey Brazer, interview with author.

68. Stanley Surrey, interview with author.

69. William Capron, interview with author.

70. For example, "Why We Must Cut Taxes," *Nation's Business*, November, 1962, pp. 40 ff.

71. New York *Times*, November 29, 1962, p. 1.

72. *Ibid.*, November 26, 1962, p. 45.

73. *Public Papers of the Presidents* (1962), pp. 879–80.

74. Walter W. Heller, letter to author.

75. Nossiter, "The Day Taxes Weren't Cut," *Reporter*, September 13, 1962, p. 28; Pechman, "The Case for Tax Reform," *Reporter*, June 6, 1963, p. 20.

76. *Public Papers of the Presidents* (1963), p. 11.

77. *Ibid.*, pp. 26 f.

78. *Economic Report of the President*, January, 1963, p. 16.

79. *Ibid.*, p. 44.

80. *Public Papers of the Presidents* (1963), p. 79.

81. Joint Committee on Internal Revenue Taxation, "Revenue Estimates Relating to the House, Senate, and Conference Versions of H.R. 8363, the Revenue Bill of 1964," Committee Report, February 21, 1964, p. 3.

82. Rowen, *Free Enterprisers*, p. 178.

83. For a more comprehensive and somewhat interpretative account of the relations between Heller and Dillon, see *ibid.*, pp. 135 ff.

84. Burns, *John Kennedy*, pp. 276–81.

Chapter VIII. The Politics of Economic Advice

1. The *Wall Street Journal* (December 10, 1964, p. 1) reports that, whereas Eisenhower's Budget Director, Maurice Stans, applied the motto "Why?" Bell and Gordon adopted the motto "How?"

2. *Federal Fiscal Policy*, p. 4.

3. *Economic Report of the President*, January, 1962, p. 69.

4. *Ibid.*, p. 17; Brown, "Federal Fiscal Policy in the Postwar Period" in Freeman, ed., *Postwar Economic Trends*, p. 183.

5. U.S. Congress, Joint Committee on the Economic Report, *Hearings on the January 1955 Economic Report of the President*, 84th Congress, 1st Session, p. 125.

6. *Economic Report of the President*, January, 1950, p. 7.

7. *Economic Report of the President*, January, 1954, p. iii.

8. *Economic Report of the President*, January, 1962, p. 7.

9. U.S. Congress, Joint Committee on the Economic Report, *Hearings on the January 1955 Economic Report of the President*, 84th Congress, 1st Session, pp. 43–44.

10. "Economic Planning Reconsidered," *Quarterly Journal of Economics*, LXXII (February, 1958), 56.

11. "Power and Administration," *Public Administration Review*, IX (Autumn, 1949), 262.

12. "Towards Improving National Policy Planning," *Public Administration Review*, XXIII (March, 1963), 11, 14.

13. John P. Lewis, interview with author.

14. Hansen, "Social Scientist and Social Counselor" in A. F. Burns, ed., *Wesley Clair Mitchell*.

15. *Economics in the Public Service*, p. 107.

16. Brown, "Federal Fiscal Policy in the Postwar Period," in Freeman, ed., *Postwar Economic Trends*, p. 155.

17. For example, *ibid.*, pp. 182–83.

18. "The Reports Prepared under the Employment Act," in Colm, ed., *The Employment Act*, p. 92.

19. "Progress toward Economic Stability," *American Economic Review*, L (March, 1960), 1.

20. Brown, "Federal Fiscal Policy in the Postwar Period," in Freeman, ed., *Postwar Economic Trends*, p. 183.

21. *Decision-Making in the White House*, p. 43.

22. *Presidential Power*, pp. 6–7.

23. "Reflections upon the Council of Economic Advisers," p. 30.

24. "Bureaucracy and Constitutionalism," *American Political Science Review*, XLVI (September, 1952), 810.   25. *Ibid.*, p. 811.

26. *Decision-Making in the White House*, pp. 14–15.

27. *Ibid.*, p. 15.

28. "Ethics and Administrative Discretion," *Public Administration Review*, III (Winter, 1943), 14.

29. *Congress Makes a Law*, p. 240.

30. "Economic Welfare and Policy," in *Economics and Public Policy*, pp. 2–4.

31. "The Economist in Government," *Forum*, I (Winter, 1957), 5.

32. *Presidential Power*, p. 155.

33. Pub.L. 304, Section 4(c,d,e).

34. "Presidential Leadership: The Inner Circle and Institutionalization," *Journal of Politics*, XVIII (August, 1958), 422.

35. "Structure and Functioning of the Council of Economic Advisers," *Commercial and Financial Chronicle*, CLXXVII (June 4, 1953), 6.

36. *Decision-Making in the White House*, p. 79.

37. *Ibid.*, pp. 22 ff.

Chapter IX. The Knowledge-Power Relationship

1. *Decision-Making in the White House*, p. 58.

2. "In Accord with the Program of the President" in Friedrich and Galbraith, eds., *Public Policy*, IV, 90–92.

3. *Economics in the Public Service*, p. 378.

4. *Presidential Power*, p. 41.

Chapter X. Conclusion: An Approach to Analysis

1. *Presidential Power*, p. vii.
2. Simon, *Administrative Behavior*, p. 71.
3. Blau and Scott, *Formal Organizations*, pp. 242–50.
4. This analysis is in part adapted from *ibid.*, pp. 60–64.
5. *Ibid.*

BIBLIOGRAPHY

Documents from the Harry S. Truman Library,
Independence, Missouri

Bell, David E. "Memorandum for Mr. Murphy." To Charles Murphy, October 3, 1950. From the files of Charles Murphy.

Blough, Roy. "Memorandum: Comment on Draft of Monthly Report," September 10, 1951. From the papers of John D. Clark.

Clark, John D. "Draft of Monthly Report," June 7, 1951; September 7, 1951. From the papers of John D. Clark.

Council of Economic Advisers. "Memorandum: Further Action on Price and Wage Controls." To the President, December 7, 1950. From the papers of Harry S. Truman.

———— "Memorandum: Monthly Report on the Economic Situation." To the President, November 9, 1949; September 12, 1950; February 15, 1951; May 17, 1951. From the papers of Harry S. Truman.

———— "Memorandum: Quarterly Report on the Economic Situation." To the President, October 19, 1950; April 6, 1951; October 15, 1951; April 21, 1952. From the papers of Harry S. Truman.

———— "Memorandum: Special Report on Economic Trends and Policies." To the President, September 26, 1950. From the papers of Harry S. Truman.

———— "Memorandum: Weekly Report on the Economic Situation." To the President, August 17, 1950; August 29, 1950. From the papers of Harry S. Truman.

———— "Sixth Annual Report to the President from the Council of Economic Advisers, December 1951." From the papers of Harry S. Truman.

Directors of Defense Mobilization. "Report to the President," December, 1951.

Houston, John C., Jr. "Memorandum: Policy Guidance to Departments and Agencies Operating under Authority of Defense Production Act."

To John R. Steelman, September 20, 1950. From the papers of Harry S. Truman.

Keyserling, Leon H. "Memorandum: Administrative Problems Discussed at Our Meeting on August 18." To Charles S. Murphy and David Stowe, August 21, 1950. From the files of Charles Murphy.

―――― "Memorandum: Comment on Draft of Monthly Report," September 7, 1951. From the papers of John D. Clark.

―――― "Record: Leon H. Keyserling" (1949). From the files of Clark Clifford.

―――― "Record in Economics Field" (1949). From the files of Clark Clifford.

―――― Blough, Roy and Clark, John D. Letter to Harry S. Truman, June 5, 1951.

McCabe, Thomas. Letter to Harry S. Truman, February 7, 1951.

Nourse, Edwin G. "Memorandum of Contacts with President Truman and White House Staff, December 3–28, 1946." From the files of Clark Clifford. White House press release, February 26, 1951.

Other Sources

Ackley, Gardner. "Selected Problems of Price Control Strategy, 1950–1952." Defense History Program. Washington, D.C., Office of Civil and Defense Mobilization Library, 1953.

American Assembly, Columbia University. Economic Security for Americans. Papers and Findings of the Third American Assembly, Arden House. New York, Graduate School of Business, Columbia University, 1954.

―――― United States Monetary Policy: Its Contribution to Prosperity without Inflation. Papers and Findings of the Sixteenth American Assembly, Arden House. New York, Graduate School of Business, Columbia University, 1958.

Appleby, Paul H. "The Influence of the Political Order," *American Political Science Review*, XLII (April, 1948), 272–83.

Bailey, Stephen K. Congress Makes a Law: The Story behind the Employment Act of 1946. New York, Columbia University Press, 1950.

―――― "Political Elements in Full Employment Policy," *American Economic Review: Papers and Proceedings*, XLX (May, 1955), 341–50.

Barnard, Chester I. Functions of the Executive. Cambridge, Mass., Harvard University Press, 1938.

Bauer, Raymond, Ithiel de Sola Pool, and Lewis Anthony Dexter. American Business and Public Policy. New York, Atherton Press, 1965.

Beer, Samuel H. Treasury Control: The Co-ordination of Financial and Economic Policy in Great Britain. New York, Oxford University Press, 1956.

Blau, Peter M., and W. Richard Scott. Formal Organizations: A Comparative Approach. San Francisco, Chandler, 1962.

Blough, Roy. The Federal Taxing Process. Englewood Cliffs, N.J., Prentice-Hall, 1952.

—— "Political and Administrative Requisites for Achieving Economic Stability," American Economic Review, XL (May, 1950), 165–78.

Boulding, Kenneth E. Principles of Economic Policy. Englewood Cliffs, N.J., Prentice-Hall, 1958.

Brigante, John E. The Feasibility Dispute: Determination of War Production Objectives for 1942 and 1943. Washington, D.C., Committee on Public Administration Cases, 1950.

Bronfenbrenner, M. "Postwar Political Economy: The President's Reports," Journal of Political Economy, LVI (October, 1948), 373–91.

Brown, E. Cary. "Federal Fiscal Policy in the Postwar Period" in Ralph E. Freeman, ed., Postwar Economic Trends in the United States. New York, Harper, 1960.

Bryson, Lyman. "Notes on a Theory of Advice," Political Science Quarterly, LXVI (Summer, 1951), 321–39.

"Budget Message of the President." The Budget of the United States Government. For the fiscal years ending June 30. Washington, D.C., 1952, 1955, 1963.

Burns, Arthur F. "An Economist in Government," Forum, I (Winter, 1957), 4–6.

—— Business Cycle Research and the Needs of Our Times. 33rd Annual Report, National Bureau of Economic Research. New York, National Bureau of Economic Research, 1953.

—— The Frontiers of Economic Knowledge: Essays. National Bureau of Economic Research. Princeton, N.J., Princeton University Press, 1954.

—— "Progress towards Economic Stability," American Economic Review, L (March, 1960), 1–19.

—— Prosperity without Inflation. New York, Fordham University Press, 1957.

—— "Some Reflections on the Employment Act." Address delivered at the annual meeting of the American Statistical Association, Minneapolis, September 7, 1962.

—— ed. Wesley Clair Mitchell: The Economic Scientist. New York, National Bureau of Economic Research, 1952.

Burns, James MacGregor. John Kennedy: A Political Profile. New York, Harcourt, Brace, 1960.

Childs, Marquis. Eisenhower: Captive Hero. New York, Harcourt, Brace, 1958.

Colm, Gerhard. The American Economy in 1960. National Planning Association Planning Pamphlet No. 81. Washington, D.C., National Planning Association, 1952.

—— "The Executive Office and Fiscal Economic Policy," *Law and Contemporary Problems*, XXI (Autumn, 1956), 710–23.

—— The Federal Budget and the National Economy. National Planning Association Planning Pamphlet No. 90. Washington, D.C., National Planning Association, 1955.

—— ed. The Employment Act, Past and Future: A Tenth Anniversary Symposium. Washington, National Planning Association, 1956.

Commission on Money and Credit. Money and Credit: Their Influence on Jobs, Prices, and Growth. Englewood Cliffs, N.J., Prentice-Hall, 1961.

Conference on Economic Progress. Pamphlets entitled "The Federal Budget" (1959), "The General Welfare" (1959), "Food and Freedom" (1960), "Inflation, Cause and Cure" (1959), "Jobs and Growth" (1961), "Tight Money and Rising Interest Rates" (1960). Washington, D.C., Conference on Economic Progress.

Council of Economic Advisers. Economic Indicators. August, 1950; March, 1953; January, 1954; February, 1954; July, 1954; January, 1961; March, 1962; April, 1962. Washington, D.C.

—— The Economics of National Defense (fifth Annual Report to the President for the year ending December 31, 1950). Washington, D.C., 1950.

—— First Annual Report to the President (for the year ending December 31, 1946). Washington, D.C., 1947.

Dale, Edwin L., Jr. Conservatives in Power: A Study in Frustration. New York, Doubleday, 1960.

"Decision on Tax Cut Teeters Back and Forth," *Business Week*, April 12, 1958, pp. 28–29.

Dillard, Dudley. The Economics of John Maynard Keynes. Englewood Cliffs, N.J., Prentice-Hall, 1948.

—— "Keynesian Economics after Twenty Years," *American Economic Review*, XLVII (May, 1957), 77–87.

Donovan, Robert J. Eisenhower: The Inside Story. New York, Harper, 1956.

Dubin, Robert, ed. Human Relations in Administration. 2d ed. Englewood Cliffs, N.J., Prentice-Hall, 1961.

Economics and the Policy Maker: Brookings Lectures 1958–1959. Washington, D.C., The Brookings Institution, 1959.

Economics and Public Policy: Brookings Lectures, 1954. Washington, D.C., The Brookings Institution, 1955.

Economic Report of the President as Transmitted to the Congress (including Council of Economic Advisers, "Annual Report to the President" and "Annual Economic Review"). Washington, D.C., 1946–63.

Elliott, John E. "Economic Planning Reconsidered," *Quarterly Journal of Economics,* LXXII (February, 1958).

Executive Office of the President. A Case Study in Peacetime Mobilization Planning: NSRB 1947–1953. Washington, D.C., 1953.

Fredlund, John R. "Keynesian Ideas as Reflected in the Domestic Fiscal and Monetary Policies of the United States, 1945–1953." Ph.D. dissertation, The American University, 1956.

Friedrich, C. J., and J. K. Galbraith, eds. Public Policy. Vol. IV. Cambridge, Mass., Graduate School of Public Administration, Harvard University, 1953.

Galbraith, John K. The Affluent Society. Boston, Houghton Mifflin, 1958.

Gore, William. Administrative Decision-Making: A Heuristic Model. New York, Wiley, 1964.

—— "Decision-Making in Federal Field Offices," *Public Administration Review,* XVI (Autumn, 1956), 281–91.

Grebler, Leo. Housing Issues in Economic Stabilization Policy. National Bureau of Economic Research Occasional Paper 72. New York, National Bureau of Economic Research, 1960.

Gross, Bertram M., and John P. Lewis. "The President's Economic Staff during the Truman Administration." *American Political Science Review,* XLVIII (March, 1954), 114–30.

Harris, T. George. "Walter Heller, 'Mr. Tax-Cut,'" XXVII (June 18, 1963), 81 f.

Hickman, Bert G. The Contraction of 1953–1954. The Brookings Institution Reprint No. 22. Washington, D.C., The Brookings Institution, 1958.

Hobbs, Edward H. Behind the President: A Study of Executive Office Agencies. Washington, D.C., Public Affairs Press, 1954.

Holmans, A. E. "The Eisenhower Administration and the Recession, 1953–1955," *Oxford Economic Papers,* X (February, 1958).

Homan, Paul T. "Reflections upon the Council of Economic Advisers." Unpublished manuscript, 1950.

Hoopes, Roy. The Steel Crises. New York, John Day, 1963.

Irish, Marion D. "The Organization Man in the Presidency," *Journal of Politics,* XX (May, 1958), 259–77.

Johnson, G. Griffith. "Reflections on a Year of Price Controls," *American Economic Review,* XLII (May, 1952) 289–300.

Keyserling, Leon H. "The American Economic Goal" ($10,000 Second Prize Winning Plan of the Pabst Postwar Employment Awards, No. 171), *American City,* LIX (June, 1944), 93.

—— "The Economic Test: Will We Act in Time?" *New York Times Magazine,* June 13, 1948, pp. 7 ff.

—— "Must We Have Another Depression?" *New York Times Magazine,* June 8, 1947, pp. 7 ff.

Lewis, John P. "The Lull That Came to Stay," *Journal of Political Economy*, LXIII (February, 1955), 1–19.

Lewis, Wilfred, Jr. Federal Fiscal Policy in the Postwar Recessions. Washington, D.C., The Brookings Institution, 1962.

Leys, Wayne A. R. "Ethics and Administrative Descretion," *Public Administration Review*, III (Winter, 1943), 10–23.

Long, Norton E. "Bureaucracy and Constitutionalism," *American Political Science Review*, XLVI (September, 1946), 808–18.

—— "Power and Administration," *Public Administration Review*, IX (Autumn, 1949), 257–64.

Lorwin, Lewis. Advisory Economic Councils. Pamphlet Series No. 9. Washington, D.C., The Brookings Institution, 1931.

Maass, Arthur, "In Accord with the Program of the President" in C. J. Friedrich and J. K. Galbraith, eds., *Public Policy*. Vol. IV, Cambridge, Mass., Graduate School of Public Administration, Harvard University, 1953.

McConnell, Grant. Steel and the Presidency—1962. New York, Norton, 1963.

Marvick, Dwaine. Career Perspectives in a Bureaucratic Setting. Ann Arbor, University of Michigan Press, 1943.

Merriam, Charles E. "The National Resources Planning Board; A Chapter in American Planning Experience," *American Political Science Review*, XXXVIII (December, 1944), 1075–88.

Merton, Robert K. Social Theory and Social Structure. 2d ed. New York, Free Press, 1957.

—— *et al.* Reader in Bureaucracy. New York, Free Press, 1952.

Mid-year Report of the President as Transmitted to the Congress (including Council of Economic Advisers, "Midyear Economic Review"). Washington, D.C., 1946–52.

Millett, John D. The Process and Organization of Government Planning. New York, Columbia University Press, 1947.

Murphy, Charles J. V. "The White House and the Recession," *Fortune*, LVII (May, 1958), 106–09 f.

Nash, Bradley de L. Staffing the Presidency. Washington, D.C., National Planning Association, 1952.

National Industrial Conference Board. An Appraisal of Official Economic Reports. Studies in Business Economics No. 16. New York, National Industrial Conference Board, 1948.

—— The Council of Economic Advisers; Retrospect and Prospect. Studies in Business Economics No. 38. New York, National Industrial Conference Board, 1953.

—— Economics of the President's Economists. Studies in Business Economics No. 20. New York, National Industrial Conference Board, 1949.

———— Pros and Cons of Council of Economic Advisers' Policies. Studies in Business Economics No. 25. New York, National Industrial Conference Board, 1950.

Neustadt, Richard E. "Presidency and Legislation: Planning the President's Program," *American Political Science Review*, XLIX (December, 1955), 980–1021.

———— "The Presidency at Mid-Century," *Law and Contemporary Problems*, XXI (Autumn, 1956), 609–45.

———— Presidential Power: The Politics of Leadership. New York, Wiley, 1960.

New York *Herald Tribune*, May 7, 1950; June 23, 1950; July 26, 1961.

New York *Times*, April 1, 1950–December 31, 1951; January 1, 1953–August 20, 1954; December 1, 1960–January 1, 1963.

Nossiter, Bernard. "The Day Taxes Weren't Cut," *Reporter*, September 13, 1962.

Nourse, Edwin G. Economics in the Public Service: Administrative Aspects of the Employment Act. New York, Harcourt, Brace, 1953.

———— The 1950's Come First. New York, Holt, 1951.

———— and Bertram M. Gross. "The Role of the Council of Economic Advisers," *American Political Science Review*, XLII (April, 1948), 283–95.

Pechman, Joseph. "The Case for Tax Reform," *Reporter*, June 6, 1963.

President's Advisory Committee on Government Housing Policies and Programs. Recommendations on Government Housing Policies and Programs. A report to the President of the United States, December, 1953. Washington, D.C., 1953.

Price, Don K. "Staffing the Presidency," *American Political Science Review*, XL (December, 1946), 1154–68.

Policies to Combat Depression: A Conference of the Universities–National Bureau Committee for Economic Research. National Bureau of Economic Research. Princeton, N.J., Princeton University Press, 1956.

Public Papers of the Presidents, Dwight D. Eisenhower 1953; 1954. Washington, D.C.

Public Papers of the Presidents, John F. Kennedy 1961; 1962; 1963. Washington, D.C.

"Reading the Nation's Economic Health," *Business Week*, December 8, 1956, pp. 141–46.

Reagan, Michael D. "Towards Improving National Policy Planning," *Public Administration Review*, XXIII (March, 1963).

Robinson, James A. "Decision Making in the House Rules Committee," *Administrative Science Quarterly*, III (June, 1958), 73–86.

Rosenberg, Herbert H. "ODM: A Study of Civil-Military Relations during the Korean Mobilization." Ph.D. Dissertation, Department of Political Science, University of Chicago, 1957.

Rossiter, Clinton. The American Presidency. 2d ed. New York, Harcourt, Brace, 1960.

Rowen, Hobart. The Free Enterprisers; Kennedy, Johnson and the Business Establishment. New York, Putnam, 1964.

—— and C. Morgello. "Forecasting Business for Ike," *Newsweek*, LI (1958), 67–70.

Sampson, Robert C. The Staff Role in Management: Its Creative Uses. New York, Harper, 1955.

Schilling, Warner R., Paul Y. Hammond, and Glenn H. Snyder. Strategy, Politics, and Defense Budgets. New York, Columbia University Press, 1962.

Schlesinger, Arthur M., Jr. The Age of Roosevelt. Vol. II: The Coming of the New Deal. Boston, Houghton Mifflin, 1958.

Seligman, Lester G. "Presidential Leadership: The Inner Circle and Institutionalization," *Journal of Politics*, XVIII (August, 1956), 410–26.

Silverman, Corinne. The President's Economic Advisers. Inter-University Case Program Series No. 48. University, University of Alabama Press, 1959.

Simon, Herbert. Administrative Behavior: A Study of Decision-Making Processes in Administrative Organization. New York, Macmillan, 1947.

—— The New Science of Management Decision. New York, Harper, 1960.

——, Donald W. Smithburg, and Victor A. Thompson. Public Administration. New York, Knopf, 1950.

Snyder, Richard C., H. W. Bruck, and Burton Sapin. Decision-Making as an Approach to the Study of International Politics. Princeton, N.J., Organizational Behavior Section, Princeton University, 1954.

Somers, Herman M. Presidential Agency: OWMR, the Office of War Mobilization and Reconversion. Cambridge, Mass., Harvard University Press, 1950.

Sorensen, Theodore C. Decision-Making in the White House: The Olive Branch or the Arrows. New York, Columbia University Press, 1963.

"Stabilizing the Economy: The Employment Act of 1946 in Operation," a symposium, *American Economic Review*, XL (May, 1950), 144–90.

Taylor, Philip. "Policy-Makers and Economic Policy," *Challenge*, VII (April, 1959), 18–23.

Thompson, Victor A. Modern Organization. New York, Knopf, 1961.

Truman, Harry S. Memoirs. Vol. II: Years of Trial and Hope, 1946–1952. New York, Doubleday, 1956.

Turner, Robert C. "Problems of Forecasting for Economic Stabilization," *American Economic Review*, XLV (May, 1955), 329–40.

—— "Structure and Functioning of the Council of Economic Advisers," *Commercial and Financial Chronicle*, CLXXVII (June 4, 1953).

U.S. Congress. House Appropriations Committee. Hearings on the Treasury, Post Office Department, and Executive Office. G-1. 87th Congress, 2d Session (1963).

———— House Committee on Banking and Currency. Hearings on H.R. 9176. 81st Congress, 2d Session (1950).

———— House Committee on Ways and Means. Hearings on Forty Topics Pertaining to the General Revision of the Internal Revenue Code. 83d Congress, 1st Session (1953).

———— House Committee on Ways and Means. Hearings on the President's Recommendations to Extend for Six Months the Excess Profits Tax. 83d Congress, 1st Session (1953).

———— House Select Committee on Small Business, Subcommittee No. 2. Hearings on the Effect of the Present Tax Structure on Small Business (pursuant to H.R. 22). 83d Congress, 1st Session (1953).

———— Joint Committee on the Economic Report. The Economic and Political Hazards of an Inflationary Defense Economy. 82d Congress, 1st Session (1951).

———— Joint Committee on the Economic Report. Hearings on the Economic Report of the President pursuant to Sec. 5(a) of Public Law 304, 79th Congress. 82d Congress, 1st Session (1951); 83d Congress, 2d Session (1954); 84th Congress, 1st Session (1955); 84th Congress, 2d Session (1956).

———— Joint Committee on the Economic Report. Report of the Subcommittee on Monetary, Credit, and Fiscal Policies. 81st Congress, 1st Session (1950).

———— Joint Economic Committee. Hearings on the Economic Report of the President pursuant to Sec. 5(a) of Public Law 304, 79th Congress. 87th Congress, 2d Session (1962).

———— Joint Economic Committee. Hearings on the Economic Report of the President and the Economic Situation and Outlook pursuant to Sec. 5(a) of Public Law 304, 79th Congress. 87th Congress, 1st Session (1961).

———— Joint Economic Committee. Hearings on Employment, Growth, and Price Levels. 86th Congress, 1st Session (1960).

———— Joint Economic Committee. Hearings on the State of the Economy and Policies for Full Employment. 87th Congress, 2d Session (1962).

———— Joint Committee on Internal Revenue Taxation.

———— Senate Committee on Appropriations. Hearings on Supplemental Appropriations Bill for 1962 (H.R. 9169). 87th Congress, 1st Session (1961).

———— Senate Committee on Appropriations, Subcommittee. Hearings on the Department of Defense Appropriations for 1952. 82d Congress, 1st Session (1951).

U.S. Congress. Senate Committee on Appropriations, Subcommittee on General Governmental Matters. Hearings for Fiscal Year 1962. 87th Congress, 1st Session (1961).

———— Senate Committee on Banking and Currency. Hearings on Inflation Control. 80th Congress, 2d Session (1948).

———— Senate Committee on Commerce, Special Study Group on Transportation Policies in the United States. Report on National Transportation Policy. Report 445, 87th Congress, 1st Session (1961).

U.S. Department of the Treasury, Tax Advisory Staff. "Taxation for Defense." Official Memorandum, December, 1952.

U.S. General Services Administration, National Archives and Records Service, Federal Register Division. United States Government Organization Manual 1953–1954; 1958–1959.

White, Llewellyn. "Mr. Wilson Goes to Washington," Reporter, IV (January 23, 1951) 28–30.

"Why We Must Cut Taxes," Nation's Business, November, 1962.

INDEX